SOCIALISM AND CHRISTIANITY IN EARLY 20TH CENTURY AMERICA

SOCIALISM AND CHRISTIANITY IN EARLY 20TH CENTURY AMERICA

✳

EDITED BY
JACOB H. DORN

Contributions in American History, Number 181
Jon L. Wakelyn, Series Editor

GREENWOOD PRESS
Westport, Connecticut • London

Library of Congress Cataloging-in-Publication Data

Socialism and Christianity in early 20th century America / edited by
  Jacob H. Dorn.
     p.   cm.—(Contributions in American history, ISSN 0084–9219
; no. 181)
    Includes bibliographical references and index.
    ISBN 0–313–30262–6 (alk. paper)
    1. Socialism and Christianity—United States—History—20th
century. 2. United States—Church history—20th century. I. Dorn,
Jacob H. (Jacob Henry), 1939–   . II. Series.
HX83.S65   1998
320.53′1′09730904—dc21   98–11104

British Library Cataloguing in Publication Data is available.

Library of Congress Catalog Card Number: 98–11104
ISBN: 0–313–30262–6
ISSN: 0084–9219

First published in 1998

Greenwood Press, 88 Post Road West, Westport, CT 06881
An imprint of Greenwood Publishing Group, Inc.

Printed in the United States of America

∞™

The paper used in this book complies with the
Permanent Paper Standard issued by the National
Information Standards Organization (Z39.48–1984).

10 9 8 7 6 5 4 3 2

In order to keep this title in print and available to the academic community, this edition
was produced using digital reprint technology in a relatively short print run. This would
not have been attainable using traditional methods. Although the cover has been changed
from its original appearance, the text remains the same and all materials and methods
used still conform to the highest book-making standards.

Copyright Acknowledgments

The editor and publisher gratefully acknowledge permission to use the following material:

American Socialism and Black Americans, Philip S. Foner. Copyright © 1977 by Philip S. Foner. Reproduced with permission.

Transcript of oral interview of Herbert Coggins by Corinne L. Gilb, Regional Oral History Office, Bancroft Library, University of California, Berkeley.

Harry W. Laidler Papers, Tamiment Library, New York University.

Henry Demarest Lloyd Papers, State Historical Society of Wisconsin.

New York County Socialist Party Papers, Tamiment Library, New York University.

Kate Richards O'Hare, "Dear Sweethearts: Letters from Kate Richards O'Hare to her Family," Missouri Historical Society, St. Louis, Missouri.

Rauschenbusch Family Papers, American Baptist-Samuel Colgate Historical Library, Rochester, NY.

Material relating to James Graham Phelps Stokes in the James Graham Phelps Stokes Papers, Rose Pastor Stokes Papers, and the Victor Jeremy Jerome Papers. Manuscripts and Archives, Yale University Library.

James Graham Phelps Stokes Papers, Rare Book and Manuscript Library, Columbia University.

Rose Pastor Stokes Papers, Tamiment Library, New York University.

Irwin St. John Tucker Papers, Special Collections, The University Library, The University of Illinois at Chicago.

Irvin G. Wyllie Papers, Wyllie Bouck White collection, courtesy of Mrs. Harriet Wyllie.

To the memory of those who worked,

as the *Christian Socialist* put it,

for the Golden Rule against the Rule of Gold

Contents

Introduction

Jacob H. Dorn

While working on this book in a second-floor study at home, I have often glanced out the window only to see a neighbor's bumper sticker proclaiming that "socialism doesn't work." That is not a message to buoy one's spirit during the often tedious work of searching notes for that just-right quotation, proofreading for misplaced commas, and double-checking of sources. The bumper sticker gives no clues as to how its creator (and the neighbor) decide what "works" and what doesn't, but it seems likely that the breakup of the Soviet Union, events in eastern Europe, and the ascendancy of conservative and neo-liberal perspectives in the United States inform their judgment.

Confusing socialism with communism is a common fallacy. So too is confusing socialism with the liberal welfare state whose foundations were laid during the Great Depression. The democratic and pluralistic socialism that attracted the subjects of this volume was a far cry from the Soviet model. It was also far more radical than the New Deal with respect to control of economic power and distribution of wealth. If socialism, loosely defined, is out of fashion, there is no reason to believe that the critique of capitalism and the aspirations for economic justice of a Kate Richards O'Hare or an Irwin St. John Tucker are uninstructive at the end of the twentieth century. They no more offer a blueprint for social reconstruction today than they did in their own day. They do offer, now as then, examples of great commitment to the good of all and of passionate efforts to spread that commitment.

In recruiting contributors to this work, I tried to find scholars who were doing intensive biographical work in the area of religion and socialism. Broad-gauged studies of social movements are fundamental to understanding them. Biography, however, gives those movements a human face. How better to help a later generation grasp the dynamics of socialist commitment than by tracing them in individual lives!

Two criteria governed the selection of subjects. The first was that Christianity played a significant part in the individual's decision to become a socialist and in the way he or she shaped the socialist message. In recent decades, the rise of the Religious Right and the enormous surge in conservative-evangelical historical writing have combined to overshadow the potential of American Christianity to stimulate social action predicated on a very different reading of the Bible than that of the Moral Majority or the Christian Coalition. The legacy of that alternative potential, whether expressed in the liberal Social Gospel or in a more radical Christian socialism, demands attention in a reliable historiography.

The second criterion was that the individual supported the Socialist Party of America in the years 1900–1920, the period of its greatest promise. The socialism in question could not be of a vaporous, diffuse kind. This emphasis seemed important because of an orientation in much of the scholarly literature on Christianity and socialism toward the theologically preoccupied and politically unfocused "Christian Socialism" of the nineteenth century. This volume is about people who understood socialism to be a political cause with a concrete program of structural changes in the public sector. In addition, it is about socialists in Progressive Era America, not in the 1930s when the Socialist Party experienced a mild but comparatively inconsequential revival under the leadership of Norman Thomas, a former Presbyterian minister.

These criteria, I believed, would bring about a bridging of the worlds of historians of religion and historians of radicalism, neither of whom has used the other's sources with great depth. The reader may judge whether these essays are actually an advance in that regard.

The seven subjects examined in Chapters 2 to 8 are not the only ones who might have been included. There are some who meet my principal criteria, but for whom inadequate sources preclude a satisfactory reconstruction of their lives and ideas. There are others for whom I could find no biographer, despite a wide casting of the net to do so.

These seven do not represent the entire range of socialist experience. They do, nonetheless, provide interesting diversity. Reflective of the fact that Christians came to socialism from many theological, liturgical, and denominational orientations, they represent the Baptist, Methodist, Congregational, Disciples of Christ, Universalist, and Episcopal traditions.[1] There are both clergymen and lay people (Kate Richards O'Hare, J. G. Phelps Stokes), and the clerical contingent includes a bishop (Franklin S. Spalding), a man who went through three denominations before founding his own Church of the Social Revolution (Bouck White), one who left the ministry (J. Stitt Wilson), and two who maintained generally stable relationships with their churches (Irwin St. John Tucker, George Washington Woodbey).

The group is also socially and geographically diverse. It includes a Kansas farm girl turned machinist (O'Hare), a Deep South rector's son transplanted to New York and Chicago (Tucker), a Tennessee slave who ended up in San Diego (Woodbey), a Canadian farm boy who gained trans-Atlantic recognition before settling in the San Francisco Bay area (Wilson), a Connecticut blueblood who wed a Russian-

Jewish cigarmaker (Stokes), the son of an upstate New York merchant who obtained Harvard and Union Seminary credentials prior to entering party work in New York City (White), and the Pennsylvania-born rector's son who became Episcopal Missionary Bishop of Utah (Spalding). It would be treacherous to attempt thumbnail personality sketches, but the reader will also find sharp contrasts in temperament from one chapter to another.

Within the Socialist Party, the seven occupied varying positions along the ideological spectrum. Some defended the confrontational Industrial Workers of the World (Woodbey, Tucker), while others were usually aligned with the party's opportunistic conservatives (Stokes, Wilson). Though a pragmatist, O'Hare was widely known as "Red Kate" for her sharp rhetoric. They differed over the proper position to take toward American intervention in World War I, Stokes and Wilson leaving the party because of its opposition to intervention and O'Hare and Tucker receiving jail sentences for their support of that opposition. Spending some time in jail was not uncommon, but perhaps it is surprising that such religiously inspired persons as Woodbey, White, Tucker, and O'Hare did so.

Finally, these radical Christians performed diverse roles within the socialist movement. A majority held office within the party at local, state, or national levels. A majority were party candidates for public office. All spoke and wrote for the party through party and non-party media.

The ways in which they embraced socialism, and their particular articulations of the Christian influence on that embrace, varied, but two commonalities are present in each account. One is an ethical interpretation of the Christian faith. This is not to say that all seven stripped the mystical and supernatural from Christianity, for they did not; but all did believe that the quest for a just society was a *sine qua non* of Christianity. The second commonality is some life-transforming experience with the realities of American society, an experience that led to the conclusion that merely meliorative efforts were insufficient to cure social ills. O'Hare had hers while trying to rescue prostitutes in Kansas City, Wilson his in the discovery in Chicago that Wesleyan holiness was impossible in an economy that rewarded selfishness, Stokes, Tucker, and White theirs in confronting social wretchedness in New York, particularly the Lower East Side, and Woodbey and Spalding theirs in similar ways.

These chapters introduce readers to material that has been neglected in the literature on both radicalism and religion in the first two decades of the twentieth century. That is true of the biographies and the broader commentary on the religious implications of socialism alike. Beyond filling gaps, however, these chapters have revisionist significance. They heighten the importance of religion as an element in the experience of socialists and as a factor in socialists' efforts to define themselves to the wider public. They also demonstrate that the Christian presence within American socialism was diverse, not monolithic, and that that Christian presence does much to explain the drawing power of socialism during the period that it was most attractive to a wide cross-section of the American public.

The contributors to this volume all owe debts of gratitude to the institutions and individuals who have supported their work. I owe particularly important debts to my wife, Carole, and my children, Jonathan and Elizabeth, for patience while I was distracted, helpful textual suggestions and proofreading assistance, and sustaining interest in the subject sufficient to overpower that dreadful bumper sticker.

NOTE

1. A rough tabulation of the denominational affiliations of 160 ministers listed as signers of a pro-socialist manifesto in 1908 ranks the eight largest as follows: Baptist (28), Episcopal (22), Congregational (20), Methodist (16), Presbyterian (16), Christian or Disciples of Christ (15), Universalist (11), and Unitarian (8). Others identified include Moravian, Church of the New Jerusalem (Swedenborgian), Reorganized Church of Jesus Christ of Latter-Day Saints (Mormon), New Thought, Reformed, and Friends. "Brave Preachers Who Give Their Names for Publication as Out and Out Socialists," *Christian Socialist* 5 (15 September 1908): 3–4.

SOCIALISM AND CHRISTIANITY IN EARLY 20TH CENTURY AMERICA

"The Oldest and Youngest of the Idealistic Forces at Work in Our Civilization": Encounters Between Christianity and Socialism

Jacob H. Dorn

It was Sunday afternoon, 31 May 1908, and 3,000 people nearly filled Carnegie Hall for the concluding mass meeting of the third annual Christian Socialist Fellowship (CSF) conference. The conference had begun on Thursday at the Episcopal Church of the Ascension at Fifth Avenue and Tenth Street. Since then, participants had listened to speeches on the coming cooperative commonwealth, sung the devotional hymn "O Master, Let Me Walk With Thee" along with "The Marxian Call," shared in a communion service conducted by William Dwight Porter Bliss, and fanned out to preach in churches throughout the metropolitan area. That these Christians were serious about their socialism was abundantly clear from their speeches. That they were taken seriously within the Socialist Party of America (SPA) was evident from the presence at CSF sessions and related functions of party luminaries like Morris Hillquit, undisputed leader of New York socialists, Algernon Lee of the Rand School of Social Science, Joshua Wanhope, editor of the *New York Call*, and writer John Spargo. A curious press covered a variety of conference activities, raising expectations for the culminating Sunday rally, which more than fulfilled the organizers' hopes.[1]

After reading greetings from the CSF's president, Episcopal Bishop Franklin S. Spalding of Utah, and R. Heber Newton, pastor of All Souls' Unitarian Church in New York, presiding member Edwin Markham set the tone for the rally by strongly affirming the fellowship's socialism and his belief in the religious goal of building God's kingdom on earth and in a Jesus who could save the economic order. Well known for "The Man with the Hoe," he recited a poem written for this occasion, "The Muse of Brotherhood."[2] Then followed speeches by two socialist ministers, Edward Ellis Carr, the Methodist editor of the *Christian Socialist*, and Charles H. Vail, a Universalist and author of widely used socialist textbooks.

The rally's highlight was the appearance of the charismatic Eugene V. Debs, who was in New York for this rally and to inaugurate the *New York Call*'s change to a daily paper. Audience members stood on their chairs, cheered, and waved hats and kerchiefs for twenty minutes to greet him. Debs had often expressed scorn for organized religion, and his embrace therefore meant a great deal to those assembled. A few years before, he observed, such an event would have been inconceivable. Admitting his past "prejudice" against the clergy "as a class," he said: "I am glad I can call you ministers of the Man of Galilee, my comrades."[3]

Editorials in friendly and unfriendly periodicals agreed that this conference marked a significant penetration of American Protestantism by socialist ideas. For the hostile *Outlook*, edited by Social Gospel pioneer Lyman Abbott, it offered "plain proof of the growth and the grip that Socialist or Socialistic principles have already gained in the churches," while Benjamin O. Flower's left-leaning *Arena* saw a "rapid change in sentiment on the part of a large and rapidly-growing body of conscience-guided American clergymen."[4]

Such statements were undoubtedly exaggerations. Even if 300 ministers belonged to the CSF, as reported, they were a small fraction of the Protestant clergy; and historians have discovered only two Roman Catholic priests, Thomas J. Hagerty and Thomas McGrady, who became socialists in early twentieth-century America.[5] A significant number of Christian lay people became socialists, but they hardly represented a trend. Socialist ministers were sometimes forced out of their parishes or for other reasons found it expedient to leave them when they took up the socialist cause. Nevertheless, for Christians to profess allegiance to the Socialist Party, even in the relatively small numbers that they did so, was noteworthy. Political socialism had not been an option ten years before for the kind of people who joined the Christian Socialist Fellowship. Debs was right. And for this change the CSF was in no small part itself responsible.

SOCIALIST CHRISTIANS AND THE SOCIALIST MOVEMENT

Organized in 1906, the Christian Socialist Fellowship grew out of the desire of a small band of ministers and lay people to bring Christianity and socialism into what they considered a natural friendly relationship. In a statement adopted at an initial meeting in Louisville, this group declared its intention to "permeate" the American churches with the "social message of Jesus," to demonstrate not only that socialism and Christianity were compatible, but that in fact socialism was "the necessary economic expression of the Christian life," and to end the struggle between social classes by establishing "justice and brotherhood" upon earth.[6] To fulfill these intentions, they necessarily had to accomplish two other things as part of their strategy to build a bridge between the Socialist Party and Americans' religious sensibilities. One was to prove that they were "straight socialists," neither purveyors of some dilution or substitute, nor factionalists who would use the party to advance a separate, internally divisive agenda. The second was to neutralize as much as possible the anti-religious rhetoric of socialists who insisted that socialism entailed a hard philosophical materialism. Such rhetoric was not only a barrier to the acceptance of socialism by religious people; it was more fundamentally, in the minds of the fellowship's founders, an unnecessary imposition upon the economic and political program of socialism.

Arguing their fidelity to socialism was no ruse. In their enthusiasm to count new recruits, fellowship leaders sometimes attributed greater socialist content to statements of sympathy than those making the statements intended. In addition, though members of the CSF had to subscribe to the socialist language in its statement of purpose, they did not actually have to belong to the Socialist Party. The CSF's constitution was very clear, however, that members were affirming both Christianity and socialism, and W.D.P. Bliss repeated this assumption in his work as the organization's general secretary.[7] It was not unusual for the *Christian Socialist* to declare:

Every one who is truly a Socialist ought to join the Socialist party. Get in and help work. If it is not exactly what you think it ought to be, get in and help make it right. . . . To vote the Socialist ticket does not make you a party member. It is necessary to join a party local and pay dues. If there is no local in your vicinity, start one.[8]

For some members of the fellowship the term "Christian Socialism" was risky and to be used only when carefully qualified. A resolution drafted by George H. Strobell and adopted at the CSF's conference in 1907 warned the Socialist Party against anti-religious propaganda, but also stated that "as active [party] members . . . we thoroughly accept the economic interpretation of social and political causes, and have no desire to qualify it by any revisionist demand." Addressing the conference, Strobell contended that "the economic truth [of socialism] was free to Christian or pagan, to monist, or theist or trinitarian." A stalwart founding member of the Socialist Party, he was a successful jewelry manufacturer in Newark, New Jersey, supporter of prohibition, women's suffrage, and direct legislation, elder in his Presbyterian church, and author of *A Christian View of Socialism,* one of several pamphlets by socialist Christians published in the Charles H. Kerr Company's "Pocket Library of Socialism."[9]

Another influential figure in the fellowship, Rufus W. Weeks, in an important paper at its 1908 conference, denied that there was any such thing as Christian Socialism, any more than there could be Christian free trade. "Socialist Christians" was a better name, he said, but the CSF's creators had wanted to pre-empt the title "Christian Socialism" to prevent its use by mere reformers or by the enemies of socialism in disguise, as had happened in Europe. Christians added to socialism only special motives: love of the church and of Jesus Christ, an understanding of Jesus' emphasis on the economic aspects of the Kingdom of God, and a "theistic passion." A wealthy vice president of the New York Life Insurance Company, Tarrytown neighbor of John D. Rockefeller, and Episcopalian, Weeks had extensive contacts with socialists of various hues on both sides of the Atlantic and was translator of an important work by a Swiss socialist pastor.[10]

The *Christian Socialist*, founded two years before the fellowship and subsequently its mouthpiece, used language much like Weeks's in answering the question: "What is the difference between a Christian Socialist and the regular kind?" The Christian kind, it said, "is the same as the ordinary kind, only more so. They agree exactly as to economics, . . . but the Christian Socialist . . . claims the additional reasons of Christian ethics and the religious spirit."[11] True to its profession, the paper carried expositions of socialist ideas by non-religious as well as religious authors, reprinted material from other socialist periodicals, advertised and distributed works by Karl Marx, Friedrich Engels, and Karl Kautsky, reported developments in the party, and gave plentiful coverage to the class struggle in America's factories and mines.

Admittedly, the paper also printed material that would have given no offense in a conventionally religious periodical: sentimental fiction and poetry, ads for books by non-socialists, and articles by individuals scouting the leftward boundaries of the Social Gospel. Admittedly also, in their enthusiasm to reconcile Christianity and socialism, socialist Christians sometimes went beyond invoking religious motives to interlace religious principles with socialist doctrine. Weeks did so in his writings.[12] Socialist adaptations of the International Sunday School lessons by William A. Prosser, a Methodist pastor in the Pittsburgh area, which began in December 1910, and a series on "Socialism in the Bible" by Carr in 1911 are other cases in point. Carr was particularly (but not uniquely) intent to show that the Bible condemned rent, interest, and profit, three pillars of capitalism.

None of this, however, invalidates the essential point of Weeks and the other professors of "straight socialism," that the Christian Socialist Fellowship's loyalty was to the political agenda of the Socialist Party. It should hardly be surprising, under the circumstances, that the CSF kept the door open to those not yet actually socialists or that the lines between its members' Christianity and their socialism could be blurred.

To the sincerity of CSF leaders' affirmations must be added the practical urgency, highlighted by Rufus Weeks, of distinguishing between their socialism and earlier forms of "Christian Socialism." In Europe and the United States, the latter term had covered non- and even anti-socialist positions. In Germany, where the gulf between churches and socialists was particularly wide, Adolf Stöcker, a Lutheran pastor and later preacher to the Prussian court, had organized in 1878 a Christian Socialist Workers Party that was antagonistic to the Social Democratic Party.[13] In Britain, an enduring tendency to call very mild reformist interests "Christian Socialist" began in 1848 with the work of Frederick Denison Maurice, Charles Kingsley, and John Malcolm Ludlow at the time of the failed Chartist uprising. Maurice's theological work, with its central emphases on divine immanence, cooperation (rather than laissez-faire competition) as the paramount Christian social principle, and gradual achievement of a reign of God on earth, had an enormous impact on Christian social thinkers for many decades, but he disdained politics and chiefly promoted cooperative societies and workers' education.[14] In this tradition, the Christian Social Union, formed in 1889 (with an American branch in 1891), though larding its publications with the term "Christian Socialism," engaged primarily in social and economic research and usually stopped short of taking positions. A prominent American interpreter of the Christian Social Union wrote: "If socialism must be defined in the terms of a programme, then the Christian

Socialists are no socialists at all"; rather, they adhered to a "a principle, . . . an attitude of mind, a point of view, a motive of conduct, the opposite of individualism."[15] In the judgment of one historian of this and other Anglican organizations, not until late in the nineteenth century did English Christian Socialists "come to regard Socialism, at least in their understanding of it, as political."[16]

Dubious terminology had also clouded previous efforts to establish a Christian socialism in the United States. W.D.P. Bliss has received considerable attention as founder of the Society of Christian Socialists (SCS) in Boston in 1889 and for tireless, wide-ranging involvement in reformist and radical circles.[17] Always a fragile organization, the SCS never grew beyond a few branches. Its organ, the *Dawn*, lasted to 1896, its final issues paralleling the *American Fabian*, which Bliss also helped found to spread an evolutionary socialism. The SCS was as forthright as the CSF in wedding socialism and the Christian faith. Its objectives included showing that "the aim of Socialism is embraced in the aim of Christianity" and informing Christians that "the teachings of Jesus Christ lead directly to some specific form or forms of Socialism."[18]

Bliss's intellectual and programmatic ecumenicity, however, often made the socialism of the SCS and the *Dawn* seem diffuse. Early on, one critic quipped that the society was "something like a society for the propagation of virtue in general." "We love the truth more than any system," Bliss wrote, promising sympathy toward any organization "moving in our direction."[19] A close reading of the *Dawn* reveals that he included Edward Bellamy's Nationalist and Henry George's Single Tax movements, producers' cooperatives, legislation to better workers' lives, and the People's Party. Socialism, he wrote in his *Handbook of Socialism,* a comprehensive survey of socialist history, organizations, and principles, was a "fixed principle": the collective ownership and cooperative operation of land and capital. That principle, however, might take diverse and unforeseen forms, and it required gradual implementation: "Society is not to be run into it as a mould."[20] With Bliss's society undoubtedly in mind, Morris Hillquit contrasted the Christian Socialist Fellowship, which endorsed the Socialist Party's "program and methods . . . in their entirety" and actively cooperated with the party, with "the Christian Socialism of the nineties," which had its own program "distinct from that of the organized political parties of socialism."[21]

The Christian Socialism of Bliss and his society did not entirely deserve the reputation it received and has subsequently borne. For one thing, the *Dawn*'s gradualism, religious idealism, and selective acceptance of Marx would not be exceptional in American socialism after the turn of the century. For another, Bliss did explicitly claim a large debt to Marx, whose "scathing and relentless analysis of the present capitalistic system of production" he praised, and testified that it was Christ who made him a socialist and Marx who made him a Christian.[22] It was little known at the time, and has since eluded historians, but he was also an active member of the Socialist Labor Party (SLP). He used the party's *Workmen's Advocate* to recruit members for his Society of Christian Socialists, and the paper in turn commended his work. Members of the SCS took part in SLP rallies on the Boston Common in the summer of 1889, and in 1890 the *Workmen's Advocate* headed a report on him, "Comrade Bliss. Honest Man, and Scientific Socialist," and bestowed on him "first place in the list" of Boston socialists.[23] What forced Bliss to leave the SLP before the end of 1891 was a collision between his desire to work with the emerging Populist movement and the ascendancy of Daniel DeLeon in the SLP. As editor of the *People*, successor to the *Workmen's Advocate*, DeLeon cut off favorable comments about Christian Socialists and Bellamyite Nationalists and in the fall 1891 election campaign sharply attacked collaboration with the People's Party. Bliss was one of several in Boston's American Section (English-speaking) who favored aiding the Populists, in order to gain a wider hearing for socialism, but the majority disagreed, and he resigned.[24] A socialist in conviction, he was outside a socialist party until a new one arose.

Bliss's predicament was not unique among Americans of Protestant heritage who became disenchanted with their society and espoused radical remedies for its deficiencies in the late nineteenth century, but found no entirely satisfactory political medium for their ideals. To be a socialist politically then meant working through the Socialist Labor Party, and it was not an organization that welcomed them, reflected their moral values, or offered grounds for hope.

Organized in 1877, the SLP had only about 3,000 members in the entire country in 1889 when Bliss formed the SCS. Not only was it extremely small, the SLP was also preponderantly foreign-born in composition and concentrated in a few large cities, primarily in the Northeast.[25] Of 100 sections and branches in 1891, eighty-eight were German, and the German language pervaded party proceedings.[26] Its immigrant members, according to one historian, were "separated from the American workers by tradition, language, and experience, and the gulf between them and the masses they sought to reach seemed to widen even as they struggled to bridge it."[27]

When Daniel DeLeon gained ascendancy in the early 1890s, he used the *People* to refashion the SLP as a more American organization. Though this meant a different approach to the application of socialist principles and less ethnic isolation, it did not mean an end to sectarianism, for DeLeon was a man of imperious temperament and devotion to doctrinal orthodoxy. One historian describes DeLeon as moving "with the savagery attributed to later Leninist rule-or-ruin internal wrangling, to close down all other avenues of Socialist approach," thus consigning socialism to "marginality" at its moment of greatest opportunity, the depressed and turbulent 1890s. Another calls DeLeon "a zealot who could not tolerate heresy and backsliding, a doctrinaire who would make no compromise with principles." The party's leadership, writes yet another, was generally "more concerned with keeping the organization untainted with unscientific ideas than in leading and teaching the great body of American workers," and party activity centered "almost exclusively around heresy-hunting in its own ranks."[28] One contemporary recalled years later that the party's "machinery was managed by a small clique in New York City who were absolute autocrats and bosses"; persons of "independent character . . . were disciplined into obedience, and, if they would not obey the chiefs, were expelled"; "no theological body could surpass Socialist Labor intolerance. There had been a Scientific Socialist revelation from some one and the Socialist Labor chiefs were its prophets."[29] Referring to "endless contentions . . . over theoretical and philosophical quibbles," Benjamin O. Flower, publisher of the *Arena*, concluded more bluntly that the SLP's propaganda did not appeal to "the Anglo-Saxon mind."[30]

As David Thelen has argued, the decade of the 1890s witnessed not only devastating economic depression, but also profound shifts in social thought and openness to new political possibilities as Americans of many stripes redefined citizenship and the public welfare.[31] W.D.P. Bliss's search for a way to socialize American democracy was repeated in countless other lives. Most came out of such searches with progressive approaches that would dominate public life for the first two decades of the twentieth century. For the minority who reached radical positions, especially if they were native Protestants, the existing socialist party was not a viable alternative.

The situation changed with the birth of the Socialist Party of America in 1901. Drawing together former Populists, Christian Socialists, rebels against DeLeon's dominance of the SLP, independent radicals, and a Social Democratic Party that Eugene Debs had organized out of the American Railway Union, the new party was broadly based and internally democratic from the beginning. Its leaders appealed to a wide public with a program that included both immediate reforms and ultimate socialist goals and with rhetoric that drew upon old American moral and political traditions. It made room for diverse ideological perspectives and regional, ethnic, and occupational groupings. Two historians with very different perspectives concur on these points. David A. Shannon calls the SPA "a broad political organization representing all shades of leftist conviction," while James Weinstein describes a "democratic and open structure," which "permitted and benefited from a wide range of doctrinal and ideological views and tendencies within its ranks."[32]

The new party was immediately attractive to socialist Christians, several of whom contributed to its creation.[33] That it had a potential for success was evident from the outset. Even before unity was achieved, Debs received almost 95,000 votes as the Social Democratic candidate in 1900—almost three times the SLP tally; in 1904 and 1908 he received over 400,000 votes, and in 1912, nearly a million. A political scientist in 1911 who found socialists in at least 435 offices in 160 municipalities and other election districts in thirty-three states believed that socialism was assuming "a position of permanent consequence in the United States"; a careful survey by a historian yields over 1,200 socialist officeholders in 340 municipalities in 1912. Paid memberships in the SPA stood at over 20,000 in 1904 and climbed to almost 118,000 in 1912.[34] The socialist press proliferated, reaching a peak of at least 323 daily, weekly, and monthly periodicals with combined circulation of over two million by 1912–1913.[35] Socialist penetration of the labor movement became significant, with socialists gaining leadership positions and membership majorities in several large unions.[36] In contrast to the SLP, this party was pragmatic, outward-looking, and vibrant.

The work that religious people did as party loyalists was far-ranging, and only suggestive examples can be given here. They served as party lecturers, editors, organizers, state secretaries, and members of local, state, and national committees. CSF founder Carr went as a delegate to the International Socialist Congress in

Stuttgart in 1907, and his wife, Ella Carr, served on the Woman's National Committee.[37] Both the Intercollegiate Socialist Society (ISS), founded in 1905 to promote the study of socialism on campuses, and the Rand School of Social Science in New York City benefited from the financial support and leadership of socialist Christians. George Strobell provided the organizational skills that enabled Upton Sinclair and other intellectuals to launch the ISS, and Rufus Weeks was for years one of the organization's financial angels. No fewer than eight identifiable socialist Christians served on its executive committee between 1905 and 1921, and J. G. Phelps Stokes was its president from 1907 to 1918.[38] Strobell was an early director of the Rand School of Social Science in New York City and its secretary from 1916 to 1922.[39] Even the iconoclastic *Masses* was subsidized during its first year, 1911–1912, by Rufus Weeks.[40]

Though a majority of the party's candidates were wage-earners, it was not unusual for ministers or former ministers to run for office on the socialist ticket. Their experience as orators and writers served them well in this regard. In Milwaukee, Wisconsin, Congregationalist Carl D. Thompson won election as a state legislator and as city clerk, and Winfield Gaylord, another former Congregational minister, almost became Wisconsin's second Socialist congressman in 1914.[41] Three of the party's most significant mayoral victories, all in 1911, were won by ministers: J. Stitt Wilson in Berkeley, California, Lewis J. Duncan in Butte, Montana, and George R. Lunn in Schenectady, New York. The examples could be multiplied.

The many American Christians who enlisted in the socialist movement early in the twentieth century did so determined to establish credibility *as socialists*. There is no mistaking the *Christian Socialist's* admonitions about party membership or the discourses of respected leaders like Weeks and Strobell. This determination reflected the belief that socialism was superior to capitalism as a social system. The frequency with which they expressed this determination, however, reflected also their sensitivity to nineteenth-century precedents: They were deeply aware of a residual suspicion of Christians who embraced socialism but qualified it as Christian socialism. When they called themselves "Christian Socialists," as many unavoidably still did, "Christian" did not signify a diminished socialism. To be sure, they varied in acceptance of Marxian economic analysis, revolutionary mood, and longevity in the movement. So, however, did non-religious socialists. People who came to the party from Christian backgrounds fanned out across the spectrum of socialist ideology, from Left to Right. Like any other socialists, they responded to questions of party policy according to many variables and were never a monolithic group.They were certainly not monolithically trimmers when it came to indicting capitalism or asserting that, though socialists should not seek a bloody revolution, they must go on "no matter through what fields of flowers or blood-soaked grass [their] pathway lead."[42]

THE ISSUE OF SOCIALIST ANTAGONISM TO RELIGION

Combating a perception that socialism and atheism were somehow logically related was a second major endeavor of the Christian Socialist Fellowship and its fellow travelers. The challenge to do so was persistent because of a significant stratum of belief, among native as well as foreign-born and middle-class as well as working-class party members, that to accept Marx's economics, one must also accept his atheism. When an author in the *New York Call* proffered guidelines for conducting socialist meetings, his most emphatic advice was: "Kill capitalism. Let the other fellow kill God, if he is able and willing."[43] One need only scan socialist periodicals—the *New York Call*, the *Chicago Daily Socialist*, the *International Socialist Review*—for significant numbers of issues to find contributions by both intellectuals and rank-and-filers arguing the falsity of religion. Even the *Christian Socialist* carried expressions of that point of view, if only to counter them. Religion was a lively issue within the Socialist Party, the subject of platform debates, songs, cartoons, poems, pamphlets, and books.

There were other strands of anti-religious opinion among socialists, sometimes but not always associated with this atheism. Most common were attacks on organized religion, particularly Christianity, as a reactionary force. The bitterness that was possible in these attacks suffuses a letter to Baptist theologian and historian Walter Rauschenbusch by a working-class woman in Oregon who had found his indictment of capitalism in *Christianity and the Social Crisis* (1907) more effective than most socialist propaganda, but objected to his appeal to the churches to be sympathetic to socialism. Describing herself as "by nature religious," she testified that it was axiomatic that those who became party members must sever ties with churches. If socialists were atheists, she contended, it was because the churches made them so; churches served the interests of the master class and "chloroformed" wage-earners, and she wished only "to see them go to pieces forever." Speaking for those who considered socialism "the most powerful force for justice, democracy, and organized fraternity in the modern world," Rauschenbusch pointed to such hostility to religion as a major impediment to involvement in "party socialism as they actually find it."[44]

Those who made such attacks commonly saw in Christianity a betrayal of Jesus' spirit of humanity and message of social justice. Socialist Christians themselves indulged in this line of thinking, often pointing approvingly to instances when working-class audiences hissed the mention of the church or Christianity but stood and cheered at the name of the carpenter of Nazareth. Attacks on organized religion—the institutions rather than the uncorrupted spirit or message—frequently singled out the clergy and the wealthy who pulled their puppet strings for special abuse. Addressing the issue of working-class "alienation" from the churches, with which Protestant leaders had struggled since the 1880s (usually ignoring not only working-class Catholicism but also huge segments of Protestantism itself), socialist authors attributed it to the fact that churches did not represent wage-earners. As Clarence Meily put it, "The workingman is outside the church of today because the church belongs to his master and voices only the interest of the capitalistic class."[45]

Whether institutional Christianity could be repristinated along New Testament lines was a matter over which opinion divided. Naturally, for those who rejected that possibility but still professed admiration for Jesus, socialism displaced the churches as the instrument of his purposes. Arguing from the perspective of economic determinism, however, a "scientific" socialist, Robert Rives LaMonte, thought that Christianity might yet "grow into the Religion of Socialism." As it had been   shaped in the past by the economic status of the earliest Christians, by feudalism, and by the rise of the bourgeoisie, so it might be transformed by the socialist revolution; then the Christian Communion would become "a banquet of brothers, ringing the globe in its embrace, joyously marking their sense of human oneness by this catholic feast of fellowship in honor of Him who first taught and lived the life of fellowship."[46]

The issue of atheism merits special consideration because it was fundamental to the very definition of socialism. Marx's atheism is indisputable. One contemporary scholar, British author David McLellan, portrays a Marx whose hostility to religion was alleviated only by indifference. Marx's father, a reluctant Jewish convert to Protestantism, was strongly influenced by Enlightenment thinkers, and whatever religious beliefs Marx had as a child were dashed at the University of Berlin. Influenced by the metaphysics of Ludwig Feuerbach, Marx considered the question of religious truth claims settled. As he developed his own "science of society," religion took a purely secondary place as part of the superstructure created by society's determinative economic forces. When he commented on religion not in metaphysical but in "functional" terms, moreover, he saw it as a fantasy (rooted in primitive social evolutionary stages) or as an instrument of class rule—but in either case, as an impediment to movements for material progress. McLellan contends that Marx condemned talk about linking the social principles of Christianity to socialism and was confident religion would disappear under communism.[47] A philosopher who has analyzed the relationship between Marx's atheism and the rest of his ideas, Peter Schuller, contends that he opposed religion not only because of historical contingencies or tactical considerations, but more fundamentally because he believed it was untrue, and because he believed it ruled out the human free agency required by a real ethical dimension in life.[48] Marx's colleague, Friedrich Engels, reared in an intensely Pietist environment, also became an atheist who saw little besides illusion in religion.[49]

Marxist accounts of religion could be more complex and nuanced than this, however, even when their authors shared the atheism of Marx and Engels, as some subsequent Marxist work illustrates. If Marx considered his philosophy and political economy inseparable, those who followed in his path did not always agree. The fact is that patterns varied in the socialist movement both in Europe and the United States. German socialism, despite some softening in the decades before World War I, carried a stronger anti-religious virus than did British socialism, which readily incorporated Christian ethical elements, as ideology bent to different national situations. In the United States socialists freely debated how much of Marx they had to accept to be socialists, their choices based on experience, temperament, and association, not logical necessity.

Few socialists were more prolific in trying to disconnect socialism from an anti-religious position than John Spargo. His views are a composite of the arguments made over and over again by those who thought religion and socialism compatible. Spargo's religious history forms a necessary backdrop to his developed views. Born in Cornwall, England, he grew up in a world of tin mines and granite quarries and of fervent Wesleyan Methodism. Joining the Social Democratic Federation ended his work as a lay preacher by the time he was eighteen. Recalling the doubts faced in the 1890s by many young people with intellectual aspirations, he spoke of flirting with atheism but really being agnostic.[50]

When he moved to New York in 1901, Spargo immediately became involved in American socialist affairs. He was a founding member and field agent of the Fellowship of the Socialist Spirit, organized in 1901 by George D. Herron, William Thurston Brown, J. Stitt Wilson, and several other newly minted socialist ministers or former ministers. He simultaneously became editor of the *Comrade*, a radical cultural journal also closely connected to Herron.[51] Under Spargo's influence the *Comrade's* tone was usually not hostile to religion. In fact, for twenty issues in 1902–1903, it carried "How I Became a Socialist" articles that treated religion in their authors' earlier lives evenhandedly. Spargo's editorials, however, occasionally lashed out at attempts to Christianize socialism. "Socialism embodies an ethical concept infinitely higher than anything that organized religion has ever known," stated one, while another found "no wrong, however terrible, which has not been justified by Christianity" and "no movement for human liberty which has not been opposed by it."[52]

For reasons that remain obscure, his writings a few years later reflect a mellower view. He never tried to "Christianize" socialism, but he did argue, frequently and at length, that there was no reason to consider socialism hostile to religion in general or Christianity in particular. He also took an interest in the Christian Socialist Fellowship, was active in its New York City center, and shared views and material with people like J. G. Phelps Stokes, Rufus Weeks, and Bishop Franklin S. Spalding.[53] As an interpreter of socialist theory and a biographer of Marx, Spargo countered the claim that Marxism entailed a materialist metaphysics or personal irreligion.

The Marx Spargo presented was winsome and nondogmatic. Spargo's biographical rendition was usually part of a broader defense of reformist socialism, but it always had important implications for religion. In a book on socialist principles he acknowledged that Marx was an atheist but added that he appreciated the ethical ideals of religion, was very tolerant toward religious believers, and opposed identifying the socialist movement with atheism. These were all claims he would repeat, as was his contention that Marx's historical materialism did not exclude human freedom.[54] A full-scale biography of Marx, for which Rufus Weeks gave help, presented a revolutionary whose goals were achievable by peaceful political means, whose proletarians welcomed allies from other classes, and whose ultimate ends did not rule out working for immediate betterment: in short, in the context of socialist debates over strategy, an "opportunist" rather than "impossibilist."[55] This was also a Marx who indicted capitalism for reducing marriage to a matter of economic calculation, not affection; his own family life was one of "singular beauty and purity" and "almost sublime devotion to his wife," and the best way to arouse his ire was "to utter vulgar remarks, or to tell stories or jokes of a questionable nature, in the hearing of women or children—especially children."[56] Though an atheist, Spargo's Marx had contempt for "professional atheists." A "great spiritual passion" actually flowed beneath his intellectual materialism, and he abhorred the spiritual as well as economic effects of capitalism upon workers.[57]

In other works Spargo explored the sources, character, and significance of socialist opposition to religion and points of convergence between socialism and religion. He offered a spiritual interpretation of the socialist movement, insisting that it could not be fully understood apart from its spiritual qualities, which included a nearly universal and "profound faith in the Brotherhood of Man," "reverence and love for Jesus" (despite invective—like his own in the *Comrade*—against churches), and other parallels to early Christianity.[58]

The antagonism between socialism and religion he considered to be adventitious and impermanent. It was adventitious largely because of the historical confluence between Marxism and naturalistic evolutionary science and the hostility of European state churches to progressive movements. It was impermanent largely because religion and socialism were both changing profoundly, religion accommodating itself to modern thought, de-emphasizing institutional and creedal priorities, and recovering the teachings of Jesus, and socialism shaking off nineteenth-century scientism and atheism.[59] Reconcilers of socialism and religion within and outside the CSF found such an interpretation reassuring.

Spargo's fullest treatment of Marx's philosophy appeared in his very important *Marxian Socialism and Religion*, in which he took considerable care to define terms. His argument distinguished between philosophical materialism, according to which "matter and its motions constitute the Universe," and historical materialism (economic determinism), according to which the economic environment is the principal shaping force in life. The former was utterly incompatible with religion, and Spargo thought Marx a philosophical materialist. He contended, however, that Marx did not think his materialistic conception of history was dependent on his philosophical views, and thus never intended to make those views a requisite of acceptance of his economic analysis.[60]

In addition, Spargo argued that Marx had a more complex understanding of causation than many realized. To begin with, the economic environment included not only the obviously economic factors of production and exchange, but also such physical factors as climate, soil, race, and geography. Furthermore, the laws, moral codes, religious ideas, and other elements of the social superstructure that rested on the economic environment became causes in turn of further developments, "reacting upon one another and upon the economic environment which produced them, functioning as co-determinants of social evolution."[61] Disentangled from philosophical materialism and a monocausal interpretation of history, the socialism that Spargo described left belief in God intact and the power of religious beliefs and values still operative for human betterment.

Though none wrote as much as Spargo on the subject, other socialists, some of considerable stature, spurned attempts to make religious faith acceptable to socialists. An anonymous early contributor to the *International Socialist Review* contrasted the artistic, scientific, and philosophical achievements of "paganism" with the mystical, authoritarian, and anti-rational qualities of Christianity, which he or she characterized as a perennial enemy of progress. Anton Pannekoek, a European contributor to the same journal, insisted that what socialists believed was of great concern in the cause—"We prefer a thorough scientific understanding to an unscientific religious faith"—but was sure that changed economic conditions would automatically bring about the demise of a religious worldview. Isador Ladoff, an activist with a long record of attacking religion, vented a variety of arguments in the *International Socialist Review*, but his central theme was simple: "Faith makes knowledge impossible. Knowledge makes faith superfluous. There can be no compromise between religion and science, mysticism and rationalism"; "Socialism is essentially . . . a free-thought movement. The thinking Socialists are all free-thinkers."[62]

Works published outside the socialist press for a wider audience also dismissed religion in the name of science and socialism. In one such work John Macy, husband of Helen Keller's teacher, Anne Sullivan, expressed the wish that the Socialist Party would proclaim officially that it and the churches were at war. William English Walling, in a work on the "intellectual and spiritual side" of socialism, championed an evolutionary explanation of religion and averred that a majority of socialists saw "no room whatever for religion in any form" in a socialist society.[63]

As for the *Christian Socialist*, its most thorough airing of the issues was an exchange in 1907 between E. E. Carr and Ernest Unterman, a prolific author in his own right and translator of German socialist classics, including works by Marx and Engels, for Charles H. Kerr Company. In a review of a posthumous book by Joseph Dietzgen, a close friend of Marx and Engels, Carr attacked Dietzgen's philosophical position, while making animadversions on his personal life. He contended that materialism was not truly scientific because it ignored evidence for the existence of God from "The cosmos, experience and utility—all fully in the realm of fact." Shortly thereafter, Carr reviewed a work by Paul Lafargue, Marx's son-in-law, repeating his contention about scientific grounds for belief in God and sharply faulting Charles H. Kerr for publishing works "purporting to be" socialist but "devoted chiefly to the spread of atheism." Unterman's response took appropriate humbrage at Carr's ad hominem nastiness, faulted his understanding of Dietzgen's work, and tartly dismissed his case for God as "a rehash of the ancient pantheistic notions, a vague and meaningless nothing without practical foundation and outside of the field of scientific perception." Most important, he denied in no uncertain terms that one could pick and choose among Marx's ideas and that any "Christian Socialism" was possible. Defending Dietzgen's attempt to "remove the last metaphysical cobwebs which still obscure the reasoning faculties of the modern proletariat," Unterman said of the elements of Marx's thought: "If you reject one, you reject them all." Carr had the last words in this exchange. Implying that Unterman was a dogmatic sectarian, he concluded that free individuals did not owe Marx unreserved allegiance, and asserted that Marx's contribution was discovering the method by which to complete "the historic struggle of the class-conscious proletariat toward the co-operative commonwealth" for which Jesus had provided the ethical impetus.[64] Such exchanges changed few, if any, minds; those predisposed to either side had too much at stake to change, even if the other side's arguments had been truly conclusive.

Despite the prevalence of anti-religious opinions, German socialists adopted statements at conferences at Gotha in 1875 and Erfurt in 1891 declaring that religion was a private matter. Socialist parties in other countries took similar actions, as did the SPA at its convention in 1908. If the party did not thereby eliminate religion as a source of controversy, it at least reduced its disruptive potential. And it set a standard to which each side could hold the other, however much both violated it. How it originated is unclear, but on 15 May the platform committee presented a resolution "That religion be treated as a private matter—a question of individual conscience." The ensuing debate, which occupied that afternoon and an evening session and fifteen pages of convention proceedings, brought some of the party's leading personalities into play: Morris Hillquit, Victor Berger, Unterman, Robert Hunter, national secretary J. Mahlon Barnes, Arthur Morrow Lewis, Spargo, Algie M. Simons, and a number of state and local leaders. About ten people associated with the Christian Socialist Fellowship were among the delegates, but this contingent apparently wished to play a minimal role, and only a few members spoke: Frederick Guy Strickland, a minister in the Christian Church; Eliot White, an Episcopal priest; and Mila Tupper Maynard, a former Unitarian clergywoman. The exchange of opinions was intense, indicating the momentousness of the resolution's implications.

The sparks began when Arthur Lewis, a popularizer of scientific naturalism who for many years held weekly Sunday meetings at Chicago's Garrick Theater billed as the Workers' University Society, moved to delete the resolution. Granting that socialist opposition to religion was an impediment to electoral success, he insisted that "if we must speak . . . we shall go before this country with the truth and not with a lie." Early in the debate Hillquit introduced substitute language that eventually passed, though only by a vote of 79–78: "The Socialist movement is primarily an economic and political movement. It is not concerned with religious beliefs." He also got the statement moved from the platform's section on program to that on principles, which would seem to have made it more basic but actually relieved some delegates' anxiety. Though the difference between the two versions does not seem significant, some believed that it was. As one delegate suggested afterward, the vote was close because some delegates strongly preferred the original wording. If he was correct, there was actually less opposition to some declaration of neutrality on religion than the close vote suggests.

The resolution cut both ways in either form. Participants in the debate complained of misuse of socialist forums to tie both atheism and Christianity to the party's economic program. The greater concern, however, was over anti-religious propaganda. Neither side, interestingly enough, was monolithic. Of the religious speakers, Strickland, a veteran of the party's founding, displayed his familiarity with the writings of German Marxists Karl Kautsky and Joseph Dietzgen to argue for the original resolution, which he saw as a way of opposing corrupted Christianity but not the pure original. White thought the resolution no more necessary for socialists than for other political parties, and Maynard considered the resolution an appropriate way to discourage attacks on religious dogmas that were giving way to a progressive "cosmic theism."

Secular participants, some of whom thought the resolution required them to juggle the respective claims of intellectual fidelity and political pragmatism, also divided over the resolution. Unterman spoke against it because he believed that the only way to truth was the "inductive, analytical method of historical materialism," though he understood the words to mean only that socialists should wait until people were inside the movement and ready before broaching its deeper principles. Several others asserted that religion was a survival from primitive superstition and opposed the resolution as deceptive. Hunter and others supported the resolution as authorization for party members to say whatever they wished with respect to religion. Affirming his agnosticism, Hillquit likewise separated religious beliefs from socialism in arguing for the statement. Barnes, probably agnostic as well, considered the statement unnecessary, but, predicting undesirable press coverage if the convention voted it down, urged passage. Ever the opportunist, Berger, who claimed that the resolution was his idea, called himself a "pronounced agnostic" but predicted a long wait indeed for socialism if its coming depended on making a majority of Americans free-thinkers.[65]

Statements like Barnes's and pointed references by others to deception and vote-chasing contributed to disagreement over the motives that led to passage of the resolution. Even counting those who did not speak, the religious contingent was too thin to have secured passage alone, and it was thoroughly secular persons who introduced and advanced it in debate. Those secular supporters were concerned to varying degrees about removing barriers to the acceptance of socialism by religious Americans, but tactical considerations were secondary in their arguments to their understanding of socialism. For socialist Christians it was a happy coincidence that many comrades agreed that philosophy and program were separable.

Controversy over religion did not end among socialists in 1908, as many previously cited statements make clear. Before the year was out, the *Christian Socialist* attacked Arthur Morrow Lewis, who presented science as the force that would liberate workers from the shackles of superstition, for "unceasing attacks upon the belief in God, upon religion and the Church" and the *Chicago Daily Socialist* for giving him undue attention. The reputation Lewis gave socialism, the editor contended, was a principal factor behind a disappointing socialist vote in Chicago that fall. Lewis's defense in the *Daily Socialist*—that he only explained religion socially, as had Marx, Engels, and others—did not satisfy the *Christian Socialist*. Under pressure within the party, he then made peace with the Christians by promising in the *Daily Socialist* not to make offensive remarks about religion.[66]

Neither side, however, could resist confrontation. In 1911 Carr debated Lewis at the Garrick on the question "Does the evidence justify belief in the existence of God?" before a crowd packed "to the dome." Four years later Lewis challenged Irwin St. John Tucker, then managing editor of the *Christian Socialist*, to two debates, the first of which turned to disaster, culminating in refunds to the audience and cancellation of the second. Lewis resorted to ridicule, according to Tucker, saying, for example, that "the Bible began when Moses had a bad dream of a burning bush, caused by eating too much gefultefish [*sic*] the night before!" A Chicago newspaper paraphrased similar remarks about the idea of a deity originating with "the 'bogey men' of prehistoric tribal life" and that of the soul, "when savages saw their shadows." However thoughtful Lewis's overall presentation may have been, such remarks could only embarrass those who were devoted to reconciling Christian faith and radical politics.[67]

A latent source of controversy within the movement throughout the first two decades of the twentieth century, the issue of whether religious belief was admissible for professed socialists remained beyond the reach of compromise. Strongly influenced by John Spargo, who had settled there, the Socialist Party of Vermont in 1912 adopted a statement about socialist parties and religion. Intended to offset stereotypes of socialist antagonism to religion, that document clearly divorced socialism from philosophical materialism, recited the positions taken by European socialist parties on religion, and cited instances of religious people who were active in socialist politics. Five years later, a party convention in Michigan adopted a strong stance against religion on the basis of philosophical materialism, one of several actions that led to its expulsion by the National Executive Committee of the SPA and eventuated in the communist schisms of 1919–1920.[68]

THE ROMAN CATHOLIC ATTACK ON SOCIALISM

The antagonistic relationship between the Roman Catholic Church and socialism turned largely but not exclusively on the disputed relationship between Marxian philosophy and Marxian economics. This antagonism preoccupied many in both church and party. Several elements in the historical context throw light on the ramifications of the standoff. To begin with, the church's centuries-old legacy of state establishment in parts of Europe and its hierarchical structure of authority gave it a socially conservative orientation and a reputation that invited suspicion on the part of secular and liberal movements of many sorts. Second, the teachings of the popes, embodied principally in papal encyclicals, set the boundaries and the distinctive emphases of Catholic social theory and its application to social policy. Though the encyclicals proved remarkably flexible, those who taught in the name of the church had to work within their framework.

A third element in the Catholic-socialist relationship was a deeply rooted and powerful anti-Catholicism, which some socialist critics of the church freely vented, and which some in the church saw in any outside criticism. While some conservative clerics reacted to the American situation with a defensive policy of institutional and cultural separateness, their more liberal colleagues sought to combat anti-Catholicism by urging the faithful to be as "American" as possible, free of associations and behaviors that might jeopardize acceptance by the Protestant majority. The Americanizing leaders in the church, moreover, generally approved the United States pretty much as it was, and some held interpretations of American "exceptionalism" that offered no ground for radical reconstruction.[69]

Finally, the overwhelming proportion of Catholics who were members of the American working class made the stakes high both for church leaders, who worried about their flock's susceptibility to dangerous ideologies and allegiances, and for socialists, who desperately wished to break down barriers to blue-collar Catholics' acceptance of their message. From the perspective of the church, if socialism even as only an economic program violated natural economic rights or fundamental moral principles, which many in the clergy thought it did, Catholic socialists would be in grave moral and spiritual error; and, of course, if socialism was inseparable from Marx's philosophical materialism, being both Catholic and socialist was utterly unthinkable. From the perspective of the party, which wished to win over Catholic workers, it was important not to let the church's anti-socialism (institutional authority) go unchallenged; it was also important to avoid being painted as anti-religious, anti-family, and atheistic. Balancing these imperatives was far from easy for the party.

The basic framework for Catholic social thought in the early twentieth century was *Rerum Novarum*, issued in 1891 by Pope Leo XIII. Expressing deep concern for the effects of industrialism upon workers and a sharp critique of laissez-faire principles, Leo insisted that private property was essential to moral development and the integrity of the family, upheld guild-like forms of cooperation as preferable to adversarial relations between employers and trade unions, and explicitly rejected socialism.[70] Pope Leo's letter left those responsible for interpreting Catholic teaching room to maneuver, but his anti-socialism was unavoidable, even if, as some contended, secondary to his other points. An author in the *Catholic World* in 1897 found enough flaws in socialist economic description to dismiss it, but, more important, insisted that its economic and philosophical components were inseparable and ran afoul of Leo's teachings. "To speak of Catholic socialism," he stated, "is an attempt to join two incongruous ideas." Twenty-one years later, the same paper carried a theological essay repudiating socialism on grounds laid out in Pope Leo's encyclicals, especially the natural right to private property, and denying therefore that a Catholic could be a socialist.[71] Between these two essays appeared many nearly identical pronouncements. The chapter title for this period in a pioneering study of Catholic social thought and action is revealing: "Not Socialism—but Social Reform." Catholics, the author finds, were "preoccupied during the whole of the Progressive era" with socialism.[72]

Some members of the American Catholic hierarchy preached and wrote with particular adamancy against any Catholic participation in the socialist movement. In 1901 Archbishop Michael Corrigan of New York preached at St. Patrick's Cathedral that "not a single leader among the Socialists [was] a Christian. . . . Their maxim is not Christian."[73] A Catholic paper reported in 1906 that nearly all American bishops had in the previous five years condemned socialism in a pastoral letter, public interview, or sermon.[74] In some dioceses anti-socialist initiatives were quite vigorous, as well as moderately effective. In Massachusetts, church attacks through the diocesan *Boston Pilot* helped stall the growth of the socialist movement very early in the century, and Cardinal William O'Connell, who believed that nothing—"neither God, nor His altars, nor His ministers, nor home, nor native land, nor wife, nor family"—was sacred to socialists, continued the campaign through the 1910s. O'Connell warned all his parishes in a pastoral letter in 1912 that it was "an utter impossibility" to be a Catholic socialist, and simultaneously gave support to a new anti-socialist organization, the Common Cause Society, formed in Boston. Bishop John P. Carroll of Helena, Montana, similarly opposed the socialist administration of Lewis J. Duncan, a former Unitarian minister who had won election as mayor in Butte in 1911, with partial effect among Irish-American voters. Milwaukee socialists struggled against the church's opposition over many years, especially in Polish and Italian wards, and they alleged that Archbishop Sebastian Messmer forbade Catholics to vote for or belong to the Socialist Party .[75]

Catholic authors approached socialism with varying degrees of erudition and patience. Bishop William Stang of Fall River, Massachusetts, had little of either. In *Socialism and Christianity* he assailed not only socialism, which "if carried to its legitimate conclusion," he predicted, would "end in the annihilation of all legitimate institutions of authority and order," but also the Protestant Reformers, public schools, uppity women and children, and birth control.[76] Beyond Stang, representing an extreme, no doubt, stood a Brooklyn priest who wrote in his parish paper that the socialist agitator was "more dangerous than cholera or smallpox—yes, he is the mad dog of society and should be silenced, if need be, by the bullet."[77]

Far more sensitive to nuances was the work of Jesuit John J. Ming, *The Characteristics and the Religion of Modern Socialism.* Yielding nothing to socialism, Ming displayed considerable familiarity with socialist sources so that his representations of what they actually said, if not his interpretations of their intentions or implications, were fair. He found socialist theory to be ultimately materialistic but noted that some authors advocated a "materialism tempered with idealistic elements." In assessing socialist antagonism to religion, he examined both European platform statements that religion was a private affair and socialist explanations of the origins of religion. His conclusion was that the antagonism was inherent. When socialist parties said religion was private, their purpose was to separate church and state, and thus strip established religions of educational and other civic functions. Moreover, the Marxist view that religion was a social-evolutionary product left no place for it in a socialist future. Ming's weakness was an inability to conceive of Christianity as anything other than a body of revealed, fixed truths and an institution embodying them. Attempts by theological modernizers working from Protestant premises to see a spiritual element in socialism or socialistic principles in Christianity were alien to him. The *International Socialist Review,* which had dismissed Stang for using "plain bare-faced lies for argument," nevertheless gave Ming's work respectful, albeit critical, consideration.[78]

There were other broad assessments of socialism by Catholic thinkers. A British Jesuit, Bernard Vaughan, in a sermon series at St. Patrick's in New York expanded into a book in 1912, drew a dreary picture of despotic statism, faulted socialists for believing that material improvements could improve character, found socialism antithetical to the family and religion, and belittled Christian socialists for having both a "feeble" socialism and an "eviscerated" Christianity.[79]

Perhaps more than any other American Catholic spokesman in the early twentieth century, it was John A. Ryan who argued that Catholics must commit themselves to improving industrial conditions while stoutly rejecting socialism. Ryan's moral arguments and statistical calculations for a "living wage" earned him a doctorate in economics from the Catholic University in 1906, where he worked with the pioneering William Kerby. As author of the famous Bishop's Program of Social Reconstruction in 1919, and subsequently the driving force in the National Catholic Welfare Conference, Ryan became the pre-eminent representative of Catholic social liberalism. A close student of the papal social encyclicals, he crafted an understanding of them fully congruent with the New Deal, which he served in official capacities.[80]

Ryan's perspective appeared in his answer to the question of whether Catholics could be socialists in a 1909 article in the Catholic *Fortnightly Review*. If "socialism" meant either the organized movement or the philosophy, both of which were overwhelmingly anti-theistic, the answer was no. If it meant the program of public ownership contained in socialist party platforms, it was yes, but he did not regard that program as economically promising. The critical point, of course, is that he in effect ruled out party membership for Catholics. Impatient with those who interpreted the Church Fathers' statements about wealth as proto-socialist, Ryan also published a short compilation and analysis of the passages usually cited, especially those from Saints Basil, Ambrose, and Jerome, to prove that this was not the case.[81]

Ryan's most widely disseminated statements about socialism appeared in debates with Morris Hillquit carried on in seven issues of *Everybody's Magazine* and reprinted as a book in 1914. Both men were razor-sharp intellectuals, and their statements were precise, cogent, and civil. There is no more comprehensive and lucid presentation of arguments for and against socialism between two covers in the literature of the period. Submitting their papers to each other for criticism in advance of publication, the authors were able to scuttle untenable positions and produce well-honed statements.[82]

Ryan agreed with harsher critics that socialism was both an economic program and a philosophical system, that private property and the motives associated with competition were ethically and socially essential, that socialist moral principles were flawed, and that the socialist movement was preponderantly irreligious. He dismissed the SPA's resolution on religion in 1908 as based on political calculation; platforms in any case were only skeletal representations of a movement whose basic literature was full of anti-religious opinion. He avoided caricature, hyperbole, and invective, however, in making his points. Hillquit's statements were in turn among the best in socialist argumentation. William English Walling believed that Ryan had won the economic argument, but Hillquit the religious argument.[83]

A debate without acrimony was rare in the history of Catholic-socialist relations.[84] Debs considered Ryan's arguments weak but Ryan interested in the truth and eminently fair. Hillquit later called him "probably the most formidable but at the same time the most gratifying opponent" he had ever debated. Ryan also respected Hillquit and, though not optimistic about the prospects, expressed his pleasure should feelings of hostility between church and socialist movement end.[85]

At the opposite extreme stood virtually all contacts between socialists and Catholic convert David Goldstein. His tactics, prefiguring those of Senator Joseph

McCarthy, included innuendo, guilt by association, misrepresentation, and fabrication. In a debate with Carl Thompson, Goldstein held up a list of 200 allegedly atheistic and free-love books by socialists. Fred Hurst, party secretary in Rhode Island, caught him reading an anti-marriage, anti-family diabtribe allegedly from the Erfurt platform at a Knights of Columbus gathering. John Spargo found forged statements from his own writings in a piece by Goldstein in the National Civic Federation's paper.[86] Goldstein helped stall the Massachusetts party's promising career in 1903 and for years thereafter aggravated socialists with his lectures and highly advertised debates.[87]

The child of immigrant Dutch Jews, Goldstein was involved in the late 1890s in the Socialist Labor Party in Boston, where he met Martha Moore Avery, who had come to socialism from Unitarianism through Nationalism. Achieving prominence as candidates for local offices, both left the SLP with Morris Hillquit's "kangaroo" faction in the late 1890s and ended up in the new SPA. The circumstances under which they left the socialist movement in late 1902 or 1903 are clouded, but both left already interested in Catholicism, to which they soon converted. Both claimed that close study of socialism led them to discover an ineradicable atheism and antagonism to marriage rooted in materialist philosophy. In particular, George D. Herron's divorce and remarriage and his denunciations of organized religion—and the blessing socialists nonetheless cast on him—completed their disillusionment. In their accounts, the Massachusetts party's defeat of a resolution to ban speakers who endorsed free love, violence, and atheism from socialist platforms was decisive.[88]

The product of Goldstein's discoveries was *Socialism: The Nation of Fatherless Children*, dedicated to the American Federation of Labor. To prove that socialism would overthrow the state, the family, and religion, he quoted socialist authors extensively. Quotation for Goldstein included stringing together highly provocative segments from original works, with frequent rhetorical asides and questions and without noting deletions. His characterizations of people, their ideas, and events were reductionist when not abusive. The book's animus against Herron and anyone associated with him—expressed in forty pages of quotations and comments—is especially striking.[89] Its rhetoric is extravagant, full of such phrases as the "slush and slime of materialism," "the pig pens of life," and "men and women broken in virtue and in health—crazed with the passions of sex." Sections on "Political Atheism" and "Free Love," the book's longest, were also the most inflamed.

After a brief period of anti-socialist activity, Goldstein withdrew from the cause for five years until asked by Cardinal O'Connell, who gave his imprimatur to a second edition of *Socialism:The Nation of Fatherless Children* in 1911, to take it up again.[90] From 1911 to 1913 Goldstein toured widely for the Central Verein of St. Louis, a German-American Catholic federation interested in promoting Catholic social principles, and from 1914 to 1917, for the Knights of Columbus, which had become concerned about socialism after the 1912 election. Both organizations also employed Peter Collins, an officer of the Brotherhood of Electrical Workers and of Boston's Central Labor Union, and the two men often worked in tandem.[91]

Catholic anti-socialism was of heightened importance because it dovetailed with a Catholic effort to influence the American Federation of Labor. As it developed in the 1910s, the church's relationship to the AFL was oriented toward keeping Catholic workers faithful but also toward keeping the AFL under non-socialist leadership. Socialist strength in some of the AFL's constituent unions, such as the brewers, miners, garment workers, and machinists, gave credibility to the latter concern. Though Catholic labor activists also opposed the open-shop campaign of the National Association of Manufacturers and other anti-union employer organizations, combating socialist influence in the AFL was arguably their primary concern.[92]

The key figure in launching this effort was Peter E. Dietz, a priest active in the Central Verein who, disappointed by the absence of an organized Catholic presence at the AFL convention in 1909, took steps to form the Militia of Christ for Social Service at the 1910 convention. With strong church support, Dietz issued Catholic labor publications, held great masses at AFL conventions, and collaborated with Catholic officers of the federation and its member unions in ensuing years. The Militia of Christ became associated with the American Federation of Catholic Societies in 1911, when Dietz took charge of the latter organization's social-service department. Along with the Central Verein and Knights of Columbus, the Militia worked with Goldstein and even more closely with Collins in their anti-socialist efforts.[93]

Socialists were sensitive to Dietz's efforts, fully understanding the centrality of anti-socialism on his agenda. The SPA's information director, Carl Thompson, issued a press release emphasizing that the Militia was an adversary, and he set about gathering information to use in the event of open conflict with Catholics in the unions. Socialist papers alleged that Dietz was using the threat of dual unionism (forming Catholic unions), as it had in Europe, to keep the AFL in conservative hands.[94] According to one report, he told a group of Catholic unionists: "If you try anything that could tend to aid the Socialists, the Catholic Church would be compelled to disown the AFL and begin organizing Catholic unions."[95]

The impact of all this on lay Catholics may not have been as great as socialists feared. Despite images of a monolithic church before the reforms of the Second Vatican Council (1962–1965), Catholics were surely not automatons. Not all Catholic observers thought that Goldstein and Collins really hurt the socialist cause. As one Catholic scholar has noted, it is naive to believe that "when the Pope coughed all Catholics at least sneezed." Yet it also undeniable that only very isolated Catholic workers in this period were unaware that their church did not want them in the Socialist Party.[96]

Undoubtedly, many thousands of Catholics voted for socialists. The party's vote in some cities is inexplicable without that assumption. Despite the official church pronouncements, a Paulist urban missionary found Catholics dismissing the clergy who criticized socialism as being unfriendly to workers. John Spargo remarked that as SPA convention delegates, "loyal Catholics, without any shame or apology to any of their comrades," could "go directly from mass to the work of shaping the policy of the socialist party."[97] Not only were Catholic workers motivated by the realities of their own situation and by the ideal of social justice, but the party also made efforts to counter the church's opposition, including publications by Catholic socialists who addressed the positions for which socialists were attacked.[98] It also produced campaign leaflets and brochures directed to Catholic voters.[99] A special Catholic edition of the *Christian Socialist*, that paper's largest ever in circulation, featured articles about a Scottish society of socialist Catholics, socialist candidates in Milwaukee, Wisconsin, and Newark, New Jersey, who were Catholics, and two priests who were willing to lend their names to supportive statements.[100]

Also in spite of official pronouncements, some priests apparently practiced benign neglect when it came to warning their parishioners about socialism. According to one account, the Massachusetts clergy early in the century were more neutral than antagonistic, and may have included a few covert sympathizers—suggesting a pattern possibly repeated in other locales and periods. Besides Fathers Hagerty and McGrady, there seem to have been a few socialist priests, including an elderly South Dakotan who identified himself as a party member after years of work for direct legislation. E. E. Carr claimed to know of priests who were socialists but considered it risky to be known as such, and George Strobell reported the conversion of a priest who, as editor of a Catholic paper, had attacked socialism. Such evidence, though skimpy, invites speculation that there may have been similar cases elsewhere.[101]

If David Goldstein made irresponsible allegations about socialists, it is imperative to note that some socialists were hardly innocent of provocative language in regard to the Catholic Church. There was, after all, a centuries-old Protestant martyrology on which to draw—and before that, the Inquisition. Struggles over public education and the mysteries of celibacy yielded more current sources for the scurrilous. The *Socialist Spirit*, representing George D. Herron's group, described a church that had "striven throughout its existence to gather into its voracious maw all the material things of this life, which its grotesque priestly keys of heaven and hell could intimidate the ignorant into yielding up to it." No organization in history had a record "besmirched with blacker crimes" or leaders who had reached "lower depths of infamy."[102] The *International Socialist Review* highlighted the case of a New York priest accused of murdering and dumping a dismembered servant girl in a river and advertised *The Roman Religion, Or How the Holy Humbug Was Hatched*, a purported exposé by Henry M. Tichenor, editor of the *Melting Pot*, a socialist paper published in St. Louis. Socialist papers as different in constituency as the *New York Call* and the *Appeal to Reason*, published by Julius A. Wayland in Girard, Kansas, carried what can only be described as attacks on the Roman Catholic Church. The vicious *Menace*, founded in 1911 in Aurora, Missouri, had many socialists associated with it, though its relationship to the movement was problematic.[103] Even the *Christian Socialist*, ordinarily devoted to persuasive tactics, could portray the Catholic Church as an authoritarian institution opposed to the public schools and individual judgment, determined to be "the mistress of the world in temporal affairs."[104] Both sides, moreover, utilized underhanded tactics in public engagements.[105]

The confrontation was commonly milder than these examples and Goldstein's words and tactics suggest. It was a confrontation, nonetheless. On one side stood a political movement with not only a radical program of economic reconstruction, but also a heritage of religion-bashing. On the other stood an ancient, hierarchical, authoritative church, accustomed in Europe to alliances with monarchy and aristocracy. Roman Catholic opposition was a force socialists could not ignore and never escaped in early twentieth-century America. It very likely kept many Catholics from joining the SPA and made the participation of those who did join more difficult to trace than Protestant participation. Loyal Catholics who shared the vision of a coming commonwealth of equality and democratic control had to pursue that vision without the sanction of the church that gave them the Christian values the vision contained.

SOCIALIST VENTURES IN PROTESTANT CONTEXTS

The Protestant denominations did not present as unbroken a front as did Roman Catholicism. Socialists nevertheless faced an uphill struggle in their effort, as the Christian Socialist Fellowship's objectives stated, to "permeate" them with their message; and members of the clergy who made their socialism public often found themselves in difficulty with their congregations or ecclesiastical superiors.

Not that the fellowship neglected the task. Over the years the *Christian Socialist* reported numerous presentations to denominational gatherings. The CSF conference in 1908 received reports of one by A. L. Byron-Curtiss, an Episcopal priest later active in the Church Socialist League and editor of its *Social Preparation for the Kingdom of God*, to a Protestant Episcopal convocation in Richmond; another by Aaron Noll, a minister in the (Dutch) Reformed Church in America, to its General Synod; and a third by a Christian Church pastor, William A. Ward, to his denomination's annual meeting. Noll had sought an exchange of "fraternal delegates" between the Reformed Church and the CSF, and, though declining the request, the synod authorized study of socialism by a special commission. Within two weeks in 1909, Carr spoke to Swedish Baptist, Congregational, and Presbyterian ministerial meetings in Chicago. A member of the German Evangelical Synod of North America ordered copies of the *Christian Socialist* sent to its approximately 1,100 ministers. Following the precedent set when it appointed George W. Slater Jr. to work among African Americans, the CSF in 1915 appointed J. G. Evert as special secretary for German-American work. Evert distributed his pamphlet *Christentum und Sozialismus*, got his writings into German-language papers in the Anabaptist tradition in Pennsylvania, Ohio, Indiana, and Kansas, and tried to answer attacks on socialism in the German-American press as a whole.[106]

The effort to influence denominations included the occasional publication of special denominational editions of the *Christian Socialist*. These issues had larger than normal press runs. Compared with a mailing list of 20,000 paid subscribers, Carr later claimed, two Presbyterian issues ran to 30,000 and 40,000 copies, two Methodist ones to 50,000 and 80,000, two Episcopal ones to about 40,000 each, a Disciples issue to 60,000, and a Roman Catholic one to 120,000.[107] There were usually special efforts to distribute these issues among adherents of these denominations.

The contents were not always very discriminating. An Episcopal edition in 1907 included articles by bona fide socialists, but also a piece on Charles Kingsley and a selection of statements by Bishop Frederick D. Huntington, a supporter of the Christian Social Union, but no socialist.[108] A Baptist edition that year had an article by Walter Rauschenbusch on the social mission of Baptists, which emphasized the lowly origins and egalitarianism of both Continental Anabaptists and English Baptists, and an article purporting to find socialist principles in Baptist polity.[109] These editions were typical. The attempt was to show people of various denominations that they had something in common with socialism—that their own theological, liturgical, ethical, or organizational traditions had, if not full-blown socialism, at least incipient socialist elements or affinities to socialism. That meant relaxing the CSF's scruples about "straight" socialism. Denominations big and small were targets of attention, Disciples and Lutherans, but also Swedenborgians.[110]

Informal bands within particular denominations also heightened morale and exchanged information and plans, but only in the case of the Church Socialist League among Episcopalians does there seem to have been any organized propaganda within a national church body, and the CSL was not strong. The northern Methodist Federation for Social Service included socialists and acquired a radical reputation but was not avowedly socialist. Annual gatherings of the largely Baptist Brotherhood of the Kingdom devoted substantial attention to socialism, but did not publicly endorse it, though some members, such as Walter Rauschenbusch, were very sympathetic. Moderates guided deliberations in the Congregational denomination, also in the Protestant vanguard on social issues, and included little discussion of socialism.[111]

The first two decades of the twentieth century were a time of wide-ranging social criticism, idealism, and reform in American society, and the Protestant churches participated *as churches* in fostering progressive advances. For them, this was, as the most thorough study of the subject makes clear, an "age of social responsibility," in which the Social Gospel reshaped institutional priorities and structures.[112] If socialists often received a respectful hearing, it was partly because of the desire—stimulated by this Social Gospel—to bring Christianity to bear on contemporary problems. Though conceptually distinct, the Social Gospel and socialist Christianity graded into each other in actual experience. Anxieties about the socialist movement had caused religious leaders to espouse the Social Gospel as an alternative since the late nineteenth century, and religious socialists commonly worked from Social Gospel perspectives, to which they gave a radical application.

Such reciprocity notwithstanding, the Social Gospel and socialist Christianity were competitors, if not antagonists, and the Social Gospel was by far the more appealing of the two in church settings. Among Congregationalists, Episcopalians, and northern Baptists, Methodists, and Presbyterians, and to a lesser extent in other quarters, supporters of the Social Gospel were successful in the early twentieth century in crafting statements of social principles and erecting agencies to give direction to Christian social action. To do so, they had to overcome complacency and institutional inertia, even on behalf of such moderate causes as child-labor reform, a living wage, and factory safety, or establishment of a social-service commission within the denomination itself. An endorsement of socialism was almost certainly impossible—in spite of attempts to ground socialism in the Bible and domesticate its reputation. With the Social Gospel, church people could satisfy the demands of justice short of social reconstruction. Major branches of American Protestantism became engaged in projects for social progress in these years, but their evolution was toward liberalism, not socialism.[113]

At the local level, for a Protestant minister to become a known socialist was risky. Faced with a choice between personal convictions, on one hand, and parish peace and job security, on the other, the socialist preacher was in a "perplexed predicament," according to one radical paper whose editor saw no easy resolution. Tailoring one's preaching to the tastes of benefactors or evading issues meant betrayal of convictions. Splitting the congregation by preaching the truth as Jesus did was ethically unacceptable because the minister was paid to build it up. One might get a working-class congregation, or find some fine line to walk between evasion and truthfulness, but neither was a promising alternative. All things considered, the editor preferred that persons in this situation leave the ministry entirely.[114]

Though no statistical analysis is possible, a fair proportion of ministers who became socialists publicly took up alternative careers. Most commonly, they became organizers or lecturers for the party or the CSF, crafted livelihoods from independent lecturing and writing, or went into newspaper work, while some formed new People's or Christian Socialist churches.[115] There were no doubt additional options.

When a pastor's politics created strife, the socialist press commonly followed the lead of Charles H. Vail, who blamed the churches' "subservience . . . to wealth."[116] According to the *Christian Socialist*, the First Congregational Church of Tampa experienced tumult after its pastor, R. Lee Kirkland, became a socialist, because wealthy members sought an injunction to bar him from preaching and, failing in that, withdrew their financial support.[117] When the preaching of John H. Bates at the Episcopal Church of the Ascension in Middletown, Ohio, produced a financial backlash among his vestrymen, the socialist paper in nearby Dayton noted: "It isn't by superior intelligence, nor superior learning, nor superior insight into the Bible that capitalism keeps its clutch on the church. It is simply by its control of the purse strings."[118]

In view of the variegated, often idiosyncratic texture of parish relationships, capitalist hegemony is far too easy an explanation of the firings and resignations that occurred. Not only might non-plutocrats, including blue-collar workers themselves, have opposed socialist clerics, but factors other than socialism could bring ministers' and congregations' expectations into conflict. In some cases, a pastor's desire for an activist community program was at odds with a congregation's desire for a more traditional "spiritual" message, even when the congregation was working class.[119] In others, a minister's changing theological views, sometimes approaching the outer borders of anything distinctively Christian, unsettled the situation. Though it was not logically necessary, radical theology and radical politics often went together.

Several examples illustrate the reciprocity between taking up unconventional religious views and radical social ideas. *Christian Socialist* editor E. E. Carr left the Methodist Church for theological reasons and became pastor of the liberal People's Church in Kalamazoo, Michigan, in the late 1890s, while also becoming a socialist. After joining the Social Democratic Party in 1900, he left parish work altogether.[120] George D. Herron, the Social Gospel prophet at Iowa College who captured national attention in the 1890s, moved similarly leftward in religious and political-economic views, ending up out of the church and a vitriolic critic of Christianity (though ever profoundly committed to spiritual experience), as well as in the socialist movement. Though complicated by the personal element of divorce and remarriage in his defrocking by Iowa Congregationalists, his story is one in which theological rethinking and an inclination toward socialism were inseparable.[121] William Thurston Brown, a Yale Divinity School graduate tried for heresy in 1896, provides another example. His "heresies" were unexceptional when set against the liberal views of Congregationalists such as Washington Gladden or the New Haven pastors and Yale professors who helped win his acquittal. His thinking continued to change, both religiously and politically, however, until even the very liberal Plymouth Congregational Church in Rochester was too confining. Simultaneously launching stinging attacks on the Christian churches and becoming a socialist, he left Plymouth by 1901–1902 to experiment with a People's Church and subsequently organized, lectured, and wrote for the socialist movement and became a Unitarian.[122]

A minister's becoming a socialist did not always sever his relationship with his congregation. The *Christian Socialist* occasionally named churches that its members served, apparently without controversy. When a minister left a congregation, it was often of his own volition, as in the cases of Carr and Brown. Moreover, the separation sometimes revealed elements of sympathy and even compassion. When Alfred W. Arundel resigned from Trinity Episcopal Church in Pittsburgh, Pennsylvania, to avoid conflict over his socialism, a petition signed by an estimated 1,500 admirers urged him to reconsider.[123]

The fascinating story of Harvey Dee Brown combines several elements discussed above: the mixture of theological liberalism and socialism, voluntary withdrawal from pastoral leadership, and an amicable separation. A graduate of Rochester Theological Seminary, a Baptist institution open to liberal theological ideas, he joined the SPA in about 1902 while serving a church in Kansas. Frustrated by obstacles to developing a working-class ministry at his second church, he went to the First Baptist Church of Kenosha in Wisconsin in 1905 with some understanding that it would be more open to his leadership. By 1907, however, that situation was unsatisfactory to him, and, making his party membership public, he resigned to try to establish a Christian Socialist Fellowship center amid Kenosha's wage-earners.[124]

Brown's resignation statement lamented the churches' failure to follow Christ's teachings with respect to economic justice for the masses. It also revealed a theological perspective from which traditional forms could no longer convey "the real things of the Christ-spirit."[125] God was to be found working within humanity, "a Universal Consciousness" humans could know "only as they cooperate with him at his universal tasks."[126] Brown soon became active in Milwaukee socialism and ran for governor in 1908; he also later served with John Haynes Holmes at New York's Unitarian Church of the Messiah (later the Community Church).[127] Far from spurning him, the Baptists in Kenosha bade him farewell with a reception, cash gift, "tastily [sic] bound copy" of resolutions of appreciation, and wishes for success in his new work.[128]

Permeating the churches with socialism was too much to expect. Denominational and ecumenical bodies were unlikely agents of a political movement to reconstruct American society, and even the moderate Social Gospel was too daring for many. Socialist ministers sometimes got along in parish situations without compromising their socialism. When conflict prevailed, theological factors often contributed to it, as a zealous minister's impatience and imprudence probably did also. Still, churches were not usually congenial places to spread socialist ideas. Despite the involvement of Protestant Christians in every aspect of the SPA's activities and the willingness of hundreds of thousands of Protestant voters to cast ballots for the party's candidates, institutional Protestantism and the socialist movement went their separate ways.

THE ETHICAL APPEAL OF SOCIALISM

When asked what attracted working-class people to socialism in Dayton, Ohio, where socialist candidates attracted from 24 percent to 44 percent of the vote in municipal elections between 1911 and 1923, Oscar Edelman, a non-religious man who was well aware of economic and other factors, answered promptly and firmly, "a strong ethical motive." Comparing two Dayton leaders, Joseph Sharts, an agnostic attorney, and Frederick G. Strickland, a minister who for three years conducted Sunday-evening "Workers' Ethical Platform" meetings with Local Dayton's blessing, Edelman concluded that Strickland was more effective because he could tap Daytonians' idealistic impulses.[129] Much of Dayton's working class was native-born and Protestant, and of course the religiously based social morality to which Edelman attributed Strickland's appeal was widely shared by non-Protestants.

It is nothing short of paradoxical, in view of attacks on socialism as a materialistic philosophy that banned God, relativized all standards of right and wrong, undermined the family, and promoted violent class conflict, that outside observers often agreed with socialists' claim that theirs was essentially an idealistic movement—that, in fact, it was deeply religious. Walter Rauschenbusch, who almost certainly voted socialist but never joined the party, described socialism and Christianity as the youngest and the oldest of "the idealistic forces at work in our civilization."[130] Socialism's "fundamental aims are righteous," he wrote: "They were part of the mission of Christianity before the name of Socialism had been spoken. God had to raise up Socialism because the organized Church was too blind, or too slow, to realize God's ends."[131] Fellow Baptist, fellow church historian, and fellow socialist sympathizer Henry C. Vedder of Crozer Theological Seminary agreed, saying, "The changes in social institutions that the socialist proposes are a wholly desirable complement to the spiritual change contemplated by Jesus," and in essence both Christianity and socialism aspired to "the common brotherhood of man, with all the corollaries of equal privilege, equal sharing of all the common gifts of the common Father in Heaven."[132]

More detached observers than Rauschenbusch and Vedder also underscored socialism's moral appeal. Congregationalist A. A. Berle testified to hearing socialists "make a finer, a more effective, a more dramatic, and a more moral use of the figures, the illustrations, and the moral teaching of the gospels, in a single evening, than he ha[d] heard from any dozen preachers in a month in the last twenty years." George S. Payson, a Presbyterian, believed that "generous souls" were drawn by socialists' "great emphasis upon altruistic and philanthropic aims. The best Socialists are inspired by an enthusiasm for humanity which, though it does not speak of Christ, reminds of Christ."[133]

It did not take a theological degree and immersion in socialist theory to see greater affinities between Christianity and socialism than between Christianity and capitalism. A poem published in 1896 for a heartland readership contrasted capitalism and Christianity in stanzas that had Christianity saying "'the earth is the Lord's" and capitalism saying "the earth is the landlord's"; Christianity, "ye are members one of another," capitalism, "free competition—man against man—the devil take the hindmost."[134] A common-sense approach to the Bible in a socialist paper in Oklahoma yielded this reflection on Jesus' prayer that God's kingdom would come on earth: "While children grow up in squalor, while exploiting and social injustice remain, the Kingdom of Heaven can never come on earth and never will."[135] Calling himself "a Socialist from the Bible and also from the political standpoint," a humble renter in Texas tapped a vein of popular millennialism when he said: "And I fully believe that the Socialist movement is the forerunner of the second coming of Jesus Christ."[136]

Socialism enjoyed the advantage, in such comparisons, of being an imagined future rather than a historical reality. Its imperfections required speculation, while capitalism's were all around. Not only had their system not been tried, but socialists usually refused to go beyond generalities in predicting how it would work. Critics considered them evasive when pressed on such matters as the extent of private ownership, compensation of capitalists for the properties the state would take over, and the freedom churches would have. In actuality, Socialists' vagueness about the future derived from a desire to avoid the criticism that nineteenth-century utopian blueprints, like Edward Bellamy's *Looking Backward*, had drawn, rather than from dishonesty. Their situation left them open to the charge of obfuscation, but it also afforded them the opportunity to counterpose the moral beauty of a society in which each was for all, and all for each, with the defects of an economic order that was fully operational—and deeply flawed.

Its ethical inspiration and the ideal elements in its proposed future led some to see socialism as a religion. Definitional problems abound in the use of both terms, as David McLellan notes in cautioning against calling Marxism a religion.[137] To be sure, generalizations about socialism as a religion, or substitute for religion, have too often been facile. Elements of religion in its Christian forms, however, did blend into the movement culture of American socialism, whether or not their functional meaning for socialists was exactly the same as for Christians.

Some socialists, for example, described becoming socialists in terms similar to religious conversion testimonies. "How I Became a Socialist" accounts focused on experiences that caused disillusionment with capitalism and a defining period or occasion of decision. Charles Edward Russell later described becoming a socialist as fundamentally different from being a Republican or Democrat: It was "a motion of solemnity and port . . . like joining a church. One must have had experience in grace, one must show that one has come out from the tents of the wicked and capitalism."[138] When socialists called each other "comrade," they were suggesting a community or experience not unlike that of evangelicals who called each other "brother" and "sister."

As in churches, music was a vital part of socialist meetings of all shapes and sizes, from singing of the "Marseillaise" in New York City labor halls to the evangelical tunes with socialist words sung in Southwestern encampments, from the parodies of Protestant hymns composed by Ralph Chaplin and other poets in the Industrial Workers of the World to the sober uplift songs in CSF member Harvey Moyer's *Songs of Socialism*.[139] The socialist movement had its martyr heroes, some borrowed from past movements for human betterment, such as abolitionism, and some close at hand in its own history—including Eugene V. Debs, whom many saw as Christ-like.[140] It had Jesus himself, sometimes simple carpenter, sometimes revolutionary, but always a man of the people—the "Comrade Jesus" of Sara Cleghorn's poem in the *Masses*, who had "paid his dues" and carried his red card.[141]

Moreover, as the biographies in this work show, the socialist message was itself religious for many party members and sympathizers. For them, this message judged the status quo by religious standards, appealed to religious motives, and promoted a more truly religious social order. "It has about it nothing new nor alarming," wrote Charles Edward Russell in the final sentence of a campaign autobiography, "and instead of being rejected by men, it should be welcomed; for the essence of its doctrine is merely the practical application of the doctrine of Jesus Christ."[142]

NOTES

1. "Program and Songs of the Third National Conference, Christian Socialist Fellowship," 28–31 May 1908, Socialist Collections in the Tamiment Library, 1872–1956, New York University; *Christian Socialist* 5 (1 June 1908): 3, and (15 June 1908): 1–3, 5.

2. "Edwin Markham on Religion and the Social State," *Arena* 40 (August–September 1908): 244–45. Though he was a valued supporter of the CSF for many years, Markham's religion was really humanism, as expressed in "The Muse of Brotherhood": "Our hope is in heroic men, Star-led to build the world again. To this Event the ages ran; Make way for Brotherhood—make way for Man." The CSF had no doctrinal test and welcomed those who, like Markham, revered Jesus.

3. Harold W. Currie, "The Religious Views of Eugene V. Debs," *Mid-America* 54 (July 1972): 147–56; "Debs in New York" and "Debs Addresses Fellowship," *Appeal to Reason*, 13 June 1908. Debs's presence and promotion for the *Call* undoubtedly enhanced the rally crowd, which included many Jews; *Christian Socialist* 5 (15 June 1908): 5. Several years

later, when recommending Carr as a speaker on socialism for the Chautauqua platform, Debs recalled Carr's speech as "one of the most eloquent and inspiring to which I have ever listened." Eugene V. Debs to [Harry P.] Harrison, 9 December 1912, University of Iowa, in Papers of Eugene V. Debs, 1834–1945 (microfilm ed., 1983), Reel 4.

4. *Outlook* 89 (13 June 1908): 319; *Arena* 40 (August–September 1908): 243.

5. Robert E. Doherty, "Thomas J. Hagerty, the Church, and Socialism," *Labor History* 3 (Winter 1962): 39–56; Thomas McGrady, *Socialism and the Labor Problem: A Plea for Social Democracy* (Terre Haute, Ind.: Debs Publishing, 1901).

6. For the CSF's full statement of purpose and origins, see *Christian Socialist* 4 (1 March 1907): 7, and (15 August 1907): 5.

7. *Christian Socialist* 6 (1, 15 June 1909): 14; *New York Call*, 19 May 1913.

8. *Christian Socialist* 8 (19 January 1911): 5.

9. *Christian Socialist* 4 (15 June 1907): 6–7, and (1 July 1907): 1. The CSF resolution was significant enough that Eliot White, a CSF officer and Episcopal priest, reported it in the *Arena* 41 (January 1909): 47. For Strobell, see Solon DeLeon, ed., *The American Labor Who's Who* (New York: Hanford Press, 1925).

10. Rufus W. Weeks, "What the Christian Socialists Stand For," *Christian Socialist* 5 (1 June 1908): 1–2. Weeks was active in Walter Rauschenbusch's Brotherhood of the Kingdom and a founder of the Collectivist Society in New York City; he translated Herman Kutter's *Sie Müssen (They Must; or God and the Social Democracy. A Frank Word to Christian Men and Women)* (Chicago: Co-operative Printing, 1908). Obituary, *New York Times*, 19 April 1930.

11. *Christian Socialist* 8 (5 January 1911): 6.

12. He helped edit and wrote for the *Christian Socialist*. His *The Socialism of Jesus: How Discipulus Learned the Lesson* (New York: Collectivist Society, 1903) went into a second edition in 1908.

13. John Cort, *Christian Socialism: An Informal History* (Maryknoll, N.Y.: Orbis Books, 1988), 198.

14. Ronald H. Preston, "The Legacy of the Christian Socialist Movement in England," in *Religion, Economics and Social Thought*, eds. Walter Block and Irving Hexham (Vancouver: Fraser Institute, 1986), 182–87. Maurice's far-reaching influence is evident throughout Paul T. Phillips, *A Kingdom on Earth: Anglo-American Social Christianity, 1880–1940* (University Park, Pa.: Pennsylvania State University Press, 1996).

15. George Hodges, "Christian Socialism and the Social Union," *Publications of the Church Social Union*, No. 30 (Boston: Office of the Secretary, 1896), 3–4.

16. Edward Norman, *The Victorian Christian Socialists* (Cambridge: Cambridge University Press, 1987), 8. See also Peter d'A. Jones, *The Christian Socialist Revival, 1877–1914: Religion, Class, and Social Conscience in Late-Victorian England* (Princeton, N.J.: Princeton University Press, 1968). For a very early emphasis on the contrasts between socialism and Christian socialism, see Paul Monroe, "English and American Christian Socialism: An Estimate," *American Journal of Sociology* 1 (1895–1896): 50–68.

17. Accounts of Bliss include Cort, *Christian Socialism*, 233–36; Peter J. Frederick, *Knights of the Golden Rule: The Intellectual as Christian Social Reformer in the 1890s* (Lexington, Ky.: University Press of Kentucky, 1976), 79–98; Charles Howard Hopkins, *The Rise of the Social Gospel in American Protestantism, 1865–1915* (New Haven, Conn.: Yale University Press, 1940), 171–83; Howard H. Quint, *The Forging of American Socialism: Origins of the Modern Movement* (Indianapolis, Ind.: Bobbs-Merrill, 1953), 109–26; Christopher L. Webber, "William Dwight Porter Bliss (1856–1926): Priest and Socialist," *Historical Magazine of the Protestant Episcopal Church* 28 (March 1959): 9–39; and

decidedly a cut above the rest, Richard B. Dressner, "William Dwight Porter Bliss's Christian Socialism," *Church History* 47 (March 1978): 66–82.

18. *Dawn* 1 (15 May 1889): 3. The society's declaration is also in Albert Fried, ed., *Socialism in America: From the Shakers to the Third International: A Documentary History* (Garden City, N.Y.: Doubleday, 1970), 348–49.

19. Nicholas Paine Gilman, "Christian Socialism in America," *Unitarian Review* 32 (October 1889): 351; *Dawn* 1 (15 May 1889): 4, 1.

20. W.D.P. Bliss, *A Handbook of Socialism: A Statement of Socialism in Its Various Aspects, and a History of Socialism in All Countries, Together with Statistics, Biographical Notes on Prominent Socialists, Bibliography, Calendar, Chronological Table and Chart* (New York: Charles Scribner's Sons, 1895), 9, 1.

21. Morris Hillquit, *History of Socialism in the United States* (5th ed., 1909; New York: Russell & Russell, 1965), 356.

22. *Dawn* 3 (4 December 1890): 4; *Christian Socialist* 4 (1 March 1907): 2–3.

23. *Workmen's Advocate*, 26 January, 23 February, 27 April, 1, 15, 29 June 1889, 3 , 17 May 1890.

24. *People,* 20 September, 11 October 1891.

25. Ira Kipnis, *The American Socialist Movement, 1897–1912* (New York: Columbia University Press, 1952), 22.

26. David Herreshoff, *American Disciples of Marx: From the Age of Jackson to the Progressive Era* (Detroit, Mich.: Wayne State University Press, 1967), 114; Howard H. Quint, *The Forging of American Socialism: Origins of the Modern Movement* (Indianapolis, Ind.: Bobbs-Merrill, 1953), 35.

27. Kipnis, *American Socialist Movement*, 19.

28. Paul Buhle, *Marxism in the United States: Remapping the History of the American Left* (London: Verso, 1987), 53, 50; Quint, *Forging of American Socialism*, 145; Kipnis, *American Socialist Movement*, 23, 26.

29. Morrison I. Swift to [Caro] Lloyd, 24 August 1910, Correspondence, Henry Demarest Lloyd Papers, State Historical Society of Wisconsin (microfilm edition, 1970), Reel 16.

30. Benjamin O. Flower, *Progressive Men, Women, and Movements of the Past Twenty-Five Years* (Boston: New Arena, 1914; Hyperion reprint ed., 1975), 85.

31. David P. Thelen, *The New Citizenship: Origins of Progressivism in Wisconsin, 1885–1900* (Columbia, Mo.: University of Missouri Press, 1972).

32. David A. Shannon, *The Socialist Party of America: A History* (New York: Macmillan, 1955), 6; James Weinstein, *The Decline of Socialism in America: 1912–1925* (New York: Monthly Review Press, 1967), 2. Both authors provide a broad survey of the party's composition and character in their first two chapters. For a briefer survey, see James Weinstein, "The Socialist Party: Its Roots and Strength, 1912–1919," *Studies on the Left* 1 (1959–1960): 5–27.

33. A case in point is the members of the Social Crusade, a predominantly Midwestern group of ministers, including J. Stitt Wilson, who though implicitly socialist before, first entered the political movement with Debs' presidential campaign in 1900. Several members participated in the convention that brought the party into being. J. Stitt Wilson, "The Political Campaign," *Social Crusader* 2 (October 1900): 4–7; "The Indianapolis Unity Convention," *Social Crusader* 3 (August 1901): 14–16.

34. The electoral figure for 1900 is from Quint, *Forging of American Socialism*, 372; figures for the other years and for membership are from Shannon, *Socialist Party of America*, 5. The estimate of officeholders in 1911 is from Robert F. Hoxie, "'The Rising Tide of Socialism': A Study," *Journal of Political Economy* 19 (October 1911): 610–11; that for 1912 is from Weinstein, *Decline of Socialism in America*, 93, 103.

35. Weinstein, *Decline of Socialism in America*, 84–102.

36. John H. M. Laslett, *Labor and the Left: A Study of Socialist and Radical Influence in the American Labor Movement, 1881–1924* (New York: Basic Books, 1970).

37. Estimates of ministers at party conventions were ten out of 216 in 1908 and eighteen out of 293 in 1912. *Christian Socialist* 5 (15 May 1908): 1–2; *International Socialist Review* 12 (June 1912): 810. For 1908, see also Charlotte Teller, "The National Socialist Convention," *Arena* 40 (July 1908): 26–39. For Carr's trip to Stuttgart, see *Christian Socialist* 4 (15 September 1907): 1–2, 8, and (1 October 1907): 1; for Ella Carr, see *Party Builder*, 31 May 1913.

38. Morris Hillquit, *Loose Leaves From a Busy Life* (1934; New York: Da Capo Press Reprint, 1971), 60–61; Max Horn, *The Intercollegiate Socialist Society, 1905–1921: Origins of the Modern Student Movement* (Boulder, Colo.: Westview Press, 1979), 1, 10, 89, 195 n. 16; Members, Executive Committee and lists of contributors for 1910–1912, Intercollegiate Socialist Society Papers, 1900–1921, Socialist Collections in the Tamiment Library, 1872–1956, New York University (microfilm ed.), Reel 27. Among those who actively participated in ISS affairs were Helen Olivia Phelps Stokes, Mary Sanford, Vida D. Scudder, and Bouck White; Union Theological Seminary Professors Charles P. Fagnani and Thomas C. Hall were also active in it, as in the CSF.

39. Minutes of Joint Meeting of Board of Directors and Advisory Board of the American Socialist Society, 9 February 1906, Rand School of Social Science Records, 1901–1956, Tamiment Library, Reel 29; Robert D. Reynolds Jr., "The Millionaire Socialists: J. G. Phelps Stokes and His Circle of Friends" (Ph.D. dissertation, University of South Carolina, 1974), 330.

40. The *Masses'* star cartoonist, Art Young, described Weeks's role in John N. Beffel, ed., *Art Young: His Life and Times* (New York: Sheridan House, 1939), 271–74. Muckraking journalist and socialist Charles Edward Russell claimed that "year in and year out, [Weeks's] was the largest individual gift of money to the Socialist Party. Never was altruism of a purer strain; he had from it nothing but the acrid criticism of his fellows, social ostracism, and at first a plenteous suspicion among those to whom he had joined himself." *Bare Hands and Stone Walls: Some Recollections of a Side-Line Reformer* (New York: Charles Scribner's Sons, 1933), 207.

41. Frederick I. Olson, "The Milwaukee Socialists, 1897–1941," 2 vols. (Ph.D. dissertation, Harvard University, 1952).

42. *Christian Socialist* 8 (9 March 1911): 8.

43. Patrick L. Quinlan, "Religion Has No Place at Propaganda Meeting," *New York Call*, 30 August 1914.

44. Margaret W. Thompson to Walter Rauschenbusch, 16 May 1912, Box 93, Rauschenbusch Family Papers, Samuel Colgate-American Baptist Historical Society, Rochester, N.Y.; Walter Rauschenbusch, *Christianizing the Social Order* (New York: Macmillan, 1912), 397–98.

45. Joseph E. Cohen, "Why the Workingman Does Not Go to Church," *International Socialist Review* 7 (July 1906): 28–32; Clarence Meily, "Why the Workingman is Without a Church," *International Socialist Review* 7 (February 1907): 459–61.

46. Robert Rives LaMonte, "Paganism vs. Christianity," *International Socialist Review* 2 (December 1901): 435–37.

47. David McLellan, *Marxism and Religion: A Description and Assessment of the Marxist Critique of Christianity* (New York: Harper & Row, 1987), Chap. 1.

48. Peter M. Schuller, "Karl Marx's Atheism," *Science and Society* 39 (Fall 1975): 331–45.

49. McLellan, *Marxism and Religion*, Chap. 2.

50. Gerald Friedberg, "Marxism in the United States: John Spargo and the Socialist Party of America" (Ph.D. dissertation, Harvard University, 1964), 1–10; "The Reminiscences of John Spargo," Oral History Research Office, Butler Library, Columbia University, 1957, 43–46.

51. *Socialist Spirit* 1 (September 1901): 17–20; "Reminiscences of John Spargo," 154–57. The *Comrade*, which merged with the *International Socialist Review* in 1905, was the first American journal to combine radical politics and culture until the *Masses* in 1911.

52. *Comrade* 2 (April 1903): 156, and (May 1903): 180.

53. In a nasty controversy in 1909, he was part of a group in New York that sought unsuccessfully to change what Carr considered essential Christian language in the CSF's constitution. *Christian Socialist* 6 (1 April 1909): 4–5. See Franklin S. Spalding to John Spargo, 8 March, 10 April 1908, 28 July 1913, John Spargo Papers, Bailey/Howe Library, University of Vermont.

54. John Spargo, *Socialism: A Summary and Interpretation of Socialist Principles*, rev. ed. (New York: Macmillan, 1909), 68–70, 87–92.

55. John Spargo, *Karl Marx: His Life and Work* (New York: B. W. Huebsch, 1910), 117–21, 331. In "The Influence of Karl Marx on Contemporary Socialism," *American Journal of Sociology* 16 (July 1910): 21–40, Spargo decried a sectarianism that made Marx infallible and his economic determinism fatalistic.

56. Spargo, *Marx*, 125–27, 192. Spargo wrote that Marx especially admired Jesus for his love of children, a love Marx shared. Ibid., 186.

57. Spargo, *Marx*, 273–75.

58. John Spargo, *The Spiritual Significance of Modern Socialism* (New York: B. W. Huebsch, 1908), 26, 33, 40–41.

59. Ibid., 85–89; John Spargo, *Marxian Socialism and Religion: A Study of the Relation of the Marxian Theories to the Fundamental Principles of Religion* (New York: B. W. Huebsch, 1915), 129, 163–70. In his first essay as book reviewer for the *International Socialist Review* in 1908, he wrote that Christianity had "largely divested itself of its theological trapping and become once again an ethical movement," while socialism had "largely passed from the influence of the philosophic materialism of the middle of the nineteenth century." "Belated rationalists" were attacking a Christianity "which has ceased to exist." John Spargo, "Whisperings in the Library," 8 (February 1908): 501.

60. Spargo, *Marxian Socialism and Religion*, 37–39.

61. Ibid., 63–64.

62. "Paganism and Christianity," *International Socialist Review* 1 (1 June 1901): 653–64; Anton Pannekoek, "Socialism and Religion," *International Socialist Review* 7 (March 1907): 555–56; Isador Ladoff, "Historical Christianity and Christian Socialism," *International Socialist Review* 9 (July 1908): 115–16. Ladoff had earlier written that religion was harmful to the working class because of

its hollowness and soullessness; its petrification and false pretense; its fostering of prejudices, superstition and narrow sectarian exclusiveness; its intolerance and bigotry; its tendency to side with the powerful and strong and preach slavish virtues to the "humble and lowly" proletarians; its blasphemous attempts to sanctify the crying injustices of the social institutions of their time and country.

From *Social Democratic Herald*, 16 February 1901, quoted in Kipnis, *American Socialist Movement*, 266. Ladoff also wrote a pamphlet, *Socialism, The Antichrist*, in English and German versions, for a German-American free-thought society (copy in Social Democratic Party Collection, Milwaukee County Historical Society).

63.   John Macy, *Socialism in America* (Garden City, N.Y.: Doubleday, Page, 1916), 115–16; William English Walling, *The Larger Aspects of Socialism* (New York: Macmillan, 1913), 391 (see Chap. 10 and Appendix B).

64.   Allen Ruff, *"We Called Each Other Comrade": Charles H. Kerr & Company, Radical Publishers* (Urbana, Ill.: University of Illinois Press, 1997), 88–89. Edward Ellis Carr, "The Folly of Materialism" and "Causes of Belief in God," *Christian Socialist* 4 (15 February 1907): 1–3, and (1 April 1907): 1–2; Ernest Unterman, "Inductive Dialectics or Metaphysical Speculation?" *Christian Socialist* (1 May 1907): 1–2; Carr, "Economic Science or Sectarian Dogmatism," *Christian Socialist* (15 May 1907): 1–3.

65.   *National Convention of the Socialist Party Held at Chicago, Illinois, May 10 to 17, 1908*, ed. John M. Work (Chicago: Socialist Party, 1908), 191–206; "Socialist Platform," *International Socialist Review* 8 (June 1908): 758–64. "National Convention of the Socialist Party," *Christian Socialist* 5 (15 May 1908): 1–2. For an account that stressed atheism in the movement, see Robert F. Hoxie, "The Convention of the Socialist Party," *Journal of Political Economy* 16 (1908): 445.

66.   "The Socialist Vote," "Echoes of the Explosion," and "Lewis Turns Over a New Leaf," *Christian Socialist* 5 (15 November 1908): 4, (1 December 1908): 5, and (15 December 1908): 4–5.

67.   *Christian Socialist* 8 (12 January 1911): 5, and 12 (March 1915): 6–7, 11; *Chicago Herald*, 8 February 1915. Tucker was a substitute for Carl Thompson, a former Congregational minister who was then the party's information director. Lewis regretted the incident, which he thought would not have occurred with Thompson. Arthur M. Lewis to Carl Thompson, 9 February, and Thompson to Lewis, 11 February 1915, Box 17, National Correspondence, Socialist Party of America Papers, Perkins Library, Duke University. In 1909 Lewis began *The Evolutionist*, which he edited in the interests of naturalistic science. See copies in Social Democratic Party Collection, Milwaukee County Historical Society.

68.   The *New York Call* published the statement on 30 July 1912; Spargo included it in *Marxian Socialism and Religion*, 148–53. For the Michigan action, see Weinstein, *Decline of Socialism in America*, 197.

69.   Robert D. Cross, who has thoroughly studied Catholic struggles over the meaning of being American in the late nineteenth century, with special emphasis on the "liberal," or Americanizing elements in the church, emphasizes these considerations in debates over Catholic conduct, cooperation with non-Catholics, political loyalties, and involvement in social reforms. Liberal leaders like Cardinal James Gibbons and Archbishop John Ireland believed American society had no serious flaws. See *The Emergence of Liberal Catholicism in America* (Cambridge, Mass.: Harvard University Press, 1958), 109–10. A strong statement of the exceptionalist view is Bishop John Lancaster Spalding's *Socialism and Labor and Other Arguments: Social, Political, and Patriotic* (Chicago: A. C. McClurg, 1902).

70.   *Rerum Novarum* is the opening document in David M. Byers, ed., *Justice in the Marketplace: Collected Statements of the Vatican and the U.S. Catholic Bishops on Economic Policy, 1891–1984* (Washington, D.C.: United States Catholic Conference, 1985), 13–41. For a highly positive assessment of Pope Leo, see Lillian P. Wallace, *Leo XIII and the Rise of Socialism* (Durham, N.C.: Duke University Press, 1966), Chap. 11. Pope Pius X reiterated Leo's anti-socialism in the encyclicals *E supremi* in 1903 and *Singulari quandam caritate* in 1912. In other respects a good cross-section of American Catholic social statements, Aaron I. Abell, ed., *American Catholic Thought on Social Questions* (Indianapolis, Ind.: Bobbs-Merrill, 1968), slights the anti-socialist strain of thought.

71.   Francis W. Howard, "Socialism and Catholicism," *Catholic World* 65 (September 1897): 721–27; Henry C. Semple, "The Case of Socialism v. the Catholic Church and the United States,"*Catholic World* 106 (February 1918): 646–53.

72. Aaron I. Abell, *American Catholicism and Social Action: A Search for Social Justice* (Notre Dame, Ind.: University of Notre Dame Press, 1960), 140.

73. Corrigan quoted in "Is Socialism Antichristian?" *Literary Digest* 24 (11 January 1902): 51–52. Corrigan's sermons and other signs of a mounting Catholic attack on socialism received attention in the *Socialist Spirit* 1 (December 1901) and *International Socialist Review* 2 (December 1901): 473–74.

74. "A Catholic Campaign Against Atheistic Socialism," *Literary Digest* 32 (9 June 1906): 875.

75. O'Connell quoted in Henry F. Bedford, *Socialism and the Workers in Massachusetts, 1886–1912* (Amherst, Mass.: University of Massachusetts Press, 1966), 214–15. Bedford covers the church's role throughout his work. "Mayor Duncan of Butte Replies to Catholic Bishop," *International Socialist Review* 13 (October 1912): 321–27; Jerry W. Calvert, *The Gibraltar: Socialism and Labor in Butte, Montana, 1895–1920* (Helena, Mont.: Montana Historical Society Press, 1988), 64–69; Olson, "The Milwaukee Socialists," I: 121–25.

76. William Stang, *Socialism and Christianity* (New York: Benziger Brothers, 1905), 11, 99–101, 151, 171, 180–90.

77. *Catholic Tribune* report, quoted in "A Foolish Priest," *Christian Socialist* 9 (16 May 1912): 5.

78. John Ming, *The Characteristics and the Religion of Modern Socialism* (2nd ed., New York: Benziger Brothers, 1908), 138–39, 148–49, 199, 223–24, 324–25; *International Socialist Review* 6 (October 1905): 250, and 10 (June 1910): 1072–73.

79. Bernard Vaughan, *Socialism From the Christian Standpoint: Ten Conferences* (New York: Macmillan, 1912), 213.

80. Francis L. Broderick, *Right Reverend New Dealer: John A. Ryan* (New York: Macmillan, 1963); David J. O'Brien, *American Catholics and Social Reform:The New Deal Years* (New York: Oxford University Press 1968), Chap. 6. For Kerby's views, see William J. Kerby, "Aims in Socialism," *Catholic World* 85 (July 1907): 500–511.

81. John A. Ryan, "May a Catholic Be a Socialist," reprinted in *Christian Socialist* 6 (15 February 1909): 2; John A. Ryan, *Alleged Socialism of the Church Fathers* (St. Louis, Mo.: B. Herder, 1913).

82. Broderick, *Ryan*, 87–89.

83. Morris Hillquit and John A. Ryan, *Socialism: Promise or Menace?* (New York: Macmillan, 1914). Walling is cited by Broderick, *Ryan*, 89. The *New York Call*, 27 September 1914, judged the debate so serious a mismatch that the book was a more effective pro-socialist document than if Ryan's arguments had been left out.

84. Another debate in an atmosphere of mutual respect, but in which the participants did not face each other, occurred in Boston in 1911 between the president of Boston College and a veteran Massachusetts socialist politician. *The "Menace of Socialism," Being a Report of an Address by The Rev. Thos. Gasson, S.J., and a Reply Thereto by Hon. James F. Carey, Delivered in Faneuil Hall, Boston, Mass., February 27, 1911* (Milwaukee, Wisc.: Social Democratic Publishing, 1912).

85. Eugene V. Debs to Morris Hillquit, 20 December 1913, Morris Hillquit Papers, State Historical Society of Wisconsin, in Papers of Eugene V. Debs, Reel 1; Morris Hillquit, *Loose Leaves From a Busy Life* (New York: Macmillan, 1934), 89; John A. Ryan to Carl D. Thompson, 10 March 1914, and Thompson to Ryan, 17 March 1914, Box 13, National Correspondence, Socialist Party Papers, Duke University.

86. Carl D. Thompson to Alphonse Olbrich, 2 July 1913, Box 10, National Correspondence, Socialist Party Papers, Duke University; Fred Hurst, *Knave? or Fool? A Reply to David Goldstein* (Providence, R.I.: H. Beck, n.d.); John Spargo to J. G. Phelps Stokes, 6 October 1919, Correspondence Files, J. G. Phelps Stokes Papers, Butler Library, Columbia University.

87. Bedford, *Socialism and the Workers in Massachusetts*, 195–96. Not all Catholic commentators agreed with Goldstein's tactics or considered him effective. "The Collins-Goldstein Anti-Socialist Propaganda," *Fortnightly Review* 23 (1 March 1916): 68–71.

88. David Goldstein, *Autobiography of a Campaigner for Christ* (Boston: Catholic Campaigners for Christ, 1936), Chaps. 1–4, 6; Debra Campbell, "David Goldstein and the Lay Catholic Street Apostolate, 1917–41" (Ph.D. dissertation, Boston University, 1982), 99–107; David O. Carrigan, "Martha Moore Avery: The Career of a Crusader" (Ph.D. dissertation, University of Maine, 1966), 24, 27, 45, 62–64, 73–74, 100, 122. Henry Bedford's careful *Socialism and the Workers in Massachusetts*, 190–91, corrects Goldstein's and Avery's statements about the state convention in 1902, showing that the party approved a resolution acceptable to Goldstein. Avery correctly placed her break with the party in 1903, but whereas she claimed that she resigned, Bedford says she was expelled. Martha Moore Avery, "Why I Left the Socialist Movement," *Common Cause* 1 (February 1912): 5–14. Socialists frequently insisted that both Avery and Goldstein were expelled.

89. David Goldstein, *Socialism: The Nation of Fatherless Children* (Boston: Union News League, 1903), 255–96.

90. Goldstein, *Autobiography*, Chap. 7.

91. Campbell, "Goldstein," 132–33, 158–63. Eugene Debs claimed that the Knights of Columbus' attacks provided free advertising for his meetings in "The Knights of Columbus," *International Socialist Review* 15 (April 1915): 600–602. For Goldstein's later work, see Debra Campbell, "A Catholic Salvation Army: David Goldstein, Pioneer Lay Evangelist," *Church History* 52 (September 1983): 322–32. One of many expressions of socialist concern about debates with Goldstein and Collins is "Goldstein and Collins. We Call Their Bluff," *Party Builder*, 21 March 1914.

92. For socialist strength in the labor movement, see Laslett, *Labor and the Left*. Abell stresses Catholic opposition to what he calls the "extremes" of both socialism and the open shop in *American Catholicism and Social Action*, 179–80.

93. Neil Betten, *Catholic Activism and the Industrial Worker* (Gainesville, Fla.: University Presses of Florida, 1976), Chap. 1; Marc Karson, *American Labor Unions and Politics, 1900–1918* (Carbondale, Ill.: Southern Illinois University Press, 1958), Chap. 9; Mary Harrita Fox, *Peter E. Dietz, Labor Priest* (Notre Dame, Ind.: University of Notre Dame Press, 1953). Karson provides much information about Catholic anti-socialism documented independently by the author in the preceding paragraphs. Another version of his work appears in John H. M. Laslett and Seymour M. Lipset, eds., *Failure of a Dream? Essays in the History of American Socialism* (Garden City, N.Y.: Anchor Press/Doubleday, 1974), Chap. 5.

94. Carl D. Thompson, "The Militia of Christ," 23 May 1913, National Correspondence, Box 9, Thompson to J. L. Engdahl, 27 February 1914, National Correspondence, Box 13, and Engdahl, "Why Fear the Catholic Unions?" typescript, Box 15, Socialist Party Papers, Duke University; "The Catholic Threat and the A.F. of L.," *International Socialist Review* 14 (January 1914): 414–15, Richard Perin, "The German Catholic Unions,"*International Socialist Review* 14 (January 1914): 397–99, and William E. Bohn, "International Notes," *International Socialist Review* 14 (June 1914): 752–55.

95. John M. O'Neill, "Something to Think About," *Miners' Magazine* 4 (December 1913): 7, quoted in Betten, *Catholic Activism and the Industrial Worker*, 15.

96. "The Collins-Goldstein Anti-Socialist Propaganda," *Fortnightly Review* 23 (1 March 1916): 68–71; Henry J. Brown, "Comment," and Marc Karson, "Reply," in Laslett and Lipset, *Failure of a Dream*, 185–99.

97. Abell, *American Catholicism and Social Action*, 148–49; John Spargo, "Christian Socialism in America," *American Journal of Sociology* 15 (1909–1910): 16.

98. Good examples are William Clancy's *Catholicism and Socialism* (Bridgeport, Conn.: Advance Publishing, 1912), and "An Appeal to the Reason of Catholic Workingmen," *New York Call*, 7 July 1912.

99. Carl D. Thompson's "Why Should Catholic Workingmen be Socialists?" *American Socialist* 1 (3 October 1914): 4, appeared also as a leaflet.

100. *Christian Socialist* 6 (15 January 1909).

101. "The Rapid Rise of Socialism in Massachusetts," *Boston Sunday Herald*, 4 January 1903; Robert W. Haire to Mr. B., 30 August 1914, Box 14, and E. E. Carr to Alphonse Olbrich, 8 August 1913, Box 10, National Correspondence, Socialist Party Papers, Duke University; *Christian Socialist* 8 (31 August 1911): 8.

102. "The Catholic Blight," *Socialist Spirit* 1 (December 1901): 10–14.

103. Phillips Russell, "When a Priest Kills," *International Socialist Review* 14 (November 1913): 272–73, 320; Elliott Shore, *Talkin' Socialism: J. A. Wayland and the Role of the Press in American Radicalism, 1890–1912* (Lawrence, Kans.: University Press of Kansas, 1988), 193–94; "Economic Significance of the 'Menace,'" *New York Call*, 14 January 1913. An example of the *Appeal* criticizing Catholicism while denying that the SPA was anti-Catholic is Fred D. Warren's pamphlet *The Catholic Church and Socialism* (Girard, Kans.: Appeal to Reason, 1914).

104. Edgar F. Blanchard, "The Roman Catholic Church and Socialism," *Christian Socialist* 10 (1 November 1913): 1–3. See also "A Priest's Debate With a Socialist," 8 (28 September 1911): 1–2.

105. For interesting examples of socialist arguments and tactics, see Joseph Husslein, "David and Goliath," *America* 6 (2 March 1912): 485–86, and "Attack of the Roman Catholic Church on Socialism Thru David Goldstein Answered by John W. Slayton," pamphlet, n.p., n.d., Widener Library, Harvard University.

106. *Christian Socialist* 5 (1 June 1908): 3; (1 July 1908): 1; 6 (15 November 1909): 7; 11 (1 April 1914): 9; 12 (February 1915): 11.

107. Judging from the frequent pleas and plans with respect to circulation, the paper's circulation varied widely. From a few hundred in 1904, it grew to about 5,000 by 1907, and to 20,000 in 1911. Carr stated that subscriptions stood at 20,000 until American entry into World War I. *Christian Socialist* 4 (1 June 1907): 5, and 8 (4 May 1911): 6. E. E. Carr, "What the Former C.S. Did," *Christian Socialist*, New Series, No. 1 (1 March 1932): 2.

108. *Christian Socialist* 4 (1 March 1907).

109. Ibid., 4 (1 November 1907).

110. Ibid., 6 (1 October, 1 December 1909); 7 (15 March 1910).

111. Paul F. Laubenstein, "A History of Christian Socialism in America" (S.T.M. thesis, Union Theological Seminary, 1925), 68–70; William McGuire King, "The Emergence of Social Gospel Radicalism: The Methodist Case," *Church History* 50 (December 1981): 436–49; Charles H. Hopkins, "Walter Rauschenbusch and the Brotherhood of the Kingdom," *Church History* 7 (June 1938): 138–56; Carl Herman Voss, "The Rise of Social Consciousness in the Congregational Churches: 1865–1942" (Ph.D. dissertation, University of Pittsburgh, 1942); Jacob H. Dorn, *Washington Gladden: Prophet of the Social Gospel* (Columbus, Ohio: Ohio State University Press, 1967), 127–39.

112. Donald K. Gorrell, *The Age of Social Responsibility: The Social Gospel in the Progressive Era, 1900–1920* (Macon, Ga.: Mercer University Press, 1988). See also Jacob

H. Dorn, "Washington Gladden and the Social Gospel," in Randall Miller and Paul Cimbala, eds., *American Reforms and Reformers* (Westport, Conn.: Greenwood Press, 1995).

113. Gorrell's *Age of Social Responsibility* suggests that consideration of socialism as an option was almost nil. See also Jacob H. Dorn, "The Social Gospel and Socialism: A Comparison of the Thought of Francis Greenwood Peabody, Washington Gladden, and Walter Rauschenbusch," *Church History* 62 (March 1993): 82–100.

114. *Coming Nation*, 29 September 1900.

115. Phyllis A. Nelson traces these patterns in "George D. Herron and the Socialist Clergy, 1890–1914" (Ph.D. dissertation, State University of Iowa, 1953), 359–63.

116. *Coming Nation*, 18 June 1898.

117. *Christian Socialist* 8 (19 October 1911): 1; (16 November 1911): 4; and 9 (1 February 1912): 2.

118. *Miami Valley Socialist*, 22 May 1914.

119. "The Workingman in His Own Church," *Literary Digest* (25 May 1912): 1105–6; Ken Fones-Wolf, *Trade Union Gospel: Christianity and Labor in Industrial Philadelphia, 1865–1915* (Philadelphia: Temple University Press, 1989), 149. Though Aileen Kraditor's argument that socialists failed to understand working-class cultures is flawed, her point that wage-earners had interests and values other than those socialists thought they should have is valid in this instance. Aileen S. Kraditor, *The Radical Persuasion, 1890–1917: Aspects of the Intellectual History and Historiography of Three American Radical Organizations* (Baton Rouge, La.: Louisiana State University Press, 1981).

120. Bliss, *New Encyclopedia of Social Reform*, 154; E. E. Carr, "Reminiscences of Eighteen Years," *Christian Socialist* 15 (July 1918): 1–2.

121. Nelson, "Herron and the Socialist Clergy"; Robert T. Handy, "George D. Herron and the Social Gospel in American Protestantism, 1890–1901" (Ph.D. dissertation, University of Chicago, 1949); Herbert R. Dieterich, "Patterns of Dissent: The Reform Ideas and Activities of George D. Herron" (Ph.D. dissertation, University of New Mexico, 1957). Herron's negativism toward the church appears in "The Recovery of Jesus From Christianity," *Arena* 26 (September 1901): 225–43.

122. William Thurston Brown, *Defense Before the Council in Reply to Charges of Heretical Teaching* (New Haven, Conn.: Tuttle, Morehouse & Taylor, 1896); William Thurston Brown to Walter Rauschenbusch, 29 April 1896, Rauschenbusch Papers; Charles D. Broadbent, "A Brief Pilgrimage: Plymouth Church of Rochester," *Rochester History* 40 (October 1978): 1–23; William Thurston Brown, "The Beginnings of a New Religion," *Social Gospel* 2 (October 1899): 9–13, "How I Became a Socialist," *Comrade* 2 (May 1903): 170–71, and "The Problem of Liberal Religion in the West," *Unitarian* 5 (April 1910): 116–19.

123. *Christian Socialist* 8 (9 November 1911): 6.

124. LeRoy Moore Jr., "The Rise of American Religious Liberalism at the Rochester Theological Seminary, 1872–1928" (Ph.D. dissertation, Claremont Graduate School, 1966); Harvey Dee Brown to M. R. Holbrook, 13 July 1905, and to Secretary, 23 August 1905, Intercollegiate Socialist Society, Tamiment Library, Reel 27; *Christian Socialist* 5 (1 March 1908): 1, 8; Church Clerk's Record, First Baptist Church, Kenosha, Wis., Frances LaMantia to author, 19 July 1990.

125. *Kenosha* (Wis.) *Telegraph-Courier*, 14 November 1907.

126. Harvey Dee Brown, "Some Spiritual Elements in the Socialist Movement," *Christian Socialist* 4 (1 November 1907): 5; 4 (15 November 1907): 3.

127. Harvey Dee Brown, "The Socialist Administration of Milwaukee," *Twentieth Century Magazine* 3 (December 1910): 195–204; *I Speak for Myself: The Autobiography of John Haynes Holmes* (New York: Harper & Brothers, 1959), 89–90.

128. *Kenosha* (Wis.) *Telegraph-Courier*, 21 November 1907.

129. Oscar K. Edelman, interview with author, 24 July 1984, Dayton, Ohio. For the Socialist vote, see John T. Walker, "Socialism in Dayton, Ohio, 1912 to 1925: Its Membership, Organization, and Demise" (M.A. thesis, University of Dayton, 1983), 13. Reports of Strickland's meetings appeared frequently in the *Miami Valley Socialist* from 1912 to 1914. An effective campaigner as well, Strickland received over 20 percent of the vote in Ohio's Third Congressional District in 1912. "Leading Socialist Congressional Districts," *National Socialist*, 11 January 1913.

130. Walter Rauschenbusch, "The Imperative Demand," *Christian Socialist* 11 (15 March 1914): 5.

131. Rauschenbusch, *Christianizing the Social Order*, 405.

132. Henry C. Vedder, *Socialism and the Ethics of Jesus* (New York: Macmillan, 1912), 383, 515.

133. Berle and Payson quoted in *Current Literature* 43 (November 1907): 537–38.

134. *Coming Nation*, 22 August 1896.

135. *Ellis County Socialist*, quoted in Garin Burbank, *When Farmers Voted Red: The Gospel of Socialism in the Oklahoma Countryside, 1910–1924* (Westport, Conn.: Greenwood Press, 1976), 21. See Burbank, Chap. 2, for a full discussion of religion and socialism in Oklahoma.

136. Quoted in James R. Green, *Grass-Roots Socialism: Radical Movements in the Southwest, 1895–1943* (Baton Rouge, La.: Louisiana State University Press, 1978), 165. For other examples of socialism and popular religion, see Green, 162–75.

137. McLellan, *Marxism and Religion*, 157–72. See "Socialism as Religion," *Independent* 55 (12 February 1903): 397–99.

138. Russell, *Bare Hands and Stone Walls*, 196. Reading socialist literature played an extremely important part in these decisions, according to James R. Green, "The 'Salesmen-Soldiers' of the 'Appeal' Army: A Profile of Rank-and-File Socialist Agitators," in Bruce M. Stave, ed., *Socialism and the Cities* (Port Washington, N.Y.: Kennikat Press, 1975), 33–34.

139. Donald E. Winters Jr., *The Soul of the Wobblies: The I.W.W., Religion, and American Culture in the Progressive Era, 1905–1917* (Westport, Conn.: Greenwood Press, 1985); Harvey P. Moyer, ed., *Songs of Socialism for Local Branch and Campaign Work, Public Meetings, Labor, Fraternal, and Religious Organizations, Social Gatherings, and the Home*, 3rd ed. (Chicago: Brotherhood Publishing, 1907).

140. Nick Salvatore, *Eugene V. Debs: Citizen and Socialist* (Urbana, Ill.: University of Illinois Press, 1982), 155, 310–11. One close associate wrote that "children used to Flock to [Debs] as they must have flocked to the Carpenter." *If You Don't Weaken: The Autobiography of Oscar Ameringer* (New York: Henry Holt, 1940), 267.

141. William L. O'Neill, ed., *Echoes of Revolt: The Masses, 1911–1917* (Chicago: Ivan R. Dee, 1989 repr. ed.), 220.

142. Charles Edward Russell, *Why I Am a Socialist* (New York: George H. Doran, 1910), 301.

2

"An Active and Unceasing Campaign of Social Education": J. Stitt Wilson and Herronite Socialist Christianity

Douglas Firth Anderson

J. Stitt Wilson confidently proclaimed, both in bold oratory and capitalized print, that "THE CHRIST COMETH THROUGH THE SOCIAL REVOLUTION." He melded an evolutionary, idealist Christianity with the socialist cooperative commonwealth: "The present Socialist movement, being the organized and militant expression of the Social Revolution, is the good Samaritan of all human history." Indeed, he asserted, socialism "is the demonstration that man—the Spirit—is master of his environment, and not victim."[1]

Above all, Wilson was an orator, or more precisely, an evangelist. He was also, for longer or shorter periods of his life, a Methodist pastor, a journalist, a graduate student, a founding member of the Christian Socialist Fellowship, and one of the few Socialist Party of America (SPA) candidates to win elected office in the party's heyday before World War I. It was his oral missionizing on behalf of his religio-social vision, though, that was the constant that tied together the various facets of his public life. His single most important written work, *How I Became a Socialist and Other Papers,* is a collection of his most popular socialist speeches. The texts are studded with lines of capitalized sentences, visually suggesting the calculated modulations of intensity that marked his oratory. At the height of his work for the SPA, he regularly attracted and moved crowds, in Britain as well as the United States. One socialist colleague recalled that Wilson "would have been a great actor. He had dramatic power. He was the best campaigner for the Party that I ever knew. . . . In a way he was trained for the work. He was a minister. He could sway people and also raise money from them. [Norman Thomas] was a good debater. A little like Stitt Wilson, too. But he could not close a sale like Stitt Wilson could."[2]

Wilson's historical significance, though, goes beyond his effectiveness as a socialist orator. First, he was one of the most important disciples of the Reverend George D. Herron, a Congregationalist pastor, college professor, and orator who stirred the waters of American Protestantism and partisan socialism between 1893 and 1901 by his explicit linkage of Christ, the postmillennial Kingdom of God, and the socialist cooperative commonwealth. Even though Herron withdrew from the public realm after 1905, Wilson sustained his central themes and his messianic style. Moreover, Wilson wedded these to the prewar program of the SPA, thereby embodying the legacy of Herronite socialist Christianity to partisan socialism in the United States. He shows with a special clarity the way in which a theological perspective can be transposed into political partisanship. He also exemplifies socialism's partial congruence with American political and religious streams, a congruence that ironically contributed to socialism's marginalization in U.S. society.

Second, Wilson's life and thought are a reminder that an emphasis on American political, economic, and social exceptionalism obscures the importance of trans-Atlantic ties for an understanding of the historical course of socialism in the United States. Born a Canadian, Wilson spent several years in Britain as a student as well as a socialist evangelist. While Wilson's conversion to a socialist Christianity was American in context and substance, British socialism and social Christianity provided him with model institutions, organizations, and developments that sustained his religious and political commitments until the crisis of the Great War. In turn, his work in Britain fed the growth of British socialism and social Christianity.

Third, Wilson's conversion to and apprenticeship in socialism in Chicago, followed by his relocation to metropolitan San Francisco, where he attained both regional and national recognition, point to the need to assess the role of place and region in the rise and decline of partisan socialism and Christian socialism in the United States. Chicago, the metropolis of the Great Lakes region, was a social, political, and intellectual maelstrom in the 1890s for many Anglo-Americans from more peripheral locales, not the least of whom were Wilson, Jane Addams, and Eugene V. Debs. As for the trans-Mississippi West, conclusions about it must be tentative. The career of Wilson, though, suggests that locales in the West at the turn of the twentieth century were receptive to radical critiques of capitalist society to the extent that they were places in which anxiety, disillusion, or disorder were juxtaposed with hopefulness, aspiration, and organization in adjusting to the developing world order.

Jackson Stitt Wilson was born in Auburn, Ontario, Canada, on 19 March 1868.[3] His father, William James Wilson, was a shoemaker who had come to Canada from Ireland; his mother, Sarah Ann Stitt, was a native of Ontario. Both parents were devout Methodists, and his father was a class leader.[4] Wilson's upbringing included not only participation in a congregation but also such marks of Wesleyan piety as Bible reading, participation in home meetings of prayer and worship, and an intense religious experience at age thirteen. The latter was probably interpreted at the time as a conventional Christian conversion. In later life, though, Wilson referred to it as a "Socialization of Personality." He interpreted it and subsequent occasions as moments when he was led "away from self" and incrementally reoriented to service to others as "the organ and instrument and agent of Universal Good, of the Kingdom of God in the Earth." These formed the experiential basis of his mature religio-social outlook: "The illuminations and enlargements of my consciousness were not created by pondering over doctrines or suffering in my conscience over certain vile sins. THE RELEASE OF MY SOUL WAS PRECIPITATED OUT OF THE WILL IN RELATION TO OTHER HUMAN LIVES." Congruent with the Wesleyan tradition, he downplayed theology and abstraction in favor of experience, will, and the fundamental moral character of existence. Yet his disparaging of individual sinfulness, the stress on consciousness, and the undertones of human perfectibility are congruent with idealist philosophy and socialist tradition. For Wilson, religious experience and socialist experience eventually converged.[5]

Before this convergence, however, the young Canadian worked at various jobs, including teaching, in Ontario and neighboring Michigan. It was not until his twenties that Wilson married and began higher education toward a career. In 1890, the year after his marriage, he began studies for the ordained Methodist ministry at Garrett Biblical Institute in Evanston, Illinois. Three years later, he became a naturalized U.S. citizen and began attending Northwestern University. While completing his B.A. in English (1893–1897), he was pastor at the Erie Street Methodist Episcopal Church in nearby Chicago. He went on to complete an M.A. in sociology and political economy, also at Northwestern, in 1901. Between his two degrees, he received full ordination as a Methodist clergyman.

Prior to 1890, Wilson's life had unfolded in and around small towns dominated by English-speaking Protestants. His move to the Chicago region, however, placed him into the social and cultural pluralism of a leading metropolis. Higher education opened up new areas of understanding for him. The most important new element in Wilson's life, though, was his pastoral work with the Erie Street congregation, for among his parishoners he was confronted with the social underside of industrialization.

Wilson found his pastoral work near "slumdom" to be a "school of Socialism." What he recalled most were the wages—too low for a single wage to enable a family to live—and the physical toll of wage-work. Nellie, who worked in a soap factory, fainted at one of his Sunday evening meetings, crying about the heaviness of the trays she had to carry at work. She committed suicide at age nineteen. And she was but one example: "Over many and many such a grave I read the burial service, 'The Lord giveth and the Lord taketh away,' WHEN I KNEW I WAS READING A LIE. I was accusing the Lord of the crime of Capitalism and sanctifying that crime with ceremonial babble."[6]

The mid-1890s was also a time of widespread economic depression. The effects of the Panic of 1893 on Chicago were delayed by the financial success of the World's Columbian Exposition—"the Great White City"—but by the end of the year, the unemployed were sleeping in City Hall and in many police stations.[7] Jane Addams, who had founded Hull House a few years earlier, recalled the time as "that terrible winter after the World's Fair."[8] Visiting English journalist, editor, and Protestant social reformer William T. Stead was moved to rally middle-class and elite Chicagoans and others through meetings and exhort them through his publications, especially *If Christ Came to Chicago* (1894). In 1894 cutbacks at the Pullman Palace Car Co. led to a bitter railroad worker strike, one of the outcomes of which was the conversion of union leader Eugene Debs to partisan socialism.

Wilson did not specifically mention the Panic of 1893 or the Pullman strike, but it is hard to conceive that the unemployed and the strikers were not additional factors in his social radicalization. It is clear that during his time at Erie Street Church, Wilson quickly turned critical of the burgeoning industrial order. He, like Washington Gladden, Walter Rauschenbusch, and others, was shaken out of his middle-class slumbers by his personal encounter with what was called "the social problem."[9]

It was also during this time that Wilson's relationship with George D. Herron began. According to Wilson, it was in 1893 or 1894 that one of his Northwestern classmates compared his developing religious and social perspectives to those of Herron. He then read about Herron in W.T. Stead's *Chicago To-Day; or, The Labour War in America* (1894). Obtaining a copy of Herron's *The Larger Christ* (1891), Wilson recalled, "I devoured and re-devoured this book." The young Methodist pastor finally met Herron in the autumn of 1895 when he was in Chicago for a lecture series. By the following winter, Wilson hosted Herron for a Friday evening meeting at the Erie Street Church.[10]

George Davis Herron, born in Indiana in 1862, was at the peak of his fame among Anglo-American Protestants during Wilson's Erie Street years.[11] Despite his lack of formal education, Herron had been accepted into the educationally conscious Congregationalist ministry in 1884. It was while he was a pastor in Minnesota in 1890, however, that Herron first began to attract attention. Through his public speaking tours and the publication of series of his sermons and lectures, the Congregationalist pastor spread a message that on the one hand excoriated American society, including religious institutions, for its fundamental self-seeking and competitiveness and on the other hand called Christians to work sacrificially with the coming Kingdom of God through following the teachings of Jesus. Herron "was obsessed," observes one historian, "with a sense of his own sinfulness, suffering, and duty."[12] In his writing and even more on the platform, these obsessions were cloaked in what another historian has termed "colossal self-assurance and passionate intensity."[13] By 1893 Herron was professor of applied Christianity at Iowa College in Grinnell. From there, he continued to develop and spread his Kingdom message, not only through his classes, at which his students saw him less and less, but also through his travels as a lecturer, through his books, through *The Kingdom*, a weekly begun in 1894, and through the American Institute of Christian Sociology, an organization that sponsored publications and summer courses in the tradition of Chautauqua.

In Herron, Wilson had found a slightly older soulmate. Herron's intensity and platform charisma undoubtedly drew the Methodist clergyman, whose own platform work came to emulate that of the Congregationalist. More important, Herron provided a model of social religiosity that was socially critical enough to see established institutions as problematic, scientific enough to claim the mantle of empiricism for its critique, yet philosophically idealist. The idealism, in turn, drew its primary sustenance from the liberal stream of Anglo-American Protestantism. As English-speaking North American Protestants coming to maturity during the late nineteenth century, Herron and Wilson were part of a religious community still largely informed by what Grant Wacker has termed a "historical hopefulness" about "the spiritual maturity of the age."[14] Although not all Anglo-American Protestants were postmillennialists, the plausibility of a belief in progress made a postmillennialism defanged of its supernaturalist bite widespread in its appeal.[15] This Protestantism also continued to bolster a universe of religious discourse and behavior that was moralist in substance, populist in aspiration, and revivalist in style.[16] Wilson and Herron were among that wing of the religious community that was most willing to jettison the element of transcendence from a traditional Christian worldview of transcendence and immanence in paradox. Their worldview was an idealist one centered on the immanence of the divine in history and human experience.[17] Herron became, in Wilson's words, a man fitted to lead a movement like "early Methodism in its passion and devotion, but divinely applying the 'word of life' to the entire actual life of man, to the whole social and industrial fabric."[18]

The precise shape of the Herron-led movement Wilson referred to did not gel before 1897. Herron had already begun a Kingdom movement that was initially dual-pronged: to socialize organized Christianity and to Christianize American society. By 1897, though, the first goal was openly running aground on a rising chorus of Protestant criticism of Herron's theological and social radicalism. Also becoming controversial was his developing relationship with Carrie Rand, daughter of a wealthy former congregant, Mrs. E.D. Rand, while his wife and children saw him infrequently. The second goal, however, remained. Since the early 1890s, Herron had been openly arguing for a Christ-imbued social democracy without using the term socialism. Drawing deeply on the Gospels and on Giuseppi Mazzini—"my best beloved master, next to Jesus"—Herron constructed an argument for the realization of the Kingdom of God in a Christian social order unified by the law of sacrificial love.[19] "As the Father sent Jesus," he declaimed in 1895 with more than a tinge of messianic self-awareness, "so he sends each of us, to bear away the sins of the world, and become completest worldly failures, that the social order of his kingdom may appear amidst the wrecks of organized selfishness."[20] Herron became an early member of the Society of Christian Socialists, organized by W.D.P. Bliss. As for partisan politics, he supported the People's Party in the mid-1890s. By 1897, though, with the demise of the Populists, he began quietly to turn to the Socialist Labor Party.[21]

What changed in 1897 was that Wilson decided to leave his congregation and Methodist Conference and launch a loose movement called the Social Crusade.[22] By then, he was also a social democrat in principle if not in formal party affiliation.[23] While the activities of the Social Crusade during its first year are not clear, Wilson apparently intended to create a religious fraternity of Anglo-American Protestant clergy that would promote through popular lectures and writing the religio-social movement he perceived to be under way but for which the American public was only partly prepared; at least, this is the organization that appeared when he launched a monthly periodical, *Social Crusader*, in September 1898.[24]

When Wilson made his decision to leave both Erie Street Methodist and the organized church, Herron was seeking rest and renewal in Europe. Wilson recalled some lonely days in which only the Gospels and one of Herron's collections of sermons, *The Call of the Cross* (1892), provided him much in the way of encouragement. But within a year, he had gathered around him a small fraternity of clergy, apparently mostly Methodist and Congregationalist. The group eventually included W. H. Wise, James H. Hollingsworth, Robert M. Webster, Carl D. Thompson, Thadeus S. Fritz, Franklin H. Wentworth, and Wilson's brother, Benjamin Franklin Wilson.[25]

The Social Crusade intended to be "an active and unceasing campaign of social education" to "herald the social ideal of Jesus, [viz.,] the kingdom of heaven upon the earth" and thereby "turn men from commercial barbarism, greed and mammon worship to social and common good and wealth; from social injustice to social justice; from industrial despotism to industrial democracy; from the lawlessness of competitive war as it is to the health and order of co-operative industrial peace." The indebtedness to Herron was particularly apparent in Wilson's proclamation of the "Five Fundamental Truths" of the Social Crusade: "The Eternal Social Idea: The Kingdom of Heaven on the Earth," "The Fundamental Law of the Kingdom of Heaven on the Earth: The Law of Sacrifice," "The Eternal Laws of Social Health: The Teachings of Jesus," "Our Immediate Social Hope: Co-operative Industry," and "The Dynamic: The Inspiration of the Divine Spirit." The Crusade managed to support a co-operative store on Lake Street in Chicago, and the formation of Social Crusade Circles was encouraged.[26]

The most successful aspect of the Social Crusade, though, was the work of Wilson and his comrades in conducting what amounted to socialist Christian evangelistic or mission meetings. The *Social Crusader* regularly referred to the tours of the fraternity to various places in the Great Lakes region.[27] Further, by 1899 the Crusade was openly taking sides in electoral politics. In February, Wilson was proclaiming that organization and education of the masses to use the ballot was the important first step to take in the necessary change from private to collective ownership. As to which party to use the ballot for, the only acceptable party, he confidently proclaimed, was the International Socialist Labor Party.[28] Later in the year, Wilson, Wise, and Hollingsworth engaged in a whirlwind of activities (including street meetings with the Golden Rule Glee Club) to help Samuel P. Jones in his unsuccessful independent candidacy for the governorship of Ohio.[29] In 1900 the presidential election elicited Wilson's open support of partisan socialism. "Our conviction is that *Socialism* is the economic expression of social righteousness," he wrote in May. Social righteousness, in turn, was one of Wilson's phrases for his by now fully developed immanenticist Christianity. The "heart of Christianity," he noted in the same May piece, is "complete self sacrifice for the sake of humanity," to the end of working for the Kingdom of God, which, in his view, was coming not by cataclysm, but by the progress of history itself gradually awakening people to set about reconstructing society.[30] The Republican Party stood for capitalism—and capitalism was "the only issue before the American people" as the source of social injustice. The Democratic Party was a "weasel" that, with a reference suggesting that Wilson had had some hopes for a Bryan victory in 1896, "sucks the meat out of every reform egg which the people bring forth." Only partisan socialism remained to address the real issues and to stand as the "natural nominee of the *workers* of America."[31]

The socialism Wilson and Herron supported openly in 1900 was that of the Social Democratic Party under Eugene Debs. It was the emergence of Debs, the Indiana-born railroad worker and union leader, and a recent convert to socialism himself, who made partisan socialism seem viable to Wilson, Herron, and other Christian social radicals. Debs Americanized socialism by stressing class conflict and side-stepping class hatred and armed revolution, using the American political idiom of democracy, natural rights, and the common good to preach the coming socialist cooperative commonwealth through a revolution by the ballot.[32]

The rise of Debs concided with Wilson's taking the Social Crusade overseas to Britain. In the late winter and spring of 1899, Wilson, Wise, and Hollingsworth traveled to London. They apparently engaged in some social mission work, but the emphasis in Wilson's report was on the various places visited, people met, and organizations encountered. Mansfield House settlement, the Independent Labor Party (ILP), and Congregationalist J. Bruce Wallace, pastor of London's Brotherhood Church, especially impressed Wilson. His trip was cut short by family illness in the United States, but in January the following year, Wilson set off for Britain again, accompanied by his wife, Emma Agnew Wilson. On this trip, Wilson spent most of his time in Bradford, an industrial city in the north of England. He conducted a Social Crusade mission in conjunction with Friends and Congregationalists as well as addressing the local Christian Social Union, the Bradford Trades Council, and the Liberal Club. The climax of his missionizing efforts was three weeks of speaking each night, the final two reportedly drawing some 4,000 people each in St. George's Hall, Bradford.[33]

Wilson's first two visits undoubtedly solidified his commitments to a gradualist, partisan socialism, for he spent the bulk of his time with like-minded British social Christians and with the burgeoning ILP. The Mansfield House settlement would have particularly interested him. He had been a resident for one year at the Northwestern University settlement and was also in close relationship with the work of Jane Addams at Hull House settlement and Graham Taylor at the Chicago Commons. The master's work he completed at Northwestern University in 1901 resulted in a social survey of a section of Chicago.[34] While in Britain, Wilson helped fuel the convergence of social Christianity, socialism, and labor with an infusion of North American Methodist social evangelism. When he returned, he had no difficulty seeing Debs as the leader to support for a similar convergence in the United States.

Wilson's time overseas and his growing partisanship between 1898 and 1901 paralleled Herron's development. The latter's journeys outside the United States, though, were primarily for rest and for escape from the pressures of criticism over his radical ideas, his commitments to his employer, Iowa College, and his relationship with the Rands versus his wife and children. The "developing fellowship" between Herron and Wilson, though, grew; Wilson characterized it as "the gravitation of two souls toward each other, both in quest of the Holy Grail."[35] The Social Crusade's commitment to support Samuel P. Jones in 1899 was also

Herron's; Wilson twice stood in for Herron in his classes at Iowa College in that fall, once while Herron helped Jones in Ohio. Herron impulsively submitted his resignation to Iowa College, which to his surprise was accepted, after which he escaped to Europe with the Rands. Similarly, the Social Crusade's support of Eugene Debs in 1900 was in line with Herron's returning from overseas in order to campaign for Debs.[36]

In the aftermath of the 1900 elections, the intertwining of Wilson and his Social Crusade with Herron's political and personal life and with Debsian socialism reached its climax. Herron, with the support of Wilson, began to work toward unifying a splintering socialist movement; he also intended, in his words, "to help spiritualize the international Socialist movement."[37] In pursuit of these goals, he issued a widely publicized call for socialist unity, which he reiterated at the convention in July 1901 that formed the SPA.[38] Second, Herron began a socialism and religion department in the Debsian *International Socialist Review*.[39]

Wilson also contributed to the *Review*. His first article, congruent with Herron's writings at the time, argued that "our time is the epoch of epochs, the transition of transitions, the revolution of revolutions" because "new ideas" and "new con-science" were struggling with "the present social and industrial system." In discussing this "moral conflict," which entailed a replacing of "old" ideas with the "new," Wilson was at his most explicit in articulating his heterodox Christianity:

God is no longer a great monarch on a distant throne . . . , but the immanent presence in all energy and life. . . . Christ is not a dying mediator paying debts to offended deity, but the living revelation of the divine possibilities of every man. Sin is social as well as individual, and evil is the pain of life unadapted to environment and in violation of the common good. . . . Salvation is character here and now and everywhere. Heaven is not a distant abode of a ransomed few, but a state of the free and harmonious here and everywhere. Hell is no longer a lurid place of eternal torment, but the state of man and of men, not punished, but suffering in consequence of the violation of the laws of life's health and harmony, here and everywhere. . . . There is no place of eternal exile in God's universe. The children will all come home sometime, somewhere.

The Christian church, therefore, "is wrong in its attitude toward the whole social problem"; "it continues to teach capitalistic morals." The "new social conscience" enables one to be "awakened to new social duties." Wilson concluded that "there is but one thing to do, viz., to protest against the social injustice and to work with the despoiled and exploited class for the new social order." The conflict "is but the birthpangs of a great and glorious liberty."[40]

Wilson's one other *Review* piece was an extended response to a previous article by "Julian" attacking Christianity and Christian socialism. On the basis of contemporary science and philosophy, Wilson challenged Julian's linking of Jesus and his teachings with the institutional church. Then, the Social Crusader argued for the abiding importance to democracy and socialism of "elemental Christianity," contrasting it with the "paganized Christianity" modern biblical criticism had unmasked. Wilson's response culminated in a variant on Herron's spiritualizing socialism: "I do not call myself a Christian Socialist. In economics I am a socialist.

But socialism and all it will mean is but a part . . . of that complete meaning to human life which I either read out of, or read into the Life and Teaching of Jesus."[41]

Beyond the contributions of Herron and Wilson to the *Review*, the Social Crusade took on a new visibility in January 1901. Wilson finally persuaded Herron to "lead" the Crusade. The latter "is the one man on the whole horizon of the social movement capable of crystallizing the rising social conscience into organic activity," Wilson gushed.[42] This meant both that the fraternity openly advertised itself as Herron's and that it sponsored Herron's speaking tours as well as those of Wilson and his previous associates.[43] In addition to his name and his rhetorical energies, Herron also introduced a term for the group's work: the Social Apostolate.[44]

However, Herron's alignment with the Social Crusade did not lead to the Holy Grail. In March 1901 Mary Everhard Herron sued for and won a divorce from her husband George on the grounds of cruelty and desertion; at the end of May, George Herron married Carrie Rand in a simple ceremony conducted by socialist Christian and Congregationalist William Thurston Brown, a new member of the Social Crusade. Mary Herron was in full agreement with her husband's religious and political principles, but she was tired of his growing attachment to the Rands, who apparently provided him with the effusive adulation that he craved. In response to the remarriage and Herron's public defense of it, the Grinnell Association of Congregational Churches expelled and defrocked him. The scandal of Herron's divorce, remarriage, and defrocking, frequently distorted by press and more conservative clergy into an example of godless socialist "free love," confirmed Herron in breaking with organized Christianity. He threw himself into the socialist unity meeting in July in Indianapolis.[45] The resulting SPA absorbed Herron's attentions when he was not retreating to Europe. Not able to run for office because of the scandal of 1901, not doctrinaire enough to be the center of a party faction, and no longer interested in defending a religious perspective, his main contributions to the SPA after 1901, besides publicity, were his drafting of the party's 1904 platform and his nominating speech for Debs. In 1905 he made a parting shot at his non-socialist critics and exiled himself and the Rands to Italy, the land of Mazzini.[46] He lived the rest of his life there, comfortably supported by the wealth of the Rands, able to view himself as a martyr to spiritualized socialism.[47]

The Herron public relations debacle undercut the Social Crusade, which still sought to appeal to Anglo-American Protestants as well as the working class. Wilson and his associates defended Herron, but Herron was no longer interested in the Social Apostolate; besides, he was too often absent from the country to provide substantive leadership to the fraternity.[48] By August, the *Social Crusader* was announcing the "dissolution" of the Apostolate, that is, Herron's leadership of the Social Crusade. The reason given was that "the coming of socialist unity" made a separate organization unnecessary. The paper would continue for a few more years under the name of the *Socialist Spirit*, edited by Franklin H. Wentworth. It took on a non-religious yet anti-clerical tone with the contributions of Herron, William Thurston Brown, John Spargo, Leonard D. Abbott, and William Mailly.[49]

Wilson, however, kept what remained of the Social Crusade fraternity in California. Wilson, his brother Ben, and Wise had headed west on a Crusade swing in the summer of 1901. The contrast with the East struck him: "The people of the east are not only physically, but morally and intellectually enslaved. There are too many colleges in the East; it is stultifying to hire one's thinking done for one;—one's brain soon ossifies when it gets into a rut. In the great West there is still much hope; the spirit has not yet become subservient."[50] Wilson's feelings about his erstwhile soulmate Herron after the summer of 1901 are unclear; Wilson made no public reference to him afterward. Given that they both remained in the SPA and given the apparent conventionality of Wilson's family life, it seems most likely that Wilson parted with Herron over the latter's handling of his marriage, divorce, and remarriage and over his turn away from religion altogether.[51] Whatever the case, upon the conclusion of the Crusade in southern California, Wilson and his family settled in Berkeley. The Social Crusade came to an end, and Wilson began the second part of his career as a socialist Christian in the West, where there still seemed "much hope."[52]

The demise of the Social Crusade ended the formative years of Wilson's socialism. Informed by the Methodist idiom of piety, between 1890 and 1901 he had immersed himself in Chicago's Methodist and working-class communities. He had come out the other end a Herronite socialist Christian, bringing with him his brother and other Methodist and Congregationalist clergy, particularly in the Great Lakes region. Further, he had honed his oratorical skills in Britain as well as the United States, contributing to the growth of the Fabian and Labour movements in the former and the movement of many socialists into support of the SPA in the latter. Finally, during all this, he had completed a B.A. and an M.A. and, unlike Herron, had managed to maintain his marriage through all the frenetic activity.

Wilson's movements and activities between 1901 and 1909 are not entirely clear, but his move to the West, his commitment to the SPA, and his ongoing ties to socialist Christianity in Britain are apparent. The Social Crusade continued into 1902 in the Los Angeles area, and in 1903 Wilson journeyed to Colorado at the invitation of moderate and conservative SPA forces worried about the strength of radicals associated with the Western Federation of Miners.[53] By 1904 Wilson was residing in Berkeley.[54] That year he represented the California SPA as a delegate to the national convention, and he campaigned vigorously for Debs throughout the state.[55] He returned to Britain for an extended period from 1906 until late 1909.[56] While there, he conducted a Social Crusade in late 1907 and early 1908, first centering in Bradford, an industrial center in the north of England west of Leeds, where he had socialist Christian and Labour friends from his earlier visits. He made a swing from Bradford through Glasgow, Halifax, Leeds, and south Wales. He also spent time in study at Oxford.[57]

The time in Britain did not lead Wilson toward the intellectual cutting edge of trans-Atlantic social democracy.[58] An eschatologically infused idealism retained its appeal, particularly in Anglo-American social Christianity.[59] Wilson's move to California allowed the hopefulness he felt in the context of the Far West to sustain his idealist religio-social perspective. A fellow northern California Christian socialist, Robert Whitaker, was also theologically heterodox and idealist. An English-born Northern Baptist clergyman, he had spent many more years on the West Coast and in California than had Wilson. He was aware of the relatively unchurched nature of California society, yet he may have been speaking for Wilson as well as himself when he exuberantly proclaimed in 1906:

Half of the irreligiousness of California is itself religious. Idealism springs naturally in this lovely land of ours. . . . When our churches come to themselves we shall find that the heart of California is religious. . . . The weakling may perish here if his imported religion is a mere veneer. But the Abrahamic soul may still find its Canaan in the west, beside the waters of the world's last Mediterranean. . . . [T]he spirit of a happy and holy inspiration broods over our land, and the world of tomorrow shall not only get its commerce by way of the Golden Gate, but forth from our city of Saint Francis, and our city of the Angels there shall go the songs and prophecies of the world's best faith, and the evangel of a blessed hope and glorious destiny for the race.[60]

California's hopefulness for Wilson and Whitaker included the rise of socialism. The population and economic centers of the United States were in the Northeast, so, not surprisingly, the historiography of socialism has also focused there. The trans-Mississippi West, though, was peculiarly unstable socially during the late nineteenth and early twentieth centuries, inasmuch as the economic and cultural core of the United States was making it, as historian William G. Robbins has observed, "an integral, albeit extractive, appendage of urban finance" and world markets.[61] California was the most populous and the most urban state in the West. Compared with other locales in the region, California's economy was less volatile overall since metropolitan San Francisco was the economic center that linked much of the West to the developing world system. Even so, the geographic remoteness of California from the core of the United States accentuated regional concentrations of economic power. Such concentrations in transportation, finance, mining, and agriculture meant that in California, local expressions of political and social radicalism could feed on both the hope and the disillusionment that sprang from what historian Kevin Starr has termed California's "symbolic connection with an intensified pursuit of human happiness."[62]

When Wilson moved to California, he brought his experience, skills, and connections to a locale that was the context for a regional socialism that had a strongly middle-class, idealist, and even Christian stream within it. Henry George's *Progress and Poverty* (1879), an American radical classic by the early 1900s, had its genesis in George's struggle to earn a living as a journalist in the Bay area. Another classic, Edward Bellamy's *Looking Backward* (1888), spawned more local Nationalism clubs in California than anywhere else in the country. Bellamyite Nationalism, in turn, became a way-station for many middle-class Californians into populism and socialism.[63] Christian socialist propagandists Herron and W.D.P. Bliss had made swings through the state, the former in 1895 and the latter in 1897–1899.[64] They had served as catalysts for the activities of people like J. E. Scott and John Randolph Haynes. Scott was a Presbyterian cleric in San Francisco who became a socialist editor and journalist about the time Wilson was leading the

Social Crusade; like Wilson, he supported the Socialist Labor and Social Democratic parties and then the SPA.[65] Haynes was a wealthy Episcopalian layman in Los Angeles; upon hearing Bliss, he underwent a socio-religious awakening and went on to become a key funder of socialism in southern California and an indefatigable proponent of direct legislation and municipal ownership as imperative steps on the way to the cooperative commonwealth.[66] Two other noteworthy California Christian socialists were Edwin Markham, author of the popular poem, "The Man with the Hoe," and African-American Baptist George Washington Woodbey, pastor of San Diego's Mount Zion Baptist Church and an outspoken lecturer for the SPA.[67]

From his new California base, Wilson made two organizational commitments. First, he joined the state SPA. Organized in 1901, by 1903 its total membership was around 1,300, spread among some seventy-four locals. Dominant among the state leadership was another former cleric (Disciples of Christ), Job Harriman, who had been Debs's running mate in 1900.[68] Second, he joined the Christian Socialist Fellowship (CSF). Founded in 1906, the organization was an outgrowth of the *Christian Socialist*, a periodical begun in 1904 under the editorship of Methodist clergyman Edward Ellis Carr. Carr had welcomed the Social Crusade to his Danville, Illinois, congregation in 1901.[69] Wilson was contributing editor to Carr's paper, and when discussing the formation of the CSF in 1905, Carr invoked Wilson's Social Crusade as a worthy precursor.[70] The founding convention of the CSF invited the attendance of all "who thoroughly believe in the Christianity of Socialism and the Socialism of Christianity,—who are loyal to *the socialist party* and believe that socialism should also have *a distinctly religious expression*."[71] National conventions brought members together, the *Christian Socialist* spread the membership's news and views nationally, and local centers and individual members worked to distribute socialist Christian literature and to promote socialist Christian speakers among Protestant churches.[72]

Wilson's religiously imbued social democracy, rooted by 1910 in the SPA and the CSF, made him an appealing socialist candidate for the California electorate. Historians have long noted the significance of California in the progressive political insurgency that worked its way from the local and state levels to the national level in the Progressive Era.[73] What has been less recognized is the significance of streams of Protestant thought, rhetoric, and style that infused the progressivism and the socialism of the state.[74]

The gubernatorial election of 1910 in California was marked by public outcry against the Southern Pacific Railroad Company, which was depicted as the dominant special interest in state politics. It was also a year of labor unrest, particularly in the "open shop" city of Los Angeles, where a strike to unionize the metal trades set the context for the bombing of the vehemently anti-union *Los Angeles Times* building on 1 October, killing twenty people.

Wilson was selected as the Socialist Party of California's candidate for governor. He received little attention from the non-socialist media, but state socialist and labor papers followed him as he indefatigably stumped the state. To tone down public stereotyping of socialism as violent revolution, he toured in a red, white, and blue car. The *Christian Socialist* trumpeted his campaign, devoting most of one issue to him. The time seemed millennial in potential. A moral revolution, radical social reconstruction, and a religious awakening were stirring. In Wilson's view: "Before Capitalism with its concomitant evils shall lift from the face of the earth, the Social Unrest will have to become a deep and irresistible Religious Movement, inspired by the most sublime Ideals and Hopes of the Human race, and backed by the consciousness that the abolition of Capitalism and the inauguration of Socialism is the Will of the Eternal."[75] Wilson doggedly emphasized in his stump speeches public control of monopolies and utilities, universal adult suffrage, the initiative, referendum, and recall, state insurance for labor and farmers, and factory inspections. He also took the labor line of supporting the exclusion of Asians. The SPA appeal made significant inroads among labor, but Wilson and the socialist slate faced opponents who were stressing many of the same issues. Even so, Wilson received 12.9 percent, or 47,819 votes, outpolling the rest of the party ticket.[76]

While the California socialists were disappointed at not doing even better, they were still confident in 1911. They felt there was a reform momentum they could steer in their direction, and they had some 6,000 members, the largest of any state at the time. Wilson was touring the state with Job Harriman in support of labor bills pending before the new progressive Republican legislature when he received a telegram from the Berkeley local. Its members wished to nominate him for that year's mayoral race. Harriman told Wilson that he did not think many Berkeleyans would vote socialist, but, after some hesitation, Wilson accepted the nomination.[77]

Berkeley was, in 1911, nearing a decade of growth, fueled in part by the devastation in 1906 of the core of San Francisco by earthquake and fire. Convenient water and rail connections linked the city of some 40,000 to San Francisco and Oakland. Except for West Berkeley, which was predominantly working class, the city was, in the words of a Presbyterian cleric of the time, "highly Anglo-Saxon." It was the only city in the Bay metropolitan area whose Protestant church membership kept pace with the population growth. It was the home of the University of California, at the time expanding toward becoming a leading public university. The city's ethos was noted for its urbane middle-class tone. The city outlawed alcoholic beverages some twelve years before the state did, it was a center of support for women's suffrage, and its 1909 charter was regarded as a model for its day.[78]

Wilson threw himself into the campaign in what had become his home town. In addition to appealing to the working class, he pitched his speeches and issues to the progressive middle class. He stressed municipal ownership of utilities, lower streetcar fares, public improvements under city supervision at union wages, progressive school reform, and the single tax. He exhorted the electorate that "the stirring of the people all over the world and all over America—and all over Berkeley—is the effort of the people to deliver themselves from privilege and monopoly of every form and to come into their own." He pledged to implement the public ownership of public utilities provided for in the new city charter. In addition, he promised to "stand for all other elements of progressive civic administration—for economy; for all needed public improvements . . .; for the 'City Beautiful,' and for all those civic attainments that a patriotic people desire to realize." Yet he also hastened to add, "I hold before the voters no rosy hopes. I am too familiar with the powerful and relentless hostility of the public service corps to think that this [program] can be accomplished in a day."[79]

Wilson won, 2,749 to 2,468. The center of his strength was in the university community and in the working-class districts.[80] He had benefited from a falling-out between Friend W. Richardson, editor of the *Berkeley Daily Gazette*, and the incumbent mayor, Beverly L. Hodghead, who ran for re-election but had offended Richardson by ousting some of the latter's friends. The *Gazette* threw its support to Wilson.[81] Ironically, later in 1911 Wilson's socialist comrade Job Harriman, who had been skeptical of Wilson's electoral chances in Berkeley, would come close to winning the mayoralty of Los Angeles.[82]

Berkeley's socialist Christian mayor, however, had only one comrade elected to the five-member city council. Given the minority position of the socialists, Wilson decided the best policy was to be efficient and non-controversial. He pressed for municipal ownership of public utilities but was unable to pass most of his proposals. The most significant accomplishment of his administration (1911–1913) was the establishment of a municipal employment bureau.[83]

Wilson made the best of the situation by accentuating his talents as a socialist evangelist. To a reporter, he said that his election "was simply the beginning of a new era in the politics of this and other nations. The sleepers have awakened, the giant has realized his strength." In his inaugural address, his socialism was virtually synonymous with progressive, scientific reform. "The one supreme issue," Wilson argued, "is the People versus the Plutocracy." He acknowledged that "a small city like ours can do little to solve this great question." There were nonetheless some things that Berkeley could do:

We are entering upon the era of scientific civic and municipal administration. Why should Berkeley not be in the van? It is replied that Berkeley is too small a city for a civic laboratory[;] perhaps the very opposite is the case. A scientific method of taxation, scientific methods and processes in administering our public utilities, and the most ideal plans for civic art and civic betterment—all of these and other developments might be more easily initiated in smaller cities than in larger. Let us at least dream of the day when Science and the Passion for Humanity shall determine civic policies.[84]

The Berkeley electorate seemed generally satisfied with Wilson. Within the SPA, however, he was criticized by some for "right-wing" socialism that, to his critics, gutted true socialist distinctions. Wilson chafed at municipal administration.[85] He leapt at the chance to promote socialism by running for Congress in 1912. His attractiveness as a candidate remained substantial; he garnered some 26,000 votes against the incumbent Republican's 35,000 and 4,000 for the Democratic nominee.[86] Declining renomination as mayor in 1913, he ran for mayor again in 1915 and 1917 (in the latter race, he was not the official socialist nominee), but he was probably content not to win either race.[87]

The California socialist's popularity with a general electorate, though, was probably the deciding factor allowing Wilson to enter the national level of SPA organization. He represented the anti-Asian views of the California party on the Committee on Immigration. More important, he was a state delegate to the 1912 national convention, and he was also a member of the platform committee. He was also a member of the SPA National Executive Commitee in 1913, a body that had some limited power of action on behalf of the national party between conventions.[88]

Wilson's electoral activity and his single victory coincided with the peak of the SPA's appeal, both in California and the nation. His Berkeley success and his creditable showings in his other campaigns underscored his skills as an orator. Yet his success supports the observation of historian Sean Wilentz about the paradox of socialism's success in the United States.[89] It was only as the SPA stressed the consonance of social democracy with traditional themes in American political discourse—the people, equality, liberty, the exploitative power of moneyed interests, and progress—that electoral success became plausible, yet this appeal could not be sustained, since these tenets were also stressed by progressives. The socialism of Wilson, when it was not stereotyped as deceptive in its protestations of revolution by ballot, could all too easily seem politically redundant when taken seriously.

Socialism underwent internal upheaval shortly after Wilson's mayoral term concluded. The Great War unmasked the power of nationalism within the movement, and the Bolshevik regime challenged gradual, democratic revolution. Initially, Wilson took the socialist line of peace, not war. By 1915, however, he had left the party. Others did so as well between 1915 and 1917, including Jack London, Upton Sinclair (who rejoined the party after the war), and Wilson's fellow seeker of the grail, Herron.[90] In Wilson's case, his Canadian birth, British ties, and democratic commitments were probably the most decisive factors leading him out of the party and to support of American involvement in the war.[91] He took to calling himself a Christian socialist rather than a party socialist, although the war also effectively ended the CSF and the *Christian Socialist*.[92] He sold war bonds for a time, and his surviving son, Gladstone (the name suggesting the importance of British political traditions for the father), was killed in an air accident while in military training during the war.[93]

Leaving the SPA, in fact, did not fundamentally alter Wilson's activities or commitments. His success as a socialist evangelist and candidate led him back toward organized Protestantism, but he had never cut all ties with churches, as had Herron. He lectured on behalf of prohibition in the California Dry campaign of 1915–1916, and he was a featured speaker at the Federal Council of Churches' World Social Progress Congress at the 1915 Panama-Pacific International Exposition.[94] He had never completely identified either the cooperative common-wealth or the SPA with the Kingdom of God, although he had, like most Christian socialists, seen them as largely overlapping.[95] In 1913 he said:

There is but one meaning of life and action to me, and that is the establishment of the Kingdom of God on the earth—the Kingdom or condition of Social Justice, brotherly love and spiritual inspiration and fellowship among men, and it has been my abiding and all-compelling conviction for nearly twenty years that the next supreme step in that coming

Kingdom is the abolition of the present capitalist system and the establishment of the Socialist co-operative commonwealth.

Six years later, and four years after leaving the SPA, he took up church membership again. He explained his action with a public statement:

I believe that never since Jesus and his disciples confronted pagan Rome has there been a period of such supreme importance to the destinies of mankind as this present hour. It is doom or deliverance now. . . .

And for myself I am ready to confess that the life and spirit and teaching of Jesus Christ, in the Christ ideal for individual souls and for society, we have the spiritual ground of truth and power and passion for that social and religious awakening which alone can save the world. . . .

I may be unduly concerned, but I can't help feeling that these are terrible years—the problems of peace more exacting than the tasks of war. And I feel that men everywhere should seek the Living God, to cease from their greed and ambition and selfish vanities and consecrate their lives to the processes of real democracy.[96]

The church by this time seemed more hospitable to his immanenticist Christianity than did the SPA. God was still working toward the Kingdom, calling people to what Wilson had elsewhere described as a "socialization of personality" that would lead to self-sacrifing service to others in the manner of Jesus.

In the 1920s Wilson lectured on college campuses on world reconstruction and education.[97] With the arrival of the Great Depression and a New Deal Democratic Party, he ran unsuccessfully for Congress as a Democrat in 1932 and 1936, and he was a state delegate to the 1936 and 1940 national party conventions. Not surprisingly, he was especially active in support of his fellow former socialist, Upton Sinclair, when the latter captured the Democratic gubernatorial nomination in California in 1934 with his End Poverty in California (EPIC) program.[98] Wilson died in Berkeley at age seventy-four in 1942.

Wilson remained a Social Crusader until his death. The vision he had worked out, under inspiration from George D. Herron in the late 1890s, of "an active and unceasing campaign of social education" for the Kingdom of God, remained relatively unchanged through the next four decades. Ironically, Wilson was a far more consistent exponent of Herronite social Christianity than was Herron. Wilson's commitment to the SPA and the CSF illustrates the importance of Wilson as well as the more famous Herron in contributing to the unification of socialist groups that created the SPA and to sustaining an outspoken tradition of socialist Christianity within the party until World War I. Further, Wilson's sustained ties to British social Christianity and the Labour political movement suggest that further research into the intellectual and cultural links between social Christianity in the United States and Europe might help us rebalance American distinctives within a larger comparative context. A reconstruction of Wilson's life and thought as a socialist Christian also suggests that the trans-Mississippi West in general, and California in particular, has an underexamined religious and political history that might well qualify generalizations largely based on studies of individuals, groups, and institutions of the Northeast.[99]

Finally, Wilson is a significant example of the persistent thread of religion in American political life and traditions. Religion and faith have been intertwined in the United States since the nation's political birth. The separation of church and state has left neither the sphere of religion nor politics devoid of significant infusions of the other.[100] Wilson's public career can remind us that the ambiguities and problematics of prominent contemporary intertwinings of religion and partisan politics on the Right have had their predecessors and counterparts on the Left. "Except this civilisation be born again," Wilson exclaimed, "we cannot enter the next phase of the Kingdom of God. That which is born of the flesh of Capitalism is Capitalism. That which is born of the new spirit is of the kingdom of the free. Marvel not that I say unto you, Ye must be socially born again."[101]

NOTES

I would like to express my special appreciation to Dr. Jacob H. Dorn for his collegial sharing of his notes on the *Social Crusader*, the *Christian Socialist*, and J. Stitt Wilson's master's thesis. This chapter could not have been attempted without this generosity.

1. "The Impending Social Revolution," in *How I Became a Socialist and Other Papers* (Berkeley, Calif.: published by the author, 1912), 18, 21. Each speech in this collection has its own pagination. For simplification, further references to these will be by speech title, page number, and the abbreviation *HIBS*.

2. Herbert Coggins, "Herbert Coggins: From Horatio Alger to Eugene Debs," transcript of oral interview conducted by Corine L. Gilb, Regional Oral History Office, Bancroft Library, University of California, Berkeley, 1957, 88, 125. Quoted by permission of the Bancroft Library. For indications of responses by British audiences, see Peter d'A. Jones, *The Christian Socialist Revival, 1877–1914: Religion, Class, and Social Conscience in Late-Victorian England* (Princeton, N.J.: Princeton University Press, 1968), 427–29.

3. Biographical sources on Wilson are scattered and often partial or ambiguous. Wilson himself is the best source: see *Who Was Who in America, Vol. 3: 1943–1950*, s.v. "Wilson, J(ackson) Stitt," and Wilson, "How I Became a Socialist," Parts I and II, and "Moses: The Greatest of Labour Leaders," *HIBS*. Other important sources include Joseph E. Baker, ed., *Past and Present of Alameda County California*, 2 vols. (Chicago: S.J. Clarke, 1914), 2:275–77; *Oakland (Calif.) World*, 8 April 1911, 1; *San Francisco Call*, 3 April 1911, 1, 2; and *Berkeley Gazette*, 29 August 1942, n.p. The single best secondary source is Michael Hanika, "J. Stitt Wilson: California Socialist" (M.A. thesis, California State University, Hayward, 1972), but it does not adequately explore, let alone highlight, Wilson in the context of either Chicago or Herronite social Christianity.

4. Baker, *Past and Present of Alameda County*, 2:275; Hanika, "J. Stitt Wilson," 37.

5. Wilson, "Moses: The Greatest of Labour Leaders," 1; "How I Became a Socialist," Part I, 1; "How I Became a Socialist," Part II, 6–9, *HIBS*. Two helpful critical overviews to the Anglo-American Wesleyan Methodist tradition, including its experiential emphasis, are Charles I. Wallace Jr., "Wesleyan Heritage" and Charles Yrigoyen Jr., "United Methodism," in *Encyclopedia of the American Religious Experience: Studies of Traditions and Movements*, eds. Charles H. Lippy and Peter W. Williams (New York: Charles Scribner's, 1988), 1:525–37, 539–53.

6. Wilson, "How I Became a Socialist," Part I, 4–8.

7. See Carl Smith, *Urban Disorder and the Shape of Belief: The Great Chicago Fire, the Haymarket Bomb, and the Model Town of Pullman* (Chicago: University of Chicago Press, 1995), Part III Strike; Matthew C. Lee, "Onward Christian Soldiers: The Social Gospel and the Pullman Strike," *Chicago History* 20 (Spring–Summer 1991): 5–21; and Gary Scott Smith, "When Stead Came to Chicago: The 'Social Gospel Novel' and the Chicago Civic Federation," *American Presbyterians* 68 (1990): 193–205, for background on Chicago and Anglo-American Protestants during the early and mid-1890s.

8. Jane Addams, *Twenty Years at Hull House, With Autobiographical Notes*, with a foreword by Henry Steele Commager (New York: Signet Classic, 1960 [1910]), 121.

9. A number of scholars have suggested—some more explicitly than others—that direct experience with the industrial urban world was *a* or even *the* decisive catalyst in the social awakening of many of the most outspoken leaders of social Christianity at the end of the nineteenth and the beginning of the twentieth centuries. To date, though, no systematic study of the encounter of educated, middle-class Protestants with wage-workers and the poor has been made. See, for example, Ronald C. White Jr. and C. Howard Hopkins, *The Social Gospel: Religion and Reform in Changing America* (Philadelphia: Temple University Press, 1976), xiii–xvi, and Ronald C. White Jr., "Social Reform and the Social Gospel in America," in *Separation Without Hope: The Church and the Poor during the Industrial Revolution and Colonial Expansion*, ed. Julio De Santa Ana (Maryknoll, N.Y.: Orbis Books, 1980), 54–55.

10. Wilson, "The Story of a Developing Fellowship," *Social Crusader* 3 (January 1901): 13–15.

11. Useful studies of Herron include Robert T. Handy, "George D. Herron and the Kingdom Movement," *Church History* 19 (1950): 97–115; Phyllis Ann Nelson, "George D. Herron and the Socialist Clergy, 1890–1914" (Ph.D. dissertation, University of Iowa, 1953); Peter J. Frederick, *Knights of the Golden Rule: The Intellectual as Christian Social Reformer in the 1890s* (Lexington, Ky.: University Press of Kentucky, 1976), 161–77; Robert M. Crunden, *Ministers of Reform: The Progressives' Achievement in American Civilization, 1889–1920* (New York: Basic Books, 1982), 40–51; and Susan Curtis, *A Consuming Faith: The Social Gospel and Modern American Culture* (Baltimore, Md.: Johns Hopkins University Press, 1991), 195–206.

12. Frederick, *Knights of the Golden Rule*, 162.

13. Handy, "Herron and the Kingdom Movement," 102.

14. Grant Wacker, "The Holy Spirit and the Spirit of the Age in American Protestantism, 1880–1910," *Journal of American History* 72 (June 1985): 58.

15. James H. Moorhead, "The Erosion of Postmillennialism in American Religious Thought, 1865–1925," *Church History* 53 (March 1984): 61–77; Christopher Lasch, *The True and Only Heaven: Progress and Its Critics* (New York: W. W. Norton, 1991).

16. On the decisive shaping of this Anglo-American Protestantism in the Early Republic, see Nathan O. Hatch, *The Democratization of American Christianity* (New Haven, Conn.: Yale University Press, 1989); for an overview of this religious community at the end of the nineteenth and the beginning of the twentieth centuries, see Ferenc Morton Szasz, *The Divided Mind of Protestant America, 1880–1930* (University, Ala.: University of Alabama Press, 1982).

17. On the shift of Anglo-American Protestant theology toward de-emphasizing transcendence in favor of an emphasis on immanence and religious experience, see William R. Hutchison, *The Modernist Impulse in American Protestantism* (Cambridge, Mass.: Harvard University Press, 1976), and Bruce Kuklick, *Churchmen and Philosophers: From Jonathan Edwards to John Dewey* (New Haven, Conn.: Yale University Press, 1985).

18. Wilson, "The Story of a Developing Fellowship," 15.

19. Herron, "At the Shrine of Mazzini," *Kingdom* 10 (24 February 1898): 379, as quoted in Frederick, *Knights of the Golden Rule*, 163.

20. Herron, *Between Caesar and Jesus* (Westport, Conn.: Hyperion, 1975), 275. This is a reprint of an 1899 collection of lectures and sermons, all of which were delivered in 1898 except for the last one, which was given in 1895.

21. George D. Herron, "Some Financial Sins," *Dawn* 1 (15 December 1889): 7; Robert T. Handy, "George D. Herron and the Social Gospel in American Protestantism, 1890–1901" (Ph.D. dissertation, University of Chicago, 1949), 52–54; Howard H. Quint, *The Forging of American Socialism: Origins of the Modern Movement* (Indianapolis, Ind.: Bobbs-Merrill, 1964 [1953]), 134. Herron was secretary of Bliss's SCS in Minnesota for a time. *Dawn* 2 (May 1890): 52.

22. *Social Crusader* 2 (September 1900): 11; *Christian Socialist* 11 (15 July 1914): 1.

23. In the fall of 1898, when Wilson began publishing the *Social Crusader*, he was recommending such socialist authors as Edward Bellamy and Henry Demarest Lloyd—and, of course, Mazzini and Herron. See *Social Crusader* 1 (15 October 1898): 15. By the following year, he had added works by Marx, Engels, DeLeon, and Kautsky. See *Social Crusader* 1 (15 January 1899): 31. Yet in October 1900, while openly urging a vote for socialism, he also claimed he was not a party member. *Social Crusader* 3 (October 1900): 5.

24. Howard H. Quint, "*Social Crusader* and *Socialist Spirit*," in *The American Radical Press*, ed. Joseph R. Conlin (Westport, Conn.: Greenwood Press, 1974), 1:43–46.

25. *Social Crusader* 1 (15 October 1898): 11; 1 (15 March 1899): 3; 1 (1 August 1899): 2; 2 (May 1900): 2; 3 (January 1901): 18–21; 3 (February 1901): 6–7, 3 (May 1901): 9, 23. See also the photo of several Social Crusaders in *Comrade* 2 (November 1902): 43. Wise and Hollingsworth were Methodist pastors from Indiana; Fritz had been a college instructor as well as pastor; Thompson and Brown were Congregationalist ministers in Illinois and New York, respectively; B. F. Wilson was pastor of Methodist congregations in Spring Valley, Chanuahon, Millbrook, and Joliet, Illinois, before resigning in 1900. B. F. Wilson returned to serving as pastor later, but as a Unitarian; see *Berkeley Daily Gazette*, 29 August 1942.

26. *Social Crusader* 1 (September 1898): 3, 4, 5–9, 9–10, 15.

27. See, for example, *Social Crusader* 1 (15 October 1898): 10–11; 1 (July 1899): 14–15; 2 (1 October 1899): 3–10; 2 (July 1900): 13–14.

28. Ibid., 1 (15 February 1899): 11–13.

29. Ibid., 2 (1 December 1899): 14–15.

30. Ibid., 2 (May 1900): 6; 3–9.

31. Ibid., 2 (August 1900): 4–7.

32. On Debs and the Americanization of socialism, see Quint, *The Forging of American Socialism*; Nick Salvatore, *Eugene V. Debs: Citizen and Socialist* (Urbana, Ill.: University of Illinois Press, 1982); and Elliott Shore, *Talkin' Socialism: J. A. Wayland and the Radical Press* (Lawrence, Kans.: University Press of Kansas, 1988).

33. *Social Crusader* 1 (15 March 1899): 3–10; 1 (June 1899): 3–7; 2 (1 January 1900): 11; 2 (March 1900): 3–8; 2 (April 1900): 3–6; Jones, *Christian Socialist Revival*, 427–28.

34. Wilson notes in passing in his "Social Value of the Religious Work of a Section of the City of Chicago" (M.A. thesis, Northwestern University, 1901), 38, that he lived in the university settlement for one year. This was probably 1898–1899, since the address of Wilson and the *Social Crusader* in 1898 was the Northwestern settlement, but by his return from England the following year, he was living in Evanston. *Social Crusader* 1 (September 1898): 1, 15, and (1 June 1899): 1. Wilson first heard Herron at Taylor's Chicago Commons. *Social Crusader* 3 (January 1901): 14. Hull House frequently hosted various activities of the

Social Crusade, and Addams obliquely refers to Wilson as "a young Methodist minister" in the area who later "took to the street corners." *Social Crusader* 2 (February 1900): 10–11, and Addams, *Twenty Years at Hull House*, 141. Later, in appealing for the electoral support of the University of California community, Wilson referred to his Northwestern University settlement experience and claimed, "I was closely in touch with the work" of Addams and Taylor; he also referred to his master's degree work, although he claimed his thesis was "Herbert Spencer's Conception of Social Evolution." Perhaps he did both a study of Spencer and the sociological study of the Chicago neighborhood in fulfillment of his degree. See J. Stitt Wilson to University of California Officers and Students, undated congressional campaign letter (1912), printed, in Berkeley Politics, 3 boxes, Bancroft Library. On Wilson's first two visits to Britain, see Hanika, "J. Stitt Wilson," 48–59.

35. *Social Crusader* 3 (January 1901): 13.

36. Ibid., 2 (1 November 1899): 9–10, and 2 (1 December 1899): 15; Nelson, "George D. Herron and the Socialist Clergy," 193–209.

37. Herron to W.D.P. Bliss, 27 December 1900, *Social Unity* 1 (1 January 1901): 10, as quoted in Frederick, *Knights of the Golden Rule*, 173.

38. Quint, *The Forging of American Socialism*, 374–75, 377.

39. See *International Socialist Review* 1 (1901): 433–37, 501–4, 574–77, and 2 (1901): 65–66.

40. Wilson, "The Present Moral Conflict," *International Socialist Review* 1 (1901): 388–89, 392, 394.

41. Wilson, "Christianity and Paganism (A Reply)," ibid., 2 (1901): 4, 7, 13.

42. *Social Crusader* 3 (January 1901): 5–7, as quoted in Nelson, "George D. Herron and the Socialist Clergy," 217.

43. A full-page ad inside the back cover opposite p. 448 of the *International Socialist Review* 1 (1901) promoted the *Social Crusader* and the Social Crusade as Herron's. Wilson described the new relationship in *Social Crusader* 3 (January 1901): 13–17. For Herron's speaking engagements as a Social Crusader, see *Social Crusader* 3 (February 1901): 3–4, (March 1901): 3–10, (April 1901): 3–4.

44. *Social Crusader* 3 (January 1901): 17, (February 1901): 5, (May 1901): 23.

45. Nelson, "George D. Herron and the Socialist Clergy," 227–40.

46. Ibid., 294–97, 309–16.

47. Quint, *The Forging of American Socialism*, 140; Frederick, *Knights of the Golden Rule*, 174–79; Herron to the Committee of the Congregational Church of Grinnell, 25 May 1901, *International Socialist Review* 2 (1901): 21–28. On Brown's affiliation with the Social Crusade, see *Social Crusader* 3 (February 1901): 6–7, (May 1901): 9, 19–23. On Herron's later brief involvment with Woodrow Wilson, the Versailles settlement, and the vision of a reconstructed post-World War I world, see Curtis, *A Consuming Faith*, 195–97, 202–6.

48. *Social Crusader* 3 (June 1901): 3–9.

49. Ibid., 3 (August 1901): 3–5; Nelson, "George D. Herron and the Socialist Clergy," 308–9.

50. *Social Crusader* 3 (June 1901): 11.

51. For a photo of Stitt and Emma Wilson and two of their four children at the time, as well as a description of the family in an accompanying interview article, see the *San Francisco Call*, 3 April 1911, 1–2. One son, Stitt, Jr., had died of diptheria, as would their surviving youngest son in 1912. Hanika, "J. Stitt Wilson," 120.

52. *Social Crusader* 3 (August 1901): 3–5; Nelson, "George D. Herron and the Socialist Clergy," 307–8; Hanika, "J. Stitt Wilson," 4.

53. Nelson, "George D. Herron and the Socialist Clergy," 307–8; Ira A. Kipnis, *The American Socialist Movement, 1897–1912* (New York: Columbia University Press, 1952), 181.

54. Between 1901 and 1904 Wilson established his residency in Berkeley. Hanika, "J. Stitt Wilson," 4, places the year as 1901, based on Wilson's reference to moving there "at the close of the Crusade in Southern California." However, the Crusade went into 1902. Further, Wilson referred in 1913 to living in Berkeley nine years, which would mean 1904. See "The Story of a Socialist Mayor," reprinted in the *Western Comrade* (September 1913), in J. Stitt Wilson, *The Harlot and the Pharisees: or, The Barbary Coast in a Barbarous Land. Also The Story of a Socialist Mayor; Letter Declining Mayorality Nomination* (Berkeley: published by the author, 1913), 24. The *Berkeley Daily Gazette*, 17 February 1906, 1, refers to him as "the well known lecturer of this city." Finally, a *Gazette* story on 29 August 1942, upon his death, states that he became a resident of Berkeley in 1903. It seems that the Wilsons' main source of income was lecturing. They were affluent enough to afford a comfortable house in the Berkeley hills with a view of San Francisco Bay. *San Francisco Call*, 3 April 1911, 2.

55. "List of Delegates," *International Socialist Review* 4 (May 1904): 686–87; Nelson, "George D. Herron and the Socialist Clergy," 404 n. 1; Ralph Edward Shaffer, "A History of the Socialist Party of California" (M.A. thesis, University of California, Berkeley, 1955), 39.

56. Wilson's brother Ben, meanwhile, was a delegate from Kansas to the 1908 SPA convention, and a member of the resolutions committee. Charles H. Kerr, "Socialist National Convention," *International Socialist Review* 8 (June 1908): 723–25.

57. Hanika, "J. Stitt Wilson," 52, 63–64; Jones, *Christian Socialist Revival*, 428–29.

58. James T. Kloppenberg, *Uncertain Victory: Social Democracy and Progressivism in European and American Thought, 1870–1920* (New York: Oxford University Press, 1986), Chaps. 6 and 7, plumbs the depths of the historicist, pragmatist philosophical outlook that leading intellectuals and social democrats in England, France, Germany, and the United States were constructing during the era.

59. Paul T. Phillips, *A Kingdom on Earth: Anglo-American Social Christianity, 1880–1940* (University Park, Pa.: Pennsylvania State University Press, 1996), 1–47.

60. Robert Whitaker, "Is California Irreligious?" *Sunset* 16 (1906): 384–85. On Whitaker, see *Who Was Who in America. Vol. 2: 1943–1950*, s.v. "Whitaker, Robert" and Robert Whitaker, *"Why Callest Thou Me Good?"* (Los Gatos, Calif.: Progressive Press, 1913). On his socialism, see his monthly periodical *Insurgent* (1910–1912), published on the San Francisco peninsula in Los Gatos, where he was pastor of the Los Gatos Baptist Church at the time. His papers are deposited in the American Baptist Seminary Archives, Berkeley. For an overview of Protestantism in California at the time, see Eldon G. Ernst with Douglas Firth Anderson, *Pilgrim Progression: The Protestant Experience in California* (Santa Barbara, Calif.: Fithin Press, 1993), Chap. 4.

61. William G. Robbins, *Colony and Empire: The Capitalist Transformation of the American West* (Lawrence, Kans.: University Press of Kansas, 1994), 14, 16.

62. Kevin Starr, *Americans and the California Dream, 1850–1915* (New York: Oxford University Press, 1973), 68. On California's society and economy in the late nineteenth and early twentieth centuries, see Walter Nugent, "The People of the West since 1890," in *The Twentieth-Century West: Historical Interpretations*, eds. Gerald D. Nash and Richard W. Etulain (Albuquerque, N.M.: University of New Mexico Press, 1989), 50–53; Gerald D. Nash, "Stages of California's Economic Growth, 1870–1970: An Interpretation," *California Historical Quarterly* 51 (1972): 315–24; William Issel and Robert W. Cherny, *San Francisco, 1865–1932: Politics, Power, and Urban Development* (Berkeley, Calif.:

University of California Press, 1986), 203–4; Lawrence J. Jelinek, *Harvest Empire: A History of California Agriculture* (San Francisco: Boyd & Fraser, 1979), 39–77.

63. Ralph Edward Shaffer, "Radicalism in California, 1869–1929" (Ph.D. dissertation, University of California, Berkeley, 1962), 74–150; Royce D. Delmatier, Clarence F. McIntosh, and Earl G. Waters, *The Rumble of California Politics, 1848–1970* (New York: John Wiley, 1970), 100–124; Robert V. Hine, *California's Utopian Colonies* (New York: W. W. Norton, 1973 [1953]), 78–100, 114–31; Kevin Starr, *Inventing the Dream: California Through the Progressive Years* (New York: Oxford University Press, 1985), 207–18. On women in California's socialism, see Sherry Katz, "Socialist Women and Progressive Reform," in *California Progressivism Revisited*, eds. William Deverell and Tom Sitton (Berkeley, Calif.: University of California Press, 1994), 117–43.

64. On Bliss, see Richard B. Dressner, "William Dwight Porter Bliss's Christian Socialism," *Church History* 47 (March 1978): 66–82.

65. Douglas Firth Anderson, "Presbyterians and the Golden Rule: The Christian Socialism of J. E. Scott," *American Presbyterians* 67 (Fall 1989): 231–43.

66. Tom Sitton, "John Randolph Haynes and the Left Wing of California Progressivism," in *California Progressivism Revisited*, eds. Deverell and Sitton, 15–33, which is a convenient summary of Sitton's full-scale biography, *John Randolph Haynes: California Progressive* (Stanford, Calif.: Stanford University Press, 1992).

67. On Markham, see Frederick, *Knights of the Golden Rule*, 187–209, and Starr, *Inventing the Dream*, 213–15. On Woodbey, see Philip S. Foner, ed., *Black Socialist Preacher: The Teachings of Reverend George Washington Woodbey and his Disciple Reverend George W. Slater, Jr.* (San Francisco: Synthesis, 1983), 1–35.

68. Shaffer, "Socialist Party of California," 36, 25–30, 45–59. On Harriman's religiosity, see Knox Mellon Jr., "Job Harriman: The Early and Middle Years, 1861–1912" (Ph.D. dissertation, Claremont Graduate School, 1972).

69. *Social Crusader* 3 (May 1901), 10.

70. Nelson, "George D. Herron and the Socialist Clergy," 321.

71. *Christian Socialist* 3 (1 May 1906): 1, as quoted in ibid., 322.

72. Nelson, "George D. Herron and the Socialist Clergy," 322–75.

73. George E. Mowry, *The California Progressives* (Berkeley, Calif.: University of California Press, 1951); Spencer C. Olin Jr., *California's Prodigal Sons: Hiram Johnson and the Progressives* (Berkeley, Calif.: University of California Press, 1968); Deverell and Sitton, eds., *California Progressivism Revisited*.

74. For an example of Protestants and Progressive Era reform in California, see Douglas Firth Anderson, "'A True Revival of Religion': Protestants and the San Francisco Graft Prosecutions, 1906–1909," *Religion and American Culture* 4 (1994): 25–49.

75. *Christian Socialist* 7 (15 September 1910): 7.

76. Shaffer, "Socialist Party of California," 84–85; Hanika, "J. Stitt Wilson," 76–84; Michael Paul Rogin and John L. Shover, *Political Change in California: Critical Elections and Social Movements, 1890–1966* (Westport, Conn.: Greenwood Publishing, 1970), 70–71, 80; William Deverell, *Railroad Crossing: Californians and the Railroad, 1850–1910* (Berkeley, Calif.: University of California Press, 1994), 169.

77. Shaffer, "Socialist Party of California," 85; Wilson, "The Story of a Socialist Mayor," in *The Harlot and the Pharisees*, 24–25.

78. For Berkeley's population, see U.S. Department of Commerce, Bureau of the Census, *Fifteenth Census of the United States, 1930: Population*, 1:22. The "Anglo-Saxon" and Protestant character of the city is assessed in [Hugh W. Gilchrist,] *A Survey of Evangelical Churches in San Francisco, Oakland, Berkeley and Alameda* (San Francisco: published by the author, 1916), 5–6. On Berkeley's history, see George A. Pettitt, *Berkeley:*

The Town and Gown of It (Berkeley, Calif.: Howell-North Books, 1973), and Phil McArdle, ed., *Exactly Opposite the Golden Gate: Essays on Berkeley's History, 1845–1945* (Berkeley, Calif.: Berkeley Historical Society, 1983).

79. *City for the People*, 28 March 1911, Berkeley election periodical; Wilson, mimeographed public letter, 30 March 1911, in Berkeley Politics, 3 boxes. Both items in Bancroft Library.

80. *San Francisco Call*, 3 April 1911, 1–2. Stanford University Professor Ira B. Cross, in his "Socialism in California Municipalities," *National Municipal Review* 1 (1912): 616, noted that there was no evidence of unusual class division in the Berkeley election.

81. James T. Burnett, "J. Stitt Wilson," in *Exactly Opposite the Golden Gate*, ed. McArdle, 279–82.

82. See James P. Kraft, "The Fall of Job Harriman's Socialist Party: Violence, Gender, and Politics in Los Angeles, 1911," *Southern California Quarterly* 70 (1988): 43–68.

83. Wilson, "The Story of a Socialist Mayor," in *The Harlot and the Pharisees*, 26; Hanika, "J. Stitt Wilson," 100–121.

84. *San Francisco Call*, 3 April 1911, 2; *Oakland World*, 8 July 1911.

85. Coggins, "Herbert Coggins," 89.

86. Hanika, "J. Stitt Wilson," 116–19; Shaffer, "Socialist Party of California," 125.

87. City for the People, 21 April 1915, Berkeley election periodical; J. Stitt Wilson, *To the People of Berkeley*, 23 April 1917, election pamphlet; various 1917 campaign materials, Berkeley Politics, 3 boxes; all in Bancroft Library.

88. Kipnis, *American Socialist Movement*, 288; "The National Socialist Convention of 1912," *International Socialist Review* 12 (June 1912): 812; "Minutes of National Committee, May 11–14," *Party Builder*, 14 June 1913.

89. Richard Wightman Fox and James T. Kloppenberg, eds., *A Companion to American Thought* (Oxford, England: Blackwell, 1995), s.v. "socialism," by Sean Wilentz.

90. Shaffer, "Socialist Party of California," 164–75; Daniel Bell, *Marxian Socialism in the United States* (Princeton, N.J.: Princeton University Press, 1967), 100–101.

91. Coggins, "Herbert Coggins," 99–100.

92. *Berkeley Pacific*, 4 October 1917, 3, a Congregationalist weekly that frequently noted Wilson's activities in the region, specifies his Christian socialism; Nelson, "George D. Herron and the Socialist Clergy," 430–39, traces the response of Herron, the CSF, and other partisan socialist Christians.

93. Hanika, "J. Stitt Wilson," 124–25; unidentified material in J. Stitt Wilson file, Biography and Reference, Bancroft Library.

94. Hanika, "J. Stitt Wilson," 124; Wilson, "The Minimum Social Program of a Militant Christianity," in *Addresses, World's Social Progress Congress, San Francisco, California, April 1–11, 1915*, ed. William M. Bell (Dayton, Ohio: World's Social Progress Council, 1915), 22–35.

95. Robert T. Handy, "Christianity and Socialism in America, 1900–1920," *Church History* 21 (March 1952): 45, argues that the convergence of the Kingdom and the socialist cooperative commonwealth is "the key" to understanding socialist Christianity after 1900.

96. *San Francisco Call and Post*, 28 January 1919; see also *Berkeley Pacific* 69 (February 1919): 18. Wilson became a member of Trinity Methodist Episcopal Church, Berkeley.

97. See, for example, J. Stitt Wilson, "A Constructive Criticism of Modern Education," in *Am I Getting an Education?*, ed. George A. Coe (Garden City, N.Y.: Doubleday, Doran, 1929), 47–60. Wilson is described as "Lecturer on Education and Social Problems."

98. Hanika, "J. Stitt Wilson," 126–27.

99. For more on how a study of Protestantism in California might modify standard interpretations of American Protestantism, see Anderson, "'A True Revival of Religion' " and also idem, " 'We Have Here a Different Civilization': Protestant Identity in the San Francisco Bay Area, 1906–1909," *Western Historical Quarterly* 22 (1992): 199–221 and "Modernization and Theological Conservatism in the Far West: The Controversy Over Thomas F. Day, 1907–1912," *Fides et Historia* 24 (Summer 1992): 76–90.

100. See, for example, Mark A. Noll, ed., *Religion and American Politics: From the Colonial Period to the 1980s* (New York: Oxford University Press, 1990).

101. Wilson, "The Impending Social Revolution," 3, *HIBS*.

3

From Slavery to Socialism:
George Washington Woodbey,
Black Socialist Preacher

Philip S. Foner

In the *Ohio Socialist Bulletin* of February 1909, the Reverend Richard Euell, a black minister of Milford, Ohio, published "A Plan to Reach the Negro." The Negro, he wrote, "belongs to the working class and must be taught class consciousness." Blacks could be recruited more rapidly into the Socialist Party if the Socialists would go to them in their churches and point out "the way to freedom and plenty." Most of them had no experience with any organization other than the church and could not think of committing themselves to action except in religious terms. The Bible and even motion pictures about the "Passion Play" could be used effectively to imbue religion with radicalism and convince the black working class of the evils of the capitalist system and the virtues of socialism.[1]

The first black socialist to conduct the type of work Reverend Euell recommended was the Reverend George Washington Woodbey (sometimes spelled Woodby). He had already been performing this function for the socialist cause for several years, even before "A Plan to Reach the Negro" was published.

Woodbey, the leading Negro socialist in the first decade of the twentieth century, was born a slave in Johnson County, Tennessee, on 5 October 1854, the son of Charles and Rachel (Wagner) Woodbey. Nothing is known about his early life except that he learned to read after he was freed and was self-educated, except for two terms in a common school, and that his life was one of "hard work and hard study carried on together." A fellow socialist who knew him wrote: "He has worked in mines, factories, on the streets, and at everything which would supply food, clothing and shelter."

Woodbey was ordained a Baptist minister in Emporia, Kansas, in 1874. He was active in the Republican Party in Missouri and Kansas. He was also a leader of the Prohibition Party, and when he moved to Nebraska, he became a prominent force in the prohibition movement in that state. In 1896, Woodbey ran for lieutenant governor and Congress on the Prohibition ticket in Nebraska.

That same year, he made his first acquaintance with the principles of socialism when he read Edward Bellamy's *Looking Backward*. His interest was further aroused by copies of the *Appeal to Reason* which he came across. Although he subscribed to the *Appeal*, he did not join the socialists. Instead, he moved into the Populist Party, and in 1900, he supported William Jennings Bryan, the Democratic and Populist candidate for president. He also heard Eugene V. Debs speak during the presidential campaign and was so impressed that when the Democratic Party asked Woodbey to speak for Bryan, he agreed to do so; the speeches he delivered, however, were geared more to the ideas advanced by Debs than to those of the Democratic candidate. After several such speeches, the Democrats stopped scheduling him and the black minister came to the conclusion that his place was in the socialist camp. He resigned his pulpit and announced to his friends that from then on his life "would be consecrated to the Socialist movement." A Nebraska socialist recalled: "We   remember him in the stirring days of the inception of the Socialist movement in Omaha. Night after night he spoke on the streets and in the parks of that city. Omaha had never had the crowds that attended Woodbey's meetings."[2]

When Woodbey visited San Diego to see his mother in the spring of 1902, he immediately made an impression on the comrades in southern California. A dispatch to the *Los Angeles Socialist* on 31 May 1902 read:

Socialism is on the boom here in this county and city. We have had Rev. G. W. Woodbey, the Colored Socialist orator of Nebraska with us for nearly a month during which time he has delivered 23 addresses and will speak again tonight, and then he will do some work in the country districts where he has been invited to speak.

Comrade Woodbey is great and is a favorite with all classes. He came here unannounced ostensibly to see his mother who resides here but as he says that he is "so anxious to be free," that he feels impressed to work for the cause constantly. He has had very respectable audiences both on the streets and in the halls. He likes to speak on the street and it is the general verdict that he has done more good for the cause than any of our most eloquent speakers who have preceded him. He is full of resources and never repeats his speeches, but gives them something new every time. He requested me to state in my notes to the "Socialist" that he desires to visit Los Angeles later on if you folks can find a place for him. He makes no charges but depends entirely on passing the hat for his support.[3]

Los Angeles did find a place for Woodbey, and he delivered a series of soap-box speeches and lectures in its leading hall. When, after one of his speeches, Woodbey was denied admittance to the Southern Hotel and Northern Restaurant because of his color, the Los Angeles Socialist Party organized a boycott of the establishments and distributed leaflets reading: "We demand as trade unionists and socialists, that every wage-worker in Los Angeles bear well in mind these two places that depend on public patronage—the Northern Restaurant and the Southern Hotel—keep away from them. They draw the color line."[4] The boycott had the desired effect.

Woodbey accepted an offer to become minister of the Mount Zion Baptist Church in San Diego, and over the next two decades, he made his home in California. He was elected a member of the state executive board of the Socialist

Party and soon became widely known in the state as "The Great Negro Socialist Orator." In a Los Angeles debate with Archibald Huntby, Ph.D., in which Woodbey took the affirmative of the topic "Resolved That Socialism Is the True Interpretation of Economic Conditions and That It Is the Solution of the Labor Problem," he was listed as a "well-known Socialist Lecturer. Quaint, Direct, Forceful. Has spoken to great audiences in all parts of the United States."[5]

An announcement that Woodbey would deliver a reply to Booker T. Washington's "Capitalist Argument for the Negro" packed Los Angeles' leading hall on 1 May 1903. He paid tribute to Washington "as a gentleman" and educator, but added: "He has all the ability necessary to make a good servant of capitalism by educating other servants for capitalism." Woodbey charged that, whether consciously or not, Tuskegee Institute fulfilled the role of providing black workers to be pitted against white workers so as to bring about a general lowering of wage scales. What Washington failed to understand, he said, was that there was basically no unity between capitalists, white or black, and workers, white or black: "There is no race division industrially, but an ever-growing antagonism between the exploiting capitalists black or white, and the exploited workers, black or white." In this "industrial struggle," the working class was bound to "ultimately triumph": "And then the men of all races will share in the results of production according to their services in the process of production. This is Socialism and the only solution to the race problem."[6]

As a socialist soap-box speaker, Woodbey was a frequent target of the police of San Diego, Los Angeles, San Francisco, and other California communities. He was in and out of jail several times between 1902 and 1908, and was hospitalized more than once as a result of police brutality. Nonetheless, he refused to retreat. When he was attacked and driven off a street corner in San Diego in July 1905 by Police Officer George H. Cooley, Woodbey led a group of protesters to the police station to lodge a complaint. There Cooley again attacked the black socialist, "using at the same time oaths and language too mean and vile to print." Woodbey was literally thrown bodily out of the station house. He immediately brought charges against the police officer for assault and battery, and informed his California comrades: "In the days of chattel slavery the masters had a patrol force to keep the negroes in their place and protect the interests of the masters. Today the capitalists use the police for the same purpose." He added that the slaves had rebelled despite the patrols and that he was following that tradition in telling the police they could not get away with their brutalities against the enemies of the capitalist system.

Woodbey's case against the police was prosecuted by the county attorney, assisted by California's leading socialist attorney, Job Harriman. All witnesses testified that the Negro socialist's conduct had been "perfectly gentlemanly" and that he had a perfectly lawful right to be at the station house. Nevertheless, the jury, composed of conservative property owners, took only fifteen minutes to find the defendant not guilty. Woodbey was furious and published the names of the members of the jury, urging all decent citizens to have nothing to do with them. He then returned immediately to the soap box in San Diego and held one of the biggest street-corner meetings held in the city up to that time. As he wrote:

The case has made more Socialists than I could possibly have made in many speeches. Had I not gone to the court with the matter the public would forever have contended that I was doubtless doing or saying something that I had no right to do or say. And when I complained I would have been told that if I had gone to the courts I would have got justice. Now, as it is, nothing of the kind can be said, and the responsibility is placed where it rightly belongs.

Many non-socialists in San Diego, Woodbey noted, were learning the truth of the socialist contention that "the police force are the watch dogs of capitalism."[7]

In more than one California city, Woodbey was arrested and hauled off to jail for trying to sell copies of his socialist booklets.[8] The writings made his name known throughout the entire party in the United States, and even internationally. A white socialist described him as "the greatest living negro in America" and noted that "his style is simple and his logic invincible. He knows the race question, and one of his most popular lectures relates to the settlement of this vexed question under Socialism." Because of Woodbey's ability to explain socialism in simple terms, he was asked to "embody some of the things he has said to the thousands who have listened to his talks, in a written form." The response was the pamphlet *What to Do and How to Do It or Socialism vs. Capitalism*. A copy of a small edition, privately printed, fell into the hands of A. W. Ricker, the socialist organizer in the West and South. While at the home of socialist publisher Julius A. Wayland in Girard, Kansas, Ricker read it aloud to the Wayland family. "At the conclusion," he wrote, "we decided that the book ought to be in the hands of millions of American wage slaves, and we forthwith wrote to Rev. Mr. Woodbey for the right to bring it out."[9]

It was published as No. 40 of the widely distributed *Wayland's Monthly* in August 1903. Ricker gave it a sendoff in the *Appeal to Reason*, writing:

The book in many respects is the equal of "Merrie England," and in the matter of its clear teaching of the class struggle, it is superior. It has been read by every negro in Girard, and has made Socialists of those who were susceptible of understanding after every other effort had failed to shake their unreasoning adherence to the republican party. A good supply should be ordered by every local in the land, and gotten in the hands of negroes especially. In our humble judgment, there is no book in the language that will excel it in propaganda value, and we expect to see it pass through one edition after another, so soon as it is read by the comrades.[10]

Since Robert Blatchford's *Merrie England*, published in England in 1894 and in the United States in 1900, was considered one of the best of the socialist educational publications, the tribute to Reverend Woodbey's pamphlet was well understood by the readers of the *Appeal to Reason*.

Woodbey's forty-four-page booklet carried this moving dedication: "This little book is dedicated to that class of citizens who desire to know what the Socialists want to do and how they propose to do it. By one who was once a chattel slave freed by the proclamation and wishes to be free from the slavery of capitalism."[11]

In his preface, Woodbey acknowledged that there was "nothing original" in his little book, his aim being simply to make the subjects treated "as plain as possible to the reader." It was not directed to those who were already convinced of the superiority of socialism over capitalism, but rather to "meet the demands of that large and increasing class of persons who have not yet accepted Socialism, but would do so if they could see any posssible way of putting it into practice." Within this framework, Reverend Woodbey's booklet is an effective piece of socialist propaganda. It was so highly thought of in socialist circles that by 1908 it had been translated into three languages and had gained an international reputation of its author.[12]

Basically, the booklet consists of a dialogue between the author and his mother, whom he has rejoined after nearly seventeen years of separation. She expresses her astonishment upon learning that her son has become a socialist. "Have you given up the Bible and the ministry and gone into politics?" she asks. Her son tries to convince her that it is precisely because of his devotion to the principles enunciated in the Bible that he became a socialist and that, as the years passed, he became more and more convinced of the correctness of his decision. When his mother points out that among his comrades are many who believe in neither God nor the Bible, he readily agrees but reminds her that he found "a still larger number of unbelievers in the Republican Party before I left it some twenty years ago" and that other parties had their "equal portion" of nonbelievers. More important, while he believed in the biblical account of God and the origin of the earth and of man, and members of his party did not, he and they were able to agree that "man is here, and the earth is here, and that it is the present home of the race, at least." To be sure, they did not see eye to eye about the "hereafter," but he was ready and willing to join hands with any who were "willing to make things better here, which the Bible teaches is essential to the hereafter." Since socialism was "a scheme for bettering things here first," he could be a "good Socialist" without surrendering his belief in God or the Bible. There was room in the Socialist Party for those who were interested only in what it could do for mankind in the present world and for those, like himself, who were "Socialists because they think that mankind is entitled to the best of everything in both this world and the next." Finally, his mother could rest assured that under socialism persons would be free to have "their own religion or none, just as they please, so long as they do not interfere with others."[13]

Having laid to rest his mother's anxiety and made her willing to listen to the fundamental principles of a movement that had obviously not destroyed her son's religious convictions, Woodbey proceeds to explain to her the evils of capitalist society and the way by which socialism, gaining power through the ballot box, would set out to eliminate these evils. After he takes his mother through such subjects as rent, interest, and profits, which are all gained from labor's production, and value, which is created only by labor but whose fruits are appropriated entirely by the capitalists, she expresses bewilderment at the meaning of these words. Her son then illustrates what they mean in simple language and in terms of daily experience. Here, for example, is his explanation of surplus value:

Why didn't the slave have wealth at the close of the war? He worked hard.
"Because his master got it," mother replied.

The wage worker's master got what he produced, too.
"But wasn't he paid for his work?" asked mother.
Yes, about seventeen cents on every dollar's worth of wealth he created.

Under socialism, he continues, the capitalist would have to turn over to the state a "large amount of capital created by labor" which he had taken from the worker. The worker, meanwhile, having been deprived of all he produced under capitalism, would have nothing to turn over. The very rich man would have no reason to complain

since he and his children, who have done nothing but live off the labor of those who have nothing to turn over, are to be given an equal share of interest with those who have produced it all, so you see we Socialists are not such bad fellows as you thought. We propose to do good unto those who spitefully use us, and to those who curse us, by giving them an equal show with ourselves, provided that they will hereafter do their share of the useful work.[14]

His mother expresses concern that the capitalists will not yield peacefully to having the "land, factories, and means of production" turned over to the cooperative commonwealth by a socialist Congress elected by the people, and that they would start a war to retain their holdings. Her son concedes that this would quite likely occur, just as the slaveholders had refused to abide by Lincoln's electoral victory and had precipitated a civil war. But the capitalists would never succeed in the war they would seek to stimulate, since the majority of the people had clearly become convinced that socialism was the only solution to their problems, or else the socialists could not have won their electoral victories. Hence, the capitalists would have no one to do the fighting for them:

The slaveholder did not dare to arm the negro, on his side, without proclaiming emancipation, and to do that was to lose his cause; so with the capitalist, if he dares to offer all to the poor man who must fight his battles, he has lost his cause; and with this condition confronting the capitalist, there is no danger in taking over the entire industrial plant as soon as the Socialists can be elected and pass the necessary laws. And the Socialist party will go into power just as soon as the majority finds that the only way to secure to itself its entire product is to vote that ticket.[15]

His mother has only one question left about the transition from capitalism to socialism: "Have the people a right to do this?" Her son reminds her of the Declaration of Independence which clearly affirms the right of the people, when any form of government becomes destructive of the rights of liberty and the pursuit of happiness, "to alter and abolish it and institute a new government" which would be most likely to effect "their safety and happiness." On this "the Socialists stand," the son declares firmly. Moreover, it was none other than Abraham Lincoln who, in his speech of 12 January 1840, in the House of Representatives had said "just what the Socialists now say." He had then declared: "Any people anywhere being inclined and having the power have the right to rise up and shake off the existing government and form a new one that suits them better."[16]

His mother by now fully satisfied, the son proceeds to describe how different departments of government—agriculture, manufacturing, transportation, distribution, intelligence, education, and health—will operate under socialism, providing for the needs of the people, and not for the profits of the capitalist as under capitalism. The mother occasionally interrupts the narrative with questions that bring answers that satisfy her. Thus, when she asks whether the workers who would own and operate the factories under socialism "would know how to do the work," the answer reassures her:

Why, the workers are the only ones who do know how to run a factory. The stockholders who own the concern know nothing about doing the work. If the girl who weaves in the factory should be told that Socialism is now established and that henceforth she is to have shorter hours of labor, a beautiful sanitary place to work in, and an equal share of all the wealth of the nation to be taken in any kind of thing she wants, do you think she would forget how to work? And if on the other hand, all she produces is to go to the girl who does nothing but own the stocks, then she can work right along? Seems to me you might see the absurdity of that, mother. "I believe I do see, now," she said, after a moment's hesitation. Then apply that illustration about the girls, to all the workers, and you will get my meaning.[17]

As might be expected, the mother asks, "Like all other women, I want to know where we are to come in." Her son assures her that it was in the interest of "the women, more than the men, if possible, to be Socialists because they suffer more from capitalism than anyone else." For one thing, the socialist platform demands "the absolute equality of the sexes before the law, and the repeal of all law that in any way discriminates against women." Then again, under socialism, each woman would, like each man, have her own independent income and would become "an equal shareholder in the industries of the nation." Under such liberating conditions, a woman would have no need "to sell herself through a so-called marriage to someone she did not love in order to get a living," and, for the first time in history, she could marry only for love. Under capitalism, the working man was a slave, "and his wife . . . the slave of a slave." Socialism would liberate both, but since it would give women political equality and economic freedom it would actually do more for women than for men.[18]

By now, his mother has been converted totally. The booklet ends with the comment: "'Well, you have convinced me that I am about as much of a slave now as I was in the South, and I am ready to accept any way out of this drudgery,' mother remarked as the conversation turned on other subjects."[19]

Here and there, *What to Do and How to Do It* reflects Bellamy's influence on Woodbey. In fact, sections of the 1903 pamphlet are somewhat similar to parts of the 1887 *Looking Backward*.[20] In the main, however, the pamphlet revealed that the black minister had broken with Bellamy's utopianism. While Bellamy emphasized "equitable" distribution of wealth under Nationalism, Woodbey was convinced that the solution lay closer to Marx's maxim, "From each according to his ability, to each according to his needs." Bellamy rejected the label socialism as dangerous and un-American.[21] In contrast, Woodbey welcomed it and believed its principles were in keeping with the best in the American tradition. Like many in the Socialist Party,

Woodbey believed that, with the capture of sufficient political offices through the ballot box, socialism could be rapidly achieved. He was one of the very few in the party in 1903, however, who recognized the danger that the capitalists would not calmly allow their control of society to be eliminated by legislative enactments, but instead would, like the slaveowners in 1860, resort to violence to prevent the people's will from being carried out. Woodbey differed from Jack London, who, in his great 1908 novel, *The Iron Heel*, predicted that the oligarchy of American capitalists would seize power from the socialists and destroy the democratic process by violence. Woodbey, on the other hand, was confident that the capitalists would fail.[22] Nevertheless, by even raising this issue in his pamphlet, Woodbey was in advance of nearly all Christian Socialists.

Early in *What to Do and How to Do It*, Woodbey assures his mother that at a future date he would tell her "more about what the Bible teaches on the subject" of socialism.[23] A year later, he fulfilled his promise with *The Bible and Socialism: A Conversation Between Two Preachers*, published in San Diego by the author. The ninety-six-page pamphlet was dedicated to "the Preachers and Members of the Churches, and all others who are interested in knowing what the Bible teaches on the question at issue between the Socialists and the Capitalists, by one who began preaching twenty-nine years ago, and still continues."[24]

As the subtitle indicates, *The Bible and Socialism* consists of a dialogue between Woodbey and another clergyman. The latter is a local pastor to whom Woodbey's mother has given a copy of the 1903 pamphlet and has invited to her home to hear her son convince him that he was wrong in contending that "there is no Socialism in the Bible." The skeptical pastor questions Woodbey about the socialist claim that Karl Marx discovered the principles of scientific socialism and points out that this was centuries after the Bible was written. In response, Woodbey notes, first, that no new idea is ever entirely new and is in some way based on what went before, and, second, that

Marx, the greatest philosopher of modern times, belonged to the same wonderful Hebrew race that gave to the world Moses, the Lawgiver, the kings and prophets, and Christ the Son of the Highest, with his apostles, who, together, gave us the Bible that, we claim, teaches Socialism. Doubtless Marx, like the young Hebrews, was made acquainted with the economic teachings of Moses, and all the rest of the Old Testament sages and prophets, whatever we find him believing in after life.

If we are able to show that the Bible opposes both rent, interest, and profits, and the exploiting of the poor, then it stands just where the Socialists do.[25]

Woodbey agrees that Marx was not a Christian but notes that this was of no significance since socialism had nothing to do with a man's religion or lack of it. He devotes the rest of his pamphlet to detailed references, quotations, and citations to convince the pastor that since the Bible—both the Old and New Testaments—did actually oppose "rent, interest, and profits, and the exploiting of the poor," it was a socialist document with close affinity to such classics as *The Communist Manifesto*, *Das Kapital*, and other writings of Marx. As a Jew, Woodbey emphasizes, Marx was able to do "the greatly needed work of reasoning out from the standpoint of the philosopher what his ancestors, the writers of the Old and New Testaments, had already done from a moral and religious standpoint."[26] This is not to say, he continues, that there is no difference between a socialism based merely on a "moral and religious standpoint" and scientific socialism, just as there was a fundamental difference between the socialism advanced by utopian reformers prior to Marx and that set forth by the father of scientific socialism. For scientific socialism was based on the class struggle which had dominated all history and all existing relationships in capitalist society. When the pastor asks Woodbey if the class struggle also exists in the church, there is the following discussion in which the mother joins:

Master and slave, before the war, all belonged to the same church. They met on Sunday and prayed together, and one church member sold the other the next day. So now, in many cases, master and wage slave belong to the same church, meet on Sunday and pray together, and the one turns the other off from even the pittance he allowed him to take out of his earnings as wages or sets him out of house and home for non-payment of rent, or under mortgage, the next day. All that, notwithstanding the Bible says love brother and the stranger as oneself.

It took the abolitionist, in and out of the church, to show the inconsistency of slavery and force a division, as the Socialists are now doing.

"Yes," said mother, "I belonged to one of that kind of churches, myself, before the war."[27]

Just as his mother was converted at the end of the 1903 pamphlet, so, too, is the pastor by the close of *The Bible and Socialism*. He confesses that he learned little of economics while in college, and since he joined the ministry, he has been too busy to give more than a casual thought to the Bible's "economic teachings" and to whether the churches adhered to them. As a result of the "interesting evening conversations," he was a changed man. "Being convinced that Socialism is but the carrying out of the economic teachings of the Bible, I shall endeavor to study it and lay it before my people to the best of my ability."[28]

Woodbey's pamphlet offered little new for white, religiously inclined socialists since the Christian Socialists had already published a considerable body of literature demonstrating to their satisfaction that the Bible and socialism were compatible. To black churchgoers, however, much of what was in the pamphlet was new and certainly must have had an impressive impact. Moreover, while many Christian Socialists preached an emotional propaganda replete with Christian ethics, they tended to ignore the class struggle or to relate their Biblical references to the contemporay scene. Not so Woodbey; he was a firm believer in the class struggle, had read Marx, and was not in the least reluctant to couple discussions of the Old and New Testaments with those about the specific evils in twentieth-century American society.

Woodbey's third and last socialist pamphlet was *The Distribution of Wealth*, published in 1910 in San Diego by the author. The sixty-eight-page booklet consists of a series of letters to a J. Jones, a California rancher friend of the author. The pamphlet describes how the distribution of wealth created by productive labor would operate "after Socialism has overthrown the capitalist method of production."

Pointing out in his preface that there was little in socialist literature about how the future cooperative commonwealth would function, Woodbey, without the slightest hesitation, declared he would attempt to fill the gap. Affirming his right to do so, he noted: "If the socialist movement is based upon truth, it cannot be destroyed by the utmost freedom of discussion, nor is the movement or the party necessarily in danger, because your views or mine are not at once adopted even should they be correct. All I ask of the reader is a fair, honest consideration of what I have written."[29]

What he wrote is an interesting elaboration of how the different institutions under capitalism would operate in the new socialist society. Some of this had already been explained in his 1903 *What to Do and How to Do It,* but here he develops it further. In 1903, it will be recalled, Woodbey had conceded that the capitalists would resort to armed resistance to prevent the socialist society from coming into being. Now, however, he appears to believe that, while the capitalists would resist the transition to socialism with "tremendous opposition," it would not necessarily lead to war. Once socialism had proved its superiority over capitalism, even the capitalists and their children would acquiesce and decide to live under it—a clear throwback to *Looking Backward.* He writes:

Let us go back, for instance, to the slaveholder, by way of illustration. He declared that he would go to war before he would permit himself and family to labor like the negro slave and live in poverty, rags and ignorance. He had been taught to believe that that was the necessary outgrowth of labor. And I submit that the condition of labor under chattel slavery was a poor school in which to teach the child of the master a desire to labor. So the capitalist of today and his children look upon the workers as he has them in the sweatshops, mines and factories of the country, putting in long hours for a bare existence, under the most unsanitary conditions, living in the worst of places, and eating of the worst of food; and, like his brother, the slaveholder, he is determined that he and his shall not be reduced to such straits. It has not yet dawned upon him that when the people who work own the industries in place of him, all of these disagreeable conditions will at once disappear. . . . It is my opinion that, notwithstanding the false education of the children of the wealthy, even they in the first generation will have so much of their distaste for labor taken away that we will have little or no trouble with them when the majority have changed conditions.[30]

Woodbey's rancher friend keeps asking whether people would work under socialism, once the fear of poverty and unemployment was removed. Woodbey's answer is interesting:

when chattel slavery prevailed, as we said, men thought that labor must continue to be always what it was then, and that because the slave sought to escape he wouldn't work for wages. So now the capitalist, and those who believe in capitalism, think that labor must continue always to be just what it is now; and that some people won't work under the new and better conditions.

It is a wonder to me that men are so willing to work as they are now under the present conditions. The fact is, the mind of the child is such that it accepts what it is taught now, and will do the same then.

The boy that was born a slave thought that it was natural for him to be one, and the young master took it for granted that he was intended to be master. But the boy that is born free, never thinks that anyone ought to own him; nor does the youngster born at the same time with him think that he ought to own him. But instead, they both go to school often in the same class. They at once accept the conditions under which they were born. No, my friend, there is no danger of the children not at once accepting the new conditions under Socialim, and we have proved there will be so little loss through idlers, even in the first generation of old folks, that it will not be found worth bothering about. And as the old and infirm should of necessity be looked after with the best of everything from the very beginning, it will be found when the time comes that the thing to do will be to let everyone work and be sure that we have abundance of everything for all, and then let everybody help themselves, wherever they may be, to what we have on hand, as we do with what the public now owns. Indeed, they can be better trusted then than now, with all fear of the future banished forever.[31]

It is perhaps significant that this is the only one of Woodbey's three pamphlets that ends with the second party still unconverted to socialism. Woodbey himself may have realized that he had tackled a difficult subject and that his presentation was too tentative to achieve total conversion. At any rate, he ends his last letter:

Hoping that I have been able to make it clear to you that under Socialism it will be possible to equitably distribute the products of industry and that you and your family will at once join the movement, I will close this somewhat lengthy correspondence by saying that I would be pleased to hear from you soon.

Yours for the cause of the revolution,

G. W. Woodbey [32]

Reverend Woodbey was a delegate to the Socialist Party conventions of 1904 and 1908; indeed, as noted earlier, he was the only Negro at these two gatherings. At the 1904 convention, Woodbey took the floor twice. On the first occasion, he expressed his opinion on the seating of A. T. Gridley of Indiana, who was being challenged because he had accepted a position in the state government after passing a civil service examination. The question at issue was whether Gridley had violated the socialist principle of not accepting a position under a capitalist government. Woodbey spoke in favor of seating Gridley, arguing that in Germany the socialists boasted of the number of comrades in the army, and noting that certainly such socialists were doing work for a capitalist government. "We all know," he continued, "that we work for capitalists when we work at all and we would be pretty poor if we did not work for capitalists at all."[33] On the second occasion, he supported the party national secretary receiving a salary of $1,500 a year, which he called "not a dollar too much."[34] He had nothing to say about the convention's failure to deal with the Negro question in the party platform or about the delegates' complete silence on the issue during the entire convention.

At the 1908 convention, Woodbey took the floor four times. On one occasion, in a discussion of franchises held by private corporations, he advanced what, for the Socialist Party, was the bold proposition that the socialists declare themselves "in favor as fast as they can get in possession in any locality, of taking everything without a cent, and forcing the issue as to whether there is to be compensation or

not. [Applause] I take the ground that you have already paid for these franchises—already paid more than they are worth, and we are simply proposing to take
possession of what we have already paid for."[35]

On another occasion, Woodbey recommended that the National Committee elect
its own executive committee from among its own members. On a third, he opposed
the imposition of a time limit before a party member could be nominated for office
on the socialist ticket in order to insure that he would not betray the movement.
Woodbey argued that the danger of such persons "selling out" was just as great if
they were members for years instead of months: "In my judgment, a man who
understand its [the party's] principles is no more liable to do it after he has been in
the Party six months than five years."[36]

The fourth occasion on which Woodbey spoke at the 1908 convention marked
the only time during the two national gatherings that he commented on an issue
related to the race question. That was when he took a firm stand, during the
discussion of the immigration resolution, against Oriental exclusion and, indeed,
against exclusion of any immigrants. His speech, coming as it did from a California
delegate, was a remarkable statement and was certainly not calculated to win friends
among socialists in his state. But it was in keeping with the tradition of black
Americans since the Reconstruction era: in 1869, the Colored National Labor Union
had gone on record against the exclusion of Chinese immigrants. Woodbey
conceded that it was generally believed that all who lived on the Pacific Coast were
as "a unit" in opposing Oriental immigration. Although he was a delegate from
California, he did not share this view:

I am in favor of throwing the entire world open to the inhabitants of the world. [Applause]
There are no foreigners, and cannot be unless some person comes down from Mars, or
Jupiter, or some place.
    I stand on the declaration of Thomas Paine when he said "The world is my country."
[Applause]   It would be a curious state of affairs for immigrants or descendants of
immigrants from Europe themselves to get control of affairs in this country, and then say to
the Oriental immigrants that they should not come here. So far as making this a mere matter
of race, I disagree decidedly with the committee, that we need any kind of a committee to
decide this matter from a scientific standpoint. We know what we think upon the question
of race now as well as we would know two years from now or any other time.[37]

Woodbey scoffed at the idea that the entrance of Oriental immigrants would
reduce the existing standard of living. He argued that, immigration or no immigration, it was the "natural tendency of capitalism" to reduce the standard of living of
the working class, and that if they could not get Oriental labor to do work more
cheaply in the United States, they would export their production to the Oriental
countries where goods could be produced more cheaply than in this country.[38]
Woodbey's prediction that American capitalists would export production to
cheap-labor countries of the Orient was, as American workers today can testify,
quite accurate.

Continuing, Woodbey spoke eloquently of the contradiction between immigration restrictions and the principles of international socialism. As he saw it, socialism

was based "upon the Brotherhood of Man," and any stand in opposition to immigration would be "opposed to the very spirit of the Brotherhood of Man." Reminding the delegates that socialists were organized in China and Japan as well as in other countries, he asked: "Are the Socialists of this country to say to the Socialists of Germany, or the Socialists of Sweden, Norway, Japan, China, or any other country, that they are not to go anywhere on the face of the earth? It seems to me absurd to take that position. Therefore, I hope and move that any sort of restriction of immigration will be stricken out of the committee's resolution. [Applause]."[39]

It is unfortunate that, while he had the floor, Woodbey did not attack delegates like Ernest Untermann and Victor Berger for the anti-Negro character of their arguments in favor of Oriental exclusion. Nevertheless, Woodbey's speech on the immigration resolution should rank high in socialist literature, even though it has heretofore been ignored by all students of the subject.[40]

Only once at either the 1904 or 1908 conventions did the delegates take public notice that Woodbey was black. That was when his name was placed in nomination as Debs's running mate in the presidential election of 1908. Delegate Ellis Jones of Ohio presented his name to the convention in a brief but moving speech: "Comrades . . . the nomination that I want to make for our Vice-President . . . is a man who is well known in the movement for many years. The Socialist Party is a party that does not recognize race prejudice and in order that we may attest this to the world, I offer the name of Comrade Woodbey of California." Woodbey received only one vote—that of Jones.[41] The nomination went to Ben Hanford, who had been Debs's running mate in 1904.[42] Possibly if Debs, who did not attend the convention, had wired the delegates that Woodbey's nomination would constitute a major contribution by American socialism to the struggle against racism, the vote might have been different. Debs, however, did not believe that the party should do anything special on the Negro question; this view was shared by everyone at the convention except for the one delegate who nominated and voted for Woodbey. Since the fact that Woodbey was even placed in nomination has escaped the attention of every historian of the Socialist Party,[43] it is clear that the significance of the one vote he received has been generally overlooked.

Following the 1908 convention, Woodbey began a tour of Northern cities with fairly large black populations and delivered a series of soap-box speeches in favor of the socialist ticket.[44] In addition, the national office of the Socialist Party circulated his four-page leaflet, "Why the Negro Should Vote the Socialist Ticket." The author was described as a member of the State Executive Commitee of the California Socialist Party, and formerly pastor of the African Church of Omaha, Nebraska. As was typical of Woodbey's propaganda technique, the leaflet consisted mainly of a speech, supposedly delivered by a Reverend Mr. Johnson, pastor of the African Baptist Church, who had called his congregation together to explain why he had decided "to vote the Socialist ticket at the coming election."

The socialist movement, he pointed out, sought to bring together all working people into a party of their own, so that through such a party "they may look after the interest of all who work regardless of race or color." Since Negroes were nearly all wage workers, surely only such a party could really represent them: "All other parties have abandoned the negro, and if he wants an equal chance with everyone else, he can get it in no other way than by voting the Socialist ticket." No other party, including the Republicans, stood for eliminating poverty, and just as at one time, the elimination of slavery was crucial for the Negro, so today was the elimination of poverty. Socialism would create a society without poverty, a society in which the land, mines, factories, shops, railroads, and the like would be owned collectively, and in which the Negro, "being a part of the public, will have an equal ownership in all that the public owns, and this will entitle him to an equal part in all the good things produced by the nation." In this future society, moreover, he would not have to abandon his belief in religion. On the contrary, by providing all with sufficient to eat and decent places in which to live, socialism would be fulfilling the fundamental ideas set down in the Bible.

Finally, Woodbey called for the unity of white and black workers, urging them to "lay aside their prejudices and get together for their common good. We poor whites and blacks have fought each other long enough, and while we have fought, the capitalists have been taking everything from both of us." The socialist movement was the embodiment of this unifying principle, for it was "part of a great world movement which includes all races and both sexes and has for its motto: 'Workers of the world, unite. You have nothing to lose but your chains; you have a world to win.'"[45]

Woodbey's first published appeal directly to his people in behalf of the Socialist Party is an excellent illustration of the black minister's ability to take a complex subject and simplify it so that even a political illiterate could understand it.

Woodbey expanded on several points in his leaflet in articles written early in 1909 in the *Chicago Daily Socialist*. In "The New Emancipation," he emphasized the common interests of black and white workers under capitalism, and he condemned black strikebreaking and the doctrine that Negrroes should seek to solve their problems by the accumulation of wealth. Even if a few Negroes could become wealthy, the fact still remained that "their brothers are getting poorer every day." What then was the answer?

Give the negro along with others the full product of his labor by wrenching the industries out of the hands of the capitalist and putting them into the hands of the workers and what is known as the race problem will be settled forever. Socialism is only another one of those grreat world movements which is coming to bless mankind. The Socialist Party is simply the instrument for bringing it about, and the negro and all other races regardless of former conditions, are invited into its folds.[46]

In another article, "Socialist Agitation," Woodbey called for the use of all forms of educational techniques to reach the black masses—"the press, the pulpit, the rostrum and private conversation." Socialist agitators had to be made to understand that they would face imprisonment and other forms of maltreatment, but such persecution was to be expected when one sought to overthrow an evil system: "For attempting to overthrow the slave system, Lincoln and Lovejoy were shot, John Brown was hung, while Garrison, Phillips and Fred Douglass were mobbed."

Naturally, socialist agitators were "equally hated and despised," and they faced constant distortion of what they stood for: "Because the Socialists recognize the existence of a class struggle they are sometimes accused of stirring up class hatred. But, instead, they simply recognize the fact that capitalism, by its unequal distribution of wealth, has forced on us a class struggle, which the Socialists are organizing to put down and bring on the long talked of period of universal brotherhood."[47]

When Woodbey advised socialist agitators to expect to be persecuted, he spoke from personal experience. At the time he was a delegate to the 1908 socialist convention, he was out on bail, having been arrested in San Francisco early in the year with thirty other socialist speakers for defying a ban against street-corner meetings. The arrest occurred in the midst of the economic crisis following the Panic of 1907 when the socialists were holding meetings to demand relief for the unemployed.

Even before the Industrial Workers of the World (IWW) made free speech fights famous, socialists had engaged in such battles and had used specific aspects of the strategy followed by the Wobblies in their spectacular free speech struggles.[48] In the case of the 1908 San Francisco free speech fight, the socialists deliberately violated a city ordinance forbidding street meetings without police permits for all organizations except religious groups. When a speaker was arrested for speaking without a permit, his place was speedily filled upon the soap box. Speaker after speaker—men and women, black and white—mounted the soap box, were arrested, and dragged off to jail. Woodbey was one of the first to be arrested and jailed. Along with his comrades, he was released on bail.[49]

"The police can't stop us," Woodbey told a reporter during the 1908 convention. "They can and do arrest us when we speak, but they can't stem the tide that has been started no more than they can the ocean. The more they ill treat us, the more Socialists there are." Despite police opposition, the socialists were determined to obtain relief for "the hordes of honest working men [in San Francisco] who are starving because they can't get the work they so earnestly desire."[50]

With the aid of liberals and labor groups, the socialists were able to force the City Council of San Francisco to repeal the objectionable ordinance, and the charges against Woodbey were dropped.[51] He continued to participate in free speech fights, and in 1912, he was a key figure in what was probably the most famous free speech fight in American history—the one in San Diego. This of course, was Woodbey's home town. Here he had been the pastor of the Mount Zion Church for several years until he was removed because, as one who knew him wrote, he "loosened up his flock with the Bible, then finished his sermon with an oration on Socialism."[52]

On 8 January 1912 the San Diego City Council passed an ordinance creating a "restricted" district of forty-nine blocks in the center of town, on which no street-corner meetings could be held. Unlike ordinances in other cities banning street speaking, the one in San Diego made no exception for religious speeches. All street speaking was banned in the so-called congested district. The reason given was that the meetings blocked traffic, but it was clear that the real purpose was to suppress the IWW's effort "to educate the floating and out-of-work population to a true understanding of the interests of labor as a whole," as well as the organization's determination to organize the workers in San Diego who had been neglected by the American Federation of Labor. Among these neglected workers were the mill, lumber, and laundry workers and streetcar conductors and motormen. The IWW's actions had infuriated John D. Spreckels, the millionaire sugar capitalist and owner of the streetcar franchise; he and other employers had applied pressure on the council to pass the ordinance. Certainly, San Diego had plenty of room for her traffic, and no one believed that this little town in southern California would suffer a transportation crisis if street-corner meetings continued.[53]

Two days before the ordinance was to go into effect, the IWW and the socialists held a meeting in the center of the restricted area at which Woodbey was a leading speaker. The police broke up the meeting but did not intimidate the free speech fighters. On 8 January 1912, the *San Diego Union* carried the following on its front page:

SOCIALISTS PROPOSE FIGHT TO FINISH FOR FREE SPEECH
Following a near-riot Saturday night during a clash between the police department, on the one hand, and Socialists and Industrial Workers of the World on the other, the Socialists and IWW members held a running street meeting last night at Fifth and H streets, but the meeting was orderly, and there was not any semblance of trouble.

During the meeting members of the organizations policed the sidewalks and kept them clear, so that the city police would have no objection to make. Among the speakers were Mrs. Laura Emerson, Messrs. Hubbard and Gordon for the Industrial Workers of the World, and George Washington Woodbey, Kaspar Bauer and Attorney E. F. Kirk for the Socialists.

The part played by the police in the affair of Saturday evening was denounced, but none of the speakers grew radical. It was announced that the fight for free speech would be waged with vigor, but in a dignified manner.

Aided by vigilantes, the police responded with more than vigor and in anything but a dignified manner. The brutality used against the free speech fighters in San Diego was so terrible that after an investigation ordered by Governor Hiram Johnson, Colonel Harris Weinstock reported:

Your commissioner has visited Russia and while there has heard many horrible tales of high-handed proceedings and outrageous treatment of innocent people at the hands of despotic and tyrannic Russian authorities. Your commissioner is frank to confess that when he became satisfied of the truth of the stories, as related by those unfortunate men [victims of police and vigilante brutality in San Diego], it was hard for him to believe that he was not still sojourning in Russia, conducting his investigation there, instead of in this alleged "land of the free and home of the brave."[54]

On several occasions, Woodbey was beaten up as he insisted on exercising his right of free speech. He filed charges of "malicious and unofficial" conduct against the chief of police, the captain of the detectives, and several policemen whom he accused of brutality.[55] As a leading figure in the Free Speech League, the organization coordinating the free speech fight, Woodbey was frequently threatened by vigilantes, and on one occasion, he barely escaped death. The *Citizen*, the official organ of the labor unions of southern California, reported in mid-April 1912:

Rev. Woodbey, a negro preacher, has been threatened for his activity. A few nights ago he was taken to his home by a committee from the Free Speech League. As the party left the car at a corner near Woodbey's home an automobile was noticed in front of the house. Upon examination it was found to contain two armed men. Across the street another vigilante was stationed, and in the alley two more armed men were found. The strength of the committee with Woodbey probably saved his life, as members of the League challenged the vigilantes to do their dirty work. The preacher's house was patrolled by armed men from the League all night.[56]

The free speech fight in "barbarous San Diego" was still in full swing in late April 1912 when Woodbey left to attend the Socialist Party national convention as a delegate from California. By the time he returned, the struggle was still continuing. He did what he could to help the cause, which was faced with certain defeat because of the power of the police, vigilantes, and state government. Wobblies continued to be clubbed and arrested, and there was little that could be done to prevent the wholesale violation of their civil rights. "They have the courts, the jails and funds," Laura Payne Emerson lamented. It was not until 1914 that the right of the IWW to hold street meetings was established. Although the ordinance still remained on the statute books, the police no longer interfered when Wobblies spoke at street corners in the forbidden district. On the invitation of the IWW, Reverend Woodbey was one of the regular speakers at such meetings.[57]

Woodbey's associations with the IWW may not have pleased some California socialists, and his role in the free speech fights probably disturbed members of his congregation. All the same, he was candidate for state treasurer on the socialist ticket in 1914, and he was still listed as pastor of Mount Zion Church in San Diego and a member of the state executive board of the Socialist Party in the *Christian Socialist* of February 1915, which published two of his articles. These Woodbey's last known writings on socialism, were "What the Socialists Want" and "Why the Socialists Must Reach the Churches with Their Message." The first was in the form of a dialogue— a familiar Woodbey technique—between the minister (here called Parker) and George Stephenson, a black mail carrier. Stephenson asks to be told "in short, and the simplest way possible, just what it is you Socialists are trying to get anyway." Woodbey proceeds to enlighten him, pointing out the features of the socialist society which he had presented in greater detail in his earlier pamphlets. When the mail carrier leaves, convinced that there was no way to answer the arguments in favor of socialism, his teacher shouts after him: "Hold on a minute, we would solve the race problem of this and all other countries, by establishing the brotherhood of man which Christ taught."

In the second piece, Woodbey insists that the socialists would never succeed unless they won over "the millions of working people who belong to the various churches of the country," and he proceeds to indicate how he did his part in this endeavor. His chief weapon was to play up the point that "the economic teaching of the Bible and of Socialism are the same, and that for that reason he [the church member] must accept Socialism in order to stand consistently by the teaching of his own religion." After having shown the church member that the Bible, "in every line of it," was "with the poor and against their oppressors," it was necessary to convince him that the solution for the ills of society was not charity, which was at best "only a temporary relief," but the collective ownership and operation of the industries. The last point had to be reached slowly and step by step, but if the socialist agitator kept using the Bible as his authority, he would carry the church member along to that conclusion. The danger was, Woodbey maintained, that too many socialists antagonized church members by linking antireligion with socialism. Therefore, he advised against using agitators "who do not understand the Christian people, to carry this message, for the reason that they are sure to say something that will spoil the whole thing."

We know nothing of Reverend Woodbey after 1915, but at this point in his career, he was still as confirmed a socialist as ever. "I would not vote for my own wife on a platform which did not have the Socialist message in it," he told an audience in December 1914.[58]

Just how many blacks Woodbey converted by the method he outlined in his last socialist writing is impossible to determine. Hubert H. Harrison, a militant black socialist in New York, said of Woodbey's work as a national party organizer: "He has been very effective."[59] At least one prominent black socialist attributed his conversion to socialism to Reverend Woodbey. In the *Chicago Daily Socialist* of 29 September 1908, Reverend George W. Slater, Jr., pastor of the Zion Tabernacle in that city, wrote: "For years I have felt that there was something wrong with our government. A few weeks ago I heard Comrade Woodbey, a colored national organizer of the Socialist Party, speaking on the streets of Chicago. He showed me plainly the trouble and the remedy. From that time on I have been an ardent supporter of the Socialist cause."

REVEREND GEORGE W. SLATER, JR.

We know little about Reverend Slater before he became a socialist. The *Chicago Daily Socialist* engaged him to write a series of articles for the paper under the general heading "Negroes Becoming Socialists," but it did not bother to introduce him to his readers with any biographical sketch. However, in the first article of this series, "How and Why I Became a Socialist," Reverend Slater reveals that during the winter of 1907–1908, a period of rising unemployment and economic distress resulting from the Panic of 1907 and the ensuing business recession, he had tried to alleviate the suffering of his black parishioners by organizing a cooperative enterprise through which they might purchase goods at savings of between 25 and 30 percent. The giant manufacturers frowned upon the venture, however, and he was unable to purchase supplies. The salesmen for the companies told him frankly that any dealer furnishing him with supplies would be driven out of business by the manufacturers.[60]

This experience opened his eyes to the futility of trying to alleviate the sufferings of poor blacks under the existing economic system. When he heard Woodbey's analysis of how only socialism could help abolish poverty, he was immediately converted and joined the Socialist Party. Once converted, Slater eagerly assumed the task of recruiting blacks for the party. This he did by means of weekly sessions in his church, by the distribution of his pamphlet *Blackmen, Strike for Liberty*, and especially through the articles he published in the *Chicago Daily Socialist*, beginning with the issue of 8 September 1908, and ending with that of 27 March 1909. Although they appeared for only a limited time, Slater's articles marked the first time in American history that a socialist organ carried writings by a black American on a regular basis.

In several ways, Slater's articles reflected the Socialist Party position on the Negro question. When asked by black correspondents what the socialists would do for the Negro, he fell back on quoting answers to these questions already published in the *Appeal to Reason* and the *Chicago Daily Socialist*, the main tenor of which was that they would do nothing except give the Negro the same opportunities as those enjoyed by whites.[61] Again, in his article "Booker T. Washington's Error," Slater leaned on arguments familiar to readers of the socialist press. He insisted that industrial training would actually hurt the black worker, since it would enable him to compete more effectively with whites. The trained black worker, being less inclined to unionization and strikes than the white worker, would be preferred by the capitalists and thus displace the whites. This, in turn, would exacerbate antiblack prejudice in white working-class circles. What, then, was the solution? It was not to deprive blacks of education and training, but "to remove from the realm of competition the exertions of men in the full liberty and the pursuit of happiness, and the right to earn an honest and adequate livelihood for themselves and loved ones, and to place such endeavors in the realm of collective cooperation wherein the government guarantees every man equal justice and opportunity."

In short, under capitalism, the education and training of black workers would only make their plight worse since it would intensify hostility toward them, while under socialism, with competition to earn a living no longer a problem, it would be a useful tool.[62]

In socialist literature, blacks trained in the industrial schools and "brainwashed" by Booker T. Washington to avoid unions and strikes were said to be preferred by capitalists and to be displacing white workers. In real life, however, the blacks with such industrial training found that, owing to the racist policies and practices of employers and unions alike, they could not obtain employment at the trades for which they had been trained.[63] Ida B. Wells-Barnett, the militant black Chicago woman, was closer to the truth than Slater when she wrote at about the same time as his article on Booker T. Washington appeared:

The black man who has a trade at his fingers' ends finds all forces combined to prevent him from making a living thereby. First, the employer tells him that he has no prejudice against color, but that his employes will object and make his business suffer. If perchance the Negro gets by, is given a chance to make good, the employes in the office, factory and workshop combine to injure his work and to make life miserable for him.[64]

Even in the South, the skilled black craftsman found it increasingly difficult to obtain employment. By 1899, the Virginia commissioner of labor reported that there were "fewer skilled Negro laborers in the state than there were before the Civil War."[65] Substantially the same picture emerged from reports from other Southern states. In the next few years, this trend intensified and was documented by W.E.B. Du Bois in *The Negro Artisan*.[66]

The trouble was that blacks as good as or better than white workers had little chance to earn a living as skilled artisans. Reverend C. S. Smith of Nashville, a critic of Booker T. Washington, asked: "How can the multiplication of Negro mechanics help to solve the so-called race problem, when those who are already skilled cannot obtain employment?"[67] Even Slater himself had a glimpse of this problem, for in his article "Pullman Porter Pity," he seemed to understand that a job as a Pullman porter was often the only work an educated, trained black could obtain.[68]

Slater's article on the Pullman porter is typical of his concern with immediate political and economic issues rather than with the religious aspects of socialism. He was more interested in trying to prove that Lincoln was a socialist than that Christ had espoused ideals similar to those advocated by scientific socialism. Of course, in the process, he exaggerated and distorted Lincoln's position. He correctly quoted Lincoln's statements on labor and capitalism such as his declaration that "labor is prior to, and independent of capital . . . in fact, capital is the fruit of labor" and that "to secure to each laborer the whole product of his labor, as nearly as possible, is a worthy object of any government." But he overlooked Lincoln's emphasis on the identity of the interests of labor and capital, and his belief that because equality of opportunity existed in American society, the laborer could easily become a capitalist. He certainly did not quote (if he knew it) Lincoln's advice to working-men: "Let not him who is houseless, pull down the house of another; but let him labor diligently and build one for himself, thus by example assuring that his own shall be safe from violence when built." While Lincoln was an advocate of the rights of labor, he was certainly no believer in socialism.[69]

Despite such exaggerations and the limitations inherent in his approach because of the influence of socialist ideology on the Negro question, Slater dealt with political and economic issues boldly and effectively. His article on the Pullman porter is not only one of the earliest discussions in print of the problems facing these workers, but it is also a masterful destruction of the myths surrounding their work. His criticism of the Republican and Democratic candidates in the 1908 election and his arguments as to why blacks should vote for Debs went beyond rhetoric. He filled his articles with statistics on the terrible conditions facing the working class, discussed the indifference of both Republican and Democratic candidates to this problem, and then contrasted this position with that of the socialist candidate. He emphasized that blacks would have the most to gain from a socialist victory:

The colored man is the worst off of all the working class of people. This is because he gets less wages, less protection, less education, pays more for food, clothing, house rent, etc.

Why is this so? It is because this government is so run that the necessities of life, such as food, clothing, houses, etc., are produced more for the purpose of permitting a few men to make profit out of them rather than to use them for the benefit of all the people. That is, that in order for the rich men to make money you must work for him for much less than you produce for him. Therefore, the colored man, being the weakest and least-protected, is at the greatest disadvantage, hence he is the most ill-treated. . . .

Let me urge you to get a Socialist Party platform and read it very carefully. and then vote for your own interests as poor people for your wife and children—by voting the Socialist ticket straight.[70]

Slater proudly announced that he had set himself the "task of reaching 1,000,000 colored people with the great message of Socialism," and he urged comrades to help him distribute his literature in black communities.[71] In the *Chicago Daily Socialist* of 4 January 1909, John H. Cummings, himself a black socialist, reported that Slater was "reaching thousands of our people with the great message of Socialism," and he urged every "colored man or woman" to "write to him." There is no way of knowing just how many blacks Slater actually reached or how many he converted. Since the number of black delegates to Socialist Party national conventions remained the same after the campaign to reach one million as it had been before—that is, one delegate—the likelihood is that he did not get very far. However, Slater certainly impressed leading white socialists. His descriptions of the welcome he received from white comrades, especially among Jewish socialists,[72] his emphasis that socialists were the "New Abolitionists,"[73] his advice to black workers not to allow themselves under any circumstances to be used as strikebreakers,[74] and his repeated insistence that only through socialism could the problems of all workers, regardless of race or color, be solved—all appealed to white socialists. Since he never criticized the Socialist Party for failing to mount a campaign against disfranchisement, segregation, lynching, and peonage in the South—subjects he himself never discussed—white comrades had little reason to feel embarrassed by his writings. At any rate, Eugene V. Debs hailed Slater as an "educated, wide-awake teacher of his race" who was "doing excellent work in educating the black men and women of the country and showing them that their proper place is in the Socialist movement." Fred D. Warren, editor of the *Appeal to Reason*, congratulated Slater on his "splendid work" and urged the party to assist him in his endeavor to reach blacks. Other white socialists wrote of how deeply they were moved by his articles and how happy they were that the socialist press was enabling such writings to appear in print. A typical letter went:

I have been reading some of your valuable articles in the Chicago Daily Socialist.

A few days ago, when I read your account of the meeting at which the Jew clasped your hand and exclaimed: "Isn't this great?" I said, "yes, that is great, that a Jew could clasp hands in so righteous a cause with the black man."

I extend to you, dear comrade, my hand across the long miles and thank you for your good work, for the greatest of all causes—Socialism. Your work is a grand one. Few of us realize what an influence for our cause you are putting into being. . . .

I am rated with the Caucasian race, but I don't think my heart or hopes are whiter than yours. I know my work can never be as grand as yours promises to be.[75]

Slater's last article in the *Chicago Daily Socialist* was a summary of his lecture on "The Race Problem" before the Labor Lyceum of Rochester, New York. In this lecture, he criticized the ideas of Booker T. Washington, dismissed emigration as a solution for the problem, assured his listeners that blacks were not "trying to secure social equality with the whites," and stressed that the "solution" of the race problem lay only in socialism. He concluded: "The Socialist party, which teaches these things in its program, is the party which will solve the problems of the black man, as well as those of his white brother."[76]

Although he stopped contributing to the *Chicago Daily Socialist* after March 1909, Slater did not cease his work for the party. When Local New York of the Socialist Party attempted to win Negro votes in the municipal campaign of the fall of 1911, it called upon Slater for aid. He furnished it with a pamphlet, "The Colored Man's Case as Socialism Sees It," which was widely distributed in Negro circles.[77] (All copies of the pamphlet, along with other pamphlets by Slater, have disappeared.) From 1912 to 1919, Reverend Slater is listed in the city directory of Canton, Iowa, as pastor of the Bethel African Church.[78] From that city, he distributed a pro-socialist monthly, *Western Evangel*, no copies of which are in existence. In addition, in the fall of 1912, the *Cleveland Citizen* reported that Slater had formed a "Negro Socialist Literature and Lecture Bureau," and was sponsoring a national conference of colored men in Chicago "to create a nationwide interest in socialism."[79] It is doubtful that the conference ever took place, since there is no report of it in the Chicago press, including the *Chicago Daily Socialist*.

In 1913, Slater was appointed secretary to the Colored Race for the Christian Socialist Fellowship. In that capacity, he published several articles in the *Christian Socialist*. One was "The Negro and Socialism," in which he assured his readers that a great opportunity existed for spreading socialist ideology among blacks. Not only were they "almost to a man . . . of the working class" and thus naturally receptive to such ideas, but even black professionals, including clergymen, were beginning to evince interest in socialism. Apart from the fact that the work of reaching them had been "woefully neglected," it could only be effectively conducted by supplying blacks with "simple literature on the subject written by some colored man. The fact that some colored person wrote it will get their attention and they will read it through carefully."[80] Fortunately, Slater indicated he had just the literature needed—his own *Blackmen, Strike for Liberty* and Dr. J. T. Whitson's *The Advantages Socialism Offers to the Negro*. He informed the comrades that they could obtain copies in quantity by writing to him in Clinton.

In the other articles, Slater again argued that Lincoln had been basically a socialist, buttressing this argument with quotations from his statements favoring labor over capital.[81] He took issue with R. R. Wright, the editor of the *Christian Recorder*, who contended that while socialism had much about it that was praiseworthy, it could not replace the social service of the church in meeting the needs of the poorer classes. Here, for the first time, Slater dealt with socialism from a religious viewpoint. In the manner made familiar by Reverend Woodbey, he pointed out that "Scientific Socialism is the only systematic expression of the social message of Jesus." Social service dealt merely with symptoms, while socialism addressed itself to the abolition of wage slavery, "the main root of our social misery." Since socialism took no account of religions, and since its doctrines were the logical fulfillment of what the prophets, Jesus, and the Apostles had sought, "should not Christians, the Church, and its social service element say Amen?" he asked.[82]

After 1919, Slater's name disappeared from the Clinton directory, but he probably remained in that area. In a letter of 27 March 1921 from that city to John Fitzpatrick, president of the Chicago Federation of Labor, he listed himself as "evangelist, Biblical, Economic, Spiritual" operating in the Iowa town, and that his special subjects were "Jesus," "The Modern Dance," "Assimilation vs. Isolation," "Courtship and Marriage," "Racial Problems," and "The Rustic City." The last-named appears to have been a cooperative interracial venture that Slater sponsored. Evidently, Fitzpatrick was sufficiently interested in "The Rustic City" to ask Slater for more information. In his reply, the Iowa evangelist enclosed a rough plan which, unfortunately, is no longer in the Fitzpatrick Papers. In his letter accompanying the plan, Slater wrote:

With great appreciation, I note what you say of our efficient activity in bringing about a better understanding between the labor unions and the leaders of the colored people. For many years I have had the opinion that a more thorough understanding and cooperation on the part of both the colored people and labor unions would do very appreciably much to eradicate the cause of the most vexatious feature of their common problems. For after all the cause of the racial element of the industrial problem is basically economic. All workers are in the same maelstrom, and it will take the combined effort of all of them to get out.[83]

OTHER BLACK CHRISTIAN SOCIALISTS

The February 1915 issue of the *Christian Socialist*, dedicated to the memory of Abraham Lincoln, was the first in that socialist monthly to devote significant attention to the Negro. In addition to articles by Reverends Woodbey and Slater, it included one by Reverend S. C. Garrison, pastor of the Negro Church of Montpelier, Indiana. Garrison's article linked Jesus, Lincoln, and John Brown to the activities of the Socialist Party, and noted particularly that "while the great Lincoln freed our bodies Socialism will free our minds, then there will be a greater spiritual development. Until we have a more sane system of production and distribution it is insane to expect further spiritual development." [84] The same issue also included the piece "A Potato Patch Philosopher: Socialism As Seen by a Negro Sage Who Works All Day in His Garden and Philosophizes All Night." The author, C. V. Auguste, was described as "a negro philosopher of St. Petersburg, Fla."

In presenting this special issue, the *Christian Socialist* announced that "the sons of the black slaves are showing white serfs how they may both be freed." It acknowledged that there might be white workers who would "scorn to read a negro's word," but it advised them to bear in mind that with black strikebreaking on the increase, white workers would only be fooling themselves if they believed they could solve their problems by ignoring those of the Negro: "If the white workers should organize, even to the last man, and leave the negro unorganized, their efforts are utterly in vain. Six million negro workmen will stand ready to leap into the places of their white brethren—unless they understand SOLIDARITY." Hence, every worker, regardless of color, should be reached with this special issue.[85]

It is open to question whether the *Christian Socialist* converted any blacks to socialism. The truth is that all black Christian Socialists overlooked the fact that their people were primarily concerned with how to earn a living, how to halt the daily threats to their lives, how to educate their children, how to escape peonage and the convict labor system, and how to end their status of disfranchised, segregated second-class citizenship. Promising them a future life in a cooperative common-wealth without these burdens was hardly conducive to winning many to the cause of socialism.

With all their shortcomings, the black Christian Socialists were outstanding propagandists for the cause. They did not hide either their hatred of capitalism or their belief in socialism. Most of them suffered for their convictions and one, Reverend Woodbey, went to jail for upholding the right of socialists and workers in general to bring their message to the people. Even though they are hardly ever mentioned in studies of American socialism,[86] and not at all in those of Christian Socialism, they deserve a high place in the history of black protest.

NOTES

American Socialism and Black Americans, Philip S. Foner. Copyright © 1977 by Philip S. Foner. Reproduced with permission of GREENWOOD PUBLISHING GROUP, INC., Westport, Conn.

1. *Ohio Socialist Bulletin*, February 1909. This is the only reference to Reverend Euell in the socialist press.

2. *Chicago Daily Socialist*, 11 May 1908; John Mather, *Who's Who of the Colored Race* (Chicago, 1921); A. W. Ricker in *Appeal to Reason*, 31 October 1903.

3. Rev. George W. Woodbey, *What to Do and How to Do It or Socialism vs. Capitalism, Wayland's Monthly* no. 40 (August 1903): 4; A. W. Ricker in *Appeal to Reason*, 31 October 1903. Correspondence with the Omaha Public Library, the University of Nebraska Library, the Nebraska State Historical Society, and the United Methodist Historical Society at Nebraska Wesleyan University has failed to turn up any information on Reverend Woodbey and his role as a Populist and socialist in Nebraska.

4. *Los Angeles Socialist*, 12 July 1902.

5. Ibid., 17 December 1904; *Common Sense* (Los Angeles), 27 October 1906.

6. *Los Angeles Socialist*, 2 May 1903.

7. *Common Sense* (Los Angeles), 5 August 1905. The *San Diegan-Sun* carried one item on the case. Under the headline "Battery Charge," it reported on 11 July 1905 that officer George H. Cooley was served with a warrant charging him with battery. "The complaining witness was Rev. G. W. Woodby, the colored Socialist orator, who has frequently been heard at the gathering of the adherents of the party in this city."

8. *Common Sense* (Los Angeles), 8 October 1904, 7 March, 11 April 1908.

9. A. W. Ricker in *Appeal to Reason*, 31 October 1903.

10. Ibid. Robert Blatchford's *Merrie England*, published in London in 1894, was a book of twenty-six chapters and 210 pages in which the superiority of socialism over capitalism is brilliantly set forth in clear, plain language.

11. Woodbey, *What to Do*, 3.

12. *Chicago Daily Socialist*, 11 May 1908.

13. Woodbey, *What to Do*, 5–7.

14. Ibid., 15–19.

15. Ibid., 20.

16. Ibid., 20–21.

17. Ibid., 24.

18. Ibid., 37–38.

19. Ibid., 44.

20. Compare, for example, Woodbey's discussion of an international credit system under socialism (pp. 36–37) with Bellamy's discussion of the same system in Chapter 8 of *Looking Backward*.

21. In a letter to William Dean Howells a few months after the publication of *Looking Backward*, Bellamy wrote that "the word socialist is one I could never well stomach. In the first place it is a foreign word in itself, and equally foreign in all its suggestions. . . . Whatever German and French reformers may choose to call themselves, socialist is not a good name for a party to succeed with in America. No such party can or ought to succeed which is not wholly and enthusiastically American and patriotic in spirit and suggestions." Quoted in Arthur E. Morgan, *Edward Bellamy* (New York: Columbia University Press, 1944), 374.

22. For a discussion of *The Iron Heel*, see Philip S. Foner, ed., *Jack London: American Rebel* (New York: Citadel Press, 1964 reprint), 87–97.

23. Woodbey, *What to Do*, 7.

24. G. W. Woodbey, *The Bible and Socialism: A Conversation Between Two Preachers* (San Diego: published by the author, 1904), Preface.

25. Ibid., 7.

26. Ibid., 69, 83, 90.

27. Ibid., 69.

28. Ibid., 96.

29. G. W. Woodbey, *The Distribution of Wealth* (San Diego: published by the author, 1910), 7.

30. Ibid., 41, 44–45.

31. Ibid., 54–55.

32. Ibid., 68. Woodbey's fellow-Californian socialist closed his letters, "Yours for the Revolution, Jack London."

33. *Proceedings of the National Convention of the Socialist Party, Held at Chicago, Illinois, May 1 to 6, 1904* (Chicago: Socialist Party), 47–48.

34. Ibid., 182.

35. *Proceedings of the National Convention of the Socialist Party, Held at Chicago, Illinois, May 10 to 17, 1908* (Chicago: Socialist Party, 1908), 208–9.

36. Ibid., 290–91.

37. Ibid., 106.

38. Ibid., 106–7.

39. Ibid., 107–8.

40. The most detailed discussion of the 1908 convention in relation to the immigration issue is Charles Leinenweber, "The American Socialist Party and 'New' Immigrants," *Science and Society* 32 (Winter 1968): 6–12. It does not even mention Woodbey's speech in opposition to the resolution calling for a study of the necessity for immigration restriction.

41. *Proceedings, National Convention . . . 1908*, 163.

42. Ibid., 164.

43. Neither Ira Kipnis nor Ray Ginger mentions Woodbey's nomination in their discussion of the 1908 convention.

44. *New York Evening Call*, 2 November 1908.

45. Rev. G. W. Woodbey, "Why the Negro Should Vote the Socialist Ticket," four-page leaflet, undated, copy in Socialist Party Papers, Duke University Library.

46. G. W. Woodbey, "The New Emancipation," *Chicago Daily Socialist*, 18 January 1909.

47. G. W. Woodbey, "Socialist Agitation," ibid., 4 January 1909.

48. Philip S. Foner, *History of the Labor Movement in the United States* (New York: International Publishers, 1965), 4:173.

49. *San Francisco Call, San Francisco Chronicle*, 1–8 February 1908.

50. *Chicago Daily Socialist*, 11 May 1908.

51. *San Francisco Call*, 12 June 1908.

52. In a letter to the author, Harland B. Adams of San Diego summarized a conversation he had with Dennis V. Allen, a black San Diegan who in the years 1912 to 1916, as a postal clerk, delivered mail to the home of Reverend Woodbey. According to Mr. Allen, Reverend Woodbey lived at 12 Twenty-Ninth Street, San Diego. He described Woodbey as "a rather dark Negro slender and about 5 feet 11 inches. Mrs. Woodbey was extremely stout, almost to the point that with her age and weight, it was difficult for her to get about. She was known by nearly everyone in the small Negro population of San Diego at that time, as Mother Mary or Mother Woodbey. She was a devout Baptist Christian and regularly attended the Baptist Church at 29th and Clay, which still exists." The Woodbeys, Allen continued, owned the property where he lived, as well as the house next door which he rented to a Negro who was a veteran of the Civil War.

According to Allen, he was in a group that drafted Reverend Woodbey as pastor of the Mt. Zion Baptist Church, and was also part of the group that had him removed. Although he was extremely popular and drew large crowds to his sermons, his dismissal "was a direct result of mixing too much Socialist with his Bible, and this the members of his church resented."

Allen organized the San Diego Race Relations Society in 1924 and held the post of president for thirty-six years.

53. Foner, *History of the Labor Movement*, 4:194–95.

54. Ibid., 4:199–200.

55. *San Diego Union*, 22 February 1912. The authorities ignored the charges.

56. *Citizen*, reprinted in *St. Louis Labor*, 27 April 1912. In her study, "The I.W W. Free Speech Movement San Diego, 1912," *Journal of San Diego History* (Winter 1973): 25–33, Rosalie Shanks does not once mention Reverend Woodbey.

57. *Industrial Worker*, 17 October 1912; *The Wooden Shoe* (Los Angeles), 22 January 1914.

58. *California Social Democrat*, 12 December 1914.

59. *New York Call*, 16 December 1911.

60. Rev. George W. Slater, Jr., "How and Why I Became a Socialist," *Chicago Daily Socialist*, 8 September 1908.

61. Cf. Rev. George W. Slater, Jr., "The Cat's Out," and "An Eye-Opener," *Chicago Daily Socialist*, 29 September, 20 October 1908.

62. Rev. George W. Slater, Jr., "Booker T. Washington's Error," ibid., 22 September 1908.

63. At a conference held at Hampton (Virginia) Industrial School in 1908, black educators pointed out that graduates of Hampton who had been trained as skilled workers "complained that they had not been able to work at their trades because [they are] excluded from the union." Quoted in Philip S. Foner, *Organized Labor and the Black Worker, 1619–1973* (New York: International Publishers, 1974), 79.

64. Ida Wells-Barnett, "The Negro's Quest for Work," *Chicago Daily News*, reprinted in *New York Call*, 23 July 1911.

65. Quoted in Foner, *Organized Labor and the Black Worker*, 124.

66. W. E. B. Du Bois, *The Negro Artisan* (Atlanta: Atlanta University Press, 1902), 180–85.

67. Philip S. Foner, ed., *The Voice of Black Americans: Speeches by Blacks in the United States, 1797–1974* (New York: Simon and Schuster, 1975), 1:640–43.

68. Rev. Geo. W. Slater, Jr., "Pullman Porter Pity," *Chicago Daily Socialist*, 22 December 1908.

69. Rev. George W. Slater, Jr., "Abraham Lincoln a Socialist," ibid., 6 October 1908. For Lincoln's statements on labor and capital, see Roy F. Basler, et al., eds., *The Collected Works of Abraham Lincoln* (New Brunswick, N.J.: Rutgers University Press, 1942), vol. 2, p. 384, vol. 3, p. 478, vol. 8, pp. 259–60. [*Editor's note*: except for the page reference to vol. 2, Foner's citation to Basler's work is incorrect.] For a discussion of Lincoln's position on labor and capital, see Foner, *History of the Labor Movement in the United States*, 1:291–92, and Eric Foner, *Free Soil, Free Labor, Free Men: The Ideology of the Republican Party Before the Civil War* (New York: Oxford University Press, 1970), 12, 16, 20, 23, 29–30, 32.

70. Rev. George W. Slater, Jr., "The Cat's Out," *Chicago Daily Socialist*, 29 September 1908.

71. Rev. George W. Slater, Jr., "Reaching the 1,000,000," ibid., 4 November 1908.

72. Rev. George W. Slater, Jr., "Mine Eyes Have Seen It," ibid., 9 November 1908.

73. Rev. George W. Slater, Jr., "The New Abolitionists," ibid., 4 January 1909.

74. Rev. George W. Slater, Jr., "The Colored Strikebreaker," ibid., 14 January 1909.

75. "The Colored Man Welcome," ibid., 4 January 1909.

76. Rev. George W. Slater, Jr., "Race Problems' Socialist Cure," ibid., 27 March 1909.

77. *New York Call*, 16 December 1909.

78. Boris Newell, Assistant Director, Clinton Public Library to author, 9 March 1966. There is no information about Reverend Slater in the State Historical Society of Iowa.

79. *Cleveland Citizen*, 14 September 1912.

80. Rev. Geo. W. Slater, Jr., "The Negro and Socialism," *Christian Socialist* 10 (1 July 1913).

81. Rev. Geo. W. Slater, Jr., "Lincoln and the Laborer," ibid., 12 (February 1915).

82. Rev. Geo. W. Slater, Jr., "Socialism and Social Service," ibid., 12 (February 1915).

83. George W. Slater, Jr., to John Fitzpatrick, Clinton, Iowa, 27 March 1921, John Fitzpatrick Papers, Chicago Historical Society.

84. Rev. S. C. Garrison, "The Lover of Humanity," *Christian Socialist* 12 (February 1915).

85. "Was He a Failure," ibid.

86. Of all the black socialists mentioned in this chapter, only one, Reverend George W. Slater, Jr., appears in any history of American socialism, and then only his 1913 article in the *Christian Socialist* ("The Negro and Socialism") is mentioned. See James Weinstein, *The Decline of Socialism in America, 1912–1925* (New York: Vintage Books, 1969), 71.

4

A Path Approaching Full Circle:
Kate Richards O'Hare

Sally M. Miller

One of the significant leaders of the dynamic, if minor, Socialist Party of America, and arguably its most popular woman speaker was Kate Richards O'Hare.[1] The daughter of a homesteading family, O'Hare while still in her twenties developed a regional following among socialists and former Populists in the Plains States and the Southwest. She was much in demand as a platform lecturer, crisscrossing the country constantly on speaking tours. By 1910 she was a national leader of the party, campaigning for and holding offices and writing for movement newspapers. O'Hare's appeal rested very much on her rural upbringing and her ability to identify with her audiences as one of them—a God-fearing farmer, working woman, and wife and mother. In fact, O'Hare's life was quite different from most of the hundreds of thousands of Americans who faithfully turned out to hear her. She was a cosmopolitan, non-churchgoing, educated writer who worked away from her family for most of each year. She lived her life on the road selling socialism, offering strong criticisms of the American social, economic, and political order. O'Hare faulted the institutions of her time, attacking society for its inegalitarian treatment of minorities, its shameless indifference to the lives of children, and its limitations on women. She challenged capitalism as exploitative, rejected the political system as plutocratic, and condemned the churches as hypocritical and un-Christian. Indeed, perhaps her most severe criticisms were leveled at organized religion. As a former church worker, O'Hare spoke out sharply at what she perceived to be clerical irresponsibility and lack of interest in human needs. During the most challenging time of her life, and indeed, for her generation, World War I, she condemned national policy and paid the steep price of imprisonment. Ultimately, she attacked economic and social exploitation and especially the lack of responsibility of clergy even more harshly than earlier, for failing to live up to the teachings of their faith and its founder. At the same time, O'Hare achieved peace with herself, believing that more than ever she as a prison inmate upheld the teachings of Jesus.

A consistent thread in the life of Kate Richards O'Hare was her own relationship to the worldview that she associated with Jesus. O'Hare was among the not inconsiderable segment of Socialist Party members who had once been religious activists—ministers, missionary workers, or zealous lay workers in a variety of capacities. One count, as noted by historian David Shannon, suggests that perhaps 300 party members were or had been ministers.[2] Such individuals had followed various paths toward deciding that the message of socialism was more ethical than that of Christianity, at least as the latter was interpreted and practiced by organized religions. Based on disillusionment with religious institutions or the attraction of the socialist message, these former church workers, many of whom had been evangelical reformers on behalf of different causes, accepted conversion to socialism. Indeed, the socialists often used the metaphors of Christianity in their rhetoric and treated as parallel the acceptance of the socialist message with a religious conversion experience.

It is likely that a greater percentage of women in the socialist movement signed on out of a religious background than did men. Given the heavy preponderance of women active in their churches and their more faithful church-service attendance than that of men in the late nineteenth century and early twentieth century, as shown in the literature, it is logical to assume that Christian commitment was more often a factor in the biographies of women party members than of men.[3] No figures exist of the percentage of party members of a religious background, and basic member-ship figures are so sketchy that a detailed profile of members is difficult to construct. But based on biographical information of individual socialists through biographical directories (for example, the *American Labor Who's Who*), this seems to be a defensible argument.[4] What one author terms the "missionary mentality of . . . Protestant women" drew some of these women from church involvement to other causes. Their religious instruction had provided them with a source of power and unintentionally had given them approval to act in the public sphere. Their evangelical Protestant values became for a them a basis for and justification of political actions. Thus, throughout the nineteenth century, church work laid the foundation for entrance into public causes for large numbers of American women, with the abolitionist and temperance movements becoming major venues of activity. The moral commitment of some of the women was easily tapped by these and other secular causes that bore an ethical component. Those with evangelical formative experiences had developed a sense of individual worth and had gained somewhat of a voice in church matters, and they were able to use those strengths in a wide variety of ways.[5]

Frances Willard (1839-1898) is the paramount example of a woman who traveled from the widely supported temperance cause to a commitment to socialism. The key individual in building the Woman's Christian Temperance Union (WCTU) into the largest organization of nineteenth-century American women, Willard virtually singlehandedly expanded the focus of the WCTU beyond the issue of alcohol to include myriad social issues. By the end of her life, this most influential and charismatic leader of thousands of American women proclaimed that to be a Christian, one had to be a socialist.[6] For Willard, a Fabian socialist in her last years, socialism had become the answer to society's ills—its intemperance, poverty, inequality, and exploitation. Her example allowed other women concerned about conditions in American society to move from a primary commitment to the WCTU to the emerging socialist movement. Accordingly, the Socialist Party of America, organized in 1901, had a visible component of women members, some of whose formative years were spent in Christian and temperance work.

Lena Morrow Lewis (1868–1950), the daughter of a small-town Illinois minister who herself taught Sunday School at a youthful age, became a temperance worker and spent several years in the 1890s as a lecturer for the WCTU. Into the new century, she became one of the most indefatigable cross-country organizers for the Socialist Party and was the first woman to win election to its National Executive Committee in 1909.[7] May Wood Simons (1870s–1947) of rural Wisconsin hoped to become a medical missionary. But with the loss of her religious certitude during her college years, she and her new husband, A. M. Simons, entered social settlement work. By the end of the century they had made the socialist movement the focus of their lives.[8] Caroline A. Lowe (1874–1933), born in Ontario but Kansas-based, was a Methodist lay leader as a young woman and a school teacher and spent years as a popular socialist speaker and party official.[9] In the South, May Beals-Hoffpauir (1879–1956), who began her adult life as a Quaker schoolteacher, was a journalist in the pre-World War I socialist movement.[10] Elizabeth Howland Thomas (1870–c.1930) of New York was another Quaker whose family background of religious-based activism led her to the social settlement movement and from there to the Socialist Party. Her life was spent in the most successful branch of the socialist movement, Milwaukee, where she held party positions, was elected on the socialist ticket to the school board, and worked on the *Social-Democratic Herald* and the *Milwaukee Leader* run by the national party leader, Victor Berger.[11]

As a final example, Ella Reeve Bloor (1862–1951), later beloved as Mother Bloor and famous as a communist activist, as a youth was involved in her church in New York. At a meeting, she met Willard, and from there followed a classic route to temperance work and then into the socialist movement in the late 1890s. For decades Bloor was an active union organizer.[12] These half-dozen individuals whose paths were charted by Frances Willard represent a minority but significant experience among women who found their way to the American Left a century ago. Certainly not all the hundreds of thousands of young, middle-class, fairly well-educated, Protestant women who immersed themselves in religious or temperance activity went on to commit themselves to the radical movements of their day, but a notable number did so, as has been suggested. Among those who traveled that route, the woman who became the most notable of her day was Kate Richards O'Hare (1876–1948), dubbed by one writer the "first lady of American socialism."[13]

Carrie Kathleen or Kate Richards was born in Ottawa County in Central Kansas in its boom years. Her first decade included formative experiences that shaped her for the rest of her years. She learned the rhythm of life on the land, the seasonal changes, and the struggle with nature over which hard-working farmers had no control. She became familiar at an early age with the heavy labor that is the norm for children on a family farm, and that training led her to appreciate and enjoy manual work. She knew intimately the ordeals but also the satisfactions of wresting a living out of the soil.[14]

The Richards family had arrived from Wales in the Colonial period, probably settling initially in Virginia, and migrated to Kentucky in the early national period, and then moved on to Kansas prior to the Civil War. On Kate's mother's side, information is scanty, but her background also suggests settlement in Colonial America. The family began a westward trek that took them through Tennessee and Kentucky. Andrew Richards and Lucy Sullivan were married in Kansas in 1866 following his service in the Union Army, and began to rear a family of five children surrounded by a kinship network encompassing both sides of the family. Kate, the oldest girl, had two brothers and two sisters, and they attended the local school and joined with the neighbors in community events.[15] Kate's family, however, avoided the revival meetings held by ministers who crisscrossed Central Kansas. Because Andrew Richards was an adherent of the Universalist fellowship, his children's religious observances were somewhat different from those of the mainly Methodist, Lutheran, and various evangelical sects of their neighbors. Andrew Richards scorned ritual and taught his children that "the only religion acceptable to God was to serve the people with all our hearts and souls," a message that Kate absorbed. But she also was influenced by a favorite uncle, her father's brother, Jim, who belonged to the Campbellite Disciples of Christ. The Campbellites, whose religion was founded in the Ohio Valley by Scottish immigrants, also minimized church dogma, and thereby reinforced Andrew Richards' teachings. But the Campbellites emphasized the New Testament as the sole source of faith, and its stress on grace appealed to the young Kate more than the intellectual approach of the Universalists to matters of faith.[16]

Whatever the distinctions, Kate's family participated in the social activities centered in the neighborhood churches, attending the picnics, bazaars, ice cream socials, and the solemn and significant Memorial Day area-wide religious services, so significant to this post-Civil War generation. Harvest and other agrarian festivals as well as civic events were typically church-related with strong religious components so that religion and patriotism were fused together. A church aura enveloped the society so that the cultural ethos of Kate's childhood could be termed overwhelmingly evangelical Protestant.[17] Because of such a background, however far Kate Richards O'Hare's views later evolved, she had a sure understanding of the ambience of the lives of Plains States and western Americans, and called on her insights to make clear to rural audiences that she knew them and was one of their own.

The idyllic childhood that Kate O'Hare fondly remembered abruptly changed when the family had to abandon its homestead during the economic collapse of the agrarian economy. Participating in a wave of farm abandonments that saw Ottawa County lose 20 percent of its population over the next few years, Andrew Richards relocated his family to Kansas City, Missouri, during the winter of 1887–1888. He found a job and within a year was able to establish his own business. In the meantime, Kate attended high school in Kansas City and, after earning a teaching certificate, embarked on a brief teaching career. Disdainful of teaching as a profession, Kate lived with her family while she pursued a variety of jobs, including work as a seamstress and a stenographer. But not simply seeking work, she was simultaneously looking for a means of satisfying a need to be of service to others. Like a great number of young women at that time, Kate was in quest of a role for herself through which she could use her education and serve society at the same time.[18]

The two pillars of her youthful idealism were a commitment to the temperance movement and a need to find a personal religious path. Kate had grown up in perhaps the most temperance-minded region in the country. Many counties of Kansas were dry, with local prohibition forces led by a Disciples of Christ minister, and the WCTU was expanding throughout the area. It is clear that Kate was affected by the atmosphere. Once, when her father went to look for one of his employees in a saloon, the young Kate was horrified by the threat to the soul of the young man.[19] At the same time, while still a student, she was drawn to religion and took several courses in religious studies. She was interested in becoming a Disciples of Christ missionary or even a minister if she, as a woman, could achieve that goal. Over twenty years later, she wrote that starting in that period of her life, she sought Jesus but without success.[20] Perhaps had O'Hare been of an earlier generation, she would have more readily found a church role for herself. Before the end of the nineteenth century, many Protestant churches, including evangelical ones, supported a range of women's activities. Women were prominent, for example, in evangelical outreach. It was her misfortune, however, to come to maturity in a transitional era when women were beginning to face increased barriers against their clerical ambitions in both mainstream and evangelical churches.[21] As religious scholar Rosemary Skinner Keller suggests, the efforts of women seeking ordination amounted to isolated and ineffective attempts.[22] Some women were led by such experiences to persist and became religious innovators, such as Mary Baker Eddy and Aimee Semple McPherson, but not Richards.[23] Encountering a ceiling on her religious quest, she became one of the thousands of young women who turned to social reform, and one of the lesser number who chose radicalism.

Kate Richards explored rescue work among a wave of women then creating a variety of voluntary associations and constructing multilayered organizations to meet the social needs of the emerging urban-industrial order. While such efforts were dismissed by Susan B. Anthony as a "patching business" that men saw as women's proper sphere, and denigrated by professional social workers who soon shunted aside the volunteers,[24] Richards immersed herself in the activities of the Kansas City branch of the Florence Crittenton Mission and Home. She and the other volunteers patrolled the central business district of Kansas City, seeking to attract the prostitutes and derelicts of the dancehalls and bars to the mission's services and programs. They successfully encouraged a thriving attendance, and yet it soon seemed to Richards that the mission's programs were not effecting meaningful change in the lives around her, for "the corner saloon still flourished . . . in defiance to [sic] church and temperance society and rescue mission."[25] She decided that the rescue mission was a hollow exercise, and that it even reeked of "smug hypocrisy."[26] Having abandoned in quick succession her religious ambitions and her commitment to volunteerism, Richards lacked a sense of direction. Without alternatives, she took a job in her father's machine shop, first in the office and then in the shop itself, and she became one of the first women to join the International Association of Machinists. That experience exposed her to the concerns and insecurities of urban workers, and she began to delve into some of the critiques of industrial society then winning a wide readership in the country, such as works by Henry George, Henry Demarest Lloyd, and Ignatius Donnelly, some of which she already knew through her father's interests. Richards became intrigued by the message of a soapbox orator who argued that workers needed their own political party, and this led her to a conversion experience that she would not have predicted only a few years before.[27]

As the twentieth century dawned, Kate Richards had found her life's work. In 1901 she attended a three-month course for socialist organizers at the International School of Socialist Economy in Girard, Kansas, administered by Walter Thomas Mills, a minister, prohibitionist, and author of a socialist classic. She married one of her classmates, Francis Patrick O'Hare (1876–1960) of St. Louis, and began a decade-long association with J. A. Wayland, publisher of the most widely read American socialist periodical, the *Appeal to Reason*, and started her career as a socialist journalist. Kate and Frank O'Hare combined their honeymoon with an organizing tour for the Socialist Party. During the next few years, they had four children, moved several times back and forth among the states of Kansas, Missouri, and Oklahoma, and maintained their party work as the framework of their marriage.[28]

Kate O'Hare became one of the most popular public speakers on behalf of the Socialist Party, perhaps second only to the party's perennial presidential candidate, Eugene V. Debs. O'Hare conducted speaking tours across the country for most of each year and drew great crowds wherever she spoke. Her appeal was the greatest in the Plains states and the Southwest, where she was a particularly effective speaker at the great summer encampment meetings of farming families. She talked to crowds and to individuals in their own vernacular about their interests and needs, and was able to advise Frank O'Hare, a "city slicker," how best to reach out to rural audiences. At the same time, she also built a following as a journalist, writing columns in a variety of movement newspapers, finally settling in 1911 into a monthly column on the staff of the *National Rip-Saw* in St. Louis, where the O'Hares finally established a permanent residence. She also ran for and won a variety of party offices. She was usually a delegate to national conventions and in 1912 became the second woman elected to its National Executive Committee. She was the one American woman to represent her party to the international socialist movement, serving on the International Socialist Bureau in 1912–1913 with Rosa Luxemburg, the only other woman to sit on that body. O'Hare was a candidate for the party's vice presidential nomination and served on the party's Woman's National Committee. Several times she was nominated for public offices on the Socialist ticket in Kansas and Missouri, campaigning for the U.S. House of

Representatives and the U.S. Senate, in the latter instance, as the first woman ever to do so.[29]

Kate O'Hare was a revisionist Marxist, as were most of her party comrades. While the party officially clung to a fiction that sidestepped any belief in modifications of Marxist teachings, like many socialist parties worldwide, the Socialist Party of America believed that socialism would inevitably triumph over capitalism, and therefore no violence would be necessary in the transformation to the new system. Forces within the capitalist system working toward concentration of industry were breaking down competitive capitalism. The party's task was to educate the American masses through propaganda and electoral campaigns to the value of the coming system, in which the workers would together own the means of production and distribution within an egalitarian and democratic political order. For O'Hare and many of her comrades, except for the orthodox Marxist minority in the party, the proper policy while anticipating the socialist millennium was the promotion of social and economic reforms enhancing the lives of the workers. She thought it was nothing short of criminal to oppose reforms in fear of diminishing the workers' appetite for wholesale change. Accordingly, O'Hare was an unequivocal reformist who lectured about and wrote of the need to improve working and living conditions. She campaigned for higher wages, protective legislation, child labor laws, female suffrage, and social ownership of transportation networks exploitative of farmers. More than perhaps any other socialist leader, virtually all of whom defined workers as solely male, urban proletarians, she was sensitive to the needs of farmers, recognizing them as typically subsistence workers rather than landowning employers, and tried to convince the party to craft a policy that met the needs of such farmers, including tenants and farmers' wives.[30]

The topics O'Hare's lectures and columns dealt with included religion. Unlike most socialists, who eschewed that subject as inflammatory, O'Hare was willing to engage the topic and even to debate with members of the clergy.[31] She clearly had a strong interest in the subject. She never debated points of theology, which, she noted, would make no sense for a layperson, but she was more than glad to challenge ministers over their attacks on and interpretations of socialism, and willingly tangled with a couple of clergy who occasionally made it a practice to follow her during her forays in their region. Reflecting on some ministerial fears of socialism, she later wrote that "the cry was always raised that Socialism would destroy Christianity. . . . [T]he clergy would preach impassioned sermons in which they would call upon the voters to save Christianity from the menace of Socialism." O'Hare sarcastically questioned what they thought the role for God was while the socialists were creating such havoc: "Perhaps they think He has lost interest." She eagerly took on such critics when they blasted the socialists as enemies of marriage and the family. O'Hare was perhaps the leading socialist commentator on society's failure to see that economic conditions entrapped women in prostitution and white slavery. She also acknowledged that women's economic vulnerability led some to accept any offer of marriage. As a result, unhappy marriages were not uncommon. More forthrightly than other socialists, she endorsed the need to establish divorce as a legal option, which opened her to attacks as anti-family.[32]

O'Hare thought of herself as a Christian who tried to reflect the teachings of Jesus without ties to a particular church. Occasionally stating that she was a granddaughter of a minister and a daughter of a Campbellite family who was educated for its ministry, she referred to herself as a "browser" among various faiths, picking and choosing as she saw value. She and Frank O'Hare tried to expose their children, Dick, Kathleen, and the twins, Victor and Eugene, to various churches, including the Roman Catholic and the Quaker faiths, so that they could find meanings of their own and so that they would not so readily absorb the prejudices of society against specific groups.[33]

O'Hare maintained that she "prefer[red] the religion of Jesus and the Prophets" to that which was usually proffered. She wrote, "I have proclaimed my loyalty to the teachings of Jesus Christ and all my work in the Socialist movement has been an effort to make those teaching[s] livable instead of unbelievable."[34] She explained to readers that the cornerstone of her faith was found in a few readings in Scripture, in chapters of Leviticus, Deuteronomy, and Nehemiah, and in the Sermon on the Mount, which, she argued, taught that everyone needed access to land and tools, and freedom from usury. She maintained that modern socialism was the one philosophy and political movement that sought to apply true Christian teachings to the lives of the people as it promoted political and economic equality and the social well-being of all God's children. It was clear, she wrote in a public letter to several ministers, that it was impossible to be individually righteous and collectively unrighteous, and any support for capitalism meant participation in its vices and inequities. Socialists were, according to O'Hare, "doing Christ's work." He was, in fact, a great labor leader and thus a disturber of the peace, which, she explained, led to the crucifixion.[35] Speaking once from a pulpit at the invitation of a rural audience, and using the language and symbols of Christianity in her talk on socialism, she was gratified by a farmer's comment that he enjoyed "that kind of gospel mighty well."[36]

She deplored what she generalized as the debauchery of the practice of Christianity ever since its embrace by the Emperor Constantine, and its subsequent institutionalization. She blasted organized religion as, at best, upholding form but lacking substance and, at worst, aligning with the powerful of society against the interests of the people.[37] Her attacks on Christianity in that vein, in fact, were the essence of her writings on religion. Organized religion stood solidly in the camp of the John D. Rockefellers, whose generosity bankrolled the churches. The outwardly Christian robber barons, whether practicing Baptist, Presbyterian, or other faiths, offered contributions and supported charities but killed and maimed their work forces at Ludlow, Colorado, and Homestead, Pennsylvania, and elsewhere as routinely as they prayed to their God.[38] Because of this unholy alliance, clergy did not feel free to support strikers, the unemployed, and the other vulnerable groups in society. It was no wonder that ministers did not lead or even join campaigns for shorter work days and better working conditions. O'Hare was vitriolic in her castigation of the clergy on this point. Too often they interpreted an industrial accident, a tenement fire, or some other calamity as an act of God rather than the result of conditions that could be improved, repaired, or changed. It was God's will, they sermonized, rather than human sins of commission or omission. Instead, she suggested, "give God a square deal and rebuild society in a decent, sane, humane manner."[39]

By 1913 Kate Richards O'Hare was flourishing in the second decade of her career as a socialist agitator and columnist. The thrust of her message, however, began to undergo modification by events abroad. Imperialism, militarism, and finally world war came to absorb her attention. At first warning of the possibility that U.S. business interests would drag the country into a full-scale war with Mexico, by spring of 1915 O'Hare focused on the European war and, at that early date, the possibility of American intervention. She condemned European socialists for their defection from international brotherhood in support of national war efforts and chided those of her own party during the preparedness campaign who spoke of being Americans first and socialists second. O'Hare proclaimed, "I am a Socialist, a labor unionist and a follower of the Prince of Peace, FIRST; and an American, second."[40] She pointedly attacked the clergy for their unflinching support of the policy of the national government as it inexorably moved closer to the British war effort against the Central Powers. She generalized that no Christian church or minister was making the slightest protest against the war. She told audiences that "the church became a recruiting office, the clergy became recruiting officers." They denied Christ, she said, as they prostituted their pulpits preaching hate and slaughter.[41] With particular venom, O'Hare derided those who celebrated as an act of God the rising employment rate due to an expanded weapons industry. Her words dripping sarcasm, O'Hare wrote: "When there are . . . fat contracts for making bullets and bombs to let, God will remember your city and send Morgan your way and flood the bank vaults of the capitalist class with gold and give your pious, God-fearing workers a job [sic] working sixteen hours a day for $1.75 . . . making ammunition to kill your brothers."[42]

O'Hare, unlike many of her socialist colleagues, clung to her antiwar posture after U.S. intervention and the passage of an espionage act in spring 1917, limiting speech that might cause military insubordination or obstruct conscription. Undeterred by the legislation, she gave the same antiwar speech again and again, which, she later decided, paralleled the just war argument of Catholic theology with which she then had not been familiar.[43] Consequently, O'Hare was indicted in North Dakota for her talk in Bowman in July, found guilty in December, and sentenced to five years in a penitentiary.

In her remarks to the court before her sentencing, O'Hare clearly tried to prepare herself for the ordeal of prison. She finished with these words:

It may be that down in the dark . . . loathsome hells we call prisons . . . there may be bigger work for me to do than out on the lecture platform. It may be that down there are the things I have sought for all my life. All my life has been devoted to taking light into dark places, to ministering to sick souls . . . ; and God knows down there in the prisons, perhaps more than any other place on earth, there is need for that kind of work. So if, as it was necessary that Jesus should come down and live among men in order that he might serve them, it is necessary for me to become a convict among criminals in order that I may serve my country there, then I am perfectly willing to perform my service there.[44]

Kate and Frank O'Hare feverishly publicized her case, hoping to convince public opinion that a jury of conservative businessmen and an avowedly anti-socialist judge had denied her a fair trial. While the O'Hares did secure some sympathetic publicity, her judicial appeals were unsuccessful, and Kate O'Hare entered the Missouri State Penitentiary on 15 April 1919.[45]

O'Hare's statement before her sentencing had signaled a renewed emphasis on a personal link to Jesus. Whether or not in this instance it was merely a rhetorical flourish, it is evident that during her incarceration she dwelled on her relationship to Jesus.

She settled into a small cell of her own in the pre-Civil War prison on the banks of the Missouri River. She was one of almost 100 women inmates in the female wing of the prison, many of whom were incarcerated for prostitution or drug use. They seemed to look on O'Hare with awe, as a "lady" who did not belong in prison, and she sympathized with them, shared the food and candies that friends and strangers showered on her, and served as confidante and letter-writer for some of the women. For the first few months, she had the companionship of Emma Goldman, one of the few other political prisoners at Jefferson City, and, despite their different political philosophies, they became close friends. But free time was limited because inmates spent nine hours on weekdays and a half day on Saturdays in the industrial shops working on overalls as contract laborers for private manufacturers. Such scab labor was appalling to O'Hare, and it was made worse by abominable working conditions—the lack of lighting and ventilation and the decrepit and unrepaired sewing machines. The health of many of the prisoners deteriorated under these conditions, and O'Hare experienced bouts of severe exhaustion and illness. The onerous routine undermined O'Hare's plan to conduct case studies on her fellow inmates, which she believed could be of great value to criminologists. Despite her preliminary work on the project before she entered prison, and the endorsement of her plans by the governor of Missouri, her schedule limited her efforts, and the notes she took for the case studies were eventually confiscated.[46]

O'Hare was allowed initially to write one letter per week, and eventually three. She directed the letters to her family, and the first months of correspondence were published by Frank O'Hare as a booklet, *Kate O'Hare's Prison Letters*, and circulated widely. Her letters were censored with paragraphs deleted and an occasional letter confiscated. But Kate O'Hare was able to use her letters to share her experience and win sympathy with the public as well as family and friends. The writing itself was cathartic, useful therapy through which she was able to review and digest her experiences and feelings and to place her situation in a useful context.[47]

O'Hare received an enormous volume of mail at Jefferson City. Letters and packages arrived not only from family and friends but also from socialist comrades. She had letters from Eugene Debs and Irwin St. John Tucker, both found guilty under the Espionage Act, Caroline Lowe, Grace Brewer of Kansas, Theresa Malkiel of New York, and many others known in the movement. But it was often the correspondence from the rank and file and their gifts that helped make bearable her isolation from her party work. The comradeship that all of these correspondents extended to her and their offers of help touched her profoundly. She was also deluged with copies of newspapers, magazines, and books. She was a voluminous reader in those months, and shared some of the periodicals and lighter readings with the literate among the other inmates, and read to those who were not able to do so.[48]

Many letters from the clergy reached her, and she was provided by them and by other correspondents with a variety of recommendations for readings, many of which she accepted. In effect, her imprisonment allowed her to expand on her prewar interest in different religions. Notes arrived from Catholic priests and nuns, who she gradually decided were an exceedingly thoughtful and caring group. O'Hare maintained a longstanding, critical relationship with the Catholic Church, which she had frequently attacked in her writings as a rich and exploitative institution indifferent to the social needs of its flock. Frank O'Hare had a Catholic background, and although he did not practice that faith, the O'Hares had sent their twin sons to a Marianist Catholic boarding school for one year because of the needed structure they believed it would give to their lives. In St. Louis, Kate O'Hare had had debates with Archbishop John J. Glennon, with whom she had often interacted in civic affairs, and had felt triumphant when he conceded to her that he agreed with the socialists in their interest in helping working people.[49] While in Jefferson City, she developed some respect for the Catholic priest who came to the prison to celebrate Mass. However, she absolutely abhorred the Protestant chaplain. In her opinion, he showed no interest in the inmates, demonstrated no human sympathy, and simply made a weekly appearance and delivered a canned sermon. She developed a sense of outrage at what she described as Protestant hypocrisy. No Protestant institution or individuals had provided the women with copies of the Bible, nor had any effort been made to offer communion to them during her entire incarceration. Any concern for the souls of these inmates was markedly absent. A critical letter from one Missouri minister incensed O'Hare, and she instructed Frank to contact him to ask how much money the local church federation spent on overseas missionary efforts compared to the energy it devoted to the welfare of delinquents in their own state. What of Jesus' message of feeding the lambs, she mused. These observations led O'Hare to decide that her contempt for "churchianity" had increased while at the same time she had developed a keener understanding of Jesus and his respect for the lowly from among whom he chose his friends and disciples. She had no doubt that her feelings toward organized religion exactly reflected what Jesus felt in his times.[50]

Despite her inclination, O'Hare sometimes attended chapel. She did so grudgingly, but chapel attendance was required in order for prisoners to qualify for an hour outdoors. Sometime she disciplined herself to forgo the fresh air, where she could freely mingle with the other prisoners, as a supplement to the usual whispered conversations between the cell bars, and at times she skipped chapel to catch up on her correspondence with her family. But when she attended the services, she steeled herself against what she considered the coarseness and bigotry displayed by the minister. She wrote to Frank that she had "too much respect for the message of Jesus" to be witness to its denigration. She, along with Goldman who never deigned to attend chapel, once responded to a midweek summons to all prisoners to report immediately to the chapel. They were treated to a guest sermon by Maud Charlesworth Booth, daughter-in-law of the founders of the Salvation Army and herself a founder of the Volunteers of America. Booth's presentation left O'Hare outraged over the audacity of such "uplifters" whose false cheerfulness, sentimentality, and sanctimoniousness revealed their ignorance of the prisoners and the depth of their experience.[51]

O'Hare's readings on the subject of religion included material on Christian Scientists, Russellites, and other lesser-known groups. She dismissed Christian Science as an "anaesthetic religion" or a spiritual opium that deadened believers to the problems of modern life.[52] She also sampled some of the reading material that she received from spiritualists of various stripes and was struck by the appeal of the psychic for some of the inmates. In fact, it seemed to her that a battle was raging over the souls of the prisoners between the old orthodoxy and more psychic appeals, and she was not surprised that orthodoxy was losing the struggle.[53]

O'Hare's own spiritual views were remarkably consistent, perhaps a hallmark of her life, as seen in her prison letters from her initial one on Easter 1919 to her Easter letter of 1920, one month before her sentence was commuted by President Woodrow Wilson. On 20 April 1919, she discussed her separation from her family and considered that perhaps the inmates needed her more than did her children. The "dope fiend" in the adjacent cell was moaning piteously, she reported, and she tried to comfort her as best she could. Perhaps, O'Hare remarked, if Jesus could be asked he might advise that it was better that she be in her cell than in some magnificent cathedral on that Easter. Three weeks later, she commented that she was at last a participant in life rather than an observer. She confessed that she could not define her conception of God except "all that is good" with "love as the creative force in the universe." She wrote that she, like Jesus, was relating to the most downtrodden, and that she would be better able to reach them after her release than in years before. She then quoted Jesus' words, "Let he who is without sin cast the first stone," and believed that the exposure she was receiving in prison was undermining any inclination she had to be judgmental.[54]

After five months in the penitentiary, O'Hare wrote repeatedly—perhaps needing reassurance—that through all the indignities, the isolation, and the distance from the socialist movement, then undergoing a worldwide schism, her soul was free for she had always tried to be true to the teachings of Jesus to beat swords into plowshares and to love her neighbors as herself. By December 1919 she reassured her family that this Christmas in prison was her most meaningful. She felt there the greatest peace and serenity, and closer to the fellowship of Jesus than she ever had.[55]

On her second Easter of incarceration, O'Hare reflected over that year and wrote that she was paying the price for her faithful adherence to the teachings of Jesus, but that she had no regrets. Prison had taught her lessons of love and service that she could learn nowhere else, she reported.[56] In the fullest development of her views, O'Hare ruminated that she had sought Jesus all her life in her various activities—in church and rescue mission work, in the labor movement and the Socialist Party, and in a variety of religions. But, she wrote: "I found myself in prison on Easter Day and there for the first time I felt that I knew Jesus; that I could sit down and talk sanely and intelligently with Him and that he could tell me out of His wide experience how to unstop deaf ears, open blind eyes, heal sick souls and bind up broken hearts! And from that day to this, Jesus and I have been good friends."[57]

To what extent these comments were shaped by her knowledge that her letters were being circulated by her husband cannot be ascertained. But even if many of her written remarks were geared to an eventual public audience, a constant and consistent theme of a relationship to Jesus, both before and during her imprisonment, is clear. While O'Hare lacked an official tie to organized religion, throughout her life she dealt with religious issues and themes and was caught up in a fascination with basic Christian teachings that only intensified during her fourteen months as a prisoner.

O'Hare's imprisonment ended abruptly when the U.S. attorney general, A. Mitchell Palmer, and President Wilson reached a consensus that O'Hare should be released from the Missouri State Penitentiary. Her release occurred not because she was the victim of unconstitutional wartime legislation or an unfair verdict, both of which arguments she had pressed, but because she was a woman with young children.[58] On 29 May 1920 she was freed to return to her family and her work as a socialist agitator and organizer. However, by then the Socialist Party had collapsed under the impact of wartime prosecutions, hostile public opinion, and the emergence of the communist movement. But if O'Hare lacked a flourishing political movement to rejoin, she had developed a new sense of direction. While she retained her party membership, over the next decade the focus of her work was penal reform and the arousal of the American public to a sense of outrage over the inhumanity of the prison system.[59]

O'Hare toured and wrote columns presenting to the public her account of prison life from the inside. She demanded decent living conditions for prisoners, the availability of physical and mental care, and the general reformation of the system through the application of the latest scientific knowledge. She especially attacked the convict labor system in which inmates worked for virtually no pay for private employers. Her efforts, along with those of others, to revise the convict labor system bore fruit when the U.S. Congress passed legislation in 1929 that undermined the flow of such prison-made goods across state lines. In the meantime, O'Hare worked in other areas as well. She pursued an earlier interest in labor education and was a founder of Commonwealth College in Louisiana and at its permanent home in Arkansas. After divorcing Frank O'Hare in 1928, a split that was at least helped along by the trauma of the couple's separation during her imprisonment, Kate O'Hare remarried that same year, settled in California, and began to lead a private life at last. Surfacing every few years when some project appealed to her, she worked in the Upton Sinclair campaign to End Poverty in California during the Depression, served briefly on the staff of a Progressive Republican in the House of Representatives from Wisconsin in Congress in 1937–1938, and immediately thereafter participated in an effort to reform conditions in San Quentin, California's infamous maximum-security prison. By the time she died of a heart attack in 1948, she was a respected civic leader in her local community who could always be called upon for a presentation on a public issue.[60]

It is impossible to trace Kate O'Hare's views on religion after her release from prison. Files of her personal papers were destroyed two different times—once by Frank O'Hare and a few years later by a young communist who judged O'Hare to be lacking in Marxist class consciousness. As a result, O'Hare left behind no statements of belief that might suggest how her views on spiritual matters may have evolved in the last twenty-five years of her life. But it is obvious that in the nearly quarter-century from the latter 1890s through her prison term, Christian ethics formed the core of her philosophy within a socialist frame of reference. Her embrace of socialism following her work on behalf of the Crittenton Mission was encased in what she considered a Christian commitment to working people. Similarly, her views of her fellow inmates were shaped by her vision of how Jesus worked among and served society's most vulnerable. The touchstone of her ideas as she expressed them was the need to share the earth's promise among all people as she read it in Scripture and understood it to be taught by Jesus.

Over those decades, O'Hare was a forceful socialist leader who touched audiences as varied as sweatshop workers in congested cities, miners in isolated sites in Michigan, Montana, and elsewhere, and especially farming men and women in their encampments in the Southwest. For the latter, her religious and moral indictment of capitalism resonated as their hard-scrabble lives mirrored that of her own family a generation earlier. It is not surprising that they were her most loyal supporters. O'Hare was an effective activist on behalf of her party because she knew the concerns and problems of those before whom she spoke, as in later years she was successful in directing public attention to the horrors of prison life which she had experienced. O'Hare's life in service to minor causes was not without its victories.

NOTES

1. No O'Hare collection exists. Because of the loss of her papers, the paucity of primary sources has been a serious problem for researchers. Her writings, however, may be found in various early twentieth-century socialist newspapers. O'Hare materials are available, if not in quantity, in the Frank P. O'Hare Papers at the Missouri Historical Society in St. Louis, in collections at the Kansas State Historical Society in Topeka, at the University of Missouri-Columbia library collections, and a few other archives. O'Hare correspondence may also be located in collections of some of her fellow socialists in various repositories.

2. David A. Shannon, *The Socialist Party of America: A History* (Chicago, Ill.: Quadrangle Books, 1967), 60.

3. Glenda Riley, *Inventing the American Woman: A Perspective on Women's History* (Arlington Heights, Ill.: Harlan Davidson, Inc., 1986), 75–76; Ann Braude, "Forum: Female Experience in American Religion," *Religion and American Culture* 5 (Winter 1995): 6–9. See for the first full discussion on this point, Ann Douglas, *The Feminization of American Culture* (New York: Avon Books, 1977), Part I.

4. See *American Labor Who's Who* (New York: Rand School of Social Science, 1925), which, unfortunately, features relatively few women; more especially useful for this topic, see the biographies of female socialist leaders in the independent monthly, *Socialist Woman*, 1907–1909.

5. Mari Jo Buhle, *Women and American Socialism, 1870–1920* (Urbana, Ill.: University of Illinois Press, 1981), 62; Ann Braude, "Women's History is American Religious History," in Tom Tweed, ed., *Narrating U. S. Religious History* (Berkeley, Calif.: University of California Press, forthcoming), 100–101; Elizabeth Fox-Genovese, "Forum," *Religion and American Culture* 5 (Winter 1995): 16–21; Rosemary Skinner Keller, "Forum," *Religion and American Culture* 5 (Winter 1995): 4.

6. Buhle, *Women and American Socialism,* 108–9.

7. "Lena Morrow Lewis," *Socialist Woman* 1 (September 1907): 2; Mari Jo Buhle, "Lena Morrow Lewis: Her Rise and Fall," in Sally M. Miller, ed., *Flawed Liberation: Socialism and Feminism* (Westport, Conn.: Greenwood Press, 1981), 61–86.

8. "May Wood Simons," *Socialist Woman* 1 (June 1907): 3; Gretchen and Kent Kreuter, "May Wood Simons: Party Theorist," in Miller, *Flawed Liberation*, 37–60.

9. "Caroline Lowe," *Socialist Woman* 2 (November 1908): 2–3; Neil K. Basen, "The 'Jennie Higginses' of the 'New South of the West': A Regional Survey of Socialist Activists, Agitators, and Organizers, 1901–1917," in Miller, *Flawed Liberation*, 92.

10. Basen, "The 'Jennie Higginses,' " 100.

11. Sally M. Miller, "Casting a Wide Net: The Milwaukee Movement to 1920," in Donald T. Critchlow, ed., *Socialism in the Heartland: The Midwestern Experience, 1900–1925* (Notre Dame, Ind.: University of Notre Dame Press, 1986), 28.

12. James Weinstein, *The Decline of American Socialism, 1912–1925* (New York: Monthly Review Press, 1967), 55.

13. Neil K. Basen, "Kate Richards O'Hare: The 'First Lady' of American Socialism, 1901–1917," *Labor History* 21 (Spring 1980): 168; for the fullest overview of O'Hare's life, see Sally M.. Miller, *From Prairie to Prison: The Life of Social Activist Kate Richards O'Hare* (Columbia, Mo.: University of Missouri Press, 1993). Rose Pastor Stokes could be called a rival of O'Hare's for that title but Stokes enjoyed greater fame outside the movement than she was prominent within it, and as an immigrant her path to radical activism was different from that of the native-born American women considered here. On the different patterns marking the lives of native-born and immigrant women socialists. see Sally M. Miller, "Other Socialists: Native-born and Immigrant Women in the Socialist Party of America, 1901–1917," *Labor History* 24 (Winter 1983): 84–102.

14. Miller, *Prairie to Prison,* 4–6.

15. Ibid., 4–7.

16. Ibid., 14; Kate Richards O'Hare, *Kate O'Hare's Prison Letters* (Girard, Kans.: Appeal to Reason, 1919), 21–23.

17. O'Hare, *Kate O'Hare's Prison Letters*, 21–23. See a biography of evangelist Aimee Semple McPherson for a similar analysis of the ambience of her girlhood: Edith L. Blumhofer, *Aimee Semple McPherson: Everybody's Sister* (Grand Rapids, Mich.: William B. Eerdmans, 1993), 12–14; David G. Hackett, "Gender and Religion in American Culture," *Religion and American Culture* 5 (Summer 1995): 127.

18. Kate Richards O'Hare, "How I Became a Socialist Agitator," *Socialist Woman* 2 (October 1908): 4–5; Kate Richards O'Hare, "The Girl who Would," *Wilshire's Magazine* (January 1903): 27–29; Miller, *Prairie to Prison,* 11–13.

19. Kate Richards O'Hare, "Drink, Its Cause and Cure," *National Rip-Saw* (September 1913): 3–6. On the dry ambience of Kansas, see Robert Smith Bader, *Prohibition in Kansas:A History* (Lawrence, Kans.: University Press of Kansas, 1986).

20. Kate Richards O'Hare, *The Church and the Social Problem* (St. Louis, Mo.: National Rip-Saw, 1911), 32, 21; O'Hare, *Kate O'Hare's Prison Letters,* 52–53.

21. David G. Hackett, "Gender and Religion in American Culture," 130; Edith L. Blumhofer, "Contexts: Evangelical Ministering Women," *Evangelical Studies Bulletin* 5 (March 1988): 8; Margaret L. Bendroth, "Fundamentalism and Femininity: The Reorientation of Women's Role in the 1920s," *Evangelical Studies Bulletin* 5 (March 1988): 1–3.

22. Rosemary Skinner Keller, in "Female Experience in American Religion," *Religion and American Culture* 5 (Winter 1995): 5.

23. Braude, "Forum: Female Experience in American Religion," 9.

24. Susan B. Anthony as quoted in Riley, *Inventing the American Woman,* 98. On the subject of female Protestant rescue work in the American West, see Peggy Pascoe, *Relations of Rescue: The Search for Female Moral Authority in the American West, 1874–1939* (New York: Oxford University Press, 1990).

25. O'Hare, "How I Became a Socialist Agitator," 4–5.

26. O'Hare, *Kate O'Hare's Prison Letters,* 53.

27. O'Hare, "How I Became a Socialist Agitator," 4–5; Miller, *Prairie to Prison,* 17–18.

28. Miller, *Prairie to Prison,* 21–23, 25–27.

29. For the best view of O'Hare's career in the Socialist Party, the necessary but painstaking way to trace her activities is through runs of socialist newspapers, such as the *Party Builder (*1912–1914*),* the *American Socialist (*1914–1917*),* the *National Rip-Saw* (1911–1917), and the *Socialist Woman* (later called the *Progressive Woman,* and then the *Coming Nation*), 1907–1913. See also Miller, *Prairie to Prison,* Chap. 5, and Basen, "Kate Richards O'Hare," 165–99. On the Socialist Party itself, of the voluminous literature, excellent overviews may be found in Shannon, *The Socialist Party,* and in Weinstein, *The Decline.*

30. See selected columns by O'Hare in the above newspapers and periodicals, and in Philip S. Foner and Sally M. Miller, *Kate Richards O'Hare: Selected Writings and Speeches* (Baton Rouge, La.: Louisiana State University Press, 1982); also see Miller, *Prairie to Prison,* 29–30. O'Hare had a distorted image in some party circles as a revolutionary or orthodox Marxist. In party factional struggles, her close ties to Debs were emphasized by some Eastern party leaders to portray her as an unsophisticated leftist.

31. Kate Richards O'Hare, "Debating With the Preachers," *National Rip-Saw* (October 1916): 20. Morris Hillquit of the East Coast reformist leadership of the party conducted one series of highly publicized debates on religion with a Catholic priest but this was an exception to the practice of avoiding engaging the clergy in debate.

32. Foner and Miller, *O'Hare: Selected Writings and Speeches,* 124–25; Kate Richards O'Hare, *Law and the White Slaver* (St. Louis, Mo.: National Rip-Saw, 1911), 30–32; Kate Richards O'Hare, *Wimmin' Ain't Got No Kick* (Chicago: Socialist Party, 1911); Kate Richards O'Hare, *The Sorrows of Cupid* (St. Louis, Mo.: National Rip-Saw, 1912), 180–81.

33. O'Hare, *Church and the Social Problem,* 21, 32; Kate Richards O'Hare, "Dear Sweethearts: Letters From Kate Richards O'Hare to her Family," 21 March, 17 April 1920, Missouri Historical Society, St. Louis, Missouri (hereafter referred to as "Dear Sweethearts").

34. Kate Richards O'Hare, "About My Infidelity," *National Rip-Saw* (September 1915): 5.

35. O'Hare, *Church and the Social Problem,* 28, 26; Kate Richards O'Hare, Letter, *Christian Socialist* 8 (30 March 1911): n.p.

36. Kate Richards O'Hare, "A Trip to Old Kentucky," *National Rip-Saw (*January 1917): 20–21.

37. O'Hare, "Dear Sweethearts," 8 February 1920.

38. Kate Richards O'Hare, "Wisdom of the Mighty," *National Rip-Saw* (March 1915): 1.

39. Kate Richards O'Hare, "Blame it on God," *National Rip-Saw* (February 1916): 18–19. O'Hare's fullest discussion of her views on organized religion is found in her booklet, *Church and the Social Problem,* cited earlier.

40. Kate Richards O'Hare, "My Country," *National Rip-Saw* (April 1917): 5.

41. Kate Richards O'Hare, *Socialism and the World War* (St. Louis, Mo.: Frank P. O'Hare, 1919).

42. Kate Richards O'Hare, "God, Billy Sunday, Morgan and Dumba," *National Rip-Saw* (November 1915): 8–9; see also Miller, *Prairie to Prison,* 130–31, 135.

43. O'Hare, "Dear Sweethearts," 21 March 1920.

44. "Speech Delivered in Court by Kate Richards O'Hare Before Being Sentenced by Judge Wade," *Social Revolution* (February 1918): 6–7.

45. No federal prison then existed for women. The Jefferson City facility where O'Hare served her sentence was a state penitentiary known to criminologists at the time as the most congested of American penal institutions, and one of the least progressive in its practices, still requiring the silence system and striped uniforms, and indifferent to hygienic standards. See Blake McKelvey, *American Prisons: A History of Good Intentions* (Montclair, N. J.: Patterson Smith, 1977), David J. Rothman, *Conscience and Convenience: The Asylum and Its Alternatives in Progressive America* (Boston: Little Brown, 1980), and Paul W. Keve, *Prisons and the American Conscience: A History of U.S. Federal Corrections* (Carbondale, Ill.: Southern Illinois University Press, 1991).

46. Miller, *Prairie to Prison,* 160–75. O'Hare, astounded that no educational program existed for the inmates, unsuccessfully volunteered to teach a few courses. See O'Hare, "Dear Sweethearts," 20 April 1919. O'Hare was not opposed to prisoners performing labor. Years later on that subject, she wrote to Emma Goldman, "I know quite well that prisoners would go mad without work to do and we are working toward the plan of employing them at making the supplies used by the state and its sub-divisions for which they will receive normal wages and be charged for their maintenance, the balance going to their families or kept for them until release." Kate Richards O'Hare to Emma Goldman, New York, 19 January 1925, Emma Goldman Archives, International Institute of Social History, Amsterdam.

47. See O'Hare, *Kate O'Hare's Prison Letters.* This booklet contains the first sixteen of the over 100 letters she wrote from prison between April and September 1919. The full set of her letters, as cited above, written between April 1919 and May 1920, may be found in mimeographed form at the Missouri Historical Society. It is necessary to review these letters with a critical eye.

48. O'Hare, "Dear Sweethearts," 28 September 1919.

49. Miller, *Prairie to Prison,* 61–62.

50. O'Hare, "Dear Sweethearts," 6 July, 10 May 1919.

51. Ibid., 21 August 1919.

52. Ibid., 1 April 1920.

53. Ibid., 21 August, 26 April 1919.

54. Ibid., 20 April 1919, 13 April, 3 May 1920.

55. Ibid., 28 September, 28 December 1919.

56. Ibid., 3 April, 13 April 1920.

57. O'Hare, *Kate O'Hare's Prison Letters,* 53.

58. Miller, *Prairie to Prison,* 190–91; minutes of a conference between the attorney general and Seymour Stedman et al., May 14, 1920, Washington, D.C., p. 24, Investigative Case Files, Bureau of Investigation, OG Files, 9–19–603, Reel 3, National Archives.

59. O'Hare wrote to her family on 14 December 1919, that "all my long hard years of training both as a writer and a speaker has [sic] merely been to fit me for the work of arousing ALL respectable people to the stupid horrors of our whole prison system." Foner and Miller, *O'Hare: Writings and Speeches*, 252. She published several works on penology, including *In Prison* (St. Louis, Mo.: Frank P. O'Hare, 1920), and a lengthier work by that title (New York: Alfred A. Knopf, 1923), and *Crime and Criminals* (Girard, Kans.: Frank P. O'Hare, n.d.).

60. Miller, *Prairie to Prison*, Chap. 8. Her second husband was Charles C. Cunningham, an apolitical Southerner who was a businessman and engineer. He was addressed as the "Colonel," but no detailed information is available on him.

5

"A Spiritual and Moral Socialism": Franklin Spencer Spalding and Christian Socialism, 1901–1914

John R. Sillito

At the time of his death in 1914, Franklin Spencer Spalding held a central place in the Christian socialist movement. Though little known today, as "the one outspoken and unqualified Socialist" bishop of the Episcopal Church and a member of the Church Socialist League, he was one of the most prominent socialist advocates of the day.[1] For more than a decade, Spalding saw his role as twofold: helping socialists appreciate the significance of a religious-based component of the coalition seeking a cooperative commonwealth, while simultaneously helping religious socialists, and the Christian community generally, realize the need for a movement for social change within the church.[2]

Spalding's support for socialism was part of a broader agenda. Like many of his generation, he advocated prohibition, peace, and progressive reforms in health, education, politics, and municipal government. Unlike some of his Christian socialist contemporaries, however, including his protégé, Paul Jones, who would succeed him as bishop, Spalding never joined the Socialist Party. At heart Spalding was a reformer, not a radical: one who believed that unless the gap between have and have-not was reduced, the fabric of American society would weaken, tensions between classes would worsen, and individuals would never achieve their full, God-given potential.

While he bristled at what he considered extremes in the socialist movement, Spalding believed that achieving, in the words of a colleague, a "spiritual and moral socialism" would bring about a better future. At the same time, his support for socialism often put him at odds with many in his own denomination, both clergy and laity. At one point Spalding "created a commotion" when he told a group of ministers in Los Angeles that he did not think it proper for ministers to "court wealth," urging them to remember that the "rich and powerful could take care of themselves" and to strive for a Christian community where the "poor were to be nourished and the helpless cared for."[3] On another occasion he recalled that a devout Episcopalian had attacked him for preaching socialism instead of biblical truths. Telling Spalding the church's proper mission was to "comfort sorrowful people, not disturb them," his critic explained that when he came to church he "wanted to be comforted, and wanted to see the poor comforted, but he didn't want to be disturbed by revolutionary preaching."[4]

Calling these sentiments typical of the views of many church members, Spalding said it was a mistake for those with "socialistic tendencies" to leave the church. What was most lacking in contemporary Christianity, he believed, was "radical thinkers": people who are "not giving up to the money interests," but are rather working from within to "build the fires of insurgency within the church to work for every social advance," while simultaneously "fighting desperately if necessary to retain [their] position within the church."[5] For all of these reasons, an examination of Spalding's road to socialism, and of the sometimes conflicting views he held on the topic, is useful in understanding the scope of early twentieth-century Christian socialism in the United States.[6]

In 1901 Spalding, then serving as a young Episcopal minister in Erie, Pennsylvania, summarized his twofold personal and political philosophy. He identified himself as a socialist who appreciated "every wise and honest effort which is being made to do away with the present competitive system," while also believing that in the Christian teaching of the fatherhood of God and the brotherhood of man would be found the means to achieve socialism.[7] Spalding shared the vision of Christian socialists who believed that socialism was embodied in the teachings of Jesus Christ, and that people could not truly be Christians until they realized that "human rights come before property rights."[8] Only under socialism, Spalding argued, could a society be created in which humane conditions would prevail and all could prosper economically and spiritually. As he expressed it, "The day is soon coming when the superabundance which is cursing the rich will be taken away, poverty and want with their deadening effect will be removed, and the higher, nobler side of life will have a chance."[9]

An examination of Spalding's early life, however, finds little to suggest a likely convert to socialism. Indeed, as he would later confess, he had gone all the way through college without knowing what socialism even meant.[10] Spalding was born in Erie on 13 March 1865, and his family on both his maternal and paternal sides had been in America since the 1650s. He was preceded in the ministry by his father, John F. Spalding, who served as rector of St. Paul's Church in Erie at the time of Franklin's birth. The elder Spalding was later elected bishop of Colorado, Wyoming, and New Mexico, and the family settled in Denver in 1874. That move marked the beginning of Franklin's lifetime interest in, and affection for, the West. Spalding, who never married, remained close to his family and would often return to Colorado for physical and spiritual rejuvenation.[11]

After attending public and private preparatory schools, Spalding graduated from Princeton in 1887, where he participated in sports and debate, served as a class officer and an editor of the school paper, and ranked scholastically in a "comfortable position about the middle of the class."[12] In 1888, after teaching in Princeton's preparatory school, briefly considering a career in the law, and spending a summer in Britain and Europe, Spalding entered General Theological Seminary in New

York to prepare for a career in the ministry, reasoning that if he had any talents that would serve him in the practice of the law, they would also help him as a clergyman. Though he did well enough scholastically, the seminary, in the words of Spalding's biographer John Howard Melish, "made no serious demands upon the students; its methods were slipshod and its standards low." In later years Spalding noted that his real education was found in the urban parishes where he served while attending seminary.[13]

Upon graduation, Spalding began his ministerial career as rector of All Saints Church in Denver. A year later his father asked him to take charge of and teach at Jarvis Hall, an Episcopal boys' boarding school in Colorado. After several years in this capacity, he returned to the city of his birth and the St. Paul's pulpit once occupied by his father. While serving in Erie, Spalding began to take an active interest in socialism, though his conversion from observer to adherent was gradual. This city served as the place of both his literal birth and of his social and political rebirth thirty years later.

When Spalding arrived in Erie in the summer of 1896, the city was solidly Republican. The young minister, however, was moving away from his traditional Republican roots. In that year's presidential race, Spalding voted for Democrat-Populist candidate William Jennings Bryan and championed the cause of Free Silver, which he believed challenged the "money power given to the banks to expand and contract as they pleased."[14] At the same time, Spalding found himself more aware of, and in increasing contact with, advocates of other reforms.[15]

Among that group was Erie's Socialist Party. Though small, the party was vigorous in its electoral activities and regularly carried several working-class districts in municipal elections.[16] Though Spalding was not a socialist at the time, Erie socialists later noted that they "admired and loved" him for his "staunch comradeliness," which allowed him to recognize the needs of any person regardless of denominational, political, or social circumstances.[17]

While serving in Erie, a series of events culminated in Spalding's first serious consideration of the importance of socialism. In the spring of 1898 he turned down an invitation to chair a meeting in Erie for socialist leader Eugene V. Debs, saying it was "out of his sphere." Spalding apparently attended the meeting, however, and was exposed to the views of America's leading socialist of the day.

By 1899 Spalding wrote to his mother that he was having "quite a controversy" with a Reverend Taylor of Warren, Pennsylvania, over socialism. Taylor, he noted, was unhappy because the local socialists were "unchristian and all out of patience with Christianity." He told his mother that while he still did not know enough about socialism, it was becoming apparent to him that something had to be done to address social and economic inequities. To that end, Spalding started a social science study group using one of Franklin Giddings' books on sociology as a text. The weekly class attracted seven "working-men but I hope some of the other class will come in soon and that it may help to bring a little better understanding between capital and labor." Such a move was timely, he believed, because several businesses in Erie were on the verge of strikes, and he was offended by the way many of the owners looked upon their workers "as so much machinery." Noting that many people were getting rich in Erie, he prayed to be delivered from the love of money and the "awful . . . way people estimate everything in terms of money."[18]

Another important early contact with the socialist movement came when Spalding attended a lecture by socialist editor and organizer Algie M. Simons at Maennerchor Hall in Erie. While the young cleric was impressed with much of Simons' analysis, in the question period he commented that "even if there was a class struggle violent and merciless in society," as a minister he belonged "to the ambulance corps and could do necessary work binding up the wounds of the combatants." Simons admitted that he too had once thought the same way but realized he had to take a stand. "What is a big husky fellow like you doing toting bandages in the rear," the diminutive Simons shot back to the six-foot-tall Spalding, "when you ought to be on the firing line?"[19] The young minister concluded that for Simons and his comrades there was "a world to win, not a world to redeem."[20] Spalding, always sympathetic to an intellectual challenge, pondered the socialist orator's questions.

As part of his pastoral duties, Spalding became more aware of conditions facing working-class families. After observing the vulnerability of day laborers and mechanics on Erie's docks when company-installed mechanical hoists led to layoffs, Spalding gradually became convinced that such changes "took the bread out of the mouths of the workers" since the "money which formerly went to labor now went to the machine, that is to capital, for capital and the owner of the machine are one and the same person."[21] Moreover, he concluded that "the actual working of the competitive system" condemned working people to a life of oppression and exploitation. Some unemployed workers were Spalding's own parishioners, which personalized the situation, and he shared their frustration toward a system that seemed inevitably to favor capitalist over worker.[22] As Spalding later observed, the competitive system was "calculated to confuse moral ideas," causing workers to believe that loyalty to their employer constituted their full duty, and making it difficult to "put moral responsibility on anyone." The challenge facing those concerned with social justice, he argued, was to examine the fundamental reasons for social injustice with a degree of moral courage

which will not be content with contemporary palliatives, but will at personal sacrifice if need be, hasten the coming of the Kingdom of God, which means human society, not organized according to the selfishness of men but according to the will of God—a will which is infinitely tender in its love for the weakest human life, but utterly indifferent to business profits.[23]

Spalding realized that under capitalism thousands who had an equally good right to the fullness of life did not have even "a ghost of a chance . . . because, even though a few might fight their way out of the ranks of manual workers, the system required others to take their places."[24]

In 1899 the young rector delivered the "principal oration" on child labor at the annual Erie Labor Day picnic. According to the *Erie Evening Herald,* the event attracted "the largest turnout in the history of local organized labor." Spalding was chosen to address the celebration, the paper reported, because he was "an enthusiastic student of economic and sociological questions" who had gained "a warm spot in the hearts of the laboring men of Erie."[25]

Spalding told his audience that while the employment of children was not as prevalent in Erie as in many other cities, it was still far too extensive in the area for the general good. Moreover, he expressed concern that some Erie foundries were "building additions with the anticipation of putting young girls to work cleaning cores." The paper concluded its report by calling Spalding's address "very comprehensive in its character and well received."[26]

Spalding probably did not realize it at the time, but he had turned an important corner in his life. The Labor Day address, and the reaction to it, would shape his future course. Many years later, a boyhood friend of Spalding's, Kemper Fullerton, recalled the significance of this event.[27] Fullerton, who had been present for the address, provides information absent from newspaper reports, and his account represents one of the most complete contemporary examinations of Spalding's developing social consciousness.

Calling Spalding's concern for the working class the passion of his life and the basis of its "prophetic character," Fullerton observed that since St. Paul's was primarily a "church of employers rather than of employees," when Spalding preached he confronted the "usual demand . . . that he should preach the simple gospel," which did not "raise perplexing questions for the conscience of the employer."[28] Noting that the most conspicuous fact of Spalding's life was his effort to give "Christianity a social interpretation," Fullerton considered the speech a "turning point" that revealed the tense situation between capital and labor in Erie.[29] According to Fullerton, the aspect of Spalding's remarks that caused the most trouble concerned those men who encouraged "their wives and children to work in the factories, not to supply their necessities but . . . only to increase their luxuries." Fullerton believed this assertion "angered many of the men, but stirred the conscience of others. Next day many of these latter refused to allow their families to return to work."[30] Some employers blamed Spalding personally for this action. One was a member of St. Paul's vestry who resigned in protest, though Spalding eventually convinced the man to rescind the decision, arguing, "What effect do you think your resignation would have upon your workers when they hear it was because you thought I took the side of your employees against you? Do you think that will lessen your difficulties?"[31]

It took courage for Spalding to follow this course of growing sympathy with labor. Not only was Erie the city of his birth as well as his current residence, but his views "brought him into collision with his personal friends and connections of his family."[32] Still, as Fullerton realized, even those who disagreed with Spalding recognized "the tremendous power with which he preached the gospel of social justice."[33]

Within two years of the Labor Day address, Spalding publicly proclaimed himself a socialist. According to Erie socialist Joshua Wanhope, Spalding came to party meetings, took part in the discussions, and "certainly [knew] Marx."[34] The process was gradual, and in some ways Spalding used the term "socialist" as a generic label for anyone advocating social change. In the election of 1900, Spalding voted again for the "honest and independent and progressive" William Jennings Bryan because he believed in "downing the trusts in the interest of private competition" and was anti-imperialist.[35] For a time, Spalding admitted, he clung to his belief that society could be made better as the church improved people "one at a time, [making] them pure, unselfish and zealous in good works" while "persuading the rich and mighty to be kind and generous and public spirited."[36] His contacts with workers and employers in Erie, however, forced Spalding to realize "that the power to make and save money carries with it the destruction of the impulse to give it away. I saw that large wages . . . and profits could not be made except by exploiting human labor, and that an employer could not rob a man of the product of his labor and still respect him."[37] Spalding admonished his parishioners at St. Paul's that business leaders should realize there is more to life than the "accumulation of money," and that working people had the right to expect more since businesses "climb to success through their efforts."[38]

Initially, Fullerton wrote, Spalding became "an enthusiastic convert to the economic theories of Karl Marx," who saw in socialism "the economic means to right the terrible wrongs and inequalities which mark the civilization of today and which my friend believed were due to the competitive system."[39] Spalding's study of socialism started with the *Communist Manifesto,* which he claimed "opened his eyes" and brought him "truth and hope" for change because while proving that "social salvation could never come through the classes, it made me see it might come through the masses."[40] Though always uneasy with what he considered the selfish and materialistic approach of some socialists, Spalding came to believe that only socialism could emancipate the working class, and that their chains would be "thrown off by laborers [themselves], not by any emancipator."[41]

Moreover, Spalding also believed that socialism provided the Christian church the way to bring real life and meaning to the teachings of Jesus Christ and to realize the society he envisioned. Taking his text from the sixth chapter of Saint Matthew, Spalding proclaimed that the church could not serve two masters, God and Mammon, and assumed the duty of persuading it to cease being the "almoner of the rich and become the champion of the poor." For Spalding, the Christian church existed for the purpose of saving the human race. While the church had failed to accomplish this, he argued, socialism, by insisting that "men cannot be made right until the material conditions of life are made right," could show the church how to succeed. Accordingly, Spalding argued, it was the duty of the church to destroy a system of society that inevitably "creates and perpetuates unequal and unfair conditions of life." Such inequalities were caused by competition, and therefore "competition must cease and cooperation take its place. Competition will not be stopped by making the victors so pitiful that they will share the spoils, but by making the vanquished so strong they can no longer be robbed."[42]

Spalding's commitment to and comprehension of socialism were considerably strengthened after his election as bishop of Utah in 1905.[43] This did not happen immediately, nor did the process lack doubts and conflict. As William Thurston Brown, a fellow minister and socialist, later recalled, Spalding grappled with the basic philosophy of socialism and seemed to approach it not "as a convinced socialist, but [as] a careful and unbiased student." Spalding, Brown believed, sought to soften what he considered to be the "materialism of Marxism."[44] Over the next few years, two factors played an important role in moving Spalding from student to advocate. First, he entered into a disagreement with Socialist Party activists, which forced him to grapple further with the meaning of socialism in a real, not simply philosophical, sense. Second, his experiences among working people, especially in the mining camps of his diocese, increased his understanding of the economic, social, and political challenges facing the American working class.

Several weeks after arriving in Salt Lake City in March 1905, Spalding addressed the Ladies Literary Club on "Christianity and Socialism." He told this elite group that no discussion of this topic could occur without careful definition of terms, noting that vagueness with reference to socialism was no longer possible. Spalding proclaimed his support for Marxian socialism, saying that Marx correctly recognized that "in every historical epoch the prevailing mode of economic production and exchange, and the social organization following from it, form the basis on which is built up and from which alone can be explained, the political and intellectual history of that epoch." Spalding told his listeners that socialism rested on a four-point program: first, abolish capital and create a common ownership of the materials of production; second, create a common management of production; third, give everyone a share of the public dividend; and, fourth, as wealth increases shorten days of labor and provide larger pleasures in leisure hours.[45]

Despite these words of solidarity, however, trouble brewed between Spalding and local Socialists over Spalding's concern about socialist motives. In a baccalaureate address to the graduates of the University of Utah in June 1905, Spalding told the students that the rhetoric of "masses and classes" lost sight of the individual, as if society was "not made up of human beings each with life and soul and heart." The country, Spalding believed, would never solve its problems "unless we place justice at the base," but to suppose that justice is a "mere matter of dollars and cents is a most inadequate conception of the matter." Turning personal, he told the graduates that he had once called himself a socialist, but as he "considered the matter more carefully," discovered he could no longer do so. Arguing that while no one really knew if the destruction of capitalism and the establishment of the cooperative commonwealth would banish "sin and misery," he insisted that it was possible to judge socialist motives, which he found "ignoble and inadequate." He then told the graduates that there was

a higher appeal than the appeal to self-interest or to class interest, there are nobler rewards than the rewards of material prosperity. I have found more kindness of heart among the poor than among the rich, and therefore the constant appeal of the socialist to the workingman's self interest seems to me a weak and unworthy appeal. I have not found that an abundance of material prosperity elevates character and therefore I cannot think but that Carlyle was right when in his blunt way he called Socialism "Pig Philosophy."[46]

Spalding's remarks sparked a firestorm. In a letter to the editor of the *Crisis,* the official paper of Utah's Socialist Party, one reader accused him of "deliberate falsehood" by "lug[ging] in the pet socio-political opinions of the ruling class" in his criticism of the socialists and their program for "the abolition of wage slavery and private ownership." Moreover, the writer, who said he assumed the remarks were quoted accurately since Spalding had failed to deny them publicly, chastised the bishop for using the graduation ceremonies as an opportunity to "attack Socialists and sit in judgement on their motives."[47]

The *Crisis* editorialized that if Spalding had once called himself a socialist, he had ceased to do so when he "discovered that Socialism proposed to make the rich get down off the backs of the workers and go to work." Spalding's distaste for appeals to class interest simply represented another way of saying that the "rich pewholders do not like it and they and he are right in disliking it. In the measure that the parasite and plutocrat dislike it, in that measure the intelligent producer and proletarian welcome it."[48]

Spalding, the paper argued, sought to poison the minds of the university students against the socialist message, which calls for the "emancipation of the Working Class and the freeing of men's minds and bodies from the chains which the rich pew-holders and their Right Reverend lackeys are so vitally interested in binding and keeping on them." The paper attacked the "Prosperous Bishop," saying that while it was not aware of the exact salary this "Protestant Episcopal ex-Socialist gets," it is a "safe wager that he receives more than the average wage of a half-dozen socially useful workers." Spalding, the paper claimed, would "shiver with horror" if he had to content himself with the material wealth "of that homeless proletarian, Jesus the Carpenter, whose follower and disciple he pretends to be."[49]

In a letter to the editor, Spalding acknowledged that press reports of the remarks were correct. Furthermore, he reiterated his belief that defenders of socialism must be more precise, saying that he believed most socialists would agree with him that the time was past when the term could be synonymous with "every effort made to ameliorate the conditions facing the wage earner; for every protest against the competitive system."[50] Showing familiarity with contemporary socialist views and publications, Spalding suggested that local socialists who disagreed with his views should examine the article "Marxian Ideals" by Emile Vandervelde, published two years earlier in the *International Socialist Review.* Spalding stated that if the position taken by the *Crisis* was true, then "my sermon was quite beside the mark. But the editor, in the same number of the magazine expressed his disagreement while admitting that it was a 'most able and scholarly presentation of that phase of Socialism.' Socialists I have been privileged to know have agreed with the editor."[51]

Spalding turned to the attacks by the editor on his salary and the allegation that he was a "fat, well-fed pulpiteer," saying that at the 1892 Socialist congress in Berlin, William Liebknecht had addressed the question of "wages paid to men who like myself are put to some extra expense by the character of his work." When criticized by workers on the staff of the socialist paper *Vorwärts* that he was making more than six times as much per year as they, Liebknecht argued "that he could not live on less; that he could make more money by going elsewhere, and that in bourgeois society equality was an impossibility, and the congress was satisfied with his position." Spalding went on to comment that in his own life he had discovered that when he was making $50 a month he could save some money, while his current salary of $275 couldn't keep up with the expenses of lodging and, "in spite of railroad passes, which I use unhesitatingly when I get them," the travel required in a diocese of 200,00 square miles. "I mention this somewhat personal matter as evidence which should be considered before a man is called 'fat and well-fed,' etc."[52]

The *Crisis* responded by denying that it had used the phrase to refer to Spalding personally, claiming that what it meant was a "state of physical and 'material' beatitude we should like to see the millions of wealth-producers attain. We are not afraid that they would lose their spirituality, incentive to progress and the higher life." The editor observed that he was sure that Spalding was "as good, high-minded and spiritual" now that he was making $275 a month as when he was making $50. But, the paper continued, it would continue to "despise and expose" the "smug hypocrisy and spiritual humbug of the $275 per month denouncing as 'pig-philosophy' the efforts of the $50 and $35 per month masses to reach the fat and well fed condition implied in $275 per. On this point we attacked his Right Reverence . . . and our columns are open to him for explanation."[53]

In addition to the exchange in the columns of the *Crisis,* Spalding accepted an invitation to meet with local Socialist Party members in April 1906. At the meeting, Spalding debated the issues with Socialist Party activist and *Crisis* editor Joseph Gilbert.[54] While he had once been proud to be labeled a socialist, he stated, his "undoing" had been the result of his criticizing Karl Marx. He told his listeners that he opposed the "criminal wastes and wickedness of capitalism" and proclaimed that the key question facing socialists was exposing the weakness of the competitive system:

How anyone can defend the present competitive system in society is more than I can understand. Capitalists, why that which they have acquired through no merit of their own, is usually squandered; the possessors have no cognizance of their duties to society. I am with you to upset the present economic system. I believe in shorter hours, but draw the dividing line where the Socialist denies Christianity. I'm a religious man and must hold up my theories by the doctrines of Christ.[55]

Spalding agreed that private capital should be abolished but said he was careful, and when someone "offered him a panacea for every ill and asked fifty cents a bottle for it . . . he saved [the] fifty cents." When socialists similarly advanced "one little bit of philosophy as a cure for all the ills that the suffering world was eenduring," he was skeptical. Where he differed was over the materialistic conception of history, which he believed to be too narrow for spiritual factors in life. Economic materialism, he argued, did not take into account the real power of religion in changing individuals and society.[56] It was important to remember that human beings need more than the power of intellect in order to understand and change society. Spalding asserted that socialism "as preached appealed to the selfish instincts of the most unselfish class of people—the poor. The cry to them to be class conscious was a cry to arouse their self-interest." Socialists, he contended, failed to recognize "the power of the spirit. To upset the present economic conditions was an ideal purpose, but it must be gone about with a spiritually quickened motive and the grace of God must leaven the effort."[57]

Gilbert responded by assuring Spalding that both the "rich plutocratic class and the poor exploited class" were materialistic. Thus, the materialistic conception of history meant that people must have nourishment for body and mind before they could turn to spiritual questions. Moreover, he argued, socialists allowed for a wide variety of opinions, and it was precisely these spiritually inspired variations that made many "socialists sacrifice their lives for the idea." Socialists were content to use materialistic arguments because they "recognize that the spiritual uplift could only come after a man [is] assured that his next meal was a certainty and not a remote possibility."[58]

After Gilbert concluded his remarks, Spalding fielded a number of questions from local party members. He defended religion as neither superstitious nor "hide bound in dogmas." Furthermore, he stated that simply because he was a bishop of the Episcopal Church he "was not bound to help in upholding the plutocracy." When the social revolution came, he said, the rich "would try to win the church against the proletariat and might come within a measurable degree of succeeding," but workers "had the opportunity to join the church and swing it the other way." At the same time, he agreed that wealthy capitalist J. Pierpont Morgan—an Episcopalian who often attended church conferences—was probably there for "selfish and earthly purposes" and constituted "quite a burden" for the church to bear. Spalding came away from the meeting convinced that the gap between his views and those of most socialists was much narrower than he had thought.[59] The arguments of real workers won him back to his previously held enthusiasm for socialism. Despite this rapprochement, however, Spalding was never really comfortable with the Socialist Party. As noted, he never joined, and despite his proclamation of 1901, he apparently voted the Socialist ticket for president for the first time in 1908. While not a party member, he saw value in lending his assistance to the party, believing its mission was to present an accurate criticism of contemporary capitalism. As he noted, if there was not a crisis in the present system, there would be no need for the Socialist Party, but in fact statistics showed that in "the United States, there [are millions] who [do] not have enough to eat and to wear and [do] not have a fit place to live in."[60]

Ultimately, however, something more important than philosophical discussions would further solidify his thinking. While serving in Erie, Spalding had been briefly exposed to the concerns and aspirations of urban labor. In the Diocese of Utah (which included parts of Nevada and Colorado), however, he came into more frequent contact with workers, especially those in the mining camps. Through his experience in these camps his understanding of, and compassion for, working people and their struggles deepened considerably.

As a consequence, Spalding advocated that since "it is the duty of the Church to win men to Christ and His righteousness," the Christian message must be actively preached to workers. It is important to help individuals in the "midst of temptation," Spalding argued in an article for the Episcopal publication *Spirit of Missions.* "Men in the mining country answer to this description," Spalding explained, for "it is very easy to be bad, somewhat lonely and conspicuous to be good." Spalding also asserted that the church must spread the gospel message by placing personal representatives in the mining camps who "have a message they believe in and without cant or indifference are living the life they recommend."[61] At the same time, he argued, it was important to recognize that the "mining camps know no distinction between Sunday and weekday." Thus, the church must provide reading rooms, shelter for the homeless, hospitals and "decent and healthful recreation," as well as spiritual guidance and other conventional Sabbath observances.[62] Moreover, clergymen must speak the working-class vocabulary and not just welcome workers when they come to church, but actively seek to bring them into full fellowship.[63]

Simultaneously Spalding called upon enlightened church leaders to embrace the socialist vision and preach it, as well. He told a group of ministers they "must be among the wage earning class not . . . the plutocrats." The clergy, he argued, must recognize that "the aristocrat who pays the bills has [no] greater right to religion than has the poor man who is kept down through force of circumstances."[64] At the same time, Spalding realized that support for socialism within the Christian community would not develop easily or quickly. "The old individualistic philosophy is gone," he argued in one sermon, and the "new socialistic philosophy is here whether we like it or not." The "rapid and radical" changes in society that he believed were coming depended on people opening their minds, but they also meant "the burning of barrels of old sermons, the consigning to the dust pile of thousands of old books, [and] the giving up of theories which nobody has been living by for the past thirty years."[65]

As a colleague noted, once Spalding was "convinced of the soundness of socialism there was nothing half-hearted in his support of the movement."[66] He rededicated himself to further study of the thought of Karl Marx, and over the next few years he was prominently and publicly identified with the socialist cause.[67] In that spirit, Spalding actively promoted socialism as he traveled throughout his diocese. Wherever he went the press emphasized the novelty of a "socialist bishop." For example, Spalding gave a lecture in Rhyolite, Nevada, in 1907, in which, indicative of his belief in gradualism, he told his audience that the system must be changed by a process of natural evolution and not by ignorant radicalism or violence. The *Rhyolite Herald* commented that the bishop was "in no way radical" but the champion of a "safe and sane brand of socialism," which could possibly provide "the means of uplifting the whole human race."[68]

While the *Herald* emphasized that Spalding did not advocate violent revolution, the bishop was, by his own definition, a Marxist who believed that the "interests of labor and capital are not the same." Rejecting sentimentality, Spalding proclaimed himself a scientific socialist who believed that socialism was "the name of a philosophy of history" predicated on the assumption that "the abolition of competition based on capitalist exploitation and the coming in of cooperation, based on the supremacy of democracy, is inevitable." To accept socialism, he argued, is to be "wise enough to see what is coming [and] . . . help it rather than stand in the way, and—to say the least—be unprepared for it."[69]

While Spalding believed that socialism had much to offer the church, particularly in understanding historical and material forces, he also believed that Christianity could help socialists better understand human nature. This is "God's world . . . and the forces outside a man's life [which] control his life in large degree . . . are from God," he said. Spalding believed that socialism would be enhanced by embracing the emphasis Christians placed on the worth of every living soul:

Where the socialists get their sublime faith in the worth of man, just common, ordinary, everyday man, without getting it from Christ, is just beyond my understanding. Without their knowing it, He must have given it to them, and it is for the Christian minister to say, "Whom therefore ye ignorantly worship, Him I declare unto you." For if we believe "that about His dignity He wrapped our humanity," we must believe in the worth of humanity. If we believe in the great Elder Brother, we cannot doubt the worth of all his brothers. And if we are Christians, we must believe that right is stronger than wrong and that God's grace is sufficient to prevent the failure of any effort to give the fullness of life to all His children.[70]

In January 1908, while preaching at the consecration of his friend, Edward J. Knight, as bishop of Western Colorado, Spalding lashed out at the church, saying it had not believed Marx's teaching, with the result that "we are the Church of the well-fed and well-clothed, and . . . we spend most of our time fattening the sheep of the fold." Spalding admonished his colleagues never to forget that they were, first and foremost, "apostles of Christ—not private chaplains to rich parishioners, not earnest men hampered with small and confining surroundings, not privates required to obey orders of others whom we are not sure of, but leaders, with no superiors, save Christ, the King."[71]

That same year, Spalding preached a series of sermons on socialism to large and enthusiastic audiences in Salt Lake City. In one presentation he argued against a system in which one-eighth of the population owned seven-eighths of the wealth and assailed the "criminal neglect" that permitted "millions of mere children to labor in factories, and . . . wastes the talents of humanity in the effort to amass wealth."[72] On another occasion Spalding told his listeners that after studying socialism for more than a decade, he was convinced that it was the most "profound question of the day."[73]

Despite this comment, Spalding was occasionally critical as well. At one point he admonished socialists in the United States that their "greatest weakness" was twofold: First, "socialism is misrepresented and often allowed to be allied with anarchy, though such is most untrue"; and second, "there is not the brains behind the movement that are found in the countries of Europe, and you must see that they are added."[74] The conservative Salt Lake City *Inter-mountain Republican* took note of these remarks and commented editorially that Spalding had "done more than give good advice to socialists" but also gave the public a better respect for socialism because "they have been told the truth about it in temperate language by a temperate man."[75] While the paper spoke kindly, if not sympathetically, Spalding's views likely offended socialists and probably seemed condescending.

As a missionary bishop in Utah, Spalding's main focus was building his denomination in Utah while dealing with Mormons and Mormonism. His activities, including his advocacy of socialism, frequently attracted the attention of the Mormon hierarchy. For example, an editorial in the *Deseret News,* owned by and representing the views of the Church of Jesus Christ of Latter-day Saints, noted that Spalding was the "honorary president" of the Christian Socialist Fellowship meetings held in New York's Carnegie Hall. While not mentioning Spalding by name, but no doubt seeking to discredit his views, the paper noted that "many church members are rapidly being influenced by socialist doctrines," and called the movement an attempt to proclaim that "Jesus was a socialist. If He had lived in our day, He would have been a Messiah of this new gospel which defends the poor against rich and opposes the domination of capitalism with an ideal of justice." Obviously Spalding realized the paper had him in mind when it cautioned its readers that Christianity endeavors to "make society what it ought to be through the regeneration of the individual." The paper further editorialized that it had always maintained that neither the "various theories of socialism, nor anarchism" contained any remedy for the "social and moral ills of mankind as long as they ignore the teachings of religion." When social reformers adopted the principles of the gospel, the paper claimed, their work assumed a different aspect entirely.[76]

Spalding's socialist views got him into trouble in other quarters as well. At one point he went to the Oregon Short Line railroad office to see about his clergyman's pass for the coming year. The manager told him he would not receive one because he had made a speech to striking workers in which he seemed to favor them rather than the company, and that in the future he would have to pay full fare. Spalding told the manager that he would never surrender his right to free speech "for a railroad pass." At the same time he confided to his mother that while he saw this as further evidence of the weakness "of our present competitive system," he also wondered "whether I am all wrong, and whether I ought to settle down and be an advocate of things just as they are." Spalding also faced difficulty with mining company officials when he sought to organize a reading room at the Utah Copper Company's Garfield Smelter. The manager told him that the church should always stand on the side of the company, and therefore any proposed meeting hall could not carry "objectionable papers" like the journal of the Western Federation of Miners and the socialist *Appeal to Reason,* or hold debates on socialism or labor questions. Spalding agreed, reluctantly, which brought criticism from local socialists. He defended his decision, saying, "If God gives me strength quietly to live and work and teach the absolute need of Social Revolution, nothing less, ten years from today I'll have done more good in Utah than stir up a strike in Garfield or bankrupt the Utah Copper Co."[77] For vastly different reasons, concerns arose among some Utah Episcopalians as well.[78] One communicant referred to Spalding's tenure as bishop as a "socialist adventure" and the "most lamentable episode" in Utah Episcopal history.[79] While such criticism did not sway Spalding, he told his fellow clergymen at a diocesan convocation that it was never his custom or intent for his opinions on issues of the day to cause division or ill-will.[80]

Despite these occasional criticisms, Spalding continued to speak out in favor of socialism as he made trips throughout Utah and around the country. An overview of the extent of his activities helps illustrates his growing commitment to the socialist cause. In February 1908 he volunteered to fill in for socialist lecturer John M. Work, speaking on socialism to a "big crowd at the Opera House."[81] In June he again spoke to graduates of the University of Utah, though his message was somewhat different from before. Returning to a familiar theme, Spalding told the graduates that contemporary American society was "money mad" and idolized "social prominence." After reminding the young people that society's standards were not where they ought to be, and that "the poor man is the only one who pays taxes," he said it was up to them in their future careers to "put duty first and profit aside" and bring about change.[82] That summer, Spalding attended the Lambeth Conference in Britain, where he spoke several times in strongly Marxist terms in favor of a socialist reorganization of society. One British paper commented that "nobody went as far as the Bishop of Utah, a slim, middle-aged prelate, with a very breezy manner." The paper observed that Spalding "expounded and enforced the principles of Marxian Socialism with immense gusto," while calling for "a revolution—an entire change in the social organization."[83]

Spalding continued his socialist advocacy in 1909, repeating a series of Lenten lectures on the subject. On May Day, 1909, he spoke to Park City's Socialist Party local.[84] By September he was in Seattle speaking to local socialists on the question: "Does the economic system depend upon religion or does religion depend upon the economic system?" He answered by saying they were "interdependent." While the rich "dominate the church and utilize its power," both Christianity and socialism have much in common, he said, and the two could be of "incalculable value" to each other in "seeking for the uplift of humanity."[85] A month later he told a reporter for the *Portland Morning Oregonian* that he was a socialist "in every sense of the word." Under the auspices of the local Socialist Party, he told a group of 300 that under the "present individualistic system of government we reach the wealthy . . . but socialism reaches the masses. I think . . . Christianity would get along better under socialism than this individualistic form of government."[86]

In the fall of 1910 Spalding made one of his periodic trips back to Erie. Each time he returned, he attracted press attention. And Spalding always spoke on socialism, which proved problematic to the local press. The *Erie Times*, for example, called Spalding a "constructive not destructive" socialist who did not expound "cant and rant," or promote the socialism "of the sledge hammer or the battering ram." Rather, the paper noted, "Bishop Spalding's socialism . . . resolves itself into the 2000 year old discourse preached by Jesus of Nazareth." Yet Spalding told Erie socialists that he was a scientific socialist who understood that "the time must come when the people must own capital. Labor must not be paid wages, but what labor creates."[87]

In May 1911 Spalding spoke at Salt Lake City's Franklin School at an evening lecture sponsored by the Socialist Party local on "The Development of a Social Conscience." He responded to the efforts of Socialist city councilman Henry W. Lawrence and others to persuade the local school board to allow the use of schools for public meetings and educational purposes.[88] That same month he told a group at St. Paul's Church in Salt Lake City that in the past it was the idea of a majority that "men were to be thrifty, accumulate great wealth perhaps, and then be the custodians of that wealth, which they should distribute among the less fortunate financially." In contemporary America, however, "the feeling is that the people do not want charity but they do want justice. A readjustment in the relationship of capital and labor will make for an improvement in the morals of the world." The real salvation of the working class, he remarked, was in direct relationship to its "class consciousness."[89]

That same year, writing in the columns of the Episcopal publication the *Living Church,* Spalding provided an extensive summary of his socialist views and sparked a lively debate that continued in the magazine's columns for several issues. Responding to criticisms from Bishop Thomas F. Gailor of Tennessee, who claimed that socialists were believers in "bald materialism," Spalding asserted that many felt that "Marx has shown them how to be better Christians." Spalding further indicated that he believed Marx had illuminated four fundamental principles: the materialistic or economic conception of history; the fact of a class struggle; the necessity of social revolution; and the "contention that this revolution must be the work of labor and not capital."[90]

Asserting that there was considerable ignorance among those who ought to know of the real feelings, motives, and policies of socialists and their supporters, Spalding observed that while he was not a party member, his extensive contacts with the "movement east and west" led him to believe that

Socialism enables me to be more patient and charitable than I could if I believed God's method of making mankind good and strong was to give a few persons great wealth in order that they might bestow it in alms upon the poor, or as benefactors support colleges, charities, and churches. I know that rich men are not their own masters, but only parts of an economic system in which fierce competition makes men selfish in spite of themselves, and in which the struggle for success demands most of their time and thought. While we honor all generous and kind-hearted men and women and are grateful to them for rising above the sordid selfishness about them, we feel that human society will not be organized according to the will of God until justice takes the place of charity, and the Cooperative Commonwealth replaces the realm of individualistic competition.[91]

Spalding's comments obviously touched a nerve among the readers. In a subsequent issue, Curtis P. Jones responded by asking Spalding and other socialists to show how "the Cooperative Commonwealth is to remedy the ills of our present social order." Jones noted that he was opposed to such a commonwealth not only because of the "initial robbery" of capitalists necessary to start it, but also because socialism was

utterly *unworkable*—would dreadfully impoverish the country, demoralize the great mass of people, and result in intolerable misery to multitudes. Men are to be relieved of the burden of supporting their families . . . and will live off the supplies furnished their dependent families by the state. Then will the state be compelled to employ a vast army of taskmasters, armed with gun or whip, to keep unwilling labor at its tasks. That will be slavery, to which the present so-called wage slavery is nothing.[92]

Support for Spalding's position came from other Episcopal socialist clergy such as A. L. Byron-Curtiss and Bernard Iddings Bell. Arguing that "the Marxian system has within it the power to convince an impartial observer," Bell asked if it was fair to judge socialists "solely by performance and not at all by profession. If we judged the Christian religion by those standards," he argued, we would have to say "good-by to all hope of converting the unchurched. Suppose some socialists have been bitter, and hateful and even immoral. Are not some Christians so?"[93]

In November 1912 Spalding told an audience at Salt Lake's First Congregational Church that "as long as the wages of the laboring classes are based on the so-called law of supply and demand, life will continue to be mostly one of merely keeping body and soul together, and the reproduction of the species. The true basis of wages is value and production of labor."[94] About the same time he returned to Erie where, as usual, he spoke on socialism. The local socialist paper reported that the daily press "carefully and painstakingly" explained that the brand of socialism advocated by the bishop was "something entirely different from the usual kind." In fact, the paper noted that "no sounder presentation of socialist theories has ever been made in this town, and Erie Socialists who were present in great numbers found nothing left out and nothing put in that was not in strict accordance with our most authoritative writers."[95]

In 1913 Spalding spoke to the Episcopal Church's General Convention in New York, angering many of those in attendance by calling it a "capitalistic convention." The bishop demanded that the church "join in the movement for industrial democracy." He told his colleagues that he hated the "unchristian and ungodlike" capitalist system that "gives to the greedy and takes from the meek." Such a system must end, he argued, and the church, which makes its money from "profit, interest and rent," must accept "the truth [that] the wealth of this country is created by the laboring classes, yet they are suffering untold misery. The worker must be rewarded on the basis of what he renders."[96]

Much of the information we have on Spalding's views on socialism is found in brief newspaper accounts. More complete statements are contained in two important articles published in the *Christian Socialist*. Both show how far his thinking had progressed since his confrontation with Salt Lake socialists in 1906. In the first, "Christian Socialism," Spalding echoed Marx's famous quotation that Christian socialism was "the holy water with which the priest consecrates the heartburnings of the aristocrats."[97] He further observed that there were many Christian ministers who claimed to be socialists simply because they did not limit their duties to preaching on Sunday, but also took an active part in reform movements. Such ministers have no right to the name socialist since individualism could never be "enlightened enough, [nor] even be Christian enough to make it socialism."[98]

Socialism, Spalding contended, must replace a contemporary society character- ized by "reckless waste, the unjust distribution of the necessities of life, when there is really plenty for all, and the undeniable tendency of the wealth of the world to become the property of a smaller and smaller number of its inhabitants." For Spalding, under capitalism

the working man does not receive the value he creates, but just as little of it as possible to keep himself alive. Indeed, if a substitute can readily be found, capital will let him die. A protest was made some months ago against the poor timbering in a Colorado coal mine. "What do I care?" said the boss. "Dagos are cheaper than crops." The Declaration of Independence committed the nation to something more democratic than a benevolent feudalism and nothing must lower our standard from the socialist ideal that every man shall have the value he creates and not depend for the return of his labor on the whim of his employer.[99]

Much of the criticism of socialism, commented Spalding, surrounded the argument that people "are not fit to rule now, much less will they be fit to carry on the proposed cooperative commonwealth." Opponents of socialism charged that "men are idle unless they are driven, dishonest unless they are watched, unambitious unless for selfish gain, and that therefore, the socialist ideal is but a silly dream."[100] In countering these arguments, Spalding maintained that scientific socialism professed complete faith in democracy and believed that the "common people are fit to govern not only the present state but a new industrial state which will, in the least, not be a simpler state than the political state we know today." Moreover, he maintained, socialism did not claim to be utopia, but rather consisted of "the discovery and formulation of social laws, and the endeavor to live by them and make them prevail. But just what the final result in social life will be, nobody can predict."[101]

In the second article, "Socialism and Christianity," Spalding expanded on several of his favorite themes. He argued that it was "conceited bigotry" for socialists to ignore the Christian church and fail to utilize "all possible power" to achieve socialism. The personal and social value of the Christian religion is "not in conflict with socialistic theory," which the socialist "rightly believes must not be weakened or diluted."[102]

Moreover, Spalding argued, there "is not the slightest doubt" that socialism preached the class struggle, for the "Manifesto states the fact with brutal frankness." The important question, however, was, if it

was right and Christian for our patriotic forefathers to stir up class feeling on the economic issue of taxation without representation, and to bring on a bloody war with the mother country, if it was right and Christian for those who did not believe in chattel slavery to create class feelings and precipitate an awful Civil War between the free states and the slave states, who shall say that it is not right and Christian for the socialist to stir up class feelings and bring on the social and economic revolution? Which alone can give life and liberty to the millions to whom now citizenship has no meaning and life confers no blessing. Let . . . no Christian preacher ever dare to say that competition is necessary to progress. For that advice is contrary to the mind of his master who said, "Blessed are the meek, for they shall inherit the earth.[103]

More than any other group, he believed, Christians should support the social revolution, because it demanded "of the body corporate what St. Paul, in the name of Christ, required of the individual, that it become, 'a new creation.'"[104]

By 1914 Spalding was at the height of his advocacy of socialism. His views were well known and widely circulated. His rejection of the materialism of contemporary American society was growing, and he criticized those people who "boast of their standing in political circles . . . their place in clubs . . . [and] their position in business," while neglecting religion and social justice.[105] Spalding took an important personal step further to solidify his support for socialism. For the first time, he publicly urged support for the Socialist Party at the polls. In that year he also published one of the most comprehensive statements of his growing socialist commitment. It is contained in a review of Winston Churchill's novel *The Inside of the Cup,* published in the *Salt Lake Herald-Republican.* Noting that the word "socialism" was mentioned several times, he could find "no indication that Mr. Churchill knows what the word means." Criticizing Churchill's failings in the novel, he argued that no thinking person in contemporary society could claim to "have an intelligent grasp of the problem of reform" without understanding

that great international movement which recognizes the fact of "the class struggle" which . . . means that in the present competitive industrial life of Europe and America there are two sharply divided economic classes. One class is composed of the workers—manual and mental—who are paid wages, which wages have no necessary relation to the value their labor creates, but depend on the supply and demand for workers. Unless raised by the power of organized labor these wages sink to a minimum sufficient to support life and maintain physical efficiency and reproduce the species. The other class is composed of the capitalists. They own the tools of industry and most of the land. They appropriate as their share of the increase of wealth produced by the workers . . . interests, profit and rent. If wages are high, profits, interest and rent are low. If profits, interest and rent are high, wages are low—actual wages which the worker can spend upon himself and his family. The "class struggle" is not a spirit but an economic fact.[106]

Accordingly, Spalding observed, the old "platitude that the interests of capital and labor are identical is untrue." Drawing on the writings of economist Scott Nearing, Spalding argued that while three-fourths of the population of the United States belonged to the "working class," the other fourth, "the capitalistic class and their parasites—corporation lawyers, real estate agents, fashionable doctors and preachers," owned 95 percent of the total wealth. And of that group, approximately 1 percent of the total population owned in excess of 70 percent of the total wealth.

In the light of these statistics, Spalding asserted that the workers of the world were slowly realizing that only the Socialist Party had a "definite and clear-cut program of reform." Only the Socialists believed in the social revolution and realized that the

present political state controlled by the capitalist class in the interest of the capitalist class must be supplanted by the industrial state controlled by the workers, in which the present economic class struggle will cease because the tools of industry and the wealth used for production of more wealth will be owned and operated by a cooperative commonwealth in which production will be for use and not profit.[107]

Moreover, Spalding observed, as one who believed in this socialist program, it was also clear that "organized religion in the United States" is supported by profits, rent, and interest, not wages. Thus, capital "controls the tools of worship and the entrepreneurs who operate them, just as it controls industry." Accordingly, workers were, with "startling rapidity," becoming aware of that fact, and were losing "confidence and interest in the church. Then they drift away, looking for religious help from other sources or doubting whether there are any spiritual values."[108]

Within a few months of publishing this review, however, his activities as a leader in the American Christian socialist movement approached an untimely and tragic end. On 25 September 1914, as he crossed a Salt Lake street on his way from mailing a letter, Spalding was struck by an oncoming automobile and instantly killed.[109]

Spalding's death produced an outpouring of grief within the Christian socialist community in particular, but also among a wider group in the cities in which he was best known—Denver, Erie, Salt Lake City.[110] Speaking for the Salt Lake Socialist Party local, Julius M. Miller proposed erecting a "tablet, monument or statue" in memory of "Comrade Bishop Spalding" to show appreciation for his "invaluable service to our class." Writing to socialists throughout the West, Miller said Spalding's death in a "preventable accident" left socialists "broken hearted" and "stunned by our calamity."[111]

Representing organized labor and the Socialist Party of Utah, William M. Knerr put aside past differences and told those attending a memorial service held in Salt Lake on I November 1914, that "Comrade" Spalding "proclaimed himself a socialist and championed the cause of labor." He was a man

whose hands were open and whose heart was full—who stood for the good things in this life—who hated caste. One who knew something about the law that governs the motion of society; who knew something about the men, women and little children who labor in our mines, mills, factories and sweat shops, knew that many were underpaid and underfed, knew that they were useful members of society, knew that the large majority of them were unable to earn sufficient food, clothing and shelter.[112]

Knerr praised Spalding for generosity, moral courage, and intellectual honesty, saying he "did not write or speak double words that might possibly be useful in retreat and contradiction." Spalding tried to "lift the many burdens of the working class . . . the friendless, the hopeless, the unfortunate . . . the suffering and oppressed. He was the friend of all the world and sought to socialize the human race."[113] In this same spirit, the November issue of the *Christian Socialist* memorialized him with articles and eulogies, condolences from Socialist Party locals around the country, and excerpts about socialism from his articles and letters to friends.

At the same time, Spalding's commitment to socialism had endeared him to many theological students who were considering where to begin their ministry after graduation. Henry Knox Sherrill, who eventually declined an invitation from Spalding to serve in Utah, noted that Spalding stirred his conscience and sympathy for the working class. Sherrill, who later served as bishop of Massachusetts and presiding bishop, remembered Spalding as "tall and spare, with a penetrating mind, skeptical of conventional ways and phrases, and a remarkable combination of fearlessness and personal humility."[114] Irwin St. John Tucker recalled that Spalding would always admonish his listeners to "[r]ead Karl Marx; there you will find the solution!" Still, Tucker also believed that Spalding was "no book socialist, but one who had thrashed the matter out in the light of his own I experience." For Spalding "nothing except the growing intelligence of the working-class" could solve society's problems and bring about the cooperative commonwealth.[115]

DuBose Murphy, president of the Yale Society for the Study of Socialism, called Spalding an "inspiration to all who came in touch with him," and a leader in the "rapidly growing army of those who are coming to believe that Socialism needs real Christianity to be effective, just as Christianity needs the continual vitalization furnished by those who see the social problem in all its significance."[116] Similarly, Charles Lewis Slattery, writing in the Episcopal magazine the *Churchman,* commented that "though exulting in his socialism and openly acknowledging it on every proper occasion, he did not repel those who did not agree with him."[117]

For more than a decade, despite occasional doubts, Franklin Spencer Spalding's life was characterized by a twofold commitment to Christianity and socialism. This duality was accurately identified by his friend, Charles D. Williams, bishop of Michigan, in a eulogy at the memorial service. These remarks provide a fitting summary of Spalding's life and work:

Spalding was a socialist in his economic creed. But his socialism was a unique kind. It was not the socialism of mere economic determinism or of materialism. . . . It was a spiritual and moral socialism, the socialism of justice and righteousness, above all the socialism of . . . Christlike love for all the weak, the disinherited, and oppressed. He was called a Christian socialist, and . . . yet I would transpose the words and call him a socialist Christian. . . . For the fundamental, underlying and determining element in all his life work and personality was his personal Christianity, his faith. It was the love of Christ that constrained him here as in every other aspect of his life, work and personality. His socialism was but the expression of his Christianity as applied to the larger problems of industrial and economic relations. But it was the same Christianity which sanctified his personal character and inspired his work as a minister of the Christian church.[118]

NOTES

1. "Bishop Spalding," *Social Preparation for the Kingdom of God* 3 (February 1915): 74–75.

2. A definitive study of socialist activities in the Episcopal Church remains to be written. A good starting point can be found in the following: James Dombrowski, *The Early Days of Christian Socialism in America* (New York: Columbia University Press, 1936); Peter J. Frederick, *Knights of Golden Rule: The Intellectual as Christian Social Reformer in the 1890s* (Lexington, Ky.: University Press of Kentucky, 1976); Bernard Kent Markwell, *The Anglican Left: Radical Social Reformers in the Church of England and the Protestant*

Episcopal Church, 1846–1954 (Brooklyn, N.Y.: Carlson Publishing, 1991); and Paul T. Phillips, A *Kingdom on Earth: Anglo-American Social Christianity, 1880–1940* (University Park, Pa.: Pennsylvania State University Press, 1996).

3. *Salt Lake Tribune*, 11 November 1912. See also *Los Angeles Examiner and Herald*, 22 October 1912.

4. Unidentified clipping. Frank Spalding Scrapbook, Colorado Historical Society, Denver, Colorado. While many of the clippings are unidentified, this collection contains important information Spalding and his immediate family. See also the Spalding Family Scrapbooks, Western History Collections, Denver Public Library, Denver, Colorado.

5. Frank Spalding Scrapbook, Colorado Historical Society.

6. This chapter expands my thinking on Spalding as explored in two earlier assessments. See John R. Sillito, "'Prove All Things, Hold Fast That Which is Good'—Franklin Spencer Spalding, A Christian Socialist Dissenter From Capitalist Values," *Weber Studies* 1 (Spring 1984): 39–49; and John R. Sillito and Martha S. Bradley, "Franklin Spencer Spalding: An Episcopal Observer of Mormonism," *Historical Magazine of the Protestant Episcopal Church* 54 (December 1985): 339–50. The Research Scholarship and Professional Growth Committee of Weber State University provided financial assistance in the research for this and the previous articles. Sarah Campbell provided important technical assistance. I also appreciate the assistance of my colleague John S. McCormick in helping me understand Spalding.

7. As quoted in John Howard Melish, *Franklin Spencer Spalding: Man and Bishop* (New York: Macmillan, 1917), 237. While flawed, Melish's account provides a basic overview of Spalding's life and thought.

8. Franklin Spencer Spalding, "A Bishop's Apologia," *Social Preparation for the Kingdom of God* 1 (January 1913): 3–5. This article was subsequently reprinted as "Bishop Spalding's Own Story of Conversion to Socialism," *Christian Socialist* 11 (November 1914): 1. The *Social Preparation* stated that its purpose was to show "churchmen and non-church socialists alike, the religious possibilities of socialism." Such sentiments obviously paralleled Spalding's views.

9. *Salt Lake Herald*, 30 November 1906.

10. DuBose Murphy, "Rt. Rev. Franklin Spencer Spalding," *Intercollegiate Socialist* 3 (January–February 1915): 14–15. The only other family member who apparently was also attracted to socialism was his sister Sarah, who served for a time as his secretary when Spalding was bishop of Utah.

11. See Franklin Spencer Spalding, *The Call of the West* (New York: Episcopal Church Mission House, n.d.). Spalding was fond of the western landscape, an enthusiastic mountain climber, and a participant in the first group to scale Grand Teton. See *Denver Post*, 19 October 1904; "Franklin Spencer Spalding, Mountaineer," *Churchman* 107 (17 December 1921): 12–13; and Chris Boileau, "Utah Bishop First to Scale Grand Teton," *Utah's Diocesan Dialogue* (January 1992): 6–7.

12. According to Melish, *Spalding,* 24, the "Princeton of the eighties was calculated to drill boys in acquiring knowledge rather than to open their minds and inspire them to think . . . . Spalding's mind was analytical rather than acquisitive, and though he worked hard, he did not attain high rank because of the methods of his day." For information on Spalding's activities at Princeton, see the Records of the Class of 1887, especially the biographical questionnaire dated 1913, Princeton University Archives, Seeley G. Mudd Library, Princeton, N.J.

13. Melish, *Spalding*, 38–40. As Spalding noted, "There is very little stimulus to work when you know the professor will hardly look at it and . . . let every one through for the honor of the institution."

14. For contemporary accounts of Erie politics, see S. B. Nelson, ed., *Nelson's Biographical Dictionary and Historical Reference Book of Erie County, Pennsylvania* (Erie, Pa.: S. B. Nelson Publishers, 1896), 260–62; and John Miller, *A Twentieth Century History of Erie County, Pennsylvania* (Chicago: Lewis Publishing, 1909).

15. As he told his sister, "Rev. Willis K. Crosby is doing really good work among the working people in the east end of Erie. When times were so hard two years ago he got up a factory and let as many unemployed as wanted to run it on a cooperative plan. They made a patent dust pan and so a good many had a living out of it. He gets the men together to study interesting facts. He asked me whether I couldn't come some evening and talk to them on some subject. I told him I didn't know anything." Gradually, Spalding began to study and speak out on questions like prison reform and juvenile crime. See Melish, *Spalding*, 61.

16. Rich Cermak, "Socialists Never in Power But Were Necessary Goad," *Erie Daily Times*, 13 June 1968, 1; William P. Garvey, "Ethnic Politics in Erie," *Journal of Erie Studies* 1 (1972): 12; and John G. Carney, *Highlights of Erie Politics* (Erie, Pa.: John G. Carney, 1986).

17. *Erie Truth*, 3 October 1914. This paper, published between 1913 and 1921, was the official paper of the Socialist Party of Erie County, Pennsylvania.

18. Melish, *Spalding*, 88–89. Giddings wrote three standard texts on sociology during this period—*The Theory of Sociology* (1894); *The Principles of Sociology* (1896); and *The Elements of Sociology* (1898). It is unclear which of these books Spalding used in the class.

19. Melish, *Spalding*, 88–89. See also *New York Call*, 27 September 1914.

20. Spalding, "A Bishop's Apologia."

21. Melish, *Spalding*, 84.

22. This was an important issue for those in the Erie labor movement and the subject of an Erie Labor Day address by Isaac Cowan in 1898. See *Erie Daily Times*, 6 September 1898.

23. *Salt Lake Tribune*, 1 June 1911.

24. Spalding, "A Bishop's Apologia."

25. *Erie Evening Herald*, 5 September 1899.

26. Ibid. The paper reported, "During his remarks he said those interested in labor reforms in this city were not as good patrons of the Free Public Library as they should be. He said that wishing to ascertain what was being read along this line, when he went to the library to get some technical books dealing with the different phases of the question . . . he was surprised to learn that they had never yet been off the shelves."

27. Kemper Fullerton was born in Cincinnati on 29 November 1865. He graduated from Princeton a year after Spalding. After graduating from Union Theological Seminary in 1891, he returned to Princeton and received a master's degree in 1894. Fullerton taught Hebrew at Lane Theological Seminary in Cincinnati from 1893 to 1904. He was Finney Professor of Old Testament at the Oberlin Graduate School of Theology from 1904 to 1934. Fullerton died on 24 March 1940.

28. Kemper Fullerton to John Howard Melish, 17 July 1915, Cathedral of St. Paul Archives, Erie, Pennsylvania. Apparently this letter was sent in response to a request by Melish for information for his biography of Spalding. Melish used much of the information though not always with attribution to Fullerton.

29. Ibid. As Fullerton explained, "If Frank had been asked to address the employers, he would have undoubtedly pointed out their shortcomings. But as he was to speak to the Unions he chose to criticize certain faults of theirs. That was always Spalding's way."

30. Ibid. Spalding later admitted he had made a "sincere error" by advising workers "to work harder and earn more so that women would not seek employment." See *Social Preparation for the Kingdom of God* 3 (February 1915): 74–75.

31. Fullerton to Melish, 17 July 1915, Cathedral of St. Paul Archives.

32. Ibid.

33. Ibid.

34. As quoted in A. L. Byron-Curtiss, "Reminiscences of Bishop Spalding," *Social Preparation for the Kingdom of God* 3 (February 1915): 15–17.

35. See Melish, *Spalding,* 89. As he told his sister, to say Bryan was socialistic was absurd: "All the Socialists here are opposed to him as bitterly as they are to McKinley."

36. Spalding, "A Bishop's Apologia."

37. Ibid.

38. *Erie Daily Times,* 30 June 1913.

39. Fullerton to Melish, 17 July 1915, Cathedral of St. Paul Archives.

40. *Erie Daily Times,* 30 June 1913.

41. *Los Angeles Herald and Examiner,* 22 October 1912.

42. Spalding, "A Bishop's Apologia."

43. A discussion of Spailding's challenges as the Episcopal bishop of Mormon-dominated Utah is beyond the scope of this chapter. For an overview of this aspect of his career, see Melish, *Spalding*, Chaps. 10–13; John R. Sillito, "Franklin Spencer Spalding on Mormonism: A Documentary Approach," *Sunstone* (July–August 1979): 33–35; and Sillito and Bradley, "Franklin Spencer Spalding: An Episcopal Observer of Mormonism." For contemporary accounts of his election as bishop, see also *Erie Daily Times,* 4 December 1904; *Erie Herald,* 7 November 1914; *Denver Republican,* 29 October 1904; *Churchman* 90 (29 October 1904); and *Living Church* 38 (29 October 1904).

44. William Thurston Brown, "Reminiscences of Bishop Spalding," *New York Call,* 21 November 1914.

45. *Salt Lake Herald,* 7 March 1905.

46. Ibid., 5 June 1905.

47. *Salt Lake Crisis,* 16 June 1905.

48. Ibid., 9 June 1905.

49. Ibid.

50. Ibid., 23 June 1905.

51. Ibid. See Emile Vandervelde, "Marxian Idealism," *International Socialist Review* 4 (February 1904): 449–61. Vandervelde noted that

historical materialism offers small welcome to those who come to socialism or are drawn toward it by sentimental reasons. For many people . . . the materialistic conception of history, that corner stone of Marxism, denies any efficacy to the ideal. Morality, law, religion or philosophy are . . . the products or subproducts of economic activity. . . . They continue to think that ideas are forces . . . [that] find their final explanation in the "Underlying Economic Factor." The socialist conscience would never submit to such a contradiction of its ideal . . . . In fact . . . those who thus interpret the doctrine of Marx only show they understand it very poorly.

52. Ibid.

53. Ibid.

54. *Inter-mountain Republican,* 2 April 1906. Gilbert, a railroad porter and active socialist, served as the party's national committeeman and was a delegate to the founding convention of the Industrial Workers of the World in 1905.

55. *Deseret News,* 2 April 1905. See also *Salt Lake Herald,* 4 April 1906.

56. Ibid.

57. *Salt Lake Telegram,* 2 April 1906.

58. Ibid.

59. The meeting also focused public attention on the question of socialist activities among the local non-Mormon clergy. The *Salt Lake Herald,* 4 April 1906, interviewed several ministers who had "similar, though varied views." For an overview of socialist activities in Utah see John S. McCormick, "Hornets in the Hive: Socialism in Early Twentieth Century Utah," *Utah Historical Quarterly* 50 (Summer 1982): 225–40; and John R. Sillito, "Women and the Socialist Party in Utah, 1900–1920," *Utah Historical Quarterly* 49 (Summer 1981): 220–38.

60. Undated clipping, Spalding Scrapbook.

61. Franklin Spencer Spalding, "The Church in the Mining Camps," *Spirit of Missions* 73 (February 1908): 97–104.

62. Ibid. See also Spalding to John W. Wood, 14 February 1908, Records of the Foreign and Domestic Missionary Society, Episcopal Church Archives, Episcopal Seminary of the Southwest, Austin, Texas. Spalding mentioned a discussion he had "with a young Baptist preacher named Stillman" over the need for a church-sponsored hall that was a "combination of a reading room, smoking room, bowling alley, game room, mortuary-chapel . . . and lodging house." Such a place, he said, represented the kind of place "the poor need to have . . . to [get] them some relief from saloons, dives, etc."

63. Undated clipping, Spalding Scrapbook.

64. Ibid.

65. *Salt Lake Herald,* 30 November 1906.

66. Murphy, "Rt. Rev. Franklin Spencer Spalding," 14.

67. For an interesting overview of Spalding during that period from the viewpoint of a fellow socialist clergyman, see the previously cited William Thurston Brown, "Reminiscences of Bishop Spalding," *New York Call,* 21 November 1914. At the time Brown knew Spalding he was minister of Salt Lake City's First Unitarian Church.

68. *Rhyolite* (Nevada) *Herald,* 12 April 1907.

69. Franklin Spencer Spalding, "Christian Socialism," *Christian Socialist* 6 (I March 1909): 1.

70. Ibid.

71. Franklin Spencer Spalding, "The Bishop of Socialism and Trade Unionism," *Christian Socialist 5* (I February 1908): 1–2.

72. *Salt Lake Herald,* 10, 27 November 1908.

73. *Inter-mountain Republican,* 10 April 1908.

74. Ibid.

75. Ibid., 11 April 1908.

76. *Deseret News,* 5 May 1908. Mormon leaders were concerned because of Spalding's activity as a critic of Mormonism. He lectured widely and wrote several articles and pamphlets on the subject most notably *Joseph Smith Jr. as a Translator* (Salt Lake City, Utah: Arrow Press, 1912), which cast doubt on the Mormon prophet's credibility. Church leaders were also concerned with a small but growing number of church members who were affiliating with the Socialist Party. For more information see John R. Sillito and John S. McCormick, "Socialist Saints: Mormons and the Socialist Party, 1900-1920," *Dialogue: A Journal of Mormon Thought* 18 (Summer 1985): 121–31.

77. Melish, *Spalding,* 223–31.

78. Henry Knox Sherrill, *Among Friends: An Autobiography* (Boston: Little Brown, 1962), 41–42. Sherrill notes that Spalding's socialism and passion for social reform did not make his task of raising funds for the missionary effort in Utah easy.

79. Kenneth S. Gutherie to Thomas Gailor, 22 March 1918, Records of the House of Bishops, Episcopal Church Archives. Spalding was followed as bishop of Utah by his protégé, Paul Jones, who was eventually forced to resign because of his socialist views and

vocal opposition to World War I. See John R. Sillito and Timothy S. Hearn, "A Question of Conscience: The Resignation of Bishop Paul Jones," *Utah Historical Quarterly 50* (Summer 1982): 209–24.

80. Protestant Episcopal Church of Utah, *Proceedings of the Second Annual Convocation of the Protestant Episcopal Church of Utah* (Ogden,Utah: n.p., 1911), 17.

81. Spalding to John W. Wood, 14 February 1908, Episcopal Church Archives.

82. *Salt Lake Tribune,* 1 June 1908.

83. *Park* (Utah) *Record,* 11 July 1908.

84. *Park* (Utah) Record, 1 May 1909.

85. *Seattle Post-Intelligencer,* 29 September 1909.

86. *Portland Morning Oregonian,* 6 October 1909. "Now by this I do not mean to infer that the Episcopal Church is preaching Socialism. . . . I am a Socialist as a man, just as you may be a Republican or a Democrat."

87. *Erie Times,* 3 November 1910.

88. *Salt Lake Telegram,* 11 May 1911.

89. Ibid., 8 May 1911.

90. *Living Church* 45 (2 September 1911): 649.

91. Ibid.

92. Ibid., 45 (16 September 1911): 674.

93. Ibid.

94. *Deseret News,* 7 November 1912.

95. *Erie Truth,* 3 October 1914.

96. Undated clipping, Spalding Scrapbook. See also "The Late Bishop Spalding's Warning to the Rich!" *New York Call,* 18 October 1914.

97. Spalding, "Christian Socialism," 1. According to the 1 November 1909 issue of the *Christian Socialist,* Spalding's "strong, scientific and religious essay" had been reprinted as a leaflet. The editor called the bishop a "real revolutionist" and urged socialists to "diligently circulate this striking leaflet."

98. Ibid.

99. Ibid.

100. Ibid.

101. Ibid.

102. Franklin Spencer Spalding, "Socialism and Christianity," *Christian Socialist* 8 (9 November 1911): 1–3. Socialist poet Edwin Markham wrote Spalding on 13 November 1911 that he "took joy" in the "courageous utterances" expressed in this article. See Spalding Scrapbook.

103. Ibid.

104. Ibid.

105. As quoted in the *Erie Dispatch,* 22 December 1914.

106. *Salt Lake Herald-Republican,* 22 February 1914.

107. Ibid.

108. Ibid.

109. Spalding's death and funeral were covered widely in the Salt Lake press. For a representative account see *Salt Lake Tribune,* 29 September 1914. See also the *Erie Evening Herald,* 30 Septembe 1914.

110. Typical is the editorial of the *Salt Lake Telegram,* 26 September 1914, which said: "Salt Lake has reason to be sorrowful today. One of her most useful citizens is dead, the kind of man whose place is difficult to fill. The manner of his death only adds to the city's great loss. Bishop Spalding . . . had great sympathy for the struggling masses. He did not limit that sympathy to mere words and imaginary dreaming; he put his sympathy into deeds. The

Socialism he taught was the Socialism of high ideas. It was based on the brotherhood of man. . . . He could rub elbows with luxury without being contaminated. Gold never caught him in its magic spell. He was the friend of the common people to the last." At the same time, while the *Deseret News* also eulogized Spalding, Mormon Church President Joseph F. Smith wrote his son Wesley, who was serving a mission in California: "You will see by the papers . . . that B[isho]p Spalding, the anti-Mormon was run down last night by an automobile driven by a daughter of Judge Wm. H. King. . . . [Spalding] will not try to 'reform' any more Mormon boys by persuading them to drink and smoke freely." See Joseph F. Smith to Wesley P. Smith, 26 September 1914, personal letterpress copybook, Historical Department, Church of Jesus Christ of Latter-Day Saints, Salt Lake City, Utah.

111. *Salt Lake Telegram*, 29 September 1914. Miller also urged "a law prohibiting minors from operating power-driven vehicles and making it murder to run down a pedestrian."

112. *See Utah Survey* 2 (December 1914): 16. See also Anna A. Maley,"A Reminiscence of Bishop Spalding," *New York Call*, 8 November 1914. Maley told of meeting Spalding in Helper, Utah, in 1911, where he addressed a group of railroad workers between shifts, and recalled their respect for him and the "power and enthusiasm" of his socialist message.

113. *Utah Survey* 2 (December 1914): 17.

114. Sherrill, *Among Friends,* 41–42.

115. Irwin St. John Tucker, "Impressions of Bishop Spalding," *Christian Socialist* 11 (November 1914): 3.

116. Murphy, "Rt. Rev. Franklin Spencer Spalding," 14.

117. Charles Lewis Slattery, "The Life of Bishop Spalding," *Churchman* 103 (14 July 1917): 42–43.

118. Charles D. Williams, "Memorial Address," *Utah Survey* 2 (December 1914): 6–14.

6

"Not a Substitute for Religion, but a Means of Fulfilling It": The Sacramental Socialism of Irwin St. John Tucker

Jacob H. Dorn

Irwin St. John Tucker was an Episcopal priest who joined the Socialist Party within days of his ordination as deacon in 1911 and devoted himself to the furtherance of the socialist cause for almost a dozen years thereafter. He did so both within party organizations and within the Episcopal Church. It was not always easy to be a priest functioning within the Socialist Party or a socialist functioning within the church, but Tucker believed the roles were complementary, not adversarial. He found the justification he needed for combining them in the Christian faith itself: in the biblical emphasis on social and economic justice in the here-and-now; in compassion for the weak and victimized; and in a distinctively Anglican-Episcopal incarnational theology that sacralized all of life.

Tucker's commitment was to the concrete program of the Socialist Party, not to an amorphous humanitarianism. He supported not only the party's "immediate" demands, reforms for which non-socialist progressives also worked, but in addition its "ultimate" demand for the collective, democratic ownership of the means of production, transportation, and distribution. In this respect, he went significantly beyond the pervasive and trans-denominational movement for a Social Gospel, as well as beyond the Anglican-Episcopal social tradition in which he had grown up.

The Anglican response to the upheavals of urbanization and industrialization had begun with the Christian Socialism of F. D. Maurice, Charles Kingsley, and J. M. Ludlow in the 1840s. Several organizations subsequently emerged to sustain this social witness: the Guild of St. Matthew (England, 1877), the Church Association for the Advancement of the Interests of Labor (United States, 1887), the Christian Social Union (England, 1889; United States, 1891), and the Society of Christian Socialists (United States, 1889). All these organizations proclaimed that Christian principles must govern all areas of human life, and some invoked socialism as an ideal, in contrast to economic individualism. None, however, explicitly and consistently endorsed a socialist party, as Tucker and a vocal minority would do in the early 1900s.[1]

If Tucker was a "regular" socialist, he was also an unwavering Christian. Despite some ebb and flow in his connection with particular parishes, he maintained his standing as a priest and a high degree of parochial activity throughout his socialist years. For him socialism was not a substitute for religion, not a new faith to fill the void left by a disintegrating old faith. It was the fulfillment of religion. Of the two commitments, in fact, the priestly was the most enduring, never really abandoned in his ninety-six years.

Tucker is little mentioned in histories of the American socialist movement. When he is, it is usually in reference to his trial with four other socialists under the Espionage Act of 1917. He was not one of the movement's luminaries or power brokers; his party roles were actually rather marginal. The neglect is therefore understandable. It is also regrettable, for he left behind a treasure-trove of materials—an unusually rich collection of poems, diary, letters, clippings, autobiographies—that reveal a great deal about what attracted a young Christian to the Socialist Party and what it was like for him to be in it.[2]

Born in 1886 in Mobile, Alabama, Irwin Tucker was brought up in the rectory of St. John's Church, a parish made up primarily of wage-earners that his father, Gardiner C. Tucker, served from 1885 until he died in 1941. Of the eight children reared by Gardiner and Melville Tucker, five were boys, four of whom began preparations for and three of whom actually entered the Episcopal ministry. The family's relationship with the church must have been intense and self-conscious, for Gardiner had left the Baptist ministry, to which his old-New England family had given many sons, after accepting the Anglican claim to direct apostolic episcopal authority. Irwin recalled a childhood permeated by Bible lessons, chants, prayers, and church bells, and when he left home he was a keen observer of liturgical differences in churches he visited.[3] The family's correspondence reflects friendly but sharp debates over Anglicanism's orientation, symptomatic of the debate in the larger church itself: Was it toward Protestantism, or toward Rome?

Childhood for Irwin also meant play, especially during vacations at Seacliff, a cottage the family bought along the eastern shore of Mobile Bay; poetry, which he was writing by the age of seven; exposure to his father's abundant library; and a wide-ranging engagement with art, mythology, and history characterized by a romanticism, that may have been primarily his mother's influence. There is no hint in this childhood of unconventional politics. A Democrat who supported the gold standard, Irwin's father strongly disapproved of William Jennings Bryan's nomination in 1896.[4]

From his graduation from high school to his decision to enter seminary in 1909, Tucker's diary and letters reflect a life of trying to get his poems and stories published, thoughts of the ministry, several romances, tensions with his father over money, and an erratic employment record. Why a precocious boy with intellectual aspirations went to work, rather than continuing his education, as had his older brothers, is unclear. Perhaps the family needed income from him. Perhaps his father believed that he needed the discipline of work.[5]

Whatever the case, in June 1902 Tucker entered the Southern Railway office in Mobile as a stenographer, a job he quit by October because of personal conflict with an agent. Soon thereafter, he quit another job after a week because it "disgusted" him.[6] A coffee company in New Orleans, where he moved in 1903 to live with his eldest brother, soon fired him, he wrote, "because I am too damned impertinent." Turning to newspapers, he worked for the *Picayune* and then for the *Item*, in both cases being discharged over the handling of assignments, before leaving New Orleans in 1906 to seek work elsewhere.[7]

Reporting in New Orleans introduced him to an urban world unlike Mobile. Covering the police beat, observing at close range the hurly-burly of politics, and meeting important people excited him, and he displayed a keen instinct for scooping other reporters and interjecting himself into dramatic situations. In particular, he found an outlet for his childhood love of the mythic and spectacular in New Orleans' Mardi Gras celebration, more elaborate than Mobile's older one. He got the *Item* to publish one of his epic poems, "The City of Dreams," which expressed his love of the city and its festival.[8]

The vicissitudes of journalism and difficulties with superiors made his search for jobs in 1906-1909—in Houston, Fort Worth, St. Louis, Chicago, Mobile, and again in New Orleans—much the same as before. Upon his return to Mobile in 1908 to restore eyes badly damaged by reading and a journalist's lifestyle, however, he became involved in mission work under his father's oversight. Finding it fulfilling, he consequently arranged to attend the General Theological Seminary (GTS) in New York City. Two brothers in the priesthood had attended the University of the South, a choice he resisted, perhaps because of its isolation in Sewanee, Tennessee.[9]

Whatever earlier factors bore upon his decision, it was Tucker's experiences at GTS and in New York that led him into the Socialist Party. Thus, his years as a seminarian deserve close attention. When he arrived in New York in 1909, he encountered an Episcopal Church with exceptional influence, visibility, and strong membership across the social spectrum. In addition to an imposing array of magnificent Gothic structures in affluent neighborhoods, there were historically working-class parishes and missions, settlements, and institutional programs sponsored by the city's Episcopal elite. Tucker's pride swelled when he considered how well Episcopalians were "holding the fort for the Master." He quickly plunged into a succession of projects—including mission teaching and a floating chapel for seamen—that introduced him to his denomination's urban ministries and brought him face to face with some of the ugly realities of urban life. Before long, he also experienced frustration and impatience with the church, as when, at a crowded St. Bartholomew's, a woman near whose pew box he was standing deliberately locked her door after the rector asked members to share unoccupied seats.[10]

At Chelsea Square Tucker found the United States' oldest and wealthiest Episcopal seminary. Patterned architecturally after Oxford and Cambridge, the GTS quadrangle of buildings—chapel, dormitories, refectory-gymnasium, classrooms, faculty houses—occupied a city block between 9th and 10th avenues and 20th and 21st streets.[11] Long a High Church bastion, yet hospitable to the whole range of Episcopal life, the school under Dean Wilford Lash Robbins strongly emphasized spiritual discipline (with three services daily) and missionary causes.[12] The seminary was less than it might have been academically, however. Some younger professors had research-based graduate training, but the faculty still contained men who were successful parish priests, not scholars. Instruction was by lecture or student recitation. Electives were available only as voluntary additions to the regular curriculum.[13]

Later, Tucker often portrayed the seminary in bleak terms. Little seemed relevant to the contemporary world. Liturgical life was stilted and lifeless, and the courses appeared "designed to equip us only for the seclusion of monastic gardens." The seminary complex itself was "a little ivy-clad island, walled off from the strong and terrible life of the great metropolis boiling and surging around us."[14] That these judgments oversimplify his experience at GTS is evident in his reactions at the time and even in some later comments.

Despite the metaphors of monastic gardens and island, Tucker was part of the most culturally vibrant, socially diverse, and politically conscious metropolis in America. From the outset, he was captivated by that larger environment and partook of its religious and cultural offerings. Seminary and city interacted as he processed—intellectually and psychologically—the information, observations, values, and cultural novelties that came his way. It is simply impossible to compartmentalize and measure, however separable they may be conceptually, the various elements that made him a socialist.

In three related matters of belief and thought, his letters suggest something other than intellectual deadness and monastic seclusion. Early on, ecclesiology took on fresh urgency as he confronted claims to Episcopal uniqueness in a High Church seminary and generally High Church diocese and related those claims to the views of his father and brothers. One letter assailed as "blasphemy against the Holy Spirit" an exclusive attitude toward other communions. Distinguishing between the "historic episcopate" and "apostolic succession," he held that Episcopalians might justifiably claim the former, the "skeleton" of the Body of Christ, but not always the latter, its "nerve center." They often blocked the movings of God's spirit, which then flowed through other channels, such as the eighteenth-century Wesleyan movement or American frontier circuit riders in the nineteenth century.[15] Dismissing "Family-Tree worshippers" preoccupied with "pedigree," he projected as the test of apostolic succession "apostolic works," without which such succession was "de jure" but not "de facto."[16] The ideal he began to articulate for the church was risk-taking, forward-looking, sacrificial, and, without forsaking Episcopal distinctives, ecumenical.

Beginning with his second year, biblical studies also assumed great relevance for social activism. His introduction to the Higher Criticism of the Old Testament, though threatening at first because it denied traditional notions about authorship and inspiration, soon made religion "a thousand-fold more believable" by giving heightened emphasis to historical context and socioeconomic implications. That Moses wrote little of the Pentateuch and there were two Isaiahs, or that Hebrew conceptions of God were initially "crude, almost barbarous," was not at all troubling. That biblical religion was evolutionary and progressive, not static, made its study "the most fascinating thing imaginable."[17]

The third area of intense interest involved Christian ethics and Christian social action. Here, Tucker's exposure to New York was primary, but the seminary was not immune to social themes. In a strong defense of ministry to people's physical needs, he wrote: "A man is not a Christian who does not relieve his brother's *physical* [emphasis added] distress. . . . I can find nothing whatever about 'spirituality' in the teaching of Christ that is not intimately connected with helping others." In an argument appropriate for a High Churchman who was contemplating entering the Order of the Holy Cross, he likened the services of modern social settlements to those of medieval monasteries, "the greatest social worker the world ever saw."[18] In his third year, he was enthralled when Bishop Franklin S. Spalding spoke to his social ethics class on Christianity and socialism. Explaining his socialism in 1914, he characterized Arthur P. Hunt and Arthur W. Jenks, his professors of ethics and history, and even Dean Robbins, as "deeply tinged with red" and recalled his discovery in the GTS library that such Church Fathers as Basil, Chrysostom, Jerome, Augustine, Gregory the Great, and Ambrose were "all in sharp conflict with the capitalistic rings of their respective days." Despite their propagandistic exaggeration, these statements confirm that the faculty and curriculum did make a difference to Tucker.[19]

Although it was not until June 1912, within days of being ordained a deacon at the Cathedral of St. John the Divine, that Tucker joined the Socialist Party of America (SPA), he had entered its orbit more than a year earlier. Even before his move to New York, he had had positive exposures to socialism. In Chicago in 1906, Ellen Dorothy (Nell) O'Reilly, later his wife, and her sister Mary, a member of the party's county committee, had taken him to party functions. In 1908 he voted for Eugene V. Debs, "or rather for the Socialist cause," in the belief that it would replace a disintegrating Democratic Party. His vote may have been due in part to his experience, while on summer encampment with the Louisiana National Guard, of being used during a strike in Birmingham to protect a trainload of "scabs" (his word). Prior to the election, his father's name appeared among 161 ministerial supporters of a pro-socialist manifesto.[20] Unfortunately, the dearth of pertinent political commentary in Tucker's diary and letters leaves the significance of these incidents uncertain.

Tucker's plunge into socialist activism began in earnest with the most notorious event in the fierce labor struggles that rocked New York's Progressive Era garment industry: the Triangle Shirtwaist Company fire of 25 March 1911, which left 146 women, mostly young Jews and Italians, dead from the flames or from jumping to the sidewalk below. Locked doors and hopelessly inadequate elevators and fire escapes suggested employer negligence, but there were no convictions. The day of an enormous march and demonstration, 5 April 1911, Tucker's poem, "It Was Suicide," a biting reflection on indifference to the lives of the poor, appeared in the *Call*, New York's Socialist daily—apparently rejected by the *New York Times*. A month later, at a mass meeting in honor of Milwaukee's Socialist congressman, Victor Berger, he sat with groups from GTS and Union Seminary on the platform. Though GTS seems not to have had a chapter of the Intercollegiate Socialist Society (ISS), formed in 1905 to promote discussion of socialism, Union had one of the most active in the nation, and Tucker's correspondence mentions occasional meetings between GTS and Union students; at the end of 1911 Tucker attended an ISS convention complete with the singing of the "Marseillaise" at a crowded banquet.[21]

Early in 1912, as Tucker was exploring post-seminary options, he won the Seymour prize for preaching what he considered a "purely socialistic" sermon that linked economics and sociology with the Gospel. One of the judges, William Norman Guthrie, rector of St. Mark's in the Bowery, apparently liked Tucker's brashness and saw in him potential for reinvigorating his parish, which was stranded in a radically changed, now heavily Jewish, neighborhood at 2nd Avenue and 10th Street. To increase attendance, but also because he believed St. Mark's had a community role to play beyond the ordinary parish, Guthrie had begun giving lectures on social and cultural topics after his Sunday evening service and opened the church hall for such gatherings as a Christian Socialist meeting and a lecture by Bouck White on his *The Call of the Carpenter*. Guthrie proposed that Tucker conduct the evening service and program.[22]

Seeing a grand opportunity to combine his dual commitments to the priesthood and to socialism, Tucker accepted the offer, which enabled him to spend a fourth year at GTS, completing requirements for the Bachelor of Divinity degree, prior to his ordination as priest in May 1913. From September 1912 through the end of 1913, he conducted what he called "The Socialist Pulpit of St. Mark's." Each Sunday night, following the standard Episcopal service, the congregation-audience moved from sanctuary to parish house for discussions, speeches, and singing that often lasted almost to midnight. Though the explicit socialism was unusual, if not unique, the structure and functions of such meetings were not. Tucker admired the drawing power of Sunday night meetings at Cooper Union, two blocks from St. Mark's, where discussions of religion and politics occurred in a secular setting. A religious variant, begun in 1907 by Percy S. Grant, rector of the Church of the Ascension, also near St. Mark's at 5th Avenue and 10th Street, had a socialist aura, if not designation, under the leadership of Alexander Irvine. Tucker had occasionally attended the "after meetings" at Ascension since his first year at GTS. The very influential Boston Baptist Social Union's Ford Hall Forum, organized in 1908, had already achieved wide recognition.[23]

Though Tucker had the examples of Grant and Guthrie, both of whom advertised their meetings in the *Call*, given his journalistic experience and penchant for attracting attention he really needed no guidance in such matters. At a huge rally for Debs at Madison Square Garden, he passed out thousands of annoucements of his first sermon, and he got the *Call* occasionally to publish Saturday notices and Monday synopses of his topics. His initial impression of Debs's human touch would later bear fruit in work in the amnesty campaign for Debs and an affectionate poem when Debs died.[24]

Though Tucker's definition of socialism was sloppy at times—finding it in the Church Fathers, for example—and his diary and letters reveal almost nothing of reading in socialist theory, the Socialist Pulpit resonated with themes of class conflict and social revolution. To begin a six-part series on "The Religion of a

Socialist," Tucker chose the Hebrew prophets, both because he had come to see their message and that of Jesus as symbiotically linked and because he wished to attract a Jewish audience. The Hebrew nation, he asserted, began when Moses successfully led captive Jewish brickmakers on strike against their Egyptian masters, and the Hebrew scriptures close with Malachi pronouncing divine judgment on oppressors. Politics was inseparable from Hebrew religion, which, in his thinking, like socialism, found its center and aim in social and economic justice and human solidarity: "Politics was a sacrament of religion: the outward and visible sign of their worship of their God."[25]

Similarly, on successive Sundays devoted to Jesus, primitive Christian communism, the Church Fathers, and the creeds, Tucker insisted on a "sacramental" complementarity between Christianity and socialism. While socialism provided the program of action essential to the fulfillment of biblical religion, religion supplied the essential spiritual dynamic. Applying a common Anglican explanation of the divine presence in the bread and wine of the Eucharist, he remarked: "One is the outward and visible sign of which the other is the inward spiritual grace; one is the temporal body of which the other is the eternal soul." Christians who opposed socialism, he argued, either misunderstood socialism or were disloyal to the spirit and message of Jesus.[26] To criticism that socialism was materialistic and thus incompatible with faith, he replied tartly that that was true of agriculture, medicine, carpentry, and "any other science"; simply "an economic program for the setting right of economic ills," socialism was "not a substitute for religion, but a means of fulfilling it."[27]

Simultaneously linking the Hebrew prophets with socialism and asserting that socialism needed Christianity, Tucker may seem to have undertaken a quixotic mission. His wide-eyed exposure to and fascination with Yiddish-speaking downtown Jews was not unique among native-born Anglo-Americans. Two starkly different cultural worlds came into close embrace in Progressive Era New York—to wit, Irvine's attractiveness to Jews at Ascension's open forums, or J. G. Phelps Stokes' marriage to Rose Pastor. Sure that she believed in Christ and the Holy Spirit and that her repugnance at any suggestion of conversion was due to "thousands of years of ancestral feeling," Tucker himself fell in love with, and almost married, Helen Schloss, a militant street-speaker and strike leader whose father had organized an Orthodox synagogue.[28]

Tucker did not expect Jews to become Christians and join St. Mark's. His emphasis on the inherent socialism of the prophets was not opportunistic but derived from his Old Testament studies at GTS, which conveniently coincided with the demography of the Lower East Side. Neither did the connection he considered necessary between Christianity and socialism give offense to many. His hearers seem to have understood that his intention was to marshal Christian support for social justice. Tucker exultantly reported what happened when one man called those present "hypocrites—me for advertising Socialism to get Jews in a Christian church, and them for sitting through a Christian service to get a chance to talk Socialism." Several Jews immediately responded, one remarking: "If Moses was for humanity, I am for Moses; if Christ is for humanity, I am for Christ."[29] Jesus was a "spiritual

Socialist," the audience decided one night, but living in a precapitalist world, he could not have been an "economic Socialist . . . had he wanted to."[30]

Tucker's love of excitement, alertness to the potential for high drama, and willingness to risk danger reinforced his newfound socialist commitment, and after organizing the Socialist Fellowship of St. Mark's, he was soon a conspicuous radical activist. The victims of "industrial wars" especially drew his support.[31] Two such "wars," both given dramatic leadership by the militant Industrial Workers of the World (IWW), occurred nearby. The first began in October 1912 with a strike of textile workers in Little Falls, New York, following a severe wage reduction. Tucker became particularly engrossed in the efforts of Helen Schloss, who became a heroine to strikers by virtue of her militant open-air speaking and arrests.[32]

During the much larger silk strike in Paterson, New Jersey, in 1913, he publicly upbraided Paterson ministers who preached law and order but showed little understanding of the suffering that caused strikes; spoke at a Sunday mass rally in Haledon, a heavily socialist neighboring town, alongside William D. "Big Bill" Haywood, Elizabeth Gurley Flynn, and Carlo Tresca; and participated in a socialist project to bring strikers' children to New York by having St. Mark's take in some twenty of them.[33] Tucker gained a deep appreciation for the "Wobblies," whom many socialists repudiated as a threat to socialist respectability and as advocates of violence. Speaking at an ISS meeting in Chicago in June 1913, he provoked discomfort by discussing the IWW from "its own viewpoint, instead of as an avowed enemy." A Christian socialist need not be a timid or conservative one.[34]

Tucker also took his cause and his fellowship to the streets. On Good Friday, 1913, with silver cross and red satin banner the St. Mark's band preached and sang near the Brooklyn Bridge. Shortly thereafter, they joined a giant May Day celebration, on whose organizing committee Tucker served, marching with cigar makers, butchers, the Finnish branch of Local New York, and other labor and socialist groups, to a culminating demonstration at Union Square at which Tucker and Helen Schloss were speakers.[35] Later in 1913, his name appears among party-authorized speakers at street meetings and as a member of the party's county committee.[36]

Immersion in party and labor affairs did not divert Tucker's attention from Episcopal social witness. Notwithstanding wide usage of the term "Christian Socialism" in its rich tradition of social concern, Episcopalians had no organization committed explicitly to socialist politics prior to the creation in 1906 of the Church Socialist League (CSL) in England, and in 1911, its American counterpart.[37] In response to the rise of reformist Social Gospel sentiment, and building on a series of earlier committees, the denomination's General Convention of 1910 created a permanent Commission on Social Service and urged dioceses to create their own commissions. Gratifying though that action was, socialist Episcopalians wanted more radical action, and beginning in 1911 their small but vocal CSL acted as a goad toward that end.

Tucker began a decade-long association with the league in 1913. After meeting its chairman, Bernard Iddings Bell, in June, he was soon involved in plans to mount a radical witness at the triennial General Convention in New York in October. He was host of a pre-convention conference on "vital issues" at St. Mark's. In protest against Episcopalians' identification with the wealthy, egregiously reflected in a new Synod Hall built especially for the convention with gifts from J. Pierpont Morgan and other millionaires, he also published a biting poem in a denominational journal, with the words

If priests profane my altar With gifts that reek of wrong,
How shall they spread My gospel, Or lift My vengeance-song?[38]

The socialist presence at the convention could not be missed. If one did not detect it in extemporaneous speeches on the social service report, it was unavoidable at daily noon recesses, when CSL speakers held a soapbox rostrum across the street from Synod Hall. Nothing captured attention, however, like Bishop Spalding's stirring addresses at the convention and elsewhere. A crowd of 600 heard one on "The Church and Socialism" at Holy Trinity Church in Brooklyn. (Holy Trinity's rector, John Howard Melish, who was at the time Bouck White's patron, spoke to the convention on the need to support workers' struggles for a just distribution of wealth.) Spalding's convention address, calling upon the church to "cease to be merely the almoner of the rich, and become the champion of the poor" by taking up the cause of industrial democracy, stunned many in the hall but elicited widespread praise among socialists.[39] Given the progressive temper of the times, the convention might have passed its remarkable final resolution demanding a social order with "a more suitable distribution of wealth" without socialist prodding. Tucker and his collaborators could well believe, however, that they had made a difference.[40]

At the beginning of 1914, in a plan to reorganize and enlarge the *Christian Socialist*, Tucker moved to Chicago to serve as managing editor.[41] Despite an occasional tiff with the vestry or Guthrie, Tucker could have remained at St. Mark's; in fact, Guthrie replaced him with another socialist priest, William Miller Gamble.[42] Several other factors made the move attractive. One was the greater influence he would have through a paper read by thousands than as a parish priest.[43] Equally important was the secure income he would have under a financial plan underwritten by William F. Cochran, a wealthy Episcopal businessman with whom he probably came into contact through the CSL. Influenced by Walter Rauschenbusch, closest of the major Social Gospel thinkers to the Socialist Party, Cochran believed that "the highest duty of a millionaire is to make the future rise of millionaires impossible."[44] To free the *Christian Socialist*'s founder and editor, Edward Ellis Carr, for an organizing drive for the Christian Socialist Fellowship (CSF), Cochran agreed to underwrite a salary for the paper.[45]

Perhaps most important was the chance to deepen his relationship, renewed during a visit to Chicago in 1913, with Nell O'Reilly. Common interests in art, theater, poetry, and—not least—socialism, and complementary personal traits made them an excellent match.[46] Having been ready to marry Helen Schloss, a Jew, it is not too surprising that this Episcopal priest should propose to a Roman Catholic—he was, after all, attracted by his own denomination's Anglo-Catholic movement. He respected Nell's sincerity and agreed (with certain provisos) that any children would be raised as Roman Catholics. Their marriage at the home of the rector of Chicago's Grace Church on July 4, which Nell's priest blessed two days later, gave them, Tucker later remarked, two anniversaries, one his and one hers.[47] He promised at the time that he "would never consider [a parish position] married or free," as she reminded him later, adding, "I couldn't be a pastoress in a church."[48]

Tucker's journalistic experience served the *Christian Socialist* well for the two and a half years of his tenure. Fluctuating income occasioned changes in periodicity and length. However, its established character as a paper loyal to the Socialist Party with a special mission to present a message yoking Christian values and motives with the socialist economic program remained constant. The approaches taken on its pages to the Christian-socialist nexus varied according to the religious traditions and perspectives of the contributors. Though widely inclusive of Christian radicals, however, it was a partisan paper with propagandistic purpose and flair.

One established feature Tucker continued to use was the special issue. A "Woman's Day Number" featured articles on capitalism's destruction of the home, the suffrage cause, and Jesus' affirmation of women. An issue on Spalding following his accidental death reflected the wide respect he had in socialist circles. An "Emancipation Number" carried articles by black ministers, including George W. Woodbey, and offered reasons for blacks to be socialists. A Labor Day edition emphasized appalling poverty, the Commission on Industrial Relations' investigation of employers' brutality, and the reactive character of labor violence.[49] Unemployment and homelessness, miners' strikes in Colorado, West Virginia, and Michigan, reviews of Bouck White's "biographies" of Jesus, Carr's travels, CSF conferences, and the formation of socialist-oriented churches were typical fare under Tucker's editorial hand, and, except for the religious elements, might have been found in any socialist paper. With his usual creativity, he arranged for the unemployed in Chicago and elsewhere to sell the paper on the streets and got the *Call* to distribute it in New York.[50]

Tucker spent the rest of his life in Chicago, involved in so many activities for so long that he became a legendary figure known as "Friar Tuck." In 1914–1915 he assisted in Episcopal services and ran another Sunday evening forum, debated Arthur Morrow Lewis on atheism and socialism in the Garrick Theater, directed publicity for a garment strike, and, except that he had not been a member of the county local long enough, might have run for alderman.[51] Nell thought that the Chicago movement was making him more a "constructive socialist," and less an "impossibilist," than he had been when he arrived from New York.[52] Such a change is not readily apparent. Tucker's understanding of class conflict remained sharp, and his willingness to work confrontationally, strong.

Unemployment and homelessness were acute problems in many American cities in 1914 and 1915, but they were especially visible in Chicago because of its function as a center for migratory workers, or hoboes. Recalling his bitter experience seeking work there in 1906, Tucker gave top priority to his efforts on behalf of the homeless and hoboes. He supported the shelter established at the

Cathedral of Saints Peter and Paul by David Gibson, who had welcomed him there in 1906, and, more important, the International Brotherhood Welfare Association of James Eads How, an eccentric St. Louis "millionaire hobo." Tucker and Nell helped advise How on spending his money; Tucker directed and taught at a Skid Row "Hobo College"; and Nell served as secretary and he as vice president and president of the association.[53] One of the most compelling of his many poems, "The Unemployed Worker," published on 16 January 1915, and addressed to a comfortable, complacent "Preacher of the Gospel," expressed his conviction that Christ would not be aloof from the poor. That Tucker could not remain aloof became evident the next day when, coming to the aid of hunger marchers whom police were attacking near Jane Addams' Hull House settlement on Halsted Street, he was jailed with twenty-one other prisoners, including anarchist Lucy Parsons. Tried for riot and unlawful assembly, he was subsequently acquitted.[54]

As a boy, Tucker had an "arsenal" in his yard, and at twelve, he gushed with pride and a sense of national mission over the Spanish-American War. He composed patriotic poems, including an ode to Admiral Dewey ("Who showed America to be The destined ruler of all lands"), and began "The Chosen Nation," an epic he would complete a few years later.[55] In 1914 the idea of America as "chosen" remained with him, but its function had changed from celebration to judgment. Despite occasional interpretive eccentricities, Tucker adopted an antiwar position consistent with that of the socialist movement as war engulfed Europe and Americans debated "preparedness" and then intervention.[56] His position contributed to a parting of the ways with Carr and the *Christian Socialist* and brought him conviction under the Espionage Act of 1917 and the prospect of a long prison sentence.

In a *Christian Socialist* "War Number" in October 1914, he applied an economic interpretation to the war and urged readers to join a war against war. A resolution he helped draft for a CSF conference in February 1915 also blamed the war on capitalism and endorsed an upcoming peace conference in Chicago. A March editorial criticized the Wilson administration for risking American lives to give "American commerce the right to rob and starve America, to feed the murderous hordes abroad" and suggested putting "a member of the firm of Morgan, of the Rockefeller family, of the Astors or of the Fields on every ship" that sailed into war zones.[57]

Tucker later claimed that Carr fired him because they differed over the war, and that may have been the key reason. In early signed articles, Carr muted criticism of European socialists who supported their nations and urged American socialists to focus on the class struggle at home; by fall 1915, he was differentiating between the warring powers in such a way as to see decided gains for democracy and international peace—if not socialism—in a German defeat. An editorial early in 1916 acknowledged tension in the CSF and called upon members not to let "pacifism" and anti-preparedness distract them.[58] Carr subsequently supported American intervention and converted the *Christian Socialist* into *Real Democracy.*[59]

Tucker's correspondence explains his firing without reference to the war. Instead, it highlights misunderstanding and controversy over personalities, finances, and personal loyalties. Carr's possessiveness toward the paper, which he had created and struggled to keep alive, was a factor. When he returned from his travels in May 1916 to become co-editor with Tucker, he probably expected deference from a man ill-suited to give it. Tucker's financial support, provided by William Cochran and Rufus W. Weeks, a wealthy insurance company executive, patron of many socialist causes, and founding member of the CSF, then provoked disagreements while Tucker was away organizing for the CSF.[60] The fact that Carl D. Thompson, a former Congregational minister, party functionary, and longtime Carr ally, needed work when the fall campaign ended added another element to an emerging crisis.[61] Cochran was upset by the move against Tucker and announced an incremental withdrawal of his contributions. An offer to keep Tucker as associate editor failed to appease Cochran, who had already begun exploring other ways of supporting Tucker.[62]

A position with the Church Socialist League was one option. Cochran was willing to provide his salary if Tucker became editor of the league's *Social Preparation for the Kingdom of God*, and Tucker envisioned combining that with a denomination-wide social service campaign.[63] The two men conferred at the Episcopal convention in St. Louis, Missouri, in October 1916, when Tucker took part in CSL-sponsored alternative meetings like those in 1913.[64] At St. Louis, Tucker decided instead to become an organizer for the Intercollegiate Socialist Society, in which he had been active in New York, while continuing his work with the hobo movement. Cochran, already an ISS supporter and fascinated by a hobo meeting to which Tucker took him, offered $1,500 to support Tucker's work.[65] Tucker did remain involved in the CSL until it dissolved in the 1920s, serving as one of its vice presidents and publishing poems in the *Social Preparation*.[66]

Tucker maintained a tiring schedule of campus appearances until American intervention in April 1917 created a repressive political climate that closed doors even in higher education. He then found work as the Socialist Party's literature director and circulation manager for the *American Socialist*.[67] By speech, poem, and article, as in the privacy of his letters, he assailed the war as a conflict over imperial commerce and bemoaned its cost in American lives and values. The loss of American lives in defense of "Morgan's loans," he wrote his mother, "is a mighty poor investment of 'National Honor.'" Not only were good reasons for involvement lacking, but the nation was becoming like autocratic Germany: conscripting men but not money, stifling a free press, and unleashing intolerance of any dissent.[68] It was sheer hypocrisy, he proclaimed in speech and book, to claim freedom and democracy as aims abroad while brutal plutocracy reigned at home.[69]

By mid-1917 he was prominent enough in the antiwar movement to be elected chairman of the Chicago branch of the People's Council of America for Democracy and Terms of Peace, an organization of socialists and liberals dedicated to a democratic, negotiated peace. In a welcoming speech to a council conference in July, he questioned Woodrow Wilson's honesty about war aims and demanded "home consumption" for the democracy Wilson was trying to export.[70] The council's convention in September, for which Tucker chaired the resolutions committee, was driven out of Minneapolis and was able to meet briefly in Chicago only because Mayor William Hale Thompson, an extravagant Anglophobe, defied Governor Frank Lowden, who then ordered in troops to break it up himself. So threatening to working-class support for the war effort did the council seem that the American Federation of Labor's chief, Samuel Gompers, collaborated with the administration in establishing a pro-war rival.[71]

Two of Tucker's mid-1917 pieces for the *American Socialist*, both reprinted for mass distribution, were the basis for his indictment, with four other socialists, under provisions of the Espionage Act broadly forbidding interference with the draft. Each offered ruinous, utterly bestial images of war. The first, "The Price We Pay," was, if not a direct incitement to draft resistance, surely provocative:

> Into your homes the recruiting officers are coming. They will
>   take your sons of military age and impress them into the army;
> Stand them up in long rows, break them into squads and platoons,
>   teach them to deploy and wheel;
> Guns will be put into their hands; they will be taught not to
>   think, only to obey without questioning.
> Then they will be shipped thru the submarine zone by the hundreds
>   of thousands to the bloody quagmire of Europe.
> Into that seething, heaving swamp of torn flesh and floating
>   entrails they will be plunged, in regiments, divisions and armies,
>   screaming as they go.[72]

Though authorities raided the Socialist Party's national headquarters and the People's Council office on several occasions in the fall of 1917, the indictment did not come down until March 1918, perhaps because of uncertainty about the strength of the government's case.[73] Tucker tempered his utterances following the indictment but did not curtail his public activities while awaiting the trial, which finally began on 9 December 1918. He raised money for the People's Council by lecturing on internationalism and got the lectures printed as a book, helped train socialist candidates for the city council, became educational director of a "labor university" named the Workers' Institute, and ran for Congress.[74]

Under the Espionage Act, the government's task was to prove conspiracy among the defendants: Victor Berger, conservative leader of the highly successful Milwaukee socialists; United Mine Workers' officer and party secretary Adolph Germer; J. Louis Engdahl, editor of the *American Socialist*; William F. Kruse, head of the Young People's Socialist League; and Tucker. Each had written, published, or circulated antiwar material, but they had done so separately and through different media. The five were not, in fact, particularly close. Their convictions on 8 January 1919 and the twenty-year prison sentences pronounced by Judge Kenesaw Mountain Landis were overturned by the Supreme Court over two years later, on 31 January 1921, on grounds that Landis had erred in denying a change-of-venue motion based on his own past prejudicial statements.[75]

Tucker saw the trial as rigged and took a bemused, spectatorial attitude toward it—reading, doodling, working on a poem, and finally, in his statement to the court, identifying the defendants with Christ, who had interfered with the Roman draft, and Landis with Pontius Pilate.[76] His public face was nonchalant, buoyant. He attended a Socialist Women's League party for the defendants, participated in several religious services, and addressed a meeting that celebrated the "new Russia" the weekend after sentencing.[77] He had felt the sting of family criticism (of his patriotism) and family analysis (of his rebelliousness and impatience); the words of Caro Lloyd Strobell, likening his sacrifice on behalf of the revolutionary movement to that of Christ, and the revolutionary movement to "the first days of Christianity," reflected better what he felt.[78]

His activism on behalf of socialism did not slacken. For over two more years, he served the cause with vigor and often at significant personal sacrifice. The spring and summer of 1919 found him in New York twice, raising money for the *Call* and lecturing on imperialism at the Rand School, and in St. Louis, where, building on earlier ties, he spoke at left-wing events.[79] Enlisting in the movement for amnesty for Debs, Kate O'Hare, and other socialist political prisoners, he faced American Legion-inspired mobs in Reading, Pennsylvania, Bridgeport, Connecticut, and other eastern cities in the fall.[80]

As James Weinstein has persuasively argued, the rapid decline of a vibrant prewar Socialist Party was due, broadly speaking, to the war and the Bolshevik Revolution. Despite increases in membership and votes in many locales due to its antiwar position, the party lost an articulate, highly visible pro-war minority. The war, moreover, brought devastating persecution, including suppression of its press, raids on party halls, and destruction of membership records. The Russian Revolution evoked strong support across the socialist ideological spectrum; it also produced an inrush of eastern European immigrants enthralled by the overthrow of a rigid autocracy. Division came, however, over the implications of Bolshevism for America: as a proletarian uprising also possible here, or were there fundamental differences between the two situations? Bitter internal struggles resulted, before 1919 ended, in the formation of two communist parties.[81] Though unhappy with caution he considered excessive, Tucker remained loyal to the Socialist Party: "I am against the Left Wing," he wrote, "and have taken part against their insane folly in public debates."[82]

His enthusiasm for the new Russia was nevertheless fervent. He was buoyed by reports of Bolshevik accomplishments from Albert Rhys Williams, a Boston clergyman who spoke as "special missioner from the Soviet of Russia" to America, and he condemned Washington's anti-Bolshevik actions. Recalling the "chosen nation" paradigm of his childhood, he published a poem by that name in which Russia replaces America as God's messenger and bearer of light to the world. His Rand School lectures on imperialism similarly contrasted an undemocratic and imperial America with a Russia in which "only workers should rule."[83]

As a member of the resolutions committee at the Socialist Party convention in May 1920, he found himself, with Engdahl, a "'leader' of the extreme left wing" in fighting for a platform with more revolutionary language and a warmer embrace of the Russian comrades than the majority of delegates would accept.[84] Defeated on the platform, he especially relished the party's nomination again of Debs, whose acceptance statement expressed his own views. As he told Nell, "[Debs] wants unconditional affiliation with the Third International, he wants friendly relations with the Communists as far as possible, he repudiates vote-catching." Tucker subsequently interviewed Debs in prison and published his views for campaign use.[85]

Tucker campaigned widely for the party in 1920 and composed a lengthy campaign pamphlet, *Now It Must Be Done*. The effects of the party fights had begun to take their toll on morale, audience size, and sales of his books in 1919.[86] The situation in fourteen states he visited was mixed: Some of his work was "awfully hard sledding, some not so hard."[87] Debs received less than a third of the three million or more votes Tucker forecast, but Tucker pressed on. In early 1921 he and Lincoln Steffens spoke widely in the Midwest and West for the Red Star League, a workers'-relief agency focusing particularly on Russian relief.[88]

By March 1921, when Tucker returned to Chicago, he was weary and discouraged. He had been on the road more than half the time since 1917. Not until 31 January 1921, when he was in Montana with Steffens, did the Supreme Court lift the weight of Landis' sentence. Two years under that sentence had drained him of "all my pep and vigor," he told Nell. To be free of it was a great relief, but the ordeal had been real. More important, he found the Socialist Party's situation increasingly bleak. The party was "dead and decomposing" in the West; communists were "everywhere busily digging rat-holes." Only Debs's reputation—"and nothing else under heaven"—kept it alive.[89] The party's drastic loss of membership made Tucker's election to its National Executive Committee in May 1921 less significant than it would have been before.[90]

A frequent speaker at socialist functions in St. Louis during this period, Tucker appeared with Kate O'Hare at a rally in opposition to the Harding administration's disarmament conference in late 1921 and was the main speaker at a July 4th picnic in 1921.[91] His most intense effort, however, was editing *Debs Freedom Monthly*, which appeared between August 1921 and April 1923. Tucker had adored Debs since first seeing him in Madison Square Garden in 1912 and published an affectionate poem upon his death; Debs in turn defended Tucker's reliability in presenting his views.[92] Renamed *Debs Magazine* following Debs's release from prison at Christmas 1921, the journal featured pieces by Debs and Tucker on many topics. Tucker's contributions assailed capitalist peace efforts as futile, condemned the Supreme Court's rejection of child-labor legislation, and supported mining and railroad strikes.[93] His most eloquent—but also most hyperbolic—article, a sequel to "The Price We Pay" titled "The Price We've Paid," rehearsed the consequences of World War I. Suffering, death, unbearable debt, economic dislocation, the loss of the nation's soul, Prussianization of American life—all these to protect an "imperial alliance of bankers."[94]

Despite these endeavors, Tucker's full-time enlistment in socialist politics had ended by the summer of 1921. He needed a less frenetic pace, to be sure. He also needed to support a family with two of the three sons he and Nell would eventually have. The quest for economic stability was long and grim. He asssisted in churches, sold advertising for a sports magazine, got a bookstore to display and sell his woodcarvings, and before the year was out designed and carved samples for a manufacturing company.[95] Nothing really succeeded, and 1922 was worse. Approaching his birthday in January 1923, he observed: "I do not own anything but a typewriter and a set of chisels, but I do know how to use them. I have a great assortment of undeserved friends and a very large accumulation of richly merited notoriety, not to say infamy. . . . Now it is up to me to begin the last half of my life with some sort of a settled business."[96] He hoped that a children's furniture company would be that "settled business," but it dismissed him in a little over a year. He had to accept family contributions to survive that crisis.[97]

Tucker's withdrawal from party activity seems less intentional—less the result of a decision—than his entrance roughly a decade earlier. There is no evidence that he concluded in the early 1920s that socialism was wrong. Rather, his involvement tapered off as socialist networks disintegrated, leaving him without a cause sufficient to give meaning to his life or means of self-support. There is no reason to believe that he would have lost interest in a healthier movement. Later, as a Republican, he told his story without recanting.

In March 1924 Tucker got a position at the *Chicago Herald-Examiner*, and, though Nell believed he had "too great a gift to be marooned on a copy desk," she found him more relaxed and happier. Approaching another birthday in January 1925, he agreed: "All my fine hopes and plans for the betterment of the world gone glimmering. . . . All the books I've written fallen quite flat, my poetry not in demand, my oratorical powers quite on the wane—and yet quite reasonably happy."[98] As head of the copy desk and in other positions, Tucker worked at this paper, which became the *Herald-American*, until retirement. A fulfillment of his earliest vocational instincts, the work seems to have kept him happy. It is significant that his *Out of the Hell-Box* uses the newspaper world to explain life and the Christian faith.

By early 1927, Tucker found a second occupation at St. Stephen's, a neglected parish in a modest North Side neighborhood. Very quickly Tucker turned a parish with a handful of communicants, not into a large one, but into a viable one—and into a hive of activity. By early 1928, he could report the first confirmation class in six years, with eleven members. Parish records indicate significant fluctuations—90 communicants in 1928, 64 in 1931, 225 in 1933, 165 in 1936—but even at worst an improvement over the conditions he had found.[99] Greater success lay in programs that drew outsiders to the neighborhood and attracted attention disproportionate to St. Stephen's institutional strength. His hours at the paper seriously limited neighborhood calling; Nell's observation that he lacked "the qualities that make the Sheperd [*sic*]" may also have been correct.[100] The congregation remained marginal, and a steel and glass structure envisioned in 1930–1931 never materialized.[101]

One focus of Tucker's work at St. Stephen's was promotion of a set of activities related to the legend of the Holy Grail. He revised "The Sangreal," a pageant he had written earlier but then taken up again in the early 1920s, attempting, mostly unsuccessfully despite support from William Cochran, to get it produced in Episcopal parishes, at the University of the South, and at the Episcopal General Convention.[102] "The Sangreal" epitomizes Tucker's susceptibility to heroic dramas and the power of myths and symbols, a fascination evident also in his love of Mardi Gras and his poem "City of Dreams," as well as in his socialism. Uncritically taking legend for history, Tucker believed that Joseph of Arimathea, consecrated by Christ as first bishop of Britain, had brought the chalice from the Last Supper and enshrined it at Glastonbury. Hidden from Saxon invaders, it was venerated by Arthur and his knights, who swore an oath of purity to it. "The distinctive epic of the Anglican church," Tucker asserted, the story proved direct episcopal succession from Christ himself, not through Rome.[103]

By 1928 Tucker established an Order of the Sangeal, with an initiation ritual, a plan for starting chapters, and a process for awarding a Cross of Honor. One of 1933's crosses went to Franklin D. Roosevelt, with a statement praising him for using his office "to protect and defend the common people" but withholding judgment on his policies "in politics, finance or industry."[104] In an effort that failed, a carload of Sangreal "pioneers" set off from St. Stephen's in 1933 to prepare for a colony of hundreds of Depression victims in Louisiana. The Arthurian motif appeared also in the church's Garden of Memory, with its "Arch of Arthur" complete with a stone from Arthur's castle at Tintagel. Playing off the tradition that when Joseph of Arimathea stuck his staff into the ground at Glastonbury it took root and blossomed as a rose tree, Ripley's "Believe It or Not" reported that a tree in Tucker's garden "bore 12 apples last year. One was bad."[105] Tucker explored outlets for his pageant decades after the 1920s. A movie seemed possible, as did an Oberammergau-like festival at Glastonbury, with the Sangreal as the "object of pilgrimage."[106]

Tucker also made St. Stephen's a shrine to culture. Starting with a service for which he got poets to post their work in the church, his vision grew to include donated etchings, woodcuts, paintings, leaded glass windows, stones from around the world embedded in the walls, the Garden of Memory with sculpture and memorial trees, which hoboes helped landscape, plans for a children's tower, and more. By the mid-1930s, Works Progress Administration-organized city tours included St. Stephen's, providing a chance to "meet Friar Tuck in person."[107] A prolific poet himself, he became poet laureate of the Chicago Diocese upon collection of another volume of his works in 1938.[108] There was more in pageantry and rituals of other sorts, including outdoor Indian ceremonies, in one of which Nell was received into the Winnebago tribe.[109]

Tucker's politics moved rightward by the mid-1930s, but his writings throw little light on the process. When in 1953 the House Committee on Un-American Activities heard testimony that hundreds in the clergy, including Tucker, were "secret reds," he responded that he had been an anti-Communist since 1921 and had voted Republican since 1936 (and even given an invocation at the Republican convention in 1944).[110] Why he turned against the New Deal is unclear and troubling, since in 1933 he had selected Roosevelt for a Sangreal cross and offered the administration program suggestions—and himself as an appointee to the Indian Bureau. When in his second autobiography he proclaimed that America was after all the "chosen nation," he emphasized the protection and economic decency it offered workers. As an explanation for his satisfaction with America, more just conditions than prevailed early in the century are certainly relevant. Given the fact that those conditions were pre-eminently a New Deal legacy, however, Tucker might well have ended up a liberal, rather than moving all the way to Republican conservatism.[111]

His employment on a Hearst newspaper may help explain Tucker's conservatism. An "old progressive" who supported Roosevelt in 1932, William Randolph Hearst soured on the New Deal by 1935, and his papers clearly reflected his hostility to the administration. Many observers considered his management style tyrannical. He used the charge of communism as a weapon on domestic issues and tendered Nazi Germany gentle treatment as a bulwark against the Soviet Union.[112]

That Hearst's policies influenced Tucker's opposition to the American Newspaper Guild is also possible. Hearst had long accepted contracts with production unions but fiercely fought the organization of writers as an infringement on freedom of the press; for its part, the guild chose his papers for important strikes.[113]

In his socialist years, Tucker had collaborated with the Industrial Workers of the World and sharply denounced Samuel Gompers and the American Federation of Labor (AFL). He had done so because of the IWW's bold actions in strikes among workers neglected by the AFL, more than because he had worked out a reasoned position on industrial as opposed to craft unionism. Still, one might have expected him to be sympathetic to the industry-wide organizing conducted in the 1930s by the Congress of Industrial Organizations and the guild. During the guild's strike in 1938–1939, however, he aligned himself with the AFL editorial union, wrote and spoke against the strike for the Chicago Federation of Labor's paper and radio station, and crossed the picket line to become what he had condemned before, a "scab." He attacked the guild both for trying to organize "anybody even remotely connected with any phase of the newspaper business" and as a communist organization.[114] Because for a time communists did control the national and some local guilds, Tucker's second point was both accurate and, given his experience in 1919–1921, understandable.[115] For his hostility to industrial unionism there is no obvious answer.

In contrast to World War I, Tucker found World War II a worthy cause and, with two sons fighting, volunteered for the chaplaincy (from which age disqualified him) and adapted a military-like organizational structure for St. Stephen's.[116] In the postwar era, he considered Richard Nixon a more reliable leader than Eisenhower, feared John F. Kennedy's "hair-brained [sic] schemes," and abhorred the upheavals of the 1960s. Consistent with his socialist antiwar sentiments, but now from the Right, he was highly critical of a globalism he saw stretching from Roosevelt and Truman to Kennedy and Johnson and eventuating in tragedy in Vietnam. Nixon received his commendation for trying both to end that war and reduce enormous concentrations of irresponsible power in Washington. His scattered comments on politics in the 1960s and 1970s seem cranky and reflexive at times, not the results of coherent reflection on his past political perspective.[117]

Tucker lived until January 1982, and his last decades contain several other stories in themselves. One involved service for several years to the Church of the

East and its patriarch Mar ("my lord") Eshai Shimun, whose people, commonly called Assyrians, had been displaced from their homeland near the intersection of Turkey, Iraq, and Iran during World War I. They used a dialect of Aramaic, the language of Jesus, and, whether Christianity came to them when the Magi returned from Bethlehem or when St. Thomas went to India, they could claim to be the oldest of Christian communities. Anglicans had an old stake in their welfare, through a mission established in the 1830s, which World War I and the breakup of the Ottoman Empire had brought to an end.[118]

Tucker met Mar Eshai Shimun in the early 1940s. Their antiquity and the authenticity of their rituals interested him as a High Churchman, and their victimization appealed to his compassion and sense of justice. It was also natural for him to identify with the Anglican mission commitment. He served as president of Mar Eshai's Patriarchal Council of America, promoted the study of Aramaic, and translated ancient liturgies. The Cambridge-educated, high-living Mar Eshai eventually disappointed him, but his enthusiasm for the language of Jesus and ancient rituals survived.[119]

Most intriguing was Tucker's conversion in late 1954 to Roman Catholicism, a decision of which he was sure his father, "always a Catholic" himself, would approve. One can only speculate whether the decision was related to Nell's health, which was deteriorating very badly more than a year before her death in February 1955, or to deep disillusionment about St. Stephen's weak condition. The reasons he gave were disillusionment with the World Council of Churches (WCC) as an instrument of Christian unity, and with Protestant shallowness in general, juxtaposed with a vision of Mary inviting him to "come home" at a great Marian Mass held in Soldiers' Field. He felt awe at the Mass's silent solemnity, so unlike the superficial pageantry the WCC had offered at its Festival of Faith in the same stadium earlier in the year. As he began instruction, attended Mass daily, and prepared to leave St. Stephen's, he ranted against his former church, rationalized papal authority, and contemplated making the Sangreal Order Catholic.[120]

His new religious life absorbed him, but the reforms of the second Vatican Council (1962–1965) were especially encouraging. The council's endorsement of more collegial governance, larger roles for the laity, and liturgical reforms (including a vernacular Mass) appealed to the Protestant in him. Without much of a base of support, he put out little mimeographed newsletters, edited the Vernacular Society's *Amen*, and taught briefly at Mount St. Mary's Seminary in Cincinnati.[121] After fourteen years, however, he sought reinstatement as an Episcopal priest, mainly because he had been unable to make friends at St. Margaret Mary's, the Catholic parish he had been attending. Following a canonical waiting period as a layman, he was reinstated in 1970.[122]

On his thirty-fourth birthday, in 1920, Tucker's mother had offered her prayer that he would find "*constructive* work in the Kingdom of God." She chided him not too gently for chafing at restraints, "seeking after the melodramatic," "liking to be in the spotlight," and yearning for direct action.[123] These were indisputable attributes of the man, not only, but especially in his socialist years. Yet what looks to one like excess or extremism, to another may be only desirable commitment or appropriate passion. Radicals are less likely to be patient, less willing to settle for the half-loaves that are inherent in negotiation and compromise, than reformers. They need, moreover, to catch public attention for their causes, to try to move those causes from the margins into the center of civic consciousness and debate, and their methods often seem uncouth, meddlesome, and self-serving.

In Tucker's case, as in many others, the question arises whether the socialist movement attracted him because by its very nature it provided outlets for the temperamental qualities described by his mother. That is, did he find socialism attractive because it offered the soapbox he needed? Affinities between his personality and the movement he served so loyally for a decade were undoubtedly strong. He was, in a more general sense, a man of causes, and a rather passionate one at that: Christian unity, the Holy Grail, incorporation of the arts in the churches, Assyrian Christians, Rome—even copy editing. Different ones engaged him with varying degrees of continuity over an extraordinarily long and complex life. As different as they were in substance, they seem to have been similar for him in function.

Yet Tucker's passion, impatience, and propensity for controversial action expressed more than the drives of personality. They expressed his commitment to an egalitarian ideal of social justice that he located in the Christian faith (with roots in the Hebrew prophetic tradition) and often phrased in the language of his Anglican sacramental theology. Christian ideals, to which he was exposed in a Mobile rectory's nursery, had taken form in his notion of what American society should be like. Experience in newspaper work in New Orleans and other cities revealed a different reality, and New York was an even more profound challenge to that notion. The disparities between rich and poor, heavy-handed capitalist hegemony, and comfortable and complacent churches drew his outrage as unacceptable contradictions to what the prophets and Jesus had had to say about human relationships. His Christianity was not the only element in his decision to become a socialist, but it was a crucial one, mingled with the experiences and contacts amid which that decision occurred.

Tucker's Christianity did not necessitate that he be any particular kind of socialist. It certainly did not align him with the SPA's conservatives, such as Victor Berger of Milwaukee. His Christian socialism was not watered down by fear of confrontation or of the disorderly, unwashed masses. Though he opposed the Left in the party battles after World War I, he was at the same time highly critical of the party's Right for timidity and vote-chasing and agitated for aid to the Bolsheviks. Eugene Debs and Kate O'Hare suited him better than Berger or Morris Hillquit. His earlier cooperation with the IWW also demonstrates his militancy, as does his vigorous public advocacy of the SPA's antiwar position at a time when some fellow Christians and non-Christians abandoned their comrades.

Finally, Tucker's Christianity was not a factor in his withdrawal from the party in the 1920s. He had not replaced his faith with socialism, and so there was no need to abandon one to recover the other. The SPA's decimation left him without a meaning-giving structure of associations within which to live with zest, as well as without means of support. The changed political culture of the United States killed any exuberance he might have retained about bringing about the cooperative commonwealth. Drawn into the socialist movement through a complex web of circumstances and experiences, he left it (with much less fanfare) because of a radically altered situation. The socialist movement had failed to achieve its goal for the United States. Though he moved on in other directions, Tucker did not regret his years in it.

NOTES

1. Paul T. Phillips, *A Kingdom on Earth: Anglo-American Social Christianity* (University Park, Pa.: Pennsylvania State University Press, 1996); Edward Norman, *The Victorian Christian Socialists* (Cambridge, England: Cambridge University Press, 1987). For these organizations, see also William D. P. Bliss, ed., *The New Encyclopedia of Social Reform* (New York: Funk & Wagnalls, 1908).

2. Tucker's two autobiographies tell his story from the perspective of journalism (*Out of the Hell-Box* [New York: Morehouse-Gorham, 1945]) and through his poetry (*The Minstrel Friar: His Legacy of Song* [Chicago: Ralph Fletcher Seymour, 1949]). The collection of his papers in the Department of Special Collections, University Library, University of Illinois at Chicago, is superb. Many of the extended family's frequent letters over the decades are here, as are Tucker's diary, copies of many unpublished as well as published writings, and extensive clippings. A secondary, less well-organized collection is at the Seabury-Western Seminary in Evanston, Illinois. Tucker's and St. Stephen's Church papers in the Episcopal Diocese of Chicago's archives, though not voluminous, contain some unique items. Unless otherwise stated, all subsequent references to the Tucker Papers in this chapter are to the collection at the University of Illinois. The only previous scholarly account of Tucker's life is Jacob H. Dorn, "Episcopal Priest and Socialist Activist: The Case of Irwin St. John Tucker," *Anglican and Episcopal History* 61 (June 1991): 167–96.

3. Irwin St. John Tucker, "'Unto My Life's End': An Appreciation of the Life of the Rev. Gardiner C. Tucker," *Living Church* (17 December 1941): 9–10. For Tucker's genealogical interests, see "The Tucker Family" and "Nil Desperandum," unpaginated typescripts, Tucker Papers, Seabury-Western Seminary.

4. Tucker, *Minstrel Friar*, 20–70.

5. His father often whipped him for his "ungovernable temper." Tucker, *Minstrel Friar*, 39–40. His eldest brother later recalled Tucker's "unusual precocity of intellect and aesthetic," but also "an unusual lack of maturity in most matters practical." Gardiner L. Tucker to Tucker, 29 December 1935, Folder 90, Tucker Papers. On the issues of college and money, see diary, 6 September, 2 October 1902, Folder 112, and Tucker to Mother, 29 August 1905, Folder 60, ibid.

6. Diary, 14 August, 2 October, 19 November 1902, Folder 112, Tucker Papers.

7. Tucker to Father, [25 February 1903], to Mother, 12 May [1903], Folder 58, to Father, 6 January 1906, Folder 61, Tucker Papers. To reduce redundancy, Tucker's letters to individual family members are cited as above, but those to multiple members are cited simply as "to Family."

8. Tucker, *Hell-Box*, 68–76, and Tucker, *Minstrel Friar*, 117–20.

9. This period can be traced in detail in Tucker's diary and in Folders 61–64, Tucker Papers.

10. Clyde Griffen, "An Urban Church in Ferment: The Episcopal Church in New York City, 1880–1900" (Ph.D. dissertation, Columbia University, 1960), 2, 11, 91–93; Tucker to Family, 25 October 1909, Folder 64, 2 January 1910, Folder 65, Tucker Papers.

11. Robert L. Kelly, *Theological Education in America: A Study of One Hundred Sixty-One Theological Schools in the United States and Canada* (New York: George H. Doran, 1924), 195-96, 318; Powell Mills Dawley, *The Story of the General Theological Seminary: A Sesquicentennial History, 1817–1967* (New York: Oxford University Press, 1969), 262, 292.

12. Dawley, *Story of the General Theological Seminary*, 309, 300, 289–91.

13. Ibid., 296, 300–309.

14. Tucker, *Hell-Box*, 78, 84, and Tucker, *Minstrel Friar*, 141.

15. Tucker to Family, 31 January [1910,] Folder 65, Tucker Papers.

16. Tucker to Family, 18 August 1910, ibid.

17. Tucker to Family, 13 October 1910, Folder 65, 25 April 1911, Folder 66, ibid.

18. Tucker to Family, 6 November 1910, Folder 65, ibid.

19. Tucker to Family, 18 March 1912, Folder 67, ibid.; Irwin St. John Tucker, "How I Became a Socialist," *Christian Socialist* 11 (1 February 1914): 7–8. It is not certain that Tucker read Francesco Nitti's *Catholic Socialism* (1890) at GTS. A work frequently cited by socialist Christians, who interpreted its accumulation of harsh pronouncements by the Church Fathers against the rich as socialist, Nitti's book invoked the Fathers in support of the moderate papal social encyclicals. Tucker continued to repeat the assertion that they were anti-capitalist in both autobiographies.

20. Tucker to Family, [10 or 16 June 1906], Folder 61, Tucker Papers; Diary, 30 July, 8, 23 August, 3 November 1908, Folder 112, Tucker Papers; "Brave Preachers Who Give Their Names for Publication as Out and Out Socialists," *Christian Socialist* 5 (15 September 1908): 3–4. Tucker was one of twenty-two Episcopalians but the only Alabamian.

21. Tucker to Father, 11 April 1911, Tucker to Family, 7 May 1911, Folder 66, and 1 January 1912, Folder 67, Tucker Papers. "It Was Suicide" is in Tucker, *Minstrel Friar*, 152. The ISS's historian says that Christians were drawn to it "as by a magnet." Max Horn, *The Intercollegiate Socialist Society, 1905–1921: The Origins of the Modern Student Movement* (Boulder, Colo.: Westview Press, 1979), 98.

22. Tucker to Father, 20 January 1912, Tucker to Family, 1 February 1912, 18 March 1912, Folder 67, Tucker Papers; *New York Call*, 7, 21 March, 27 April, 11 May 1912. For Guthrie's subsequent experiments, see his "Unique Services at St. Mark's, New York," *Churchman* 114 (9 December 1916): 764–65, and, for some truly exotic rituals, three boxes of materials at General Theological Seminary.

23. Tucker to Family, 18 March 1912, Folder 67, 19 March 1910, Folder 65, and 8 July 1912, Folder 67, Tucker Papers; Percy Stickney Grant, "The Open Forum Movement," *North American Review* 203 (January 1916): 81–92, and Percy Stickney Grant, "Working-Men and the Church—An Experiment," in *Socialism and Christianity* (New York: Brentano's, 1910), 193–203; Reuben L. Lurie, *The Challenge of the Forum: The Story of Ford Hall and the Open Forum Movement* (Boston: Richard G. Badger, 1930).

24. *New York Call*, 30 September, 7 October 1912, and subsequent dates; Tucker to Family, 1, 7 October 1912, Tucker Papers.

25. *New York Call*, 13 October 1912. Later series covered "The Economic Basis of Religion," "Great Revolutionary Priests," and "The Truth in World-Religions." "The Socialist Pulpit," pamphlet (n.p., n.d.), Folder 67, Tucker Papers. Tucker also used guest speakers, such as Charles P. Fagnani, a Union Seminary professor who spoke on "Socialism and the Gospels," and W. E. B. Du Bois, who spoke on "Socialism and the Negro." Tucker to Family, 25 November 1912, Folder 67, Tucker Papers; *New York Call*, 15 February 1913.

26. *New York Call*, 13 October, 17 November 1912. Later, Tucker remarked: "Socialism without Christianity is a corpse, and Christianity without Socialism is little better than a ghost." *New York Times*, 19 May 1913.

27. Tucker to Family, 14 December 1912, Folder 67, Tucker Papers.

28. Tucker to Family, 30 January 1913, 10 February [1913], 13 March 1913, Folder 68, ibid. For Schloss' admiration for Jesus, but not Christianity, see *New York Call*, 18 June 1913 and 3 March 1914.

29. Tucker to Family, [October 1912], Folder 67, Tucker Papers.

30. Tucker to Family, 7 October 1912, Folder 67, ibid.

31. *New York Call*, 11 November 1912; Tucker to Family, 25 November 1912, Folder 67, Tucker Papers.

32. Anne H. Tripp, *The I.W.W. and the Paterson Silk Strike of 1913* (Urbana, Ill.: University of Illinois Press, 1987), 34–35, 92–94. Tucker to Family, 30 January 1913, Folder 68, Tucker Papers. For Schloss, see *New York Call*, 21 October, 9 November, 15, 18 December 1912, and 5 January 1913; for St. Mark's Fellowship, *New York Call*, 20 January 1913, and Minutes of Executive Committee, Local New York, 16 December 1912, Socialist Party Minutes, 1900-1936, Socialist Collections in the Tamiment Library, 1872–1956, New York University (microfilm ed.), Reel 9.

33. *New York Call*, 20 April 1913; Tucker to Family, 16 May 1913, Folder 68, Tucker Papers; Tucker, *Hell-Box*, 92; *New York Times*, 19 May 1913.

34. Tucker to Family, 15 June 1913, Folder 68, Tucker Papers.

35. Tucker to Family, 30 March, 24 April 1913, Folder 68, ibid.; *New York Call*, 14, 30 April, 1, 2 May 1913.

36. "Local New York Street Meetings," weeks of 15 September, 25 October, 1 November 1913, and "Minutes of the Meeting of the Seventh Assembly District Committee," 22 August 1913, Socialist Party Papers, New York State, 1906–1912, Socialist Collections in the Tamiment Library, Reel 6.

37. Peter d'A. Jones, *The Christian Socialist Revival, 1877–1914: Religion, Class, and Social Conscience in Late-Victorian England* (Princeton, N.J.: Princeton University Press, 1968), 243–49; "Church Socialist League," in Bliss, *New Encyclopedia of Social Reform*, 225–26.

38. Tucker to Family, 9, 15 June, 5, 13 August 1913, Folder 68, Tucker Papers; *New York Call*, 13 September, 7, 8 October 1913; *Living Church* 49 (18 October 1913): 859. "Exsurgat Deus!" appeared in *Living Church* 49 (4 October 1913):793; see also Irwin St. John Tucker, *Poems of a Socialist Priest* (Chicago, 1914; repr., Sunrise, 1975), 58–59, and Tucker, *Minstrel Friar*, 172–73.

39. *Churchman* 108 (1 November 1913): 599; *Living Church* 50 (1 November 1913): 28; *Christian Socialist* 10 (1 December 1913): 5, 11; *New York Call*, 15, 16, 20 October 1913.

40. *Living Church* 50 (8 November 1913): 47; *Christian Socialist* 10 (15 December 1913): 4.

41. *Christian Socialist* 11 (1 February 1914): 13, and (1 March 1914): 1.

42. Tucker to Family, 28 May 1913, Folder 68, Tucker Papers; *New York Call*, 29 March, 17 May 1914.

43. Tucker, *Hell-Box*, 96.

44. Tucker to Family, 5 December 1913, Folder 68, Tucker Papers; William F. Cochran to Walter Rauschenbusch, 10 March 1915, Box 29, Rauschenbusch Family Papers, American Baptist—Samuel Colgate Historical Library, Rochester, N. Y. For Rauschenbusch, see Jacob H. Dorn, "The Social Gospel and Socialism: A Comparison of the Thought of Francis Greenwood Peabody, Washington Gladden, and Walter Rauschenbusch," *Church History* 62 (March 1993): 82–100. Ray Stannard Baker featured Cochran in "Seeing America: A Rich Young Man Who Began to Believe in Jesus Christ," *American Magazine* 78 (July 1914): 16–17, 76–80.

45. *Christian Socialist* 11 (1 March 1914): 4, and (15 March 1914): 10. Cochran's contributions appear in Carr's reports, Christian Socialist Fellowship, September and October 1914, Box 14, and 1 June 1915, Box 18, National Office Papers, 1896–1969, Socialist Party of America Papers, Perkins Library, Duke University.

46. The poems they exchanged over the years reveal the depth of the bond between them.

47. Tucker to Family, 9 June 1914, Tucker to Bernard Iddings Bell, 9 June, 17 July 1914, and Tucker to Ernest Tucker, [1914], Folder 69, and Diary, 4 July 1955, Folder 112, Tucker Papers.

48. Nell to Tucker, 22 August [1916], Folder 71, ibid.

49. *Christian Socialist* 11 (15 March 1914) and (November 1914), 12 (February 1915) and (September 1915).

50. Tucker to Family, 6 January 1914 [1915], Folder 70, Tucker Papers; *New York Call*, 10 March 1915; *Christian Socialist* 12 (April 1915): 10.

51. Tucker to Family, 25 October 1914, Folder 69, Tucker Papers; *Chicago Herald*, 8 February 1915; Tucker to Family, 19 December 1915, Folder 70, Tucker Papers; Minutes, Delegate Committee, 13 February 1916, Folder 5, Cook County (Ill.) Socialist Party Records, Department of Special Collections, University of Illinois at Chicago.

52. Nell to Father, 31 January 1915, Folder 70, Tucker Papers.

53. Irwin St. John Tucker, "Father Gibson's Twenty Years," *Living Church* (4 October 1939): 9; Tucker to Family, 28 November 1915, Folder 70, 2 March, 7 April, 21 December 1916, Folder 71, 27 January, 6 May, 25 December 1917, Folder 72, Tucker Papers; Hobo College clippings, Folder 6, Tucker Papers; Tucker, *Hell-Box*, 100–105. For How, see "'Millionaire Hobo' is Dead," *Christian Century* 47 (20 August 1930): 1020.

54. William Cochran first got the poem published in the *Baltimore News;* it appears also in Tucker, *Poems of a Socialist Priest*, 39–41; and Tucker, *Minstrel Friar*, 176–77. See "Hull-House Riot" clippings, Folders 9–11, Tucker Papers.

55. Tucker, *Minstrel Friar*, 49–54, and for "The Chosen Nation," 80–90.

56. Nell's Irish nationalism and nationalist associations also undoubtedly influenced his thinking about the British cause. Alexander Trachtenberg, ed., *The American Socialists and the War* (New York: Rand School, 1917), is a compendium of socialist statements from August 1914 to June 1917.

57. *Christian Socialist* 11 (October 1914): 3–4, and 12 (April 1915): 5–6, 13, and (March 1915): 2.

58. Tucker, *Hell-Box*, 105; and Tucker, *Minstrel Friar*, 173–74. *Christian Socialist* 11 (October 1914): 11, 16; 12 (October 1915): 3–4; 13 (February 1916): 7–8.

59. Carr remained a socialist in economic orientation but concentrated on public-ownership issues. In 1932 he made a short-lived effort to revive the *Christian Socialist*.

60. Nell to Tucker, [27 June 1916], and Tucker to Nell, 14 August 1916, Folder 71, Tucker Papers; Cochran to Rauschenbusch, 5 August 1916, Box 30, Rauschenbusch Papers; Rufus W. Weeks obituary, *Tarrytown* (N.Y.) *Daily News*, 18 April 1930.

61. Tucker to Nell, 18 August 1916, Folder 71, Tucker Papers; *Christian Socialist* 13 (10 May 1916): 5, and (21 June 1916): 4.

62. Cochran to Rauschenbusch, 5 August 1916, Box 30, Rauschenbusch Papers; Nell to Tucker, [13 August 1916], Nell to Family, 25 August 1916, and Tucker to Nell, 18, 26 August, 21 September, 21 October 1916, Folder 71, Tucker Papers.

63. Tucker to Nell, 15, 16, 18, 26 August 1916, Folder 71, Tucker Papers.

64. *Living Church* 55 (28 October 1916): 910, and 56 (4 November 1916): 21–22; *Churchman* 114 (4 November 1916): 611; *Christian Socialist* 13 (6 December 1916): 1.

65. Tucker to Nell, 21, 23, 24 October 1916, Folder 71, Tucker Papers.

66. *Social Preparation for the Kingdom of God* 7 (October 1920): 15; Irwin St. John Tucker, "Incense Hymn" and "The Liturgy of God," ibid., 8 (January 1921): 14, and (April 1921): 7–8.

67. Tucker to Mother, 14 February, and Tucker to Family, 25 March, 6 May, 28 June, 3 July 1917, Folder 72, Tucker Papers. Tucker had previously published articles in the *American Socialist* on 4, 11, and 18 September 1915, and 28 October 1916. In a "Suggested War Program" published on 31 March 1917, he had proposed in the event of intervention, confiscation of incomes over $10,000, nationalization of railroads and mines, making speculation in food treasonous, and a role for unions in running industries.

68. Tucker to Mother, 19 June, 30 August 1917, Folder 72, Tucker Papers.

69. Irwin St. John Tucker, "The Flag Day Speech," *American Socialist*, 23 June 1917, and Irwin St. John Tucker, *Have We Made Good? After 141 Years of Democracy* (Chicago: Socialist Party, [1917]).

70. Tucker to Mother, 19 June 1917, Folder 72, Tucker Papers; "Address of Welcome to Second American Conference on Democracy and Terms of Peace," typescript, n.d., Folder 36, Tucker Papers; *American Socialist*, 14, 28 July 1917.

71. Tucker to Family, 23 August, 6 September 1917, Folder 72, Tucker Papers; *American Socialist*, 1 September 1917; *St. Louis Labor*, 15 September 1917; Frank L. Grubbs Jr., *The Struggle for Labor Loyalty: Gompers, the A.F. of L., and the Pacifists, 1917–1920* (Durham, N.C.: Duke University Press, 1968), 58–64.

72. Irwin St. John Tucker, "The Price We Pay" and "Why You Should Fight," *American Socialist*, 5 May, 9 June 1917.

73. Tucker to Family, 6, 30 September 1917, and Tucker to Father, 12 December 1917, Folder 72, Tucker Papers. Two court cases in 1917 involving distribution of "The Price We Pay" produced contrary results. Walter Nelles, ed., *Espionage Act Cases* (New York: National Civil Liberties Bureau, 1918), 56–65; and H. C. Peterson and Gilbert C. Fite, *Opponents of War, 1917–1918* (Madison, Wis.: University of Wisconsin Press, 1957), 33–35.

74. Tucker to Family, 12 March, 29 July, 21 August, 18 September, 10 October 1918, Folder 73, Tucker Papers; Irwin St. John Tucker, *Internationalism: The Problem of the Hour* (Chicago: Privately published, [1918]).

75. Victor Yarros, "The Chicago Socialist Trial," *Nation* 108 (25 January 1919): 116–18; *Victor L. Berger et al., vs. United States of America* (U.S. Circuit Court of Appeals for the Seventh Circuit, October Ten, A.D. 1918. No. 2710).

76. Tucker to Family, 12, 26 December 1918, Folder 73, and 1 January 1919, Folder 74, Tucker Papers; *Chicago Evening American*, 9 January 1919; *100 Years—for What? Being the Addresses of Victor L. Berger, Adolph Germer, J. Louis Engdahl, William F. Kruse, and Irwin St. John Tucker to the Court* (Chicago: Socialist Party, [1919]).

77. Tucker to Family, 14 January, 24 February 1919,Folder 74, Tucker Papers.

78. Tucker to Family, Good Friday 1918, Folder 73, Ernest Tucker to Family, 13 January 1919, and Tucker to Family, 21 January 1919, Folder 74, ibid.

79. Tucker to Family, [March 1919], 10 June 1919, Folder 74, ibid., *St. Louis Labor*, 23 August 1919.

80. With customary wit, he reported being "chased over most of New England by the Gadarene Swine, whose name was Legion." Tucker to Nell, 5 December 1919, Supplement 1, Box 1, Folder 3, and Tucker to A. Mitchell Palmer, 25, 26 November, 12 December 1919, Folder 28, Tucker Papers; *St. Louis Labor*, 6, 13 December 1919.

81. James Weinstein, *The Decline of Socialism in America, 1912–1925* (New York: Monthly Review Press, 1967), Chaps. 3–4.

82. Tucker to Family, 23 July 1919, Folder 74, Tucker Papers.

83. Tucker to Family, 24 February 1919, and Tucker to Gardiner Tucker, 14 June 1919, Folder 74, ibid.; Irwin St. John Tucker, *The Chosen Nation* (Chicago: Privately published, 1919), 42–44, and Irwin St. John Tucker, *A History of Imperialism* (New York: Rand School, 1920), 374–401. Williams published *The Bolsheviks and the Soviets* (New York: Rand School, 1919).

84. Tucker to Nell and children, 19 May 1920, Folder 75, Tucker Papers; *St. Louis Labor*, 15 May 1920; *New York World*, 12 May 1920; convention clippings, Folder 21, Tucker Papers.

85. Tucker to Nell, 30 May 1920, Supplement 1, Box 1, Folder 3, Tucker Papers; *St. Louis Labor*, 12 September 1920; Nick Salvatore, *Eugene V. Debs: Citizen and Socialist* (Urbana, Ill.: University of Illinois Press, 1982), 321–23.

86. Tucker to Family, 13, 23 July, 12 September, 3 November 1919, Folder 74, Tucker Papers.

87. Tucker to Father, 11 October 1920, Folder 75, ibid.

88. Tucker to Nell, 29 January, 6, 7 February 1921, Supplement 1, Box 1, Folder 3, and tour clippings, Folder 33, ibid.; Irwin St. John Tucker, *Soviet Russia and the Red Cross* (Chicago: American Red Star League, n.d.). Tucker bitterly contended that the Red Cross was controlled by the House of Morgan and had sabotaged relief supplies to Russia. Steffens' *The Autobiography of Lincoln Steffens* (New York: Harcourt, Brace, 1931) makes no mention of this trip; Justin Kaplan gives it only a passing reference in *Lincoln Steffens: A Biography* (New York: Simon and Schuster, 1974), 266.

89. Tucker to Nell, 26 January, 1 March 1921, Supplement 1, Box 1, Folder 3, Tucker Papers.

90. Tucker to Family, 11 May 1921, Folder 76, ibid.

91. *St. Louis Labor*, 19 November 1921, 7 July 1923.

92. Eugene V. Debs to Theodore Debs, [22 August 1922], Indiana State University, Terre Haute, Papers of Eugene V. Debs, 1834–1945 (microfilm ed., 1983), Reel 4; Debs to Otto Branstetter, 3 September 1922 (from Indiana State Library), Debs Papers, Reel 4; Debs to David Karsner, 3 December 1922 (from David Karsner Papers, New York Public Library), Debs Papers, Reel 4. Debs to Tucker, 9 September [1922], Folder 27, Tucker Papers. Tucker's poem about Debs, first printed in the *Chicago Herald-Examiner*, appears in Tucker, *Minstrel Friar*, 157–58.

93. *Debs Freedom Monthly* 1 (October 1921): 10–11; *Debs Magazine* 1 (June 1922): 4, 1 (August 1922): 5, 15, and 2 (September 1922): 4, 15.

94. *Debs Freedom Monthly* 1 (September 1921): 8–9, 20–21.

95. Tucker to Family, 19 August, 20 December 1921, Tucker Papers.

96. Tucker to Family, 18 January 1923, Folder 78, ibid.

97. Tucker to Family, 20 February, 26 December 1922, Folder 77, 17 October 1923, Folder 78, 3 January, 14 February 1924, Folder 79, ibid.

98. Nell to Mother, 27 March 1924, Folder 79, and Tucker to Family, 15 January 1925, Folder 80, Tucker Papers.

99. Tucker to Family, 23 March 1928, Folder 83, ibid.; Parochial Reports, 1920–1985, Box 3, Folder 7, and Tucker to Diocese of Chicago, 28 January 1936, Box 1, Folder 19, St. Stephen's Church Papers, Episcopal Diocese of Chicago.

100. Tucker to Family, 5 August 1929, Folder 84, and Nell to Mother, 27 March 1924, Folder 79, Tucker Papers.

101. *Chicago Herald and Examiner*, 29 November 1931; Building Program, 1930–1931, Box 2, Folder 6, St. Stephen's Church Papers, Episcopal Diocese of Chicago.

102. Tucker to Family, 10 September 1921, Folder 76, 28, 31 March, 17 July 1922, Folder 77, Tucker Papers.

103. Irwin St. John Tucker, *The Quest of the Sangreal* (Chicago: Witness Publishing, 1928); Tucker to Family, 10 September 1921, Folder 76, Tucker Papers.

104. Tucker to Family, 25 June 1928, Folder 83, Tucker Papers; typescript, "Awarding the Cross of Honor," [1931], and unsigned copy of letter to Franklin D. Roosevelt, 1 November 1933, Folder 18, ibid.

105. Clipping, [*Chicago Herald-Examiner*, 7 February 1933]; Pamphlet, "The Little Church at the End of the Road" (Chicago: Wild Onion Press, 1941), Folder 15, Tucker Papers; "Believe It or Not," *Chicago Herald and Examiner*, 19 July 1933.

106. Grace M. Byrne to Tucker, 1 December 1952, Folder 107, and Diary, 6, 23, 31 August 1953, 13 January 1954, Folder 112, Tucker Papers.

107. Irwin St. John Tucker, "St. Stephen's Is a Little Church," *Readers Digest* 17 (September 1930): 399–401; St. Stephen's materials, Folders 15–17, Tucker Papers; Beatrice Plumb, "My Peace I Give Unto You," *Christian Herald* (April 1935): 20–21, 37–38.

108. "Friar Tuck," *Time*, 3 October 1938; Irwin St. John Tucker, *Friar Tuck's Breviary: Hymns and Ballads of the Little Church at the End of the Road* (Chicago: Frederick H. Jaenicken, 1938).

109. Tucker to Family, 12 March 1929, Folder 84, 12 June 1930, Folder 85, Tucker Papers.

110. Chicago newspaper clippings, 12 September 1953, Folder 7, ibid. Elizabeth Dilling included him in *The Red Network: A "Who's Who" and Handbook of Radicalism for Patriots* (Kenilworth, Ill.: Privately published, 1934), 328.

111. Harold L. Ickes to Tucker, 21 March, 6 April 1933, Folder 88, Tucker Papers; Tucker, *Minstrel Friar*, 244–45.

112. Rodney P. Carlisle, *Hearst and the New Deal: The Progressive as Reactionary* (New York: Garland Publishing, 1979).

113. Ibid., Chap. 8; Daniel J. Leab, *A Union of Individuals: The Formation of the American Newspaper Guild, 1933–1936* (New York: Columbia University Press, 1970), 243–60.

114. *Federation News*, 11 February 1939, clipping, Folder 49, Tucker Papers. For controversy over Tucker, see Thomas Hendrick to Bishop George Craig Stewart, 17 December 1938, Folder 7, Charles H. Mitchell to Stewart, 23 December 1938, and Tucker to Mitchell, 26 December 1938, Folder 3, and Harry Read to Tucker, 19 June 1939, Folder 4, Irwin St. John Tucker Papers, Episcopal Diocese of Chicago.

115. Leab, *Union of Individuals*, 222, 268, 282.

116. Tucker, *Hell-Box*, 26–30; St. Stephen's Church clippings, Folder 17, Tucker Papers.

117. Diary, 29 November 1957, 8 November 1960, and summer 1968–June 1971 passim, Folder 112, Tucker Papers. The United Nations, he wrote, was chiefly devoted to recognizing "tiny tribal 'republics' hardly more than territorial gangs." 1 July 1970, ibid.

118. J. F. Coakley, *The Church of the East and the Church of England: A History of the Archbishop of Canterbury's Assyrian Mission* (Oxford, England: Clarendon Press, 1992).

119. "I Meet the Patriarch of the East," "A Nestorian Book of Prayers," and other manuscripts, Tucker Papers, Seabury-Western Seminary; Diary, 1, 3 September 1953, Folder 112, Tucker Papers. Several copies of the Patriarchal Council's *Light from the East* are at Seabury-Western. Mar Eshai Shimun was assassinated in 1975. The Church of the East, a constituent member of the World Council of Churches, continues to have a difficult existence in Iraq. Coakley, *Church of the East*, 362.

120. Diary, 1 October 1954, 16 February 1955, 17 August 1953, Folder 112, Tucker Papers; Irwin St. John Tucker, "Mother Mary Opens the Door," *Extension* 49 (March 1955): 12–13ff., and "I Was Converted Through Mary," *Our Lady's Digest* 10 (May 1955): 23–34; Diary, 1 October-5 December 1954, Folder 112, Tucker Papers. Tucker announced his resignation to his bishop and asked him to raise a purse for his retirement before letting the bishop or anyone at St. Stephen's know the reason. Tucker evidently found breaking old ties difficult, for months later the bishop insisted that he stop visiting the church. Tucker to Gerald Francis Burrill, 27 October, and Burrill to Bishop's Committee, St. Stephen's, 5 November 1954, Box 2, Folder 20, St. Stephen's Church Papers, Episcopal Diocese of Chicago; Burrill to Tucker, 2 May 1955, Box 1, Folder 19, ibid.

121. *The Briefery* seems to have appeared in 1961–1962, *Sunrise* from 1964 to 1973, and some issues of *New Sunrise* in 1976. *Sunrise* also reflected Tucker's long interest in Aramaic. Tucker wrote articles for the Catholic periodicals *Christian Family*, *Ave Maria*, *Marianist*, and *North American Voice of Fatima*. He went to Cincinnati thinking he would seek Roman Catholic ordination, but the experience changed his mind. Diary, 2 January 1967, Folder 112, Tucker Papers.

122. Diary, 2, 16 March 1968, Folder 112, Tucker Papers; "Priest Pioneers Unity," *Chicago Today*, 7 July 1970.

123. Mother to Tucker, 3 January 1920, Folder 75, Tucker Papers.

7

Christianity, Democracy, and Socialism: Bouck White's Kingdom of Self-Respect

Mary E. Kenton

Bouck White, one of New York City's most notorious radicals in the World War I era, was born in Middleburgh, New York, on 20 October 1874.[1] He was christened Charles Browning in honor of his father and paternal grandfather. His birth completed the family of Charles Addison and Mary Jane White; their only other child was a daughter, Alice. When noticing that the Whites had been "son struck," the local newspaper mentioned that "Charlie," a dry-goods merchant in the small Catskill village, had ordered a case of boots in honor of the occasion.[2] In this prosaic way was the fiery and visionary personality of Bouck White introduced to the world. But certainly the editor of the *Middleburgh Gazette* had no reason to suspect that the son of the well-to-do Methodist and prohibitionist Whites would grow up to declare commerce the root of all evil, to proclaim Jesus a socialist, and to advocate New York City's secession from the United States to become an independent wet republic.

The Whites' roots in upstate New York went back to colonial times. Though mostly farmers, laborers, and blacksmiths, the family had produced a Democratic governor in the 1840s, Mary Jane's great-grandfather, William C. Bouck.[3] There is also family lore of a distant ancestor marrying an "Indian maid," a theme that Bouck returned to much later in his life.[4] Bouck's paternal grandfather, Brownen White, was notoriously shrewd, hardworking, and parsimonious. When he died intestate in 1878, he left a small fortune of $20,000 to Charles, enough for him to sell his store and live the life of a country gentleman. A proud and vain man, he enjoyed rumors of his great wealth and later bragged that he had never worked a day in his life.[5]

Left with nothing useful to do, Charles devoted himself to managing his family and his money. A petty tyrant who bought his wife's clothes and often humiliated her in public, Charles made all the decisions concerning the two children. Fortunately for everyone, he took a long trip each winter to Florida to oversee his orange grove and real estate investments. The rest of the family joined him for a few weeks each year, so everyone had a break from small-town family life and the gossip that their unusual arrangements generated.[6]

It was common knowledge that Bouck was the favored child in the White household with the person who counted, Charles. As one villager put it: "Bouck could ask for a dime and get a dollar, while Alice could ask for a dollar and get a dime."[7] Charles's tightfistedness was no match for Bouck's tenacity. He could always wheedle what he wanted from his father. Alice and Bouck were never close as children. That Alice was three years older perhaps played a part in their lack of affection, but their father's obvious preference for his son must have engendered resentment. As an elderly woman, Alice recalled how she had begged her father for years for a bicycle and never got one. Bouck, however, with patient coaxing was successful. Alice's summation of the incident has more than a tinge of bitterness in it: "He had a way of making everyone come across."[8] Alice was the rebellious child in the White family. A relative characterized her as "Peck's bad boy in skirts." She became so uncontrollable in public school that she was sent away to a private academy. As a young woman Alice was an active participant in Middleburgh's social scene and had "a great round of love affairs."[9] She shared none of Bouck's love of books.

Bouck was always an outstanding student. He received the Regents' Diploma from Middleburgh Academy in 1887 when he was just thirteen.[10] The principal of the academy, Roland Keyser, who held a Ph.D. from Syracuse University, urged Bouck to continue his education there. Bouck attended classes at Syracuse from 1891 to 1894 but was dissatisfied with its "narrow, rigid curriculum." He decided to transfer to Harvard, where, under the elective system introduced by President Charles W. Eliot in 1869, he could get the courses he wanted.[11]

White entered Harvard with junior standing in 1894.[12] In addition to his course work, he was active in the Forum (debate club) and the Total Abstinence League, a continuation of his parents' activity in the Prohibition Party. In a class of 274, White was one of only nine Methodists. Only one other student claimed the Prohibition Party. Most of his classmates were older and did not abstain from liquor.[13] Perhaps these differences help to explain the fact that White spent two years at Harvard without establishing any lasting friendships.

White's ambition was to be a journalist, and the courses he chose were suited to that goal. He took several semesters of English literature, composition, and rhetoric. American history and economics were strong interests. His economic classes are suggestive of his later career: from Edward Cummings he had "The Social and Economic Condition of Workingmen in the United States and Other Countries," and under F.W. Taussig he studied "Railway Transportation."[14] But like so many other students, White fell under the spell of William James. He fancied himself a pragmatist, and there are echoes of James scattered throughout his writings.

Despite his father's pleadings that he become a businessman, White's heart was set on journalism. Shortly after graduation from Harvard in 1896, he went to work for the *Springfield* (Massachusetts) *Republican* as a reporter assigned to the city desk.[15] His stay there was short and undistinguished. He made no friends and impressed his editor as slightly eccentric.[16] White later said, "The *Springfield Republican* made a man of me," and he always counted his year as a reporter as one of the most important in his life.[17]

Lucy Weeks Trimble, White's only published biographer, reports that while in Springfield White received a call from an "unseen Power" to enter the ministry. He insisted that "he was called to the ministry in a Paul-like experience." While lying in a hammock, "he heard a voice tell him to begin preaching the word of God." He continued to hear the voice for several days. According to Trimble, this call came at a crucial point in his life. In a passage tantalizing for its brevity, she describes White's dilemma:

The call that came to him was sudden, unexpected, and of almost dramatic intensity. It had in it, moreover, a number of features that were unwelcome to him. There had come to him the temptation, and from the worldly point of view, the opportunity of his life: a successful career as a lawyer for a great corporation, wealth, and with these the fulfillment of Love's young dream, all were his for the taking. But when he realized that this meant a service, not to protect the poor from the injustice of the law, but to protect the great corporation from paying to the poor what they would justly receive under the law, he made his final choice, and decided to serve his Master in the ministry.[18]

Anxious to heed the "inner voice," White applied for and received a local preacher's license from the Methodist Episcopal Church. Both of his parents were totally opposed to his decision to become a clergyman. His father believed he had already spent too much on his son's education. But, as usual, Charles gave in to his son's determination. White left Springfield in 1898 to enroll in the Methodist-affiliated Boston Theological Seminary. After completing a special one-year course, he transferred to Union Theological Seminary in New York.[19]

At the turn of the century, the Social Gospel was entrenched at Union, which had been "in the vanguard of the movement" for the sociological study of religion. As early as 1894 the seminary provided its students with the opportunity to gain first-hand knowledge of urban problems through participation in the Union Seminary Society for Christian Work.[20] The alumni organized the Union Settlement Association in 1895 "for the maintenance of Settlements in New York City for the assertion and application, in the spirit of Jesus Christ, of the principles of brotherhood along the lines of educational, social, civic, and religious well-being." The Union settlement was "for many years . . . one of New York's most significant social-service establishments."[21] No seminary outdid Union's attempts to make Christianity responsive to social problems and to bring it to the community.

White was privileged to study under a remarkable group of men at Union. It seems fair to suggest that in education and scholarship, Union's faculty was rivaled only by the group assembled by William Rainey Harper at the University of Chicago's divinity school. White made good use of his opportunities; he was, on the whole, a fine student. In the days when a C was still a respectable grade, he managed to graduate with an average of 87.39. It would have been above 90 had he not received a 48 from Charles Augustus Briggs in biblical theology. There is no explaining White's miserable failure; in two other courses with Briggs, he earned high marks.[22]

Briggs was one of the more controversial members of Union's faculty. An outstanding scholar, by the 1890s he was recognized "as the leading Presbyterian exponent of critical views."[23] Briggs believed that the church had become so preoccupied with sanctification and salvation in a future life that it was "unresponsive to modern life, with the result that most humanitarian enterprises [had] been carried on outside the church and sometimes against the opposition of its leaders."[24] Briggs' inaugural address as professor of biblical theology offended conservative Presbyterians and led to his trial for heresy in 1892. Acquitted by the Presbytery of New York, he was later tried by the General Assembly, condemned, and suspended from the ministry. Among those who came to his defense was fellow Social Gospel adherent Washington Gladden, who preached a sermon titled "Heresy Trials and What They Prove."[25] The two-year struggle became an international event marked by "publicity, controversy, and bitterness." The faculty and board of directors stood behind Briggs and "Union emerged from the struggle as a champion of freedom for scholarship in matters of faith and religion."[26] As a result of the controversy Union broke off its loose affiliation with the Presbyterian Church.

Another of White's teachers at Union, Arthur Cushman McGiffert, was driven from the Presbyterian Church for his liberal beliefs. McGiffert's offense came in his classic study, *History of Christianity in the Apostolic Age*. In this moderate account of the New Testament period, McGiffert questioned in a footnote whether Christ had meant to establish the Lord's Supper as a perpetual rite. After censure by the General Assembly in 1898 and again the following year, McGiffert withdrew and joined the Congregationalists. He served ably as president of Union from 1917 to 1926.[27]

A strong socialist and ardent suffragist, Charles Prospero Fagnani was probably the most politically liberal of White's teachers at Union.[28] He was named instructor of Hebrew at Union in 1892. Fagnani was noted as a dynamic speaker and a man of great personal charm. In 1926 the *Alumni Bulletin* paid tribute to the strength of his social vision: "In his indignation over all that savors of oppression and exploitation, the spirit of the prophets of the old dispensation seems to speak again; and in his sympathy for the poor and neglected and his zeal for the universal brotherhood, one feels the spirit of the new."[29] Perhaps at least part of the credit should go to Fagnani for White's lifelong willingness to fight the battles of the underdog.

Years later, when he was under fire from almost all sides, White liked to point out that he had been certified by two of the best schools in the country, which he hinted were responsible for his social theories.[30] Certainly he had been exposed to some of the most progressive thinking of his time at Harvard and Union. Indeed, the seeds of his later radicalism may have been planted in his student days, but when White left Union in 1902 he was no socialist.

Union encouraged settlement work as a way for students to gain practical experience as ministers.[31] Instead of working with the huddled masses of New York City, White chose to spend his school vacations ministering to a small group of forgotten mountaineers.[32] His field was in the Ramapos, "the picturesque mountains where the Erie Railroad winds up from New York City."[33] His flock were the descendants of the Scots, English, and Hessians who had settled there in the Revolutionary War era. White became so attached to these sturdy, proud individualists that after his graduation he spent a year living among them. His home was an isolated woodchopper's cottage "in a clearing in the forest far from the railroads."[34] The year was one of solitude and unaccustomed privation. White was befriended by "Aunt Hale," whom he credited for helping to keep him alive "during that year in 'Doodletown' in the woods, among the deserters still hiding (as they supposed) from the Officers of General George Washington's army."[35]

White published his first book, *Quo Vaditis? A Call to the Old Moralities*, in 1903. Much of it was probably written while he was in the Ramapos. *Quo Vaditis* reveals that White had not yet come to a socialist position. In it he supported neither labor nor capital and condemned ministers who take sides.[36] More than anything else, *Quo Vaditis* is a Whitmanesque paean to Jeffersonian America. It pours out White's love of the land, his reverence for the Constitution, and his despair over the materialistic bent of modern society. Although *Quo Vaditis* hints at White's later position on many issues, much more time had to pass before he was ready to declare revolution the highest spiritual act.

White left no clues as to why he went to the mountains or why he chose to leave when he did. Trimble records only that the experience "deepened his life appreciably."[37] Sometime during the first half of 1904 White was hired as minister of the First Congregational Church in Clayton, New York, a small resort community on the St. Lawrence River. This position necessitated his ordination. The service was held Friday evening, 1 July 1904, at his new church.[38] He had finally fulfilled his father's sarcastic prediction that all of the expensive education he had given Bouck would qualify him for nothing more than "to preach in some deserted rural church."[39]

During White's ministry at Clayton, he established several themes that would in variations recur throughout his career. He learned the value of advertising almost immediately. Attendance at his services rose dramatically after he contracted with the local paper to advertise church matters. He identified most strongly with the young people. His personal eccentricities and air of high culture made him an object of ridicule among the town's working classes, but the children and the wealthy summer colonists took an immediate liking to him.[40] He established an outstanding Boys' Club, "the only thing of its kind in the whole North Country," replete with meeting rooms, a gym, bowling alleys, and a printing press.[41]

White's success with the Boys' Club also precipitated the problems with the Catholic community that eventually drove him out of town. Clayton's sizeable Catholic minority was French in ancestry and poor and unassimilated. White's anti-Catholicism is apparent in all his writings and probably originated in his rural Protestant upbringing and his visceral reaction against anything with an authoritarian structure. His club was popular with all the boys in town. Catholic parents feared he was luring their sons to the club to ply them with Protestant teachings.[42] A local school board election provoked the final confrontation. A discussion of the issues degenerated into name-calling on both sides. White preached against the Catholics and printed his sermon and distributed it throughout the community.[43] A campaign developed to force him to leave; vandalism against the club and his sailboat and threatening letters surely contributed to his decision to take a position at Lewis Avenue Congregational Church in Brooklyn.

White had met the senior pastor, Robert J. Kent, during the summer season at Clayton. Kent was obviously impressed with White's accomplishments at Clayton and hoped that he could work similar miracles with Lewis Avenue's large Sunday school. But White had a new idea. Somewhere he had picked up Episcopal Bishop Henry C. Potter's notion that young people should take citizens' oaths, following the example of ancient Athens.[44] Potter conceived of the oath as a symbolic act against governmental corruption. A citizen, he believed, "must do more than maintain the integrity of the soul; [he] must aim to save his country as well as himself."[45] White became so entranced with the idea that he decided to devote his life to it. But dedication was not sufficient to keep the oath crusade from total failure within a few months. The Lewis Avenue congregation found him too odd, and he was not kept on.[46]

In addition to bringing him his first crushing defeat, the citizens' oath crusade left White broke and without any means of support.[47] If he followed past patterns he surely next would have appealed to Charles for money. But the evidence seems to indicate that for once Charles stood firm. He had warned his son that he could not succeed in the ministry, and the failure at Lewis Avenue seemed to validate his position. Charles had a vindictive streak, and it is not hard to imagine him rubbing salt into his son's wounded ego. This scenario depicts a plausible explanation for the drastic action that White now took: He disinherited his father! A few years later White declared: "No person ever lived who needed a father over him," but for the present he was content to shed his own.[48]

On 15 November 1907, White appeared before Judge Norman S. Kike in Kings County Court and changed his legal name from Charles Browning White to Bouck White.[49] Bouck, of course, was his mother's maiden name. He wrote to Harvard almost immediately, giving notice of the legal action and requesting the necessary changes in his official record. Always proud of his Harvard diploma, but no longer comfortable with the one bearing the discarded name, he inquired about the cost of securing a replacement, one that would recognize his new identity.[50] Thus did White repudiate his father, embrace his mother, and move on with his life.

With this dramatic gesture and in a state of destitution, White entered the most productive and influential decade of his life. Before fading into obscurity after World War I, he would publish several influential and controversial books, found his own church, run for Congress on the Socialist Party ticket, and spend three terms in jail for putting his principles into practice. But first, he had to find another job.

White appealed to John Howard Melish, rector of Holy Trinity Episcopal Church in Brooklyn, for whatever work might be available. Although they had been classmates at Harvard, apparently their first meeting had taken place some months earlier when Melish allowed White and Potter to use his church to promote the citizens' oath crusade. Melish immediately offered him a job working with the young men of Trinity Club. Melish confessed embarrassment at offering a man of White's experience and training only room, board, and fifty dollars a month. "Experience," White told him, "does not give you something to eat, and my ability at present is unable to furnish me with a bed. I will take the job for whatever you pay." Their arrangement was to last five years.[51]

According to Melish, White's work at Holy Trinity was superb. Formed in 1906, Trinity Club had approximately 300 members when White took charge. Many of the members were Catholic or Jewish boys who paid ten cents a week to have a hot shower and play on Trinity's powerful athletic teams.[52] White, always the ardent democrat, spent his energy teaching democracy to the sons of New York immigrants. He decided to let the boys run their own club. They elected an executive committee, held debates and discussions, and, in true democratic fashion, published their own newspaper. Melish concluded that White's methods achieved a high level of group cohesion and practical results.[53] Once again, White proved he could work miracles with young people.

White's duties at Trinity Club were not overtaxing. He had plenty of time to wander New York's streets and to think deeply about what he saw. The poverty of the tenement dwellers touched him for the first time, especially as it stood in sharp contrast with the opulence of the city's fashionable neighborhoods. White's "daily work in caring for the social debris thrown down by the grinding of the economic machine, rapidly brought [him] into the Socialist position."[54] No doubt he also heard socialist speakers and read the socialist press. Socialism was in the air. It was the next logical step for a young intellectual already primed with the latest in liberal and progressive thought. The research and writing he was doing surely also helped to focus his thinking. Always a passionate advocate for any cause he embraced, he decided to formalize his conversion to socialism. It was probably in 1909 or 1910 that he joined a branch of Local New York and became a regular speaker on behalf of the Socialist Party. His liberal education at Union had paved the way, but it took direct, daily contact with the squalor of city life to push White to a radical position.

White kept his efforts for the Socialist Party separate from his work at Trinity. He never mentioned his new sympathies to Melish, nor did he discuss his latest project: "a loosely rendered" life of one of the founding fathers of Wall Street and the principal benefactor of the Methodist Drew Theological Seminary. When *The Book of Daniel Drew* went on sale in April 1910, it caused an immediate sensation.[55] As the first comprehensive account of Drew's career, the book received wide attention. It was written in autobiographical form, and most reviewers took the first-person voice literally, assuming that Drew actually wrote the book, with White playing only editorial and promotional roles. During the discussion of the authenticity of the book, someone revived a 1905 story from the *New York Tribune* on the discovery of the Drew diaries. The story concluded that the diaries were being readied for publication.[56] Drew's family denied the existence of any diary, and the subsequent raucous debate over the validity of the book kept the family and the seminary in an embarrassing spotlight for weeks.

White's portrayal of Drew as a totally unscrupulous businessman who would lie, cheat, and steal if a dollar could be made in the process naturally stung Daniel's son, William Henry. He and his attorney, Frederick S. Barnum, explored the possibility of seeking an injunction to forbid Doubleday, Page, and Company from continuing to issue the book. Unperturbed by the threat and probably glad of the publicity, the publishing house issued a statement denying legal culpability in any libel case. In the opinion of Doubleday's lawyers, the only legal recourse available to William Drew was a personal libel suit against White. Contending that his father was practically illiterate and had left behind no writings of any character, William Drew filed a complaint of criminal libel against White with Manhattan District Attorney Charles S. Whitman. White welcomed the chance, he said, to prove in open court that what he had said about "Uncle Dan" was true. On 7 May, just ten days after initiating the action, William Drew formally withdrew his charges. He was unable to specify an offensive passage.[57]

White obviously enjoyed watching those associated with the Drew name squirm—and squirm the Methodists did. The *Brooklyn Eagle* reported that "Methodist circles [were] in an uproar, especially Drew Seminary."[58] White subsequently claimed he was not attacking the Methodist church; rather he was trying to save it from its connection with a corrupt businessman so that it could play its destined role in the redemption of America. His objective, he said, was to decanonize Daniel Drew. He wanted the seminary to drop Drew's name and return to the Erie Railroad (from which it was originally stolen) the money Drew had donated. White concluded that "if the authorities of Drew Seminary could persuade themselves to this act of justice, their deed would stand as a lighthouse, whose rays would pierce the spiritual and moral darkness that is now covering the country, and reach to the uttermost parts of these United States."[59]

The seminary was in bad financial shape, largely because Drew had failed to pay the entire $250,000 he had pledged as an endowment. Most likely, the trustees never considered returning the donations, but they feared they would be obliged to change the seminary's name if White's charges were proved. Since changing the name "would involve the institution in expensive legal complications with respect to the legacies with which it [had] been endowed," President Henry Anson Buttz was anxious to avoid this, as yet, "unnecessary expense."[60] The faculty and administration managed to weather the humiliation of awkward questions from mischievous students and New York reporters; they were, no doubt, relieved when William Drew dropped the charges, and the story faded from public consciousness.

The validity of White's portrait of Drew is open to serious question. He never produced the mysterious diary and, when asked about it in 1948, denied its existence.[61] How then did he put together an account accurate enough to dissuade Drew's family (probably on advice from the District Attorney's Office) from pressing suit? Several explanations have been offered. The truth probably takes something from each. Minnie Hotaling, White's friend since his pastorate at Clayton, maintained that he acquired his information "by roaming around the old Drew haunts, interviewing old codgers who knew him."[62] James R. Joy, assistant editor of the *Christian Advocate*, concluded in his review of the book: "Mr. White has brought forth nothing new. The contents of his book appear to be largely a recapitulation of the newspaper stories which were printed in Mr. Drew's day."[63]

Although Clifford Browder, who published a scholarly biography of Drew in 1986, never found evidence of the missing diary, he was able to identify several literary sources from which White borrowed liberally.[64] The conclusion is inescapable that White deliberately misled the public. He may not have been legally guilty of libel, but he certainly perpetrated a fraud.

Obviously, *The Book of Daniel Drew* does not espouse socialism, but it is a book that would gladden the heart of any Marxist. White's decision to tell the story from Drew's point of view makes the anti-capitalist message even stronger. The reader is drawn into the narrative and the powerful characterization of Uncle Dan. The stories that illustrate capitalist depravity are colorful, memorable, and entirely believable. *Daniel Drew* was White's first effort to synthesize his opposition to both predatory capitalism and a Christianity organized to keep the monied classes in power.

The measure of his success is that the book has taken on a life of its own. It has been reprinted several times and was translated into German. In 1937 RKO released a film, *The Toast of New York*, loosely based on White's book. The Hollywood version, staring Cary Grant and Frances Farmer (herself persecuted as a radical during the McCarthy era), pushed Drew into the background and made Jim Fisk the main character to give some romance and glamour to the story. Frank S. Nugent reviewed the film for the *New York Times,* dismissing it as "only moderately entertaining," unhistorical, and overly romantic.[65] *Daniel Drew* is the only creation of White's to survive, and it is in many ways his best writing. It is wickedly funny, and White's telling points about untempered capitalism and evangelical religion have contemporay relevance.

The furor over *The Book of Daniel Drew* had barely died down when White created another sensation with the publication in 1911 of *The Call of the Carpenter*, another loosely rendered biography. It was, by all accounts, White's most influential book. No one who read it could remain neutral. Melish had agreed to introduce it without having read the manuscript. When he finally did, he learned for the first time of his colleague's socialist connections. Despite the fact that he disagreed with many of White's conclusions, he kept his promise and wrote a favorable introduction, which unfortunately appears only in the rare first edition of the book. A friend of radicals in the Episcopal Church Socialist League, Melish believed the book had real merits but thought White's journalistic training had caused him to sensationalize his arguments. When he asked why he had not been allowed to see the manuscript prior to publication, White replied: "I was afraid you would take the edge off of it."[66] Skirting the theological issues, Melish said of *The Call of the Carpenter*:

The aim of this book is to make Jesus the most interesting person in history, and it succeeds splendidly. It is a book which everyone interested in the religion of Christ should read in order to get the social basis of the gospel. It is a book which everyone interested in the social question should read that he may have a new view of the religion of Christ.[67]

Others were even less restrained. George D. Herron, author of *The Call of the Cross* (1892) and one of the first to synthesize Marxian socialism and Christianity, concluded: "Bouck White has spoken a word that once it goes forth, will never return. *The Call of the Carpenter* will not only prove to be an historic book, but it is a book that will assuredly be one of the makers of history."[68] The Reverend W.D.P. Bliss, prominent Christian Socialist and founder of the Church of the Carpenter in Boston, endorsed it as "a book unquestionably of genius and prophetic fire."[69] Socialist politician Eugene V. Debs found in *The Call* a portrait of Jesus that confirmed his own sense that Jesus was a friend and comrade of the working man. Debs concluded that *The Call of the Carpenter* was the greatest book since *Les Miserables* and urged everyone to read it.[70] In summing up "one of the most widely read books of recent years," Doubleday, Page, and Company announced: "Clergymen endorse it as voicing the true spirit of religion, reformers endorse it as voicing the spirit of social reform, and yet others attack it as revolutionary and inflammatory. But it is not blasphemy any more than it is orthodox. It is a reverent and modern interpretation of the greatest character the world has ever known."[71]

The book was indeed talked about. It spawned several spin-off articles and one book-length rebuttal.[72] It brought White to real prominence in radical circles. The first edition of 2,000 sold rapidly, and it reportedly went through ten printings. It was widely advertised in the socialist press, and was sometimes offered as a premium for subscription. Many on both sides saw the book as a successful attempt to capture Jesus for the workers in the ongoing battle between capital and labor. Its popularity made the conservatives even more incensed. The vestry at Trinity did not like the publicity or the associations the book's author brought to the church, and members demanded that White be tried for heresy. Melish pointed out that since White was not an Episcopal clergyman a heresy trial was not possible.[73] What was it about this book that aroused such passionate feelings on both sides?

White claimed for *The Call of the Carpenter* that it was based on the latest scholarship, but it was clearly not a scholarly work. Totally without the usual scholarly paraphernalia, this work aimed for a popular audience. White took what he had learned at Harvard and Union and applied his own imagination and point of view with abandon. In its passionate advocacy of a religion that demanded a more just society, *The Call of the Carpenter* made a valiant attempt to fuse Marxian socialism, Jeffersonian democracy, and the message of the Galilean carpenter.

The first part of the book is a biography of Jesus in the tradition of the search for the historical Jesus. White retold the gospel stories in naturalistic terms. In White's gospel, there was no virgin birth, no heavenly father, no miracles, no bodily resurrection. White stripped the gospels of any theological overlay and recast the stories as examples of class conflict. Everything is interpreted in relation to the despotic Roman Empire. White found in Judaism a strong democratic tendency. This tendency came to fruition in Mary, who possessed an "uncommon force of character."[74] Proud, independent, unconventional, and fierce minded, Mary passed her hatred of Roman oppression and her yearning for economic justice on to her sons, Jesus and James, and to their cousin, John the Baptist. Without Mary there would have been no Jesus movement.

As Rome's grip tightened, poverty grew more desperate in Palestine. Few were able to make a living no matter how hard they worked. The working classes feared they were being pushed daily toward slavery. In this context, John the Baptist gathered a following. He inveighed against the ruling order, but according to White had no constructive view of the future. That is why, with John's encouragement, Jesus took over leadership of this nascent working-class movement. Jesus, "one of the master intellects of all time," had a vision of making " the Jews the nucleus of a federation of the world's proletariat against the world's oppressor." He meant to have a revolution, not start a religion. White concluded that Jesus' thinking was not clouded by theology. The main message of "the Carpenter of Nazareth was economic and only secondarily religious." The dominant religious group, the Pharisees, were little more than a tool of the Romans, in White's view. The Pharisees were guilty of "class hatred" toward the working people of Galilee. They kept for themselves all the privileges of their learning and had nothing but contempt for those who worked with their hands. Ignorance was tantamount to sinfulness. Between Jesus and the Pharisees there could be no rapport: "The Pharisees aimed at building up a church, Jesus aimed at building up society."[75]

As the people responded more and more to the revolutionary message Jesus proclaimed, the Romans began to see him as a threat to the social order that provided them with a life of material abundance. They sent spies to his meetings to ask tricky questions, but Jesus always managed to avoid their traps. Parables allowed him to get his message across without giving the Pharisees or Romans direct evidence of his seditiousness. Jesus became more daring against the Temple priests who enriched themselves at the expense of the populace, protected by a Roman garrison. When Jesus drove the money lenders from the Temple, he became "the hero of the city."[76] His enormous popularity offered some protection from the authorities, who determined to kill him. But all his precautions were subverted with a bribe and a trap, and he was hauled into a hastily convened night court and sentenced to die before the city's masses awoke from their Passover feasting.

White emphasized that it was the Romans who killed Jesus: "Crucifixion was characteristically Roman. It was the method by which those lords of the earth put their slaves to death." Jesus, who tried to inspire self-respect among the masses, was the "fatal enemy" of a system built on and maintained by human degradation. It was the Romans who committed "the greatest crime in history."[77] Even as he was dying on the cross, Jesus thought about the movement. He would live on in the cause so long as his disciples carried the message. When the people awoke to find their hero dead, the ensuing riot rocked the city like an earthquake and was not quelled by the Romans until the Temple veil was rent asunder.

Despite the best efforts of the Galileans, Jesus' message was eventually subverted by Paul and Greek philosophy. What the Romans could not accomplish with persecution, Paul in all sincerity achieved with conversion: Paul "was in culture a Hellenist, in religion a Pharisee, in citizenship a Roman."[78] By the time his writings and influence had reshaped Christianity, it was barely recognizable as the revolutionary movement for economic justice and radical egalitarianism started by a poverty-stricken, uneducated, manual laborer. Paul made Christianity fit for proper Roman citizens. Women were pushed back into their subordinate place, slaves were cautioned to serve their masters, and patience, suffering, and poverty became virtues. Paul preached peace with the status quo and encouraged Christians to focus on another world. The philosophers, clients of the Roman state, completed the process in the second century: "The Carpenter [was] worked into a theological system modeled faithfully on Roman lines."[79] The Trinity was created to reflect Roman ideology. God the father corresponds to the emperor, "Jesus was made into the patrician patron, and the common people were the plebs who had no recognition at the court in their own right, but obtained it only through the patron. 'If any man sin we have an advocate with the father'—there is Rome's social organization transfigured into a theology."[80]

Once Rome adopted Christianity and created the Holy Roman Empire, religion was for centuries nothing more than a tool of the ruling class and the opiate of the masses. White concluded *The Call of the Carpenter* with a heartfelt appeal to the churches to return to their roots in social democracy. For White material sufficiency could never by itself be adequate. Humans require self-respect and fellowship. It was this dimension that the religion of the Carpenter could add to the socialist movement. For White, it was not only possible but absolutely essential to link true religion and socialism. Each was incomplete without the other: Socialism was the head, Christianity the heart. Like those other romantics of the Left, the Wobblies (Industrial Workers of the World, or IWW), White wanted bread and roses too.

The Call of the Carpenter was in many ways typical of the Social Gospel era; it left few of the liberals' principles untouched. But on almost every issue White took theological stands that placed him to the left of the Social Gospel movement. One of the passions of the liberals was to put Jesus into historical context, but White clearly carried his historical explanation much further than the existing evidence would support. Almost universally the liberals emphasized Jesus' ethical teachings, but in White's reading his life had meaning only in ethical terms. White totally discounted his role as savior and redeemer—a stand even a pronounced ethicist like Walter Rauschenbusch would not have taken. His portrayal of Mary infuriated not only the conservatives but also some of those who were willing to view the virgin birth as myth. His treatment of the Jehovah of the Old Testament as nothing more than community spirit or national pride diminished the authority of God more than most liberals thought necessary. The liberals strove to preserve the uniqueness and primacy of Christianity as a religion, but White stripped it of every distinguishing doctrine. As he explained Christianity, it was not even a coherent system of ethics but simply a local political movement. Paul was not (and still is not) a favorite of the liberals, but few then or now could dismiss him so cavalierly as a tool of the Roman Empire. White called on the names of the great liberal pioneers—Albrecht Ritschl, Adolf von Harnack, and Arthur Cushman McGiffert—implying that his ideas were in tune with theirs, but, in truth, he often exaggerated, oversimplified, or distorted their work.

As dated as it is by today's scholarly standards, there are yet elements of *The Call of the Carpenter* that speak to contemporary sensibilities. White insists on an ethical reading of the Bible, a passion that resonates with feminist scholars, process theologians, and liberationists.[81] He has, perhaps, most in common with Walter Wink, who also analyzes the Bible in terms of patterns of domination.[82] His view of Jesus as disinterested in theology would find many contemporary adherents. His sense that the New Testament contains a variety of voices, and that the Gospels and the Revelation of John have more in common with each other than with the letters of Paul are not foreign ideas to such New Testament scholars as David Barr and Dennis Duling.[83] Were he alive today, White would no doubt find friends in the Jesus Seminar[84] and make common cause with the most radical of the feminists. He needed to be on the edge, looking to the future, preparing to jump. He changed his focus as he grew older, but he never lost his radical way of thinking about and living life.

White's life followed a pattern of reflection, writing, and social action. Trimble reported that the research White did for *The Book of Daniel Drew* and *The Call of the Carpenter* deepened his understanding of and commitment to the socialist cause. During 1912, when his pen was silent, White was building his reputation as a Socialist Party speaker. Local New York invested time, money, and energy in seeing that the citizens of that metropolis regularly heard the word. White gained experience in the lecture hall and on the soap box. The *Brooklyn Eagle* followed his public speaking rather closely, but, whenever the editor was unable to assign a reporter, White obligingly provided an account, usually exaggerating his positions for effect. Once again, Melish blamed a disturbing trait on White's training in journalism. He was so impressed by White's work with Trinity Club that his patience with his assistant's extracurricular activities, though sorely tried, never ran out.[85]

White had the first of his many encounters with the New York City Police Department in February 1913. He was arrested while speaking to a group of striking garment workers. When police Officer Regan tried to arrest him for disturbing the peace by causing a crowd to collect, White exacerbated his problems by calling Regan a scab. White was released to Melish's custody in lieu of a $200 bond. During his hearing White told the judge that he was a revolutionary, but that the revolution could be accomplished "peaceably if the police were taught not to take the side of the capitalists."[86]

The apex of White's career as a socialist speaker occurred on 7 May 1913, when he debated the Reverend John Wesley Hill on the statement: "Resolved, That Socialism is a peril to the State and the Church." The editors of the *New York Call* commented on the event in a lighthearted manner. Hill was characterized as an "eat-em-alive hater of socialism," but they were convinced that White could handle him. "Bouck White is skilled," they opined, "and he will not fall into any traps." All proceeds from the debate were to go to *The Masses*, a new socialist monthly.[87]

Inez Millholland, a socialist leader in the women's suffrage movement, presided over the "good-natured audience." Webster Hall was filled to capacity for the event. Although the audience was primarily made up of socialists or sympathizers, a Republican club attended en masse, and three detectives were assigned to protect Hill in the event of a riot. Added to this potpourri were John Hammond, a local millionaire, John Reed, boy socialist, and Joseph Ettor and Big Bill Haywood, leaders of the ongoing IWW strike in Paterson, New Jersey.[88]

Hill spoke first in defense of the resolution. He argued that economic determinism was incompatible with revealed religion and that socialism would destroy the basic unit of Christian society, the family. When White's turn came to argue the negative, he abandoned Hill's logical, calm style and made a series of insulting personal remarks about his opponent. The audience, at first hostile to Hill, began to turn, and, by the time he finished his rebuttal, it was clear that he had won the crowd over, if not to his position, at least to his personality and style.[89]

After the debate, Haywood was introduced to make an appeal for the Paterson strikers. Just a year before he had been recalled from the Socialist Party of America's Executive Committee, and his Wobblies were driven from the party's rank and file. The issue had been violence. Still stinging from the rebuke and contemptuous of the tactics of what he called parlor socialists, he made an impassioned speech against White and his kind. Haywood couldn't understand how anyone could contend that religion and socialism went together. He concluded that he was going back to Paterson to fight. "You know what that is, don't you?" he taunted the crowd. "But there are a lot of you who haven't the nerve to advocate it. This is sabotage. We believe in advocating it. Sabotage is anything that will break off the profits of capitalism." Haywood's caustic remarks were greeted with sustained applause.[90]

In all, the evening was a tremendous embarrassment to Local New York. The party and the major New York City socialist daily, the *Call*, had sanctioned and promoted the debate, probably thinking that a sympathetic audience and victory were assured. Seven hundred people saw the party buffeted from the Right by the affable Hill and from the Left by a fiery Bill Haywood. Thousands more read about the fiasco in the next day's papers. The party closed ranks around White, however, and no public word of censure was uttered against him.

White's public-relations problems were only beginning. Nineteen thirteen was also the year that he published a novel about country life, *The Mixing*.[91] It was the story of a small, backward community being brought around to unity, Christian charity, and civic pride. The setting of the story, the imaginary town of Hillport, bore a remarkable similarity to Clayton, and the characters were drawn from White's native village. White portrayed the villagers as bigoted, selfish simpletons who had to be tricked into the right direction by the more sophisticated summer colonists and their shy young minister. White changed the setting and situations enough to mollify the town of Clayton, but then his imagination failed him. According to a libel suit filled in January 1914, he used the real names of the townsfolk of Middleburgh and portrayed them as peasants. Matthew D. Wood, who had law offices in New York City but maintained a residence in Middleburgh, filed the suit on behalf of the town. He and White had grown up together, but Wood now considered himself White's bitter enemy. The whole town was up in arms against the man who was fast becoming its most notorious native son.[92]

In 1914 White published a sequel to *The Call of the Carpenter* titled *The Carpenter and the Rich Man*. In this book he amplified the themes set forth in *The*

Call of the Carpenter with more emphasis on Jesus' thinking, especially as exemplified in the parables. If anything, *The Carpenter and the Rich Man* was even more blatantly Marxist in interpretation. "So pivotal in him was the economic," White says of Jesus, "that there alone is to be found the clue to his character-unity; the integrating purpose of his life." White devoted a chapter to debunking the middle class and concluded with chapters on the uselessness of reform and the necessity for revolution: "Naught else but revolution can save us."[93] White was unclear about what kind of revolution would come; he hinted that it could be bloodless if his and Jesus' words were heeded. Like many sequels, *The Carpenter and the Rich Man* added little of substance to the ideas presented in *The Call of the Carpenter*. Without the structure that the biographical format provided in *The Call,* White was scattered, repetitive, and even more verbose than usual. *The Carpenter and the Rich Man* earned White few additional followers and further alienated those who thought he had already gone too far.

According to the papers, the Trinity vestrymen were ready to force White's resignation, and White always insisted that he was fired. But Melish recalled the situation differently. White came to Melish and demanded that he be given complete control of Trinity's evening service. While Melish was not the most orthodox of Episcopal clergymen, he respected the restrictions of the Prayer Book and felt sure White would not. After careful consideration he decided to deny White's request, fully realizing that his decision would lead to White's resignation. Melish flatly denied that the vestry had asked White to resign. In spite of the fact that Melish believed White to have misconstrued his departure from Trinity and misrepresented his statements to the press, the rector was still sorry, because of the club, to see him go.[94] After his severance from Trinity, White was never again to have any connection with official religion. Spurning in turn the Methodist, the Congregational, and the Episcopal traditions, White, ever the individualist, established his own church—the Church of the Social Revolution. He had forged a unique theology in *The Call of the Carpenter* and its companion volume, *The Carpenter and the Rich Man*, and he now had a pulpit from which to preach his gospel.

White's church held its first service at Berkley Theater in New York City on Easter Sunday, 5 April 1914.[95] White invested the savings accumulated from his book royalties in establishing the church. It evolved from a group that had gathered in Greenwich Village on Sunday afternoons to sing socialist songs. Group singing, a unifying force in White's view, was a crucial part of every service at the Church of the Social Revolution. On Sunday mornings the faithful would gather at the church, assemble behind the American flag and the red flag of the revolution, and march, singing all the way, to a predetermined street corner. There they sang some more, preached the evils of capitalism, and invited passers-by to join them. This was called the Mud-Gutter Meeting. Its goal was to increase attendance at the regular service, and it was usually successful. Trimble reports that the Mud-Gutterers often brought back "from five to six times the number which left the church."[96]

Two weeks after the advent of the Church of the Social Revolution, New York City was in a turmoil over the treatment of striking miners in Ludlow, Colorado. The situation there was tense, and on 20 April 1914, following a skirmish with the strikers, the state militia fired into the tents the miners were using as temporary homes. When the one-sided battle was over, eleven children, two women, and six miners had been killed. While the battle raged for days across the state, it became clear that the Rockefellers owned a controlling interest in the Colorado Fuel and Iron Company. As the details of the "ugly story" of the company's treatment of the miners came to light, "public opinion at once declared itself strongly on the side of the workers."[97] Many held John D. Rockefeller personally responsible for what came to be known as the Ludlow Massacre and were further enraged when he refused to have the dispute settled by arbitration. Throughout May 1914 the situation dominated the New York papers. By no means united on tactics, the city's left-wing community was, however, unanimous in condemning the situation in Colorado. They held rallies and demonstrations in support of the strikers almost daily.

The New York Local of the Socialist Party of America (SPA) refused to become involved in such things as picketing Rockefeller's house in mourning garb, but it was effective in the more mundane activity of coordinating relief efforts. On 27 April the party sponsored a "monster rally" at Carnegie Hall to stimulate public sentiment for the strikers and raise money. Several prominent clergymen were sent box-seat tickets—Melish and John Haynes Holmes, a liberal Unitarian, were so honored—but there is no record that White was invited. So volatile a person as he, however, could not stay silent.[98] White believed that everyone was missing the larger implications of the Colorado situation. Most protesters focused on Rockefeller's individual guilt, but to White, Ludlow was just one more example of the evil of the system. In an attempt to raise the discussion of the Ludlow Massacre to a spiritual and universal level, White used the Church of the Social Revolution as the vehicle for his protest against wealth and institutional religion, both of which he saw as inimical to a truly Christian society. The Ludlow controversy gave him a golden opportunity to put himself on the line just as Jesus had done. White too longed to drive the money lenders from the temple. With a small band of disciples, he invaded Calvary Baptist Church, a bastion of wealthy parishioners and evangelical theology, and demanded a discussion of the morality of money.

The story of White's invasion of Calvary Baptist Church as told on a day-to-day basis by the *New York Times* is high melodrama liberally laced with irony. It and its aftermath are the quintessential defining events of White's career. On 7 May 1914, the *Times* reported that White had been authorized by his church to issue a letter to the Reverend Cornelius Woelfkin, then pastor of the temporarily combined congregations of the Calvary and Fifth Avenue Baptist churches, challenging him to debate Christ's attitude toward the rich.[99] White singled out Woelfkin because he was the beloved pastor of the Rockefeller family. To White, John D. Rockefeller represented the epitome of hypocrisy. White had made it clear in *The Call of the Carpenter* and *The Carpenter and the Rich Man* that great wealth and true religion were incompatible. That one could, in good conscience, serve as pastor to one of the city's most fashionable congregations was inconceivable.

White's rigidly held view that salvation was social or it was nothing made it difficult for him to believe Woelfkin sincere. But Woelfkin was not a hidebound, unfeeling conservative, or a puppet of the Rockefellers. Woelfkin was the son of German immigrants. His gracious manners and elegant language were self-acquired. His youth was spent painting signs rather than in the classrooms of the nations's finest universities. For Woelfkin, culture and learning came as byproducts of his commitment to religion and his consequent study of theology. He was baptized a Baptist in 1882 at the age of twenty-three and ordained four years later. Early in his career Woelfkin was an evangelical, but, contrary to cliche, he became more liberal as he grew older. During the 1920s he led the Modernists in their struggle against the Fundamentalist faction of the Northern Baptist Convention. His guiding creed, he was fond of saying, was love of one's neighbor.[100]

Woelfkin held several pastorates and taught at Rochester Theological Seminary before coming to Fifth Avenue. The senior Rockefeller recommended him for the pulpit after the two had met by chance while fishing in the Catskills. Before Woelfkin accepted the post he confessed to Rockefeller that he had no college training. Rockefeller reassured him that his learning, however acquired, was equal to the task, and thus began a friendship that deepened to intimacy through the years. The close relationship Woelfkin enjoyed with the entire family, coupled with Rockefeller's high visibility as a Baptist churchman, led almost inevitably to his becoming known as "the Rockefeller pastor." To his credit Woelfkin always resented the tag.[101] Naturally, the leftists delighted in using it as a jab, along with such scathing, but understandable, sarcasm as referring to him as the "Pastor of Standard Oil," and to his church as the place "where the plutes pray."[102]

Worlds apart in temperament, background, and beliefs, White and Woelfkin might have staged a fascinating debate. On the surface White's request for a discussion seems entirely reasonable. Given the temper of the times, however, it would have been impossible to hold such a debate with even a modicum of decorum. Woelfkin obviously thought that to ignore White and others like him was best. Woelfkin's deeply held belief in personal salvation and the promise of a new life gave him the serenity to tolerate the degradations and inequities of life in the world. Like White, Woelfkin preached and lived his version of the gospels; to ask him to breach the dignity of his worship service to argue with what must have appeared as a ragamuffin band of half-cocked, wrong-headed idealists was too much for his strong sense of propriety.

Although Woelfkin did not receive White's letter until moments before the Sunday service was to begin, he could not have been ignorant of its contents. The New York papers were filled with the challenge, and the wire services broadcast it to Europe. He deliberately chose not to respond. Had he received the letter in time to read it before the disturbance, it seems unlikely that he would have acted differently. White did not ask to participate in the service at Calvary on 10 May; he merely announced at the letter's outset his resolution to do so. After assuring Woelfkin that he and his parishioners were coming only in friendship, he condescendingly asserted that "it will surely be helpful to some in the churches of the older school to get our viewpoint as to the discoveries which scholarship is making concerning the economic side of the teaching of Jesus." This, coming after a reference to White's Harvard and Union education, could only have been intended to remind Woelfkin of his own educational inadequacies. Following more protestations of friendliness, White concluded that he and his followers were coming, in part, to prevent other, more violent, raids on the church. Receive us, he suggests, or "the wilder spirits in the revolutionary movement" will descend en masse.[103]

Saturday night, 9 May, there was another enormous rally in support of the miners led by Alexander Berkman and other anarchists, with the majority of its support coming from the IWW. However, Upton Sinclair, head of the short-lived Free Silence League (the picketing mourners), was there, as was Bouck White. White's challenge had won him center stage, and he gladly discussed its possible ramifications with reporters who thronged about this ominous gathering of the angriest and most unpredictable revolutionaries. He confidently proclaimed that he did not think the police would dare arrest him when he went to Calvary. The *Times* reported threats on Rockefeller's life.[104] The situation seemed to be moving to a climax, and perhaps White, heady with the size of the crowd and its intense feeling, actually believed that he had the power to humble Rockefeller and bring about his conversion to the social revolution.

The bizarre story of White's visit to Calvary appeared on Monday's front pages in huge headlines. The *Times* article read, "Rockefeller's Foes Invade His Church," while the socialist *Call* proclaimed, "Police and Church Ushers Hold Orgy of Brutality in Rockefeller's Church." Although the *Call* focused more on the violence perpetrated against White and his followers, both papers told essentially the same story. White and several of his group entered the church with the other worshipers. Suspecting trouble, the New York Police Department had assigned twenty detectives to attend the service. They were directed to take seats "near each person identified" and ordered "not to disturb the intruders until they attempted some disorderly act." Early in the service White rose to speak. He was asked to sit down and he did. He waited until the announcements were being read, and then he walked to the front of the church and said, "I am here to speak the truth."[105] Woelfkin continued to ignore him, and the organist tried to drown his words with music. White sat in a front pew only to rise a few moments later and say: "I come here as a pastor of a neighboring church. I come to bring peace and not war."

Woelfkin replied, "No, no, no! This is not the time or the place to ask such questions."[106] By this time two ushers had grabbed White and were trying to eject him from the church.

As they wrestled him to the floor, White held on to a pew and shouted, "I want you to let me speak so that I can tell you about one member of your congregation who is guilty of the murder of women and children in Colorado."[107] At this point, Calvary Church, whose frontispiece proclaims, "We preach Christ crucified," became the scene of general pandemonium.

White's followers, who further identified themselves with shouts of "I protest," were attacked by the ushers. The carefully placed detectives were hardly needed. The *Times* reported that it was "the ushers who became the aggressors." Most members of the congregation were standing on the pews to escape the melee that reigned on the floor. Most were shouting, "Put him out," but a minority wanted to "let him speak." Two of White's parishioners, Milo and Mary Woolman, had somehow escaped detection. At the height of the scuffle, Milo opened his Bible and read aloud, "It is easier for a camel to pass through the eye of a needle than for a rich man to enter the Kingdom of Heaven." Woolman's indiscreet reading of the Scriptures provoked the wrath of the outraged ushers and detectives. While they beat him with fists and clubs, his distraught wife flailed away at John D. Rockefeller Jr. She too was accosted and dragged from the church. The violence intensified in the vestibule and outside the church, where a large crowd had gathered. When the patrol wagon finally arrived, White's torn clothes were hanging from his body and two of his followers required the services of an ambulance surgeon. Throughout the outburst Woelfkin remained in his pulpit calmly surveying the scene. Once everything quieted down, "he went on with the service as if nothing of an unusual nature had occurred." Woelfkin refused to comment after the service, but he reportedly told one of the deacons, "They interfered with the order of our service, and no one has a right to do that."[108]

White and ten followers were hauled off to Night Court. Martha Rembaugh and Mary Toole, his attorneys, secured an adjournment on the grounds that they needed time to subpoena witnesses. Several hundred supporters awaited White's release outside the packed courtroom. When the magistrate granted the stay, White's jubilant followers hoisted him to their shoulders and carried him from the courtroom. The hearing was set for Tuesday morning (12 May) in West Side Court with Magistrate George Campbell presiding.[109]

The charges against White and the others were disorderly conduct and disrupting a church service. White came to court uncharacteristically dressed in clerical garb. Campbell cut his testimony short, ordering him to give only brief, factual replies. White's defense was built around the fact that he had sent Woelfkin the letter. Since he had received no reply, he assumed he was welcome. Woelfkin testified that he had not received the special delivery letter until Sunday morning and that he hadn't read it until after the service. Rembaugh then moved to drop the charges, arguing there was nothing illegal about asking a clergyman a question in public. Campbell denied the motion, found seven of the eleven defendants guilty, and set sentencing for the next day.[110]

Before sentencing, Mayor John Purroy Mitchell called for a more vigorous police policy toward disturbers of the peace. Referring to White directly, he said, "You can't handle a situation like that at Calvary Church with kid gloves." Apparently Campbell got the message. For "overstepping himself," White was sentenced to six months in the workhouse. Milo Woolman received the same. Emanuel Lopez was sentenced to ten days of compulsory labor. The five remaining defendants were placed on probation and ordered "not to go near any church of which they were not a regular member." As the surprisingly brief trial (ten minutes) came to a close, White and Campbell made lengthy speeches explaining their positions. Thus was justice served. Progressive Republican Amos Pinchot hit the mark when, in a letter of protest to Mitchell, he called Campbell's sentence "entirely uncivilized."[111]

The following Sunday Woelfkin discussed the disturbance from the pulpit. Speaking for the congregation, he addressed the entire city. "We deeply regret the episode," he said. "In no sense do we gloat." He denied he had set a trap for White, explaining that officers often attended services when a disturbance was feared. He repeated his testimony that he didn't receive White's letter in time to read it before the service. But White's letter was public knowledge several days before the incident. Might not Christian charity have prompted Woelfkin to warn White about the police? As White accurately observed in his summary of the episode, at any point in the proceedings against him one word from Woelfkin would have brought them to a halt.[112] Instead Woelfkin chose to serve as star witness for the prosecution. His self-defense has more the cold air of legalistic accuracy than total soul-searching truthfulness. It certainly falls short of what the public might have expected from a Christian minister on whose church steps the week before Emanuel Lopez had been clubbed senseless while the fashionably dressed onlookers shouted, "Kill the Jew! That's what he deserves."[113]

While White's parishioners, joined by those who were appalled by the severity of the sentence, were working to get him out of jail, he was trying to adjust to the harsh conditions at Blackwell's Island. It was a difficult task for the genteel agitator, and, despite his protestations to the contrary, imprisonment seemed to have a lasting and deleterious effect on his personality. First there was the horror of being packed into a tiny, airless room in the prison ship's hold with 39 foul-smelling, vermin-infested derelicts. Thirty-five to forty-odd prisoners were lodged in the same small room with no running water or toilet facilities. Lice were a constant problem. He was eventually transferred to Queens County Jail, where he was allowed a private room and time to write.[114] While finishing his term, he refined and articulated his views on the relationship of religion to the Socialist Party and evolved sacramental rituals and a catechism for the Revolution Church.

White wanted to actualize his intellectual union of religion and socialism. The purpose of the Church of the Social Revolution was "to revolutionize the world's idea of religion." White hated the idea of submission; he wanted a religion of strength, one that would not grovel or beg: "The one whom we worship is not a fatherly potentate dispensing titbits to those who beg the loudest. Our God is a Man of War!" He urged workers to enlist in God's cause, but he did not promise them victory. Sounding very much like William James, White conceded that the outcome was uncertain, but in that very uncertainty "lies the zest of the conflict, its piquancy and pungent joy." The rejoining of religion and political action would "make the social revolution a certainty, and at the same time steer its energies into beneficent constructive channels."[115]

White recognized the extraordinary power that ritual can exercise over the human mind. He believed that if socialism were to triumph, it would need to build rituals to replace the dethroned ones of traditional society. He created an order of service for the Church of the Social Revolution that included congregational singing, an invocation, recitation of the covenant, an offering, invitation into the fellowship, and the benediction, "And now may the Lord-of-the-uprising-of-labor keep us in the Fellowship." The congregation responded, "Forevermore."[116] The consecration ritual focused on bringing up the child to work for justice in the world. Late in November 1914 White baptized Russell Palmer, dedicating the infant to "the cause of human freedom" and "a career of social revolutionary teaching, preaching, and thinking."[117]

White believed a marriage service that would openly recognize divorce was necessary, not because of declining moral values but because of changing economic circumstances. The family, he explained, was no longer the basic social unit. It had been replaced by the individual. No longer was it necessary for the sexes to pair off for a lifetime in order to survive economically. White did not advocate promiscuity, but he believed that divorce could be a positive step. In White's opinion marriage vows were binding only so long as the love endured. He called his system "monogomy tempered by divorce." He scorned the Roman Catholic position on marriage, which, he thought, reduced it to a breeding institution. Singing in the same key as William Blake and other Romantics, White eschewed centuries of social tradition and declared, "Marriage is so sacred that nothing but love can sanction it."[118]

White was adding substance to the Church of the Social Revolution, and his friends were working to get him out of prison. Woelfkin and other prominent clergy were persuaded to write letters and visit the mayor. Court appeals failed, and the governor ignored pleas from his friends for a pardon as well as a passionate letter from White demanding a new trial.[119] Although White never gained official vindication, he took pride in the fact that while he was in prison, membership in the Church of the Social Revolution more than doubled, increasing to about 500. One of the new converts was reported to be a disgusted defector from Woelfkin's congregation. During White's confinement, Solomon Fieldman, well known in the city as a socialist agitator, gradually took over the direction of the church's day-to-day activities.[120] He frequently spoke following the Mud-Gutter meetings, but guest speakers were also common. Both John Haynes Holmes and William English Walling, the socialist journalist, spoke from White's pulpit.[121]

Fieldman also coordinated the Bouck White Defense Fund. He saw to it that White's case received attention in the radical press outside New York. As the news of White's daring and his rough treatment spread, Local New York found itself in an increasingly embarrassing position. White was a member in good standing in the party. He was an officer in the Intercollegiate Socialist Society, and he was attracting a great deal of attention to the miserable situation in Colorado. Nevertheless, the party leadership, no less than the IWW, hated his tactics. Morris Hillquit, the socialist boss in New York, and Julius Gerber, secretary of the Local's executive committee, were openly anti-religious.[122] Neither had any use for White's spiritualism, and they considered his Revolution Church schismatic. Hillquit never became publicly involved in the controversy over White, but the actions of the executive committee surely had his blessing.

In July 1914 White was nominated by the party to run in the Thirteenth Congressional District, which included Greenwich Village. White lived at 42 Washington Square, and much of his following was centered in the Village.[123] Whether his nomination was a cynical vote-getting ploy based on his notoriety or whether the rank and file nominated him over the objections of the leadership is unclear. In either event, White accepted. An official campaign leaflet had nothing but praise: "The workers need in Congress a strong voice to speak for them fearlessly. In electing Bouck White they will secure such a voice. . . . He typifies the principles and policies of International Socialism, the hope of the world. . . . Vote for Bouck White and all the nominees of the Socialist Party."[124] White's nomination gives a far more favorable impression of his relationship with the party than was actually the case.

Late in August the church engaged the Hippodrome for a 13 September meeting to protest White's treatment. Local New York was invited to send speakers.[125] The secretary's response illustrates clearly intra-party tension over attempts to infuse socialism with religion. Julius Gerber waited until 11 September to inform Fieldman that the party would not send a speaker, because that might "imply an indirect endorsement of the Church of the Social Revolution." Gerber went on to say that the Socialist Party was the proper vehicle for the revolution. Organizations like White's church tended to splinter socialists' efforts and "prolong the present system." This hardly seems an appropriate way to treat one of the party's nominees, but it was entirely in character with the ruthless way Gerber, a jealous keeper of the party's dignity and authority, operated.[126] But this is not the worst example of the executive committee's attempts to sabotage White's growing popularity.

The Appeal to Reason, the mass-circulation socialist paper of the Midwest and Southwest, and the *National Rip-Saw,* associated with Debs, were far more supportive of White than his hometown *Call.* Though all were socialist papers, they appealed to different populations. The New York City Local was dominated by immigrants and led by Jews. As socialism moved west, native-born Protestants were more active. Naturally, White's perception of socialism played better with them. Despite the fact that the Midwesterner Debs was the socialists' quadrennial presidential candidate and by far its most popular representative, the leaders in New York did not want him infringing on their territory, especially on behalf of the maverick White. Fieldman had successfully negotiated for Debs to speak at the church on 10 October, but the SPA's Central Committee canceled the engagement upon request from New York's executive committee. In a letter of explanation to Debs, Gerber claimed that the party was plagued by "constant interference by outside organizations" that "made it a point to interfere with the work of the Party Organization as much as possible." He complained: "If Local New York arranges a meeting in one large hall, they proceed and arrange another a week or so before or after, with the result that both meetings are failures." Gerber concluded by telling Debs that he "should not speak at that meeting."[127]

Debs was not one to countenance such cavalier treatment. Although he never did make it to New York (his speaking tours were incredibly complicated), he made certain that Local New York knew what he thought of the way it had behaved in the

White incident. White's supporters were planning a welcome-home rally for him at Carnegie Hall on 13 November, the day following his release from prison, and they wanted Debs as keynote speaker. Debs fired a letter back to Gerber saying that he saw no reason why he shouldn't speak at the meeting in White's behalf. White was suffering under an "outrageous sentence" for what was in Debs' opinion a "lawful and orderly way to advance the propaganda of the Socialist movement." Debs acknowledged that White's "particular method had been criticized by Socialists," and then delivered the sarcastic conclusion: "I am bound to say in his behalf that his method in this instance, foolish as it may seem to his critics, is still far preferable to the methods of those who sit back and do nothing but talk and find fault with those who actually do things." He observed that "petty jealousy and factional envy" were the real plagues of Local New York, not interference, as Gerber had complained. He asked the local to work to make the meeting a success; the "best thing the socialists can do is to stop objecting and pitch it." Debs concluded his rebuke by stating that it was impossible for him to understand how anyone could object to helping "poor Bouck White" who had "served our cause."[128] Not a word of this factional strife leaked into the papers until the *Times* got wind of it after the celebration at Carnegie Hall.

White invited Woelfkin and Campbell to join him on stage to discuss the case. Needless to say, neither accepted. Meyer London, Socialist congressman-elect from the Twelfth District, made the opening remarks.[129] London was in a sticky situation. He had accepted the role of chief eulogist, but he could not sing White's praises too loudly or he would be in trouble with the Socialist Party machine. He equivocated nicely. London called White a dreamer and said he loved him for it. Dreams made the world progress. Of course, the world needed both dreamers and practical men. "It is for the Socialist movement," London concluded, "to realize the dreams of the prophets."

When London introduced White, the crowd of 3,000 gave him a three-minute ovation and sang the "Marseillaise" and "John Brown's Body." Charles White, who had been devastated by his son's imprisonment, pushed as close to the stage as he could get. He must have viewed the reception as Bouck's long-sought vindication. He told Alice that it was the proudest moment of his life.[130] After the hall quieted, White paid notice to all of the empty seats that had been reserved for the city's clergymen. The ministers "would rue the day they found it convenient to be silent in the face of issues such as he brought to the Protestant Church."[131] Then he launched into a lengthy review of the incident at Calvary and presented the defense of his actions that he wanted preserved for posterity. Printed in *Letters From Prison,* the address rivals *Daniel Drew* for sustained excellence and coherence of style. It had precisely the outraged, sardonic, and slightly malicious tone that the occasion demanded.

After defining "extortion" as "squeezing all you can get out of the other fellow," he went on to "prove" that the Baptist church taught it and that its members admitted to the practice. He contended that the Fifth Avenue Church (while he was in prison, Calvary and Fifth Avenue had decided against a permanent union)[132] "delights to honor" successful extortionists, Rockefeller being a case in point. By squeezing every cent he could out of the other fellow—that is, by extortion—he had amassed the most extensive private fortune known to history.

And he is also clothed by his Church with every preferment in its power to bestow. His membership on their roll is celebrated with anthems of joy. Not a post of honor in that organization but would be conferred upon him with bell-ringings of delight. The Fifth Avenue Church has given to extortionate riches a clean bill of health. Yes, has enhaloed it with a radiance from the heaven of the highest; consecrating the code with sanctions the most holy within the mind of man to conceive or within the heart of man to cherish.

Speaking of the Colorado Fuel and Iron Company, he condemned absentee ownership as inhuman and the perfect tool of extortion; it prevented both owner, who could not see "the cruelties that are enacted," and manager, "but a hired man," from exercising their "natural human sympathies." White's imaginary conversation between the two is biting parody.

> Says the owner to the superintendent, "I have promoted you to this coveted post. Now it is for you to make good. The superintendent before you jacked the dividend up from 4 ½ to 6 percent. See if you can do as well."
>
> "Will do my best," replies the superintendent. "I'll keep an eye on the dividend; be sure of that. Of course there is—er—the workmen and their families. Just what procedure do you—er—think—"
>
> "What procedure?" exclaims the owner. "Adopt the Christian procedure. I've got a heart, I have. Be good to the workmen."
>
> "Er—even at the expense of—er—lowering the dividends, sir?"
>
> "Now, see here, Mr. Superintendent, I've appointed you to the management of an industrial plant, not to the head of a charity. I keep my business and my philanthropy distinctly separate. Business means dividends."
>
> "And the heads of families?"
>
> "Give them all you can. But don't reduce the dividend."
>
> "The women?"
>
> "Treat the women well. But don't reduce the dividend."
>
> "The boys and girls?"
>
> "Be tender towards them. But don't reduce the dividend."
>
> The Dividend is the one deity in the business kingdom. . . . Maintain the dividend even at the price of massacre, was the order that came, directly or indirectly from Tarrytown. . . . Poncantico Hills got its dividends. And the Fifth Avenue Church, its pew rent and missionary contribution.

White brought his "history of that Fifth Avenue Church affair" to a close with an assessment of who should bear the guilt for the miserable condition of American society.

I do not blame the rich for their covetousness. I blame the Church that has taught them the falsified gospel that covetousness is ethical and christianly. There is going to be more hope for John D. Rockefeller at Judgment Day than for Cornelius Woelfkin. Rockefeller is an offender against humanity. But he doesn't know it. . . . Rockefeller is a moral idiot. . . . Through the perverted religious teachings in which he has been immersed since boyhood, he is stone blind to the price in the misery of multitudes that has been paid for his wealth.

In true socialist fashion, White concluded on a note of optimism. Like thousands of other radicals, he believed the European war proved that capitalism was in a state of rapid decline. Before the large audience he rededicated his life to revolution and repeated the covenant of its church:

I enlist under the Lord of the blood-red banner to bring to an end a scheme of things that has enthroned Leisure on the back of Labor, an idle class sucking the substance of the poor. I will not be a social climber, but will remain with the workers in class solidarity till class shall have been done away in fellowship's glad dawn. I will seek recruits of the Church of the Social Revolution, unto the overthrow of present-day society and its rebuilding into fellowship.[133]

It must have seemed to White, standing before an admiring throng in the temple of popular culture, that he had finally achieved the status his message deserved. Now, everyone would listen. And for a short while they did, but the drums of war drowned out the message of international socialism and American society made dissent too costly for most. White had dropped from view by the fall of 1917. He regained public attention only sporadically after the war, and, when he did it was usually as an object of derision or curiosity.

White had another turn in the public spotlight when he held a flag-melting ceremony at his church on 1 June 1916. White had been charged with flag desecration in March when he distributed a flier depicting the American flag and a bag of money intertwined with a serpent. The flag-melting took place on the eve of his court appearance. At 10:00 p.m. those attending the regular church service were ushered into the church's back yard, where they found an altar covered with a red cloth proclaiming "It is God's command" and a kettle marked "Melting Pot" hanging from a tripod. After a rousing speech by Ned Ames denouncing European nationalism, natives of several countries placed their flags in the burning melting pot and embraced in their place internationalism and universal brotherhood. The crowd gasped when Albert Henkel entered the yard carrying the American flag. It too went into the melting pot. While the American flag burned, the participants stretched a banner proclaiming internationalism over the altar. The *New York Times* reporters who had been invited to the ceremony gave the police a blow-by-blow account.[134]

White was arrested just before sentencing was scheduled on his previous flag desecration charge. He and his followers have the distinction of being the only people prosecuted anywhere in the nation for flag burning in the period 1900 to 1965.[135] Theoretically White was in tune with the antiwar stand of the party. Once again, however, his tactics were too extreme and flamboyant for their tastes. Before White came to trial the Socialist Party found a way to rid itself of his embarrassing presence. He was charged with supporting a non-socialist candidate. Already disillusioned by the way European socialists supported their national governments in the war effort, White was happy to sever ties with the party.[136]

White's trial started in March 1917. Granted permission to defend himself, he tried to make even jury selection a lesson in American radicalism, asking prospects if they knew about William Lloyd Garrison, Roger Williams, John Brown, and Thomas Jefferson. When he rejected a juror who had never heard of John Brown, White explained, "I realize that a man has never been refused before for jury service because of his ignorance of John Brown. But we are concerned with the formation of American precedent."[137] The prosecution called the reporters who had been present and rested with the testimony of a nine-year-old child who had watched the service from his fire escape: "I asked mamma what right they had to burn the American flag, and I said I didn't think it was right."[138]

White tried to convince the jury that the flag-burning had been a religious ceremony. He called a Harvard Divinity School student who affirmed that the ceremony was conducted with "reverence, humility, and prayer." The judge refused to allow the young man's testimony that the teachings of Harvard Divinity and Union Theological Seminary were compatible with those of the Church of the Social Revolution. In his opinion they were not. "At any rate," the assistant district attorney chimed in, "they don't teach their students to burn the American flag." White put himself on the stand, denounced militarism and John D. Rockefeller, and conceded under cross-examination that "life is a vale of trouble." He called forth a phalanx of character witnesses who testified that he was a man of peace and affirmed his excellent reputation. The judge hurried them along with a caution about the expense of the trial.[139]

The jury deliberated five hours before returning a guilty verdict against White and two of his followers, Ned Ames and Albert Henkel. The jury requested clemency for all three. Ignoring their recommendation, Judge McIntyre levied the maximum sentence of thirty days in the work house for all three and fined White $100 as well. The sentence was accompanied by a stern warning to all radicals:

If there ever was a time in this great Republic when every American should be true and loyal to the flag, it is now. I regret that I haven't the power to make this sentence a matter of years. In recent years there has [sic] been coming to this country certain elements from lands where there has been oppression. Instead of enjoying the opportunities offered by America they have dared to suggest destruction of our institutions. To these and all others this court sends the warning that hereafter it must be hats off to the flag.[140]

McIntyre ignored the fact that the three defendants he sentenced were native-born Americans. The seven immigrants tried had been acquitted. Each day in confinement White had to raise and lower the American flag that flew over the Tombs.[141]

White emerged from prison armed with yet another plan for social regeneration. Twice imprisoned for antiwar activities, he now urged all radicals to support America's war effort. He had come to view the war as a tremendous opportunity for social change. "Tis the most wonderful moment, probably, since time began for remaking the social map. To fritter an hour such as this," he warned, "in a campaign of splutter and nagging would be a crime against the human race." He urged all his "fellow-malcontents" to join with him in working for a Constituent Assembly as provided for in Article V of the Constitution.[142] White apparently believed there was sufficient unrest in America to make his plan feasible. He changed the name of his church to the Association for a Constituent Assembly (thus removing any recognition of it as a religious institution) and attempted to mount a publicity campaign.[143] But, as with the citizens' oath crusade, the idea did not catch on, and he faded from the public view.

White never gave up his search for the solution to society's problems. In 1919 he published his last book, *The Free City*. More clearly written and closely argued than much of his work, it represented the turn his thinking was to take for the rest of his life. The free city, White concluded, was the only political order that had God's blessing. Following his pattern of putting ideas into action, White organized a group called the Free City to work for home rule for New York City. White wanted the police to form the nucleus of a citizens militia to resist enforcement of federal prohibition. The Brewery Workers Local 59 joined the home-rule crusade for a time, but the city found prohibition less bothersome than secession.[144]

Charles White died in 1918, leaving his son enough money to buy a small farm and travel in Europe. On one trip to France to study pottery, White, 47, met and married a 19-year-old French student, Andree Emilie Simon. The marriage was a disaster and lasted barely a month before Andree fled White's rustic farmhouse and filed for an annulment on the grounds of fraud. Once again the *Times* delighted to have White in its headlines. Andree's testimony indicated the marriage was never consummated, and that, in fact, White did not believe in marriage "in that way." He was looking for a companion, a union that would produce books, not children. The locals drove him from his farm with taunts and tarring and feathering.[145] He wandered for a while, opening a pottery studio in Paris and working for the English language *Paris Tribune*. After the stock market crash, he returned to America broke, but with a secret method of making unfired glazed pottery.[146]

White lived for a time with his sister, Alice, but they got along no better than when they were children. At the height of the Depression, he persuaded an old friend from Middleburgh to lend him $500. With that be bought five acres in the Helderberg Mountains near Albany. He rescued two Swedes from the Albany unemployment office, and together they began constructing a complex of stone buildings White called Federalburg.[147] By 1935 White's retreat had become a popular tourist attraction. Thousands climbed up rugged trails to tour the bizarre buildings, meet White—the Hermit of the Helderbergs—and buy souvenir postcards or pieces of pottery.

White seemed content with the life he made for himself in the mountains. He published nothing after 1932, but he was able to satisfy his need for a public forum by speaking about his pottery to women's clubs and on local radio. On these excursions he was always immaculately dressed, perfectly charming, and reasonably lucid. But those who knew him well couldn't help noticing that his mind wasn't always in tune with reality. He fantasized that he was a full-blooded Iroquois and for a while wore only a loincloth.[148] Despite the fact that his pottery sold very well, he was miserly to the point of begging rotten vegetables from the village grocery.[149]

The flurry of publicity that greeted the release of *The Toast of New York* prompted a retrospective interview and feature article in the *New York Herald Tribune*. By 1937 White "had arrived at a mellow view point." He no longer hated the capitalists but felt compassion for them. Still convinced that he knew the answer to the world's problems, he was content to wait for its leaders to come to him. He felt confident that the world would soon "revert to a 'society of cities.'" He looked back on his days as an agitator with regret. "I want to make that plain," he said: "My protest . . . took the form of wild, ineffectual demonstrations. In its fruiting, it didn't amount to a hill of beans and, therefore, it was unsound. The only way to explain it is that collective lunacy was getting into my nerve centers along with those of all the rest. It made me unwise." Though the reporter found him "strong and tanned at sixty-two," the question of growing old and dying crept into the interview. White's answer revealed that he had given the matter some thought.

Death has to come to us sometime. . . . And I feel that disease could be met better in a beautiful spot like this than in any other area I can think of. If you've got to pass away slowly it is more natural to do so here in the sun than in some city tenement. Up here you become accustomed to the idea that decay is as natural as growth—that if spring is natural, so is autumn. Age with the aching tooth will come upon me. I am ready for them. I expect them.[150]

White's dream of living out his time in the mountains was not realized. In 1945 he suffered a stroke and was admitted to the Menands Home for Aged Men in Albany. He died there in January 1951. Praying for the world's salvation to the end, he left little behind but a tortuously written plan for the beautification of the Hudson River Valley.[151]

NOTES

1. *Who Was Who in America with World Notables* 5 (Chicago: Marquis Who's Who, 1969–1973): 773. Although White was known as Charles or Charlie until he was past thirty, he will be referred to as Bouck throughout to distinguish him from his father and because he preferred that name.

2. *Middleburgh* (New York) *Gazette*, 24 October 1874, Irvin G. Wyllie papers, hereafter cited as IGW. The historian Irvin G. Wyllie collected materials for a scholarly biography of Bouck White in the period 1948–1950. He laid the project aside and did not return to it before his death in 1975. Consisting largely of correspondence, interview notes, clippings, pamplets, and photographs, the Wyllie Bouck White collection was donated to the author in 1977 by the professor's widow, Mrs. Harriet Wyllie.

3. *Schenectady Gazette,* 25 August 1934, IGW; Henry J. Carman, "William C. Bouck," *Dictionary of American Biography* (New York: Charles Scribner's Sons, 1964), I: 476–77.

4. Lucy Weeks Trimble, introduction to *Letters From Prison: Socialism, A Spiritual Sunrise,* by Bouck White (Boston: Richard G. Badger, 1915), 3.

5. Office of the Surrogate, Schoharie, N.Y., "Petition for Letters of Administration and Official Oath in the Matter of Goods, Chattels, and Credits of Brownen White, 26 November 1878," IGW; Roland Bouck, interview by Irvin G. Wyllie, at Schoharie, N.Y., 7 August 1950, IGW.

6. Alice White and Charlotte Bouck, interview by Irvin G. Wyllie, Middleburgh, N.Y., 25 July 1950; Louise Meinhardt and Bouck White, interview by Irvin G. Wyllie, Middleburgh, N.Y., 7 August 1950, IGW.

7. Meinhardt, in Louise Meinhardt and Bouck White interview, IGW.

8. White, in Alice White and Charlotte Bouck interview, IGW.

9. Bouck, in Alice White and Charlotte Bouck interview, IGW.

10. *Middleburgh* (New York) *Gazette,* 30 June 1887, IGW.

11. White, in Louise Meinhardt and Bouck White interview, IGW.

12. Marion C. Belliveau, Registrar, Harvard University, to the author, 3 March 1977.

13. *Harvard University Class of 1896, Secretary's First Report* (Cambridge, Mass.: Harvard University Press, n.d.), 14–15.

14. Belliveau to the author.

15. Waldo L. Cook to Irvin G. Wyllie, 15 February 1949, IGW.

16. Edwin A. Field to Irvin G. Wyllie, 2 February 1949, IGW.

17. White, in Louise Meinhardt and Bouck White interview, IGW; Trimble, introduction to White, *Letters,* 4.

18. Trimble, introduction to White, *Letters,* 4.

19. Ibid.; White, in Louise Meinhardt and Bouck White interview, IGW. Photocopy of White's transcript and license courtesy of Union Theological Seminary.

20. Aaron Ignatius Abell, *The Urban Impact on American Protestantism, 1865–1900* (Cambridge, Mass.: Harvard University Press, 1943; reprint ed., Hamden, Conn.: Archon, 1962), 238.

21. Charles H. Hopkins, *The Rise of the Social Gospel in American Protestantism, 1865–1915* (New Haven, Conn.: Yale University Press, 1940), 157.

22. Union Theological Seminary transcript.

23. Jacob H. Dorn, *Washington Gladden: Prophet of the Social Gospel* (Columbus, Ohio: Ohio State University Press, 1967), 162; for detailed discussions of the Briggs case see Lefferts A. Loetscher, *The Broadening Church: A Study of Theological Issues in the Presbyterian Church Since 1869* (Philadelphia: University of Pennsylvania Press, 1957), 48–62; Carl E. Hatch, *The Charles A. Briggs Heresy Trial* (New York: Exposition Press, 1969); Robert T. Handy, *A History of Union Theological Seminary in New York* (New York: Columbia University Press, 1987), 69–93.

24. Hopkins, *Rise of the Social Gospel,* 137.

25. Dorn, *Washington Gladden,* 162.

26. Handy, *History of Union,* 69.

27. Roland Bainton, "Arthur Cushman McGiffert," *Dictionary of American Biography* (New York: Charles Scribner's Sons, 1944), Supplement One, 11: 527–29.

28. John H. Melish, interview by Irvin G. Wyllie, at New York, 13 July 1950, IGW.

29. Union Theological Seminary, *Alumni Bulletin* I (June–July 1926): 155.

30. White, *Letters,* 25.

31. Hopkins, *Rise of the Social Gospel,* 157.

32. Trimble, introduction to White, *Letters,* 5.

33. Bouck White to Irvin G. Wyllie, 20 February 1949, IGW.

34. Trimble, introduction to White, *Letters*, 5.

35. Bouck White to Minnie and Lorenzo Hotaling, 31 January 1949, IGW.

36. Bouck White, *Quo Vaditis? A Call to the Old Moralities* (New York: Civic Press, 1903), 83.

37. Trimble, introduction to White, *Letters*, 5.

38. Typed copy of invitation to White's ordination, IGW.

39. Meinhardt, in Louise Meinhardt and Bouck White interview, IGW.

40. Minnie Hotaling, interview by Irvin G. Wyllie, at Home for Aged Men, Albany, N.Y., 30 July 1948, IGW.

41. Corinne Morse, interview by Irvin G. Wyllie, at Clayton, N.Y., 20 July 1959, IGW.

42. Montrose Hungerford and Mrs. Clay Dick, interview by Irvin G. Wyllie, at Clayton, N.Y., 20 July 1950, IGW.

43. Typed notes from White's brochure, "The Coming School Board Election," IGW.

44. John H. Melish to Irvin G. Wyllie, 18 May 1948, IGW.

45. George Hodges, *Henry Codman Potter* (New York: Macmillan, 1915), 244–45.

46. Florence Epworth to James Cruikshank, 4 April 1949, IGW.

47. Melish to Wyllie, 18 May 1948, IGW.

48. Bouck White, *The Call of the Carpenter* (New York: Doubleday, Page, 1911), 291.

49. Bouck White clipping folder, Harvard University Archives, Widener Library, Cambridge, Mass.

50. Bouck White to Harvard Registrar, 22 November 1907, Harvard University Archives, Widener Library.

51. Melish to Wyllie, 18 May 1948, IGW.

52. *New York American*, 3 January 1909; John H. Melish, interview by Irvin G. Wyllie, 22 July 1950, IGW.

53. Melish to Wyllie, 18 May 1948, IGW.

54. Trimble, inroduction to White, *Letters*, 7.

55. Bouck White, *The Book of Daniel Drew* (New York: Doubleday, Page, 1910).

56. *New York Tribune*, 8 February 1905.

57. *New York Call*, 29 April 1910, 1; *Brooklyn Eagle*, 25, 29 April, 7 May 1910, IGW.

58. *Brooklyn Eagle*, 25 April 1910, IGW.

59. Ibid., 29 April 1910, IGW.

60. Ibid., 27 April 1910, IGW.

61. White, in Louise Meinhardt and Bouck White interview, IGW.

62. Hotaling interview, IGW.

63. Quoted in *Brooklyn Eagle*, 28 April 1910, IGW.

64. Clifford Browder, *The Money Game in Old New York: Daniel Drew and His Times* (Lexington, Ky.: University Press of Kentucky, 1986).

65. *New York Times*, 23 July 1937.

66. Melish to Wyllie, 18 May 1948, IGW.

67. Doubleday advertising brochure, IGW.

68. Advertisement in 1914 edition of Bouck White, *The Carpenter and the Rich Man* (New York: Doubleday, Page). Other endorsements were by John Haynes Holmes and Michigan Governor W.N. Ferris.

69. W.D.P. Bliss, *Literary Digest* 45 (17 August 1912): 264.

70. Eugene V. Debs, "Bouck White's Great Book," *Coming Nation*, 10 May 1913.

71. Advertising brochure, IGW.

72. Katherine S. Trask, *The Mighty and the Lowly* (New York: Macmillan, 1915).

73. Melish to Wyllie, 18 May 1948, IGW.

74. White, *Call of the Carpenter*, 19.

75. Ibid., 68, 73, 95, 118.

76. Ibid., 162.

77. Ibid., 183–89.

78. Ibid., 227.

79. Ibid., 254.

80. Ibid., 255.

81. Elisabeth Schüssler Fiorenza's Presidential Address, "The Ethics of Interpretation: De-centering Biblical Scholarship," *Journal of Biblical Literature* 107 (March 1988): 3–17.

82. Walter Wink has elaborated his understanding in three books: *Naming the Powers: The Language of Power in the New Testament* (1984); *Unmasking the Powers: The Invisible Forces That Determine Human Existence* (1986); and *Engaging the Powers: Discernment and Resistance in a World of Domination* (1992). All are by Fortress Press in Minneapolis.

83. Dennis C. Duling and Norman Perrin, *The New Testament: An Introduction* (New York: Harcourt Brace Jovanovich, 1993); David L. Barr, *New Testament Story: An Introduction* (Belmont, Calif.: Wadsworth, 1995).

84. Both John Dominic Crossan and Marcus Borg present a naturalistic interpretation of Jesus' life and focus on his concern for the common people. See Borg's *Conflict, Holiness, and Politics in the Teachings of Jesus: Studies in the Bible and Early Christianity* (Lewiston, N.Y.: Edwin Mellen Press, 1984) and *Meeting Jesus Again for the First Time: The Historical Jesus and the Heart of Contemporary Faith* (San Francisco: Harper, 1995); and Crossan's *The Historical Jesus: The Life of a Mediterranean Jewish Peasant* (Minneapolis: Fortress Press, 1991).

85. Melish to Wyllie, 18 May 1948, IGW.

86. *New York Times*, 7 February 1913, 9; and 12 February 1913, 8.

87. *New York Call*, 7 May 1915, 6.

88. Ibid., 8 May 1913, 2.

89. Ibid.; *New York Times*, 8 May 1913, 3.

90. *New York Call*, 8 May 1913, 2.

91. Bouck White, *The Mixing: What the Hillport Neighbors Did* (New York: Doubleday, Page, 1913).

92. *New York Times*, 23 January 1914, 5.

93. White, *The Carpenter and the Rich Man*, 17, 327.

94. Melish to Wyllie, 18 May 1948, IGW.

95. Quoted in Mary A. Stuart, "Bouck White—Interpreter of Christ," *Forum* 57 (May 1917): 597–609.

96. Trimble, introduction to White, *Letters*, 13.

97. Allan Nevins, *John D. Rockefeller: The Heroic Age of American Enterprise*, 2 vols. (New York: Charles Scribner's Sons, 1940), 2:669–72. For more detailed coverage of the labor war in Colorado, see Graham Adams Jr., *Age of Industrial Violence* (New York: Columbia University Press, 1966), Chap. 7, "Massacre in Colorado," 146–75; Leon Stein and Philip Taft, eds., *Massacre at Ludlow* (New York: Arno Press and The New York Times, 1971).

98. Socialist Party, New York County Local Papers, 1907–1914, Socialist Collections in the Tamiment Library, 1872–1956, New York University (1962 microfilm edition, 4 reels), Reel 3.

99. *New York Times*, 7 May 1914, 7.

100. Nevins, *Rockefeller*, 2:700; *New York Times*, 7 January 1928, 17.

101. *New York Times*, 7 January 1928, 17.

102. Upton Sinclair, *The Profits of Religion* (Pasadena, Calif.: Published by the author, 1918), 192; *New York Call*, 11 May 1914, 1.

103. White, *Letters*, 253, 26.

104. *New York Times,* 10 May 1914, sec. 3, 11.

105. Ibid., 11 May 1914, 1, 4.

106. *New York Call*, 11 May 1914, 2.

107. *New York Times*, 11 May 1914, 4.

108. *New York Times*, 11 May 1914, 1, and 13 May 1914, 22; *New York Call*, 11 May 1914, 2.

109. *New York Call*, 11 May 1914, 2.

110. Ibid.

111. Ibid., 14 May 1914, 6, and 15 May 1914, 11.

112. White, *Letters*, 128.

113. *New York Tribune*, 11 May 1914, 5.

114. White, *Letters*, 114–19.

115. Ibid., 97, 99, 100, 105.

116. Ibid., 141.

117. Ibid., 146; *New York Times*, 23 November 1914, 14.

118. *New York Times*, 11 October 1914, 7.

119. Ibid., 23 June 1914, 7; White, *Letters*, 33–34.

120. Many advertisements in the *New York Call* list Solomon Fieldman as director and lecturer of the church.

121. John Haynes Holmes to Irvin G. Wyllie, 11 August 1948, IGW; *New York Times*, 1 June 1914, 5.

122. Julius Gerber to Mrs. Katie A. Butchelder, 29 December 1914, NewYork County Local Papers, Reel 4. In this letter Gerber gives advice on religion and socialism:

We have made it a practice not to mix religion with Socialism. . . . Religion is a thing apart. . . . Religion is the affair of the individual and not of the state or party. . . . [It is] dangerous for the Socialist Party to preach religion. . . . Socialism is universal—all embracing, where religion is narrow, dogmatic, and sectarian. . . . [Socialists should not] divert our energies to side shows, which may perhaps help in the realization of our aim, but are equally liable to divert us from the straight course and liable to divide our forces.

123. Julius Gerber, interview by Irvin G. Wyllie, 5 July 1950, IGW; New York County Local Papers, Reel 4.

124. Leaflet in IGW.

125. Unsigned letter from the church to the Local's Executive Committee, 21 August 1914, New York County Local Papers, Reel 4.

126. Julius Gerber to Solomon Fieldman, 11 September 1914, ibid. Even a cursory reading of the party's official correspondence reveals Gerber as a man of little patience and tolerance. At best he was curt and to the point; at his worst he was insufferably arrogant, insulting, and domineering. Apparently was also efficient, hard-working, and unswervingly loyal to the party organization.

127. Julius Gerber to Eugene V. Debs, 20 July 1914, ibid.

128. Eugene V. Debs to Julius Gerber, 22 July 1914, ibid.

129. *New York Times,* 13 November 1914, 7. White lost his race to a Democrat, G.W. Loft. *New York Times,* 3 November 1914, 4. Neither the *Times* nor the *Call* reported White's vote or anything about the campaign. Apparently White's defeat was a foregone conclusion.

130. *New York Call*, 14 November 1914, 3; White, in Charlotte Bouck and Alice White interview, IGW.

131. *New York Times*, 14 November 1914, 15.

132. The *New York Times* covered the proposed merger over several years.

133. All quotations are from White, *Letters from Prison*, 123–39.

134. *New York Times*, 2 June 1916, front page.

135. Robert Goldstein, *Desecrating the American Flag: Key Documents of the Controversy from the Civil War to 1895* (Syracuse, N.Y.: Syracuse University Press, 1996), 3.

136. *New York Times*, 28 December 1916, 18.

137. *New York Call*, 6 March 1917, 5.

138. Ibid., 10 March 1917, 2.

139. *New York Times*, 10 March 1917, 11; 13 March 1917, 7; 14 March 1917, 9; *New York Call*, 14 March 1917.

140. *New York Times*, 16 March 1917, 12.

141. Ibid., 18 March 1917, sec. 2, 3.

142. *Outlook* 116 (22 August 1917): 613.

143. *New York Times*, 3 September 1917, 5.

144. Bouck White, *The Free City* (New York: Moffat, Yard, 1919).

145. *New York Times*, 29 May 1921, sec 1, 5; 30 May 1921, 1; 1 June 1921, 12.

146. *New York Herald-Tribune*, 17 May 1937.

147. Mrs. Calla Engle, interview by Irvin G. Wyllie, Middleburgh, N.Y., 7 August 1950, IGW.

148. *Watertown* (New York) *Daily Times*, 16 September 1937, IGW.

149. Bouck, in Charlotte Bouck and Alice White interview, IGW.

150. *New York Herald Tribune,* 17 May 1937.

151. Handwritten manuscript on Hudson River beautification in IGW.

8

Millionaire Socialist and Omnist Episcopalian: J. G. Phelps Stokes's Political and Spiritual Search for the "All"

Robert D. Reynolds Jr.

In 1895 James Graham Phelps Stokes's life changed. A student at the College of Physicians and Surgeons of Columbia University, Stokes had expected to combine his two great interests, medicine and the church, by becoming a medical missionary. But his father, Anson Phelps Stokes, head of the family company with widespread real estate and railroad properties, was in failing health and needed his second eldest son to help oversee the family's financial holdings. The request that he abandon a life of "service" to become a "mere man of business" shocked the younger Stokes. He would now have to search for new outlets for his dream.

The guiding principle in Stokes's search, in both his religious and his temporal activities, was "a REALITY so transcendent that upon approach to it every vestige of separate awareness vanishes, and one becomes awake in That Which Is All." For Stokes the key was: "All the higher centers awake to functional activity automatically as man succeeds in leading a selfless life; and it is only through such selfless living, and selfless devotion to that One Purpose which seeks equally the welfare of all its seeming parts that the higher forms of vision can be attained."[1] Stokes sought this vision in politics and in religion, ultimately finding solace only in the spiritual realm. The Socialist Party in America ultimately failed to provide the selfless political system he was seeking. Only the Episcopal Church and other of the world's religions provided an unsullied forum for Stokes's study and devotion.

Wealth, religion, and civic responsibility had been part of the Stokes and Phelps families for generations. Stokes's great-grandfather Thomas Stokes was a successful merchant and one of the founders of the London Missionary Society. Another great-grandfather, Anson Greene Phelps, created the company that evolved into the industrial giant Phelps Dodge and Company but also had time to be one of the founders of the American Board of Commissioners for Foreign Missions. Throughout the nineteenth century, the families participated in the activities of the American Bible Society, the American Tract Society, the Domestic Missionary Society, and a number of similar organizations.

Stokes's father, Anson, married Helen Phelps, daughter of a successful banker, the two families having close ties for more than 200 years and sharing a common forebear, George Phelps. Stokes was born on 18 March 1872, and, like his six siblings, was christened in the Episcopal Church with the family cognomen of Phelps. He had a happy childhood living in luxury on Madison Avenue in Manhattan; in the New York City suburb of Noroton, Connecticut; at the family's summer estate in Newport, Rhode Island; or at the family mansion in Lenox, Massachusetts.

In the fall of 1888 he enrolled in the biology program at Yale's Sheffield Scientific School, expecting to become a physician. His extracurricular activities during his undergraduate years centered on church-related organizations, especially the Young Men's Christian Association (YMCA). He was one of two "class deacons" who led classmates in prayer services. While at college, Stokes became interested in the work being done by evangelist Dwight L. Moody, and he attended summer programs at Moody's recently established private secondary schools in Northfield and Mount Hermon, Massachusetts. These gatherings for college students had direct links to the YMCA, and a large portion of the agenda had by the late 1880s evolved into proselytizing work in the foreign missionary movement. The Student Volunteer Movement, with strong ties to the YMCA and Moody's summer conferences, became a spearhead in the Anglo-American effort to spread Christianity to the non-Western world.[2]

Stokes's spiritual commitment at Yale won him the nickname of "Deacon" or "Deac." A good student and a hard worker, his senior year he received several votes as class "grind." He did not cloister himself, however. Stokes participated in track athletics, served as editor of the *Yale Record*, and was named the best dancer of the class of 1892.[3]

After a year of world travel following graduation from Yale, Stokes began his medical training at the College of Physicians and Surgeons of Columbia University. By the time he entered medical school, Stokes had begun to realize that there were environmental factors to consider in studying the growth of disease and human suffering. As an undergraduate he had written his departmental thesis on "The Heredity of Disease" but had been troubled by what he considered controllable factors contributing to sickness and ill health. He came to believe that human ignorance or error created a "moral factor" underlying an exceedingly large proportion of human suffering. Stokes included under "moral factors" environmental conditions caused by poverty and ignorance beyond the control of the sufferer but not society as a whole. In the antiseptic classrooms of Columbia, all Stokes could do was pencil in the margins of his textbooks the letter "m" next to paragraphs discussing ailments for which he believed a "moral" factor entered into the picture. During Stokes's junior year, he was offered the exceptional privilege for a medical student of spending a few weeks as an ambulance doctor at Roosevelt Hospital, where, especially on the night shift, he was able to view disease-producing environments created by human error.[4]

One of the areas served by the hospital was "Hell's Kitchen" on the West Side of midtown Manhattan. It was here the sheltered son of privilege saw for the first time the effect of deep and unrelenting poverty on the physical well-being of people. Even after the passage of over fifty years he could still remember such horrors as retrieving an almost dead woman from an airshaft in which she had jumped from the sixth floor to escape a brutal husband. Stokes was appalled at the horrible sanitation facilities that included open privy sheds a few feet from wells where drinking water was obtained.[5]

Immersed in his medical studies and the impact of poverty on health, Stokes in 1895 received the crushing news from his father that he must give up the study of medicine and help out in the family business. He decided to finish medical school and then accede to his father's wishes. That summer while lounging around home, engrossed in the Sunday newspaper, Stokes spied an article about the activities of James Reynolds and a group of associates who were working to help the residents of Manhattan's Lower East Side ghetto. While attending Yale, Stokes had previously worked with Reynolds, a member of the class of 1885 who retained ties with his alma mater by holding the post of first secretary of the YMCA at the university.

The newspaper story that caught Stokes's attention described the phenomenon of the social settlement movement. Based upon the model of Toynbee Hall in London, centers had sprung up in several cities where the underprivileged could participate in educational and recreational programs. Some settlements provided a place for the well-educated, well-to-do to immerse themselves by taking up residence in them. Totally captivated by what he read about the work of the settlements, Stokes wrote Reynolds asking if he could join in it.

The transition to settlement work was not difficult for Stokes because in addition to his stint as an ambulance surgeon, he also had been active in the Young People's Church at Fifth Avenue and Fifty-fifth Street, where he had become involved in a settlement-type project. Disillusioned by the lack of parishioner response to the needs of the poor, Stokes and other young churchgoers to the area rented an abandoned saloon on Tenth Avenue known as the "Tub of Blood," and, after making certain alterations, renamed it the Neighborhood Club for Boys and Girls.[6]

Stokes soon joined the board of directors of the University Settlement Society of New York, which oversaw the running of the Neighborhood Guild at 26 Delancey Street, where Reynolds was the head worker. Fellow council members included such notable city reformers and philanthropists as Seth Low, Franklin H. Giddings, V. Everit Macy, Henry Holt, Henry D. Sedgwick, and R. R. Bowker. But Stokes was the one board member who totally immersed himself in the settlement house and its Lower East Side neighborhood. Obtaining a list published by the Board of Health of the tenements with the highest death rates, he visited each apartment in the various buildings. The horrible conditions he witnessed equaled or exceeded those he had seen in Hell's Kitchen.[7]

Shortly after Stokes became associated with the Guild he headed a committee that proposed erecting new premises to replace the condemned settlement center on Delancey Street. His elder brother's architectural firm drew up plans for a five-floor dwelling, which included a lecture hall, kindergarten, library, classrooms, and residents' rooms. The new quarters, erected at 184 Eldridge Street, opened in 1889 at a cost of $90,000. After the move to the new building, the name University Settlement came into wide usage.[8]

Stokes's association with the settlement movement revealed other reform organizations to which he invariably gave his time and his name. At the University Settlement, he became acquainted with Charles Stover, one of the earlier rescuers of the Neighborhood Guild, who in 1898 was helping to form the Outdoor Recreational League of New York. Stokes joined the organization and was instrumental in helping to establish playgrounds and small parks in all areas of the city. Another group, first brought to Stokes's attention through his contact with the University Settlement, was the Prison Association of New York. He not only became a member of the board of directors but eventually received appointment as state inspector of prisons. Before the new century appeared, Stokes joined many such organizations seeking to promote the public good. Among the most noteworthy were the League of Political Education (later known as Town Hall), the City Club, the Citizens Union, and the New York State Conference of Charities and Correction.[9]

Perhaps the project closest to Stokes's heart—one in which he could combine settlement work and family ties—was the development of Hartley House. For many years Marcellus Hartley lived across the street from the Stokes house on Madison Avenue, and his daughters married into the Stokes and Dodge families. Hartley's father had organized the New York Association for Improving the Conditions of the Poor (AICP), an organization dedicated to miscellaneous philanthropic work. After Stokes had become interested in the settlement house movement, he joined the board of managers of the AICP and launched an effort to organize a new social work building. Collaborating closely with Hartley and Dr. William R. Huntington, rector of Grace Church in New York, Stokes helped to establish, under the AICP's auspices, Hartley House on Forty-sixth Street between Ninth and Tenth Avenues.[10]

Shortly after the center opened Stokes wrote an article about the enterprise for the *New York Times Magazine*, later expanding it into pamphlet form. The essay explained the innovations underway at Hartley House and gave an account of his beliefs on the role to be played by wealthy reformers. Sounding very much like a typical charity bureaucrat, Stokes wrote that Hartley House, in order to diminish "the evil of indiscriminate almsgiving . . . [which] produces and sustains a host of vagrants and chronic impostors," was issuing work tickets at a nominal fee to applicants for relief. A woman who presented a ticket was "given ample food and clothing in *exchange for an equivalent in work.*"[11] A slightly modified plan served the men who needed help. But neither men nor women could receive aid more than twice in one week since the object was only to tide the "worthy poor" over when they could not find work elsewhere. Under no circumstances did Hartley House ever give money directly to the people it served; however, in addition to food and clothing, it offered standard settlement house services such as baths and industrial training.[12]

In writing about Hartley House Stokes denied the contention of his socialist acquaintances who claimed the gulfs between the social classes would never be obliterated. According to Stokes, "If the classes could become the friends of each other, the 'gulfs' would not exist." He went on to state that the role of Hartley House was to bring the well-to-do and the poor, especially the young of each group, into "kindly, sympathetic, helpful relations one with another; and to do all that it can toward overcoming social prejudices by the spread of kindly Christian friendliness."[13] At this point in his life Stokes had a long way to go before he could accept the socialist view of the class struggle.

As the new century started, Stokes strengthened his ties with the University Settlement. Although Hartley House occupied much of his time, it had no any male living quarters, so he resided at the University Settlement during the spring of 1899 and in the spring and summer of 1900, and by the summer of 1902 decided to stay on a full-time basis.

Stokes participated fully, not only in University Settlement projects but also in other related activities. During this period he associated himself with approximately thirty committees, movements, and societies promoting the "public good." His more recent positions included serving as treasurer of the Manhattan Trade School for Girls, trustee of the Northern Dispensary of New York, and director of the Juvenile Asylum.[14] Most dramatic was his work for the newly formed New York Child Labor Committee for which he made a hasty "midnight trip" to Albany in April 1903 to argue before the state legislature for passage of committee-sponsored laws.[15]

Despite the enormous degree of success achieved in the child labor fight and similar causes by the University Settlement workers and their allies, there was growing internal friction among the settlement hierarchy. For a number of years there had been criticism of the institution's governing council. Stokes, long an opponent of "charitable work by proxy," decided to have a showdown with the council.

The brouhaha created by Stokes's dissatisfaction with the council set in motion a chain of events that resulted in his meeting someone who altered the course of his public and private life. Among the newspapers interested in the rumor that Stokes had resigned from the governing board and planned a rival settlement was the *Jewish Daily News*. The paper's English department editor assigned a fledgling staff member, Rose Pastor, to interview Stokes. In the published article, Stokes denounced the "uptown friends" of the settlement who knew little about its operation, and he left open the possibility of a new settlement. He also addressed the role of Jews in the organization's hierarchy, taking the position that Christians and Jews must work together because sectarianism breeds class consciousness, which is not desirable in democracy. Avoiding sectarianism and searching for universal ideals became a lifelong quest for Stokes. He looked for these ideals in both religion and politics, achieving success in the former and failure in the latter. He fell in love with Rose Pastor and together they sought answers.

Wealthy entrepreneur and gadfly radical Gaylord Wilshire opened the pages of the March 1903 issue of his socialist magazine, *Wilshire's*, to Stokes in order that the settlement worker could elaborate his philosophy in some detail. Describing his thoughts as "Omniism; or We and Company, Limited," Stokes explained that there were various types of partnerships, the most important being the partnership among the people of a society as a whole and individuals, both acting in their own self-interest. A person might own land or business, but "we," the public, acting through government, could place certain restrictions on the uses of that property. Stokes cited several examples of this private and public partnership, found in such diverse projects as constructing a tenement dwelling or running a railroad. He postulated that selfishness was the reason for endless public laws, that the individual, desiring to promote his own interests, inevitably disregarded the rights of "All." Additionally, Stokes cautioned against altruism because too often in its zeal to help a few helpless people it ran counter to the "Whole." For his solution Stokes suggested a philosophy that "looks primarily to the well-being of that Whole of which the Others and Self are but parts." His philosophy of the All or "Omniism" he summed up by calling for "word, effort, deed and life . . . devoted to the advancement of the welfare not merely of Self, nor of Others, but of that Whole which embodies All."[16] Although Stokes was to confront the concept of selfishness and change his definition of the term as his political life evolved, he remained steadfast in regarding his Omniism as a guiding principle.

Stokes had time for contemplation and abstractions during the summer of 1904 when the Barrows, a well-to-do couple who were occasional visitors to the University Settlement, invited him and Rose to stay with them at their "summer camp" in Quebec. Arriving on 29 July 1904, Stokes and Miss Pastor soon took advantage of the quiet and solitude of the outdoors to compare their respective backgrounds and tell each other their hopes, dreams, and ambitions.[17]

It would be hard to imagine a more dissimilar couple. In physical appearance Stokes stood six feet four inches and had a thin, angular face and deep-set eyes. Most photographs show him with a somber Lincolnish expression as though he was carrying the troubles of others. Brother-in-law Robert Hunter said that Stokes's "ascetic face" reminded him of Hans Holbein's portrait of Erasmus.[18] Rose was almost a foot shorter at five feet five inches; her most notable features were her red hair and expressive brown eyes.[19] These physical differences were minor, however, compared to their disparate family backgrounds and lifestyles.

Rose had none of Graham Stokes's wealth and social status. Born Rose Harriet Wieslander on 18 July 1879, in the small Jewish settlement of Augustow, Russian Poland, she was the granddaughter of a fisherman, daughter of a bootmaker, and the niece of three cantors. Her childhood centered on the Torah, poverty, and emigration. After her parents separated, Rose's mother moved first to Germany and then to a London East Side slum. Her mother married Israel Pastor, a Romanian immigrant who relocated the family to Frying Pan Alley, where, soon after the Pastors arrived, "Jack the Ripper" deposited a torso of a victim in a nearby courtyard. Rose remembered a childhood spent in the Whitechapel district of London where she never saw a tree or a blade of grass except in graveyards.

In 1890 Rose's stepfather resettled the family in Cleveland, Ohio, where life proved to be as difficult as in London. Rose took a job in a cigar factory, and although she tried other jobs, such as sewing shirtwaists and selling women's bonnets, wrapping cigars provided the most stable income for the family. In 1901 her life changed when she responded to a request from the *Jewish Daily News* in New York City for letters from factory workers. The paper published her letter and hired her as a columnist to write "talks" for working women. Within two years, Rose had a full-time job in New York as assistant to the editor of the English section of the *News*. Soon after she met and fell in love with Graham Stokes.[20]

During their stay at the Barrows' Quebec residence, Graham spent time explaining to Rose his belief that "all disease had its root in social causes." He also covered religious and philosophical topics and read the *Light of Asia* to her. Rose did not find it difficult to compare Graham to the book's description of Siddhartha—the given name of Buddha—who, at the age of twenty-nine, had left the home of his rich parents to become a wanderer and to seek a cure for the afflictions of mankind.[21]

At this point in his life Graham Stokes was immersed not only in reading about Buddha but also in charting out an omnistic religious life for himself. Around this time, he joined the American branch of the Vedanta Society, an outgrowth of the Hindu reformer Svämï Vivekänanda's visit to the 1893 World's Parliament of Religions in Chicago and his subsequent three-year tour of the United States. The Vedanta Society declared that all religious prophets preach the same truth under different forms—and that the basic gospel is the same. A recent study notes that the "Vedanta is above all a spiritual outlook, an attitude of mind, and not so much a closed religion with well-defined doctrines. . . . [I]f a prize were offered for the most universal religious system, Vedanta would have a good chance of winning it."[22] A leader in the movement who often wrote to Stokes remarked in 1906, "I almost believe you were a Hindu ascetic in your last incarnation and you have been reincarnated in American flesh for some good work by the Lord's will for this country."[23]

Although becoming immersed in Eastern religions and philosophy, Stokes retained a strong adherence to traditional Christianity. He had strong ties to the Episcopal Church, especially through his younger brother Anson, who became a minister in the church and ultimately canon of the National Cathedral in Washington, D. C. Their parents had originally been members of the Presbyterian Church but changed to the Episcopal Church later in life. Stokes was baptized in the Episcopal faith, was confirmed in 1885, and took his first communion at the Episcopal Church of Heavenly Rest on Fifth Avenue. Throughout his young adulthood, he remained "a member in good standing" in the Episcopal Church but ventured into many other Protestant faiths and nondenominational Christian movements. In addition to his YMCA ties, he was secretary of the Federation of Churches and Christian Workers, was active in the Young People's Association of the Fifth Avenue Presbyterian Church, and was an Honorary Member of the Men's Association of the Fifth Avenue Baptist Church. He attended with deep devotion many services in churches of other denominations.[24]

Graham and Rose married on her twenty-sixth birthday, 18 July 1905. The groom's brother, the Reverend Anson Phelps Stokes Jr., performed an Episcopal ceremony but omitted the word "obey" at the bride's request.[25] The engagement and wedding had produced newspaper headlines. Realizing they had the ultimate fantasy of every working girl—to marry a millionaire—the papers considered it one of the most newsworthy events of the era. Besieged by reporters, Stokes was forced to explain how he and his fiancee could reconcile their different backgrounds. He defined their attitude toward Judaism and Christianity as identical, with each considering himself or herself Christian. The issue was not important to them, Stokes said, because "neither religion as preached to-day contains the entire truth."[26] Another newspaper quoted him as saying, "We are one and have been for months past—spiritually, of course. The marriage is merely to satisfy the world. I can imagine no more beautiful nor purer democratic union than that of Miss Pastor and myself."[27] The publicity continued unabated, the public following every facet of the storybook couple's life. Everyone seemed to be saying about Rose, there goes "the luckiest girl in America!"[28]

After a European honeymoon, Graham and Rose rented a top-floor apartment at the corner of Norfolk and Grand Streets, not far from the University Settlement. Stokes still maintained his ties with the settlement and various other charitable agencies, yet increasingly devoted most of his energies to political activities.

The previous year he had dabbled in the national election of 1904 by allowing his name to be used as a presidential elector supporting Tom Watson, the candidate of the Populist Party. This was an almost totally passive action by Stokes, requiring little of his time. In 1905, however, he became an active participant in a historic New York City election, running for president of the Board of Aldermen on the Municipal Ownership ticket headed by William Randolph Hearst. The newspaper mogul ran for mayor because he wanted to build a national movement for his presidential ambitions. Stokes ran because "gas and water socialism" had interested him for the past four years and he had been a member of the Municipal Ownership League for the previous two years.[29] In his statement accepting the nomination, Stokes repeated the word "morality" several times and followed the line of thought he had expressed in his *Wilshire's* article on Omniism two years before: "The people as a whole have nothing to lose from fair-dealing; the possessors of inequitable 'rights' would in many cases lose much. Both expediency and morality require that *rights* should be emphasized less, and that *right* should be emphasized more. Nothing that is wrong is worth conserving."[30]

Most of Stokes's Socialist Party friends considered the Municipal Ownership campaign detrimental to their cause. John Spargo wrote the nominee: "You know I can't enthuse over your nomination nor bid you success. But I can believe in you and do!" Stokes replied that he was convinced his course of action would accrue unforseen benefits to the Socialist Party and win it new friends.[31] But running against a Tammany Hall-backed Democratic ticket, Hearst and Stokes fell a few thousand votes short of election. The result remained in doubt for some time due to the justifiable charge that Tammany engaged in widespread voter fraud. In replying to post-election charges that Hearst was himself building a political machine, Stokes stated that "the old-fashioned machine is coercive; Mr. Hearst's is educative." He also praised the publisher as "a democrat with a small 'd' and a socialist with a small 's.'" Although an inaccurate description of the enigmatic and politically ambitious Hearst, Stokes's statement aptly described himself.

Education and socialism became recurring themes in Stokes's thought as 1906 approached. He had been impressed by socialist theory but repelled by the intense quarreling over doctrine at party meetings he had attended as a spectator. But a proposal advanced in late 1904 by fledgling novelist Upton Sinclair for formation of an organization that would seek to interest college students and teachers in the subject of socialism captured his interest. He later wrote that Sinclair's declaration appeared to be "closely akin" to his own philosophy of Omniism, expressed in 1903 in *Wilshire's* magazine.[32]

In September 1905 Stokes became one of the vice presidents of the newly created Intercollegiate Socialist Society (ISS), which would, according to one of the participants, "not aim to produce Socialists, but to create students of Socialism."[33] Stokes believed that if people learned the precepts of socialism, an "inner revolution" would occur and they would "make the common welfare rather than private profit the aim and goal of all!"[34]

As the national appeal of municipal ownership waned after the 1905 election, Stokes moved closer to embracing the Socialist Party. His long association and friendship with socialists began to erode most of his moral indignation against the idea of a class struggle. As 1906 began, the answers he received from Socialist Party adherents at a conference he co-hosted in Connecticut and at meetings of the X Club in New York City became increasingly difficult for him to refute in light of the failure of other organizations to which he belonged to solve society's ills.

Stokes's circle of friends from settlement work and journalism was also moving to adopt socialism as its creed. Like Stokes, many belonged to the X Club, an organization formed in 1903 to serve as a "clearing house of ideas" about socialism and related topics. The group met every two or three weeks at various midtown restaurants for debate about some aspect of socialism. Some members, such as W. J. Ghent, Algernon Lee, and Rufus W. Weeks, belonged to the Socialist Party; others, such as historian Charles Beard, journalist Lincoln Steffens, and editor Norman Hapgood, had strong interest in Marxist theory. X Club member John Martin, an Englishman and supporter of the socialist Fabian Society, often hosted club gatherings at his home in rural Staten Island or his summer place in the Adirondack Mountains.[35]

The revolutionary activities in Russia captured the attention of this circle of friends, some of whom had set up a cooperative housing venture called the A Club on lower Fifth Avenue at Washington Square. When the writer Maxim Gorky visited New York City in early 1906 to raise money for the Russian Revolution, the A Club provided sanctuary when the author and his common-law wife were thrown out of their hotel, which expressed indignation over their unmarried status. Stokes's friend and X Club member William English Walling traveled to Russia in 1905–1906 to see and report on the revolution in person.

In 1905 and again in 1906 Stokes and his brother-in-law, Robert Hunter, the author of *Poverty*, an outgrowth of his settlement work, hosted conferences similar to the ones held at John Martin's Adirondack retreat, with X Club members, writers, and liberal politicians making up the guest list. Brick House, the Noroton, Connecticut, home of Stokes's parents, served as the meeting place. The first conference passed almost unnoticed by the press, but the second in March 1906 became a media circus when an invited participant, the wealthy young heir to the

Chicago Tribune, Joseph M. Patterson, announced two days before the meeting that he was abandoning his support of municipal ownership to join the Socialist Party. Although Patterson never attended the Brick House meeting, the newspapers headlined it "Men of Millions in Socialists War" and "Socialist Talk Feast."[36]

The unwelcome publicity focused new attention on Stokes, whose marriage less than a year earlier had him on newspapers' front pages. The similarity of his social standing and wealth to Patterson's could not be ignored. Was he also a socialist? Brick House participant and socialist Leonard D. Abbott characterized Stokes and some others at the meeting as "demi-semi-socialists" who were "hesitating on the brink like a man who cannot quite make up his mind whether to plunge or not."[37]

Stokes was not yet ready to declare himself a socialist. He had to make his semiannual visit to Nevada to oversee the family business holdings. After completing the necessary work there, Rose and he planned to visit San Francisco, but the famous earthquake disrupted their plans. Instead, they detoured to Pasadena, California, where they met and heard the Reverend J. Stitt Wilson, a spellbinding apostle of socialism who later became mayor of Berkeley. Wilson's views about the Socialist Party particularly impressed Rose, who thought about his ideas on the return trip across country. A few days after arriving back in New York City, Stokes was one of the speakers at the fifteenth annual meeting of the Walt Whitman Fellowship. He and others denounced the suppression of free speech by those who would not allow a series of lectures attempted by anarchist Emma Goldman.[38]

During that summer of 1906, Stokes was ready for a change. Rose and he were abandoning the Lower East Side of New York for a beautiful rustic home on an island off the coast of Stamford, Connecticut. Also preying on his mind was the fall gubernatorial election, when the Independence League (the renamed Municipal Ownership League) would, according to Rose's autobiography, probably ask him to be its candidate for governor.[39] These and other influences since the Brick House conference probably played a part in his coming to a decision.

The third week of July 1906, Stokes announced his plans to join the Socialist Party in a letter of resignation to the Independence League. He applauded the aims of the league and wished it well but thought the Socialist Party offered him a more direct base from which to awaken the public to its responsibilities to society. He further commented that his fears about the party's hatred of those who approved of capitalism while allowing gross materialism in its own ranks had been overcome. Stokes expressed disgust at the idle rich and called for collective ownership of capital for the public welfare.[40]

Socialist Party stalwart and friend John Spargo, who opposed Stokes's municipal ownership political foray, immediately welcomed him to party membership: "Never have I written the word 'Comrade' to any man with profounder joy." On the same day, Stokes's Uncle Will Stokes, the wealthy and volatile owner of New York City's Ansonia hotel, reacted rather differently to the announcement. He used a political-theological metaphor, saying he expected his nephew soon to become an anarchist, then a terrorist, and finally an imperialist, like the converts who leave "Methodism for Presbyterianism, then Episcopalianism, then take up Catholicism and become the most extreme Catholics."[41] Ironically, though he repeated Spargo's view when he wrote, "*I believe in you*," Uncle Will saw the future for his nephew in very different terms: "You are yet young, and the sooner you become a Nihilist and a Terrorist the better for you. That is my theory of your case, you have a chance to grow and change your mind, and the quicker you go through these changes and these 'isms' the better."[42]

The Socialist Party opened its arms to Graham and Rose Stokes, dispensing with the requirement that they appear at the East Fourth Street Local to meet party members in their district. New York party treasurer U. Solomon felt this formality was unnecessary since the district organization where the couple lived "transacts its business mostly in Jewish" and the Stokeses' announcement had been "met with a hearty welcome by our members."[43] The party lost little time in recruiting the new converts to be the principal speakers in the coming New York gubernatorial campaign. Graham and Rose joined John C. Chase, the New York party secretary and Socialist candidate for governor, in touring the eastern part of the state in late September and early October 1906.[44]

After Stokes announced his joining of the Socialist Party, individuals and organizations inundated Rose and him with requests to speak and for financial assistance. The party expressed a desire to use his celebrity status. In making arrangements for a talk by the Stokeses, the secretary of the state party of Pennsylvania admitted: "I hope you do not object to my exploiting the idea of your being millionaires, as I think that will prove a strong card in securing a class of persons that we do not usually reach with our Socialist Lectures." In reply, Stokes strongly objected to this idea, proclaiming the "millionaire story false and misleading."[45]

The socialist press also quickly made overtures to Stokes based on his supposed wealth. Milwaukee's *Social-Democratic Herald* broached this "very delicate matter" by writing that, in order to pay off a debt of over $2,000, it would "have to depend on a half dozen well-to-do comrades." The *Chicago Daily Socialist*, New York City's *Worker*, Oakland's *The World*, and doubtless others all asked for funds.[46]

Stokes's wealth was an issue the moment he joined the party. The phrase "millionaire socialist" became almost part of his name in the numerous newspaper articles about him throughout the next decade. He was not alone in this regard. Chicagoans Joseph Patterson and William Bross Lloyd, son of reformer Henry Demarest Lloyd, came from wealthy families and joined the Socialist Party in 1906. Stokes's brother-in-law Robert Hunter and close friend English Walling were widely assumed to be party members although they did not join the party for several years, and they also were characterized as "millionaire socialists."[47]

Unfriendly newspapers from the start called for Stokes to be consistent and back up his political and social beliefs by dividing his wealth with the poor. Stokes replied that he was not a millionaire and received an income from investment of between $2,000 and $2,500 a year. But since he could not realistically locate each individual who worked to supply this unearned revenue, he contributed all of it to organized efforts to spread socialist doctrines among the working class. Most of the money Stokes used for his own benefit came from a salary from the family business and from the very limited medical practice he conducted on semiannual business trips to Nevada mining towns where doctors were few and the barroom brawls numerous.[48]

After Stokes joined the Socialist Party, far more gratifying than the appeals for money or exploitation of his name were the numerous requests from religious organizations desiring his presence. A church in Montclair, New Jersey, wrote soon after Stokes joined the party: "There are some of us who want to learn how the church can really minister more than it does to the life of the community" and that one way to do this is "bringing men like you to speak to a community like this."[49] Stokes believed that it was important to get "socialist theory before the church members of our country" but questioned whether the Christian Socialist movement was going about it correctly. Writing to the Reverend E. E. Carr, editor of the *Christian Socialist*, Stokes remarked that it seemed "quite possible for Christian Socialists to do more harm than good by separating themselves into a different Socialist organization from those Socialists who do not admit the divinity of Jesus."[50]

In a widely published interview explaining why he was a Socialist, Stokes said that he did not think Socialists were any less religious than Republicans or Democrats, and supporters of those parties usually had both their politics and religious beliefs handed down to them from their forebears. A Socialist, on the other hand, is "a human machine that thinks . . . . [and] is never a Socialist because his father was one." In answer to a question about his religious affiliation, Stokes replied: "I was an Episcopalian. . . . Now I think more highly of religion than I did before and controversly [*sic*], less of the church."[51] In divesting himself from the numerous groups devoted to "furtherance of the common good" he had served in some executive capacity, Stokes remarked to the Tuskegee Institute that he expected now to be a "student and teacher" of socialist principles and regarded "Socialism as but the most logical application to social and industrial life of the social teachings of Jesus."[52]

After the initial wave of publicity about Stokes's conversion and the party's exploitation of it through speaking engagements and appeals for funds, he became a member of its National Executive Committee in January 1908. At the party's national convention in May, Stokes participated in the executive committee hearings on delegate credentials, which gave a preview of the serious factional disputes that would rack the convention over such questions as the role labor unions should have in achieving a socialist state. Stokes did not become involved directly in debates over such issues, but his brother-in-law Robert Hunter was one of the leading spokesmen of the conservative wing of the party, one that had ties to the American Federation of Labor. With his philosophy of seeking the universal or "the All," Stokes would not have been pleased by the bitterness among the factions.[53]

Shaking off any doubts, Stokes in late July accepted the nomination of the New York State party to run in the Eighth Assembly District, an area that encompassed much of Manhattan's Lower East Side. Hunter gained the nomination for the adjoining Sixth District. Optimism remained high in the Stokes camp as Election Day approached. One newspaper reporter, who despaired at what he considered the illogical arguments of the Eighth District Socialists, nevertheless admired their dedication and sincerity, which he found to be contagious. He wrote that although Stokes and his followers might be considered "parlor socialists," each talked until his or her voice went hoarse, storming over the district from noon until midnight, "from hall to hall and cart tail to cart tail." The results proved disappointing. Although Stokes had the highest assembly vote total for any Socialist running, he finish third, a few hundred votes behind the Republican candidate.[54]

As the Socialist Party headed into 1909, the issue of trade unionism surfaced again as one of the major points of disagreement among the organization's warring wings. Stokes did not serve again on the National Executive Committee, but Hunter did, and he became one of the leading proponents of a labor party. In November, English Walling, whom Stokes had recently invited to bring his family to live on the Stokeses' island home, charged that there was a plot by Hunter and the right wing to take over the party. Because Walling alluded to having Stokes's support, much of the furor about the charge descended upon Stokes, who was caught in the middle between his brother-in-law, Hunter, and his close friend, Walling.

When it became necessary to state his position in the controversy, Stokes explained that he had tried to temper some of the language in Walling's letter of accusation but did share some of Walling's apprehension regarding the executive committee's close ties with the idea of a labor party. Stokes stressed the need for party harmony based on publication of all the facts in the case.[55] The controversy reached a climax in late January and early February 1910 with the annual election for the committee. All but one of Walling's opponents were re-elected. What rankled most was that Hunter received the highest vote total and seemingly complete vindication. Walling criticized Stokes and others for not being more optimistic and "serious" revolutionaries and wildly blamed his setback on opposition from the "German machine, Russian machine, the A. F. L. machine, and the Christian Socialist machine."[56]

By 1910 the bitter party disputes had taken their toll on Stokes. He had wearied of endless rounds of speaking engagements Rose and he had undertaken since joining the party and consequently drastically curtailed his schedule of public appearances. His island home, a few hundred feet off the coast of Stamford, had become a mecca for socialists to gather. Named Caritas Island by the Stokeses, from the Latin *caritas*, meaning charity or brotherly love, the home served a function similar to that of the earlier X Club, A Club, and John Martin's summer camp in the Adirondack Mountains.

Transient visitors were always welcome, and the permanent residents included the Wallings and the writer Leroy Scott and his family. Painter Rockwell Kent and his wife joined the community in the fall of 1909 and stayed almost a year. Elizabeth Gurley Flynn and her infant son spent the summer of 1910 on the island. The idyllic atmosphere on the island coincided with the personalities of Graham and Rose. Kent claimed that "they were as spiritually disembodied and generally impractical a pair as one might ever meet." Frequent visitor Horace Traubel, socialist and Walt Whitman chronicler, echoed this sentiment, stating that the Stokeses in their idealism "were not of this world."[57]

More and more, Stokes retreated to the library to study economic issues. Years earlier he had spent time after graduation from medical school studying economics at Columbia University. Now foremost in his mind was the belief that economic factors motivated the formation of the United States Constitution. Stokes had spent countless hours in the recently opened New York Public Library at 42nd Street collecting and cataloging data to be used in a projected book when his friend Professor Charles Beard published in 1913 *An Economic Interpretation of the Origins of the Constitution.* Stokes was not disappointed but relieved that Beard had done such an admirable job on so necessary a task.[58]

Stokes had little reason to be unhappy over his unproductive historical research because a scientific project captured his interest, one that was destined to provide him with handsome financial rewards. All his life Stokes had suffered from hay fever, so in the summer of 1913 he set out to develop an ophthalmic solution that would relieve the constant eye irritation caused by pollen. He worked on the project for several years and in 1916 successfully approached a pharmaceutical firm to market his results under the name Estivin.[59] Stokes, who many believed lived only on inherited wealth, created considerable income for himself from this research project.

Stokes did not abandon activity in the Socialist Party completely. In 1911 he became a member of the Connecticut State Executive Committee and in 1912 ran for local office on the party ticket. Running a campaign in a well-to-do suburb was more in keeping with his educational lecturing about socialism than his 1908 campaign on the Lower East Side, which was a political battle.

While Stokes's devotion to the Socialist Party waned, his interest in socialist theory remained strong. He spent considerable time helping his friends with their writing projects on the subject. Walling thanked Stokes for a "careful reading" of his manuscript for the 1912 book *Socialism as It Is* and for "numerous and vital changes made at his suggestion." Earlier, Stokes had provided similar help to Hunter with the manuscript of *Socialists at Work.* Later, in 1916, he, Walling, and others connected with the ISS edited *The Socialism of To-Day: A Source-Book of the Present Position and Recent Development of the Socialist and Labor Parties in All Countries, Consisting Mainly of Original Documents.*[60]

The Intercollegiate Socialist Society, with its broad educational agenda, became the focus of Stokes's socialist activities as World War I approached. President of the organization since 1907, he faithfully fulfilled his duties to the organization except when he had to be out of town on business. This was made easier because he and Rose purchased a residence in Greenwich Village next door to his sister Helen.

Although Stokes supported the left wing of the Socialist Party in denouncing the attempt by the New York State Socialist Party to recall Bill Haywood from the National Executive Committee and expel him from the party in 1913, Stokes was in all likelihood influenced by Walling's and by Rose's militant positions.[61] While Walling fought for his brand of socialism and then, like Stokes, retreated to study and write about socialism, Rose headed in the opposite direction. The picket line and the lecture platform had transformed the shy ghetto immigrant who married

Stokes into a mature, sophisticated woman. The New York City hotel and restaurant workers' strike of 1912 and the Paterson, New Jersey, silkworkers' strike the following year captured her energies and dedication. In her diary, Rose noted that Graham "dreads the thought of my going into the strike without him. Yet he feels that he is not especially fitted for that *kind* of work in the movement."[62]

In 1914 Stokes was reticent about expressing his opinion about the outbreak of war in Europe. In part this was due to a business crisis with the family railroad in Nevada that occupied his attention to the exclusion of other matters. Stokes stressed the need to present "carefully reasoned" differing viewpoints on the war question, and he regarded the Intercollegiate Socialist Society as the key organization to do this.

After the war reached its second year, Stokes became more and more a partisan of preparedness but did nothing to undermine the Socialist Party's opposition to arming the country because he still regarded the organization as "a very useful instrument in the democratic movement" whose efficiency should not be diminished.[63] His attitude changed in 1917 as the United States moved close to declaring war on Germany. When the Socialist Party's emergency convention voted not to support the war effort, Stokes and like-minded friends such as Walling gathered at the Stokeses' home on 26 April and organized the pro-war Social Democratic League. Stokes announced it was a poor citizen "who refrains from public service while awaiting the millennium."[64] For Stokes, the "All" was his country and its allies. Public service and the war effort had become one and the same.

On 9 July, the day after the Socialist Party's members voted to support the antiwar position of the convention, Graham and Rose left the party. He undoubtedly was the author of their resignation letter, which cited loss of faith in the party because it departed from democratic ideals internally and externally. True socialists, it said, could no longer tolerate the dictatorial rule of the organization's leaders and the party's opposition to the war being waged for democracy.[65] At this time, Stokes also supported the efforts of the Social Democratic League to link with the American Federation of Labor's pro-war American Alliance for Labor and Democracy (AALD). In addition, he worked to create a new political party, the National Party, out of the patriotic remnants of Socialists, Progressives, Prohibitionists, and Single Taxers.

Amid the rising animosity between socialist supporters and critics of the war, however, Stokes retained his ties to the ISS because he believed that it constituted neutral ground where the sides could debate. At a November 1917 ISS conference, he gave a lecture titled "Universal Service in Peace and War" that stressed the need to battle selfishness through service to the community.[66] For Stokes, a pacifist in the United States was a selfish individual and not part of the "All." The concept of a classless world representing the "All" had receded almost totally in Stokes's mind.

After being turned down five times for overseas military service on account of his age, Stokes was able to enlist in the New York Coast Artillery. His support of the military was in conflict with many in the ISS. He tried unsuccessfully to resign from the ISS and its presidency. He remained as the president only because he feared leaving would wreck the society.[67]

Stokes's views about the war and the Socialist Party began to create strains in his marriage. While he supported Woodrow Wilson's Fourteen Point program, Rose applauded the Bolshevik ascendancy in Russia, and in December 1917 she rejoined the Socialist Party. Six months later she was convicted and sentenced to ten years in prison for speaking out against the war but remained free on bail pending an appeal.

Meanwhile, Stokes devoted his energies to the Social Democratic League, but not as shrilly as many historians have claimed. David Shannon in his book, *The Socialist Party of America* (1955), incorrectly attributed to Graham Stokes letters that his uncle W. E. D. Stokes sent to government officials suggesting that any possibly treasonous activities by antiwar senators or congressmen be investigated and adding, "If any are guilty, let the guilty be shot at once without an hour's delay." Obviously drawing on Shannon, other books have repeated this historical inaccuracy about Graham Stokes, leaving the impression that during the war he was a bloodthirsty fanatic.[68]

Stokes was not a fanatic but he did pursue what he considered his patriotic duty with great zeal. A compilation of his "unofficial war activities" indicates that he furnished the State Department many times with information about alleged German spies, the activities of socialists, and the antiwar Left in general.[69] When in July 1918 he withdrew from the ISS, Stokes proclaimed: "I draw a sharp distinction between liberty that is democratic and that which is or which I conceive to be individualistic or anarchic." Of the latter type, he said: "In time of crisis . . . it may and should be restrained."[70] Stokes had hardened his view that following one's conscience in opposing the war in any way was selfish and not part of the "All."

After Germany capitulated, Graham and Rose Stokes found that politics irrevocably divided them. Content with Wilson's foreign and domestic policies, Graham bitterly opposed Rose's allegiance to the newly created Communist Party movement that developed in 1919. Although the government reversed her wartime conviction and ordered a new trial, the case was not dismissed until 1921. Domestic tranquillity by then proved impossible between the Stokeses. After a series of uneasy truces, Graham received an interlocutory decree of divorce against Rose in 1925. The two political foes were free to go their separate ways.

A year after his divorce from Rose, Stokes wed Lettice Lee Sands, daughter of a railway executive. As in his first marriage, the word "obey" was not in the marriage vows.[71] After so many years in the public eye Stokes relished his newfound anonymity. In the years to follow, he considered his occupation that of an "executive" and continued to oversee the Stokes family's real estate and other holdings. He lived a routine existence, each day working about six hours and walking about two miles.[72] An inveterate joiner, he continued to be involved in the social and cultural life of New York City, maintaining membership in countless civic and educational organizations, few of which had any political agenda.

The patriotism he preached during the war carried over into peacetime. Military activities replaced political causes in his life. His career in the armed forces had predated his devotion to socialism and his World War I service. During his senior year at Yale, Stokes had enrolled in a military training program. In 1896 at the age of twenty-four he enlisted for five years in the New York State National Guard and, though not leaving the country, served on active duty as a private in the cavalry during the Spanish-American War. After the war, he transferred to the Hospital Corps and received his honorable discharge in 1901.

After the end of World War I, Stokes remained in the Ninth Coast Artillery Corps, New York Guard until 1936, when he retired with the rank of major. He won a number of medals for marksmanship and state decorations for "long and faithful service" and for "service in aid of civil authority." In the 1930s he became chairman of the National Defense Committee of the Military-Naval Club of New York and continued in that capacity throughout World War II. After that war he became active in promoting and supervising extensive recreational facilities and activities for troops at the military base on Governors Island in New York Harbor.

He held memberships in a number of organizations and clubs with military connections, but perhaps his greatest and most longstanding interest in this area was his research into the lineage of his own regiment, New York's Ninth, and into the lineage of the more famous Sixty-Ninth Regiment. After Stokes's death, the Sixty-Ninth offered to "make space in the Regimental Museum for a permanent display of his uniforms, camp kit, medals and photographs."[73]

After Stokes abandoned his devotion to socialism, the only aspect of life that rivaled the military was his religious convictions and actions. Whereas his military endeavors proved a mirror image of his earlier passion for left-wing political activity, his religious beliefs continued to reflect his lifelong search for the "All."

Stokes's interest in the world religions remained strong. He retained his ties to the Vedanta Society and other similar movements. He maintained close contact with Sri Swami Omkar, founder in 1917 of a holy retreat in the Himalayas "where Hindu, a Mohammedan, a Jew, a Christian, a Buddhist, and one all, find a heaven of Peace, worshipping God in his own way and custom. Here caste, creed, color, religion and nationality, are forgotten in the spirit of Oneness and Brotherhood." In their correspondence over many years, Omkar often referred to Stokes as "a living Buddha."[74]

In the 1920s Stokes and Lettice visited Ommen, Holland, the site of the Order of Star, an eastern religious organization run by a leader who, Stokes exclaimed to his mother, "I have no doubt whatever, is so often used as a special vehicle by *the Christ*." The Stokeses supported and remained close to the group until it disbanded in the 1930s. The Stokeses were also in contact in the 1920s with the Islamic mystic Sufi movement.[75]

These and other religious movements that espoused a universal spiritual message attracted Stokes's interest and support. For him,

the evidence is so overwhelming as to be beyond argument, that Jesus did live, not only in Palestine, but elsewhere. But whether or not his actual period was that usually supposed is, to me a matter of no moment whatever. If our views or understandings of the matter happen to differ, what of it? That the vision of man is limited at best; that no one sees the whole truth; that some see relations with one another, or make the least difference in their friendly regards for one another.[76]

Stokes's spirituality manifested itself in the monthly "Gatherings" he conducted at his Greenwich Village home for twenty-five years. Friends visited for a talk by Stokes and meditation when all experienced "flights of the alone to the Alone."[77] The Gatherings ended in the late 1940s so that Stokes could spend more time researching and writing to "break down the barriers that still seem to cause so many earnest people both in the East and in the West to imagine themselves much farther apart respecting 'things spiritual,' than in truth they are or ever should be!"[78]

Although Stokes sought spiritual answers outside Christianity, he remained a strong adherent of it. He continued his pre-World War I interest in a variety of denominations, including liberal Catholicism. But he and his wife also considered themselves devoted Episcopalians and were members of the congregation of Grace Church on Eighth Street and Broadway, near their Greenwich Village home. In the late 1940s, Stokes joined the vestry and became interested in the welfare of the church's grade school. In 1951 he deeded to the church a Nevada iron mine he owned, allowing the school to be renovated and expanded.[79]

When he ventured into religious endeavors outside the Episcopal Church, however, Stokes felt it necessary to obtain his minister's consent so as not to harm "the designation of 'member in good standing' in that Church for the rest of his days." Stokes's vision was "to continue to be as truly 'catholic' in all my church relations as the Episcopal Church itself so rightly endeavors to be."[80] Graham Stokes carried on this ambition until he died on 8 April 1960.

Throughout his long life, Stokes pursued the universal over the narrow and sought the selfless answer to the meaning of life. Although a person of spiritual temperament, he was trained in the political and medical sciences to deal with the temporal world. Perhaps his friend English Walling's sister-in-law, Rose Strunsky, expressed it best when she observed that Graham Stokes considered "life a consecration."[81]

For the first half of his life Stokes sought the "All" in both the religious and the political worlds. He found the oneness he was seeking in the former but ultimately found what he considered to be selfishness in the latter. For the period 1906 to 1910 he believed that the Socialist Party of America was the organization that spoke for the brotherhood of man, that it was not selfish but a universal organization. For a much longer period, from 1905 (or earlier) to late 1918, he thought socialist theory could be studied unfettered by party politics and petty ambition, national chauvinism, and class warfare. He hoped that if one educated the population in the socialist theory of the universal, this knowledge would serve the temporal needs of the All. He was doomed to disappointment.

Only in the religions of the world did Stokes find the All he was seeking. Near the end of his life he wrote to Swami Omkar, a leading Vedanta, expressing his creed: "According to my incomplete understanding, real Peace of lasting character is never possible except as there is Realization in the human heart of the Oneness of All! Such Realization cannot be attained (as I understand the Truth) except in proportion as one understands and becomes ONE WITH THE LORD WITHIN; and through Him, and in Him, *and even as He*, One with in and as All That Is!"[82]

NOTES

1. J. G. Phelps Stokes to Thomas A. Watson, 23 November 1932, Box 88, James Graham Phelps Stokes Papers, Columbia University (hereafter JGPS Papers, Columbia University). Watson was the individual who helped Alexander Graham Bell create the telephone.

2. James F. Findlay Jr., *Dwight L. Moody: American Evangelist, 1837–1899* (Chicago: University of Chicago Press, 1969), 339–55.

3. *Class Book of 1892: Sheffield Scientific School* (New Haven, Conn.: Yale University, 1892), 86, 97.

4. J. G. Phelps Stokes, "My Narrative," unpublished autobiography dictated by Stokes between 1950 and 1956, 66–67. The copy dated 3 October 1967 was in the possession of Mrs. J. G. Phelps Stokes in the 1970s when the author used it in his research. After her death, Columbia University received many additional J. G. Phelps Stokes papers, but "My Narrative" was not included. At present, the author does not know its whereabouts but assumes it is held by a relative of Stokes.

5. Ibid., 68.

6. Ibid., 115, 259–60.

7. Ibid., 70–71; Letterhead, V. Everit Macy to J. G. Phelps Stokes, 6 October 1898, Box 4, JGPS Papers, Columbia University.

8. *New York Herald*, 5 June 1898, clipping, Box 4, JGPS Papers, Columbia University. Stokes; "My Narrative," 262.

9. List of "Sundry Movements in and about New York City 1895– 1918 seeking to promote wider Cooperation in furtherance of the Common Good," Box 83, JGPS Papers, Columbia University.

10. Stokes, "Narrative," 124. Pamphlet issued on the fifteenth anniversary of Hartley House, February 1912, Box 9, JGPS Papers, Columbia University.

11. J. G. Phelps Stokes, *Hartley House: And Its Relations to the Social Reform Movement* (New York: 1897), 24, pamphlet in New York Public Library.

12. Ibid., 32.

13. Ibid.

14. J. G. Phelps Stokes to Albert Kennedy, 15 May 1931, Box 4, JGPS Papers, Columbia University. See also Boxes 11, 21, and 63.

15. Paul Keneley to J. G. Phelps Stokes, 1 May 1902, and Robert Hunter to Governor-elect Frank W. Higgins, 22 November 1904, Box 11, JGPS Papers, Columbia University.

16. J. G. Phelps Stokes, "Omniism; or We and Company, Limited," *Wilshire's* 5 (March 1903): 52. See also untitled "autobiographical notes," p. 16, Box 25, JGPS Papers, Columbia University.

17. Rose Pastor Stokes, "Autobiography," pp. 113–14, Victor Jerome Papers, Yale University. It was at the camp that Rose met the person who became her closest lifelong friend, Olive T. Dargen, who wrote novels under the pen name Fielding Burke.

18. "Robert Hunter Autobiography," portion held by Mrs. Henry C. Gray, Terre Haute, Indiana.

19. Rose Pastor Stokes's 1931 New York State Driver's License, Box 3, Rose Pastor Stokes Papers (hereafter RPS Papers), Yale University. Rockwell Kent, *It's Me O Lord: The Autobiography of Rockwell Kent* (New York: Dodd, Mead, 1955), 187. See also photo collection in RPS Papers.

20. Rose Pastor Stokes, "Autobiography," pp. 1–80, 95–106, Victor Jerome Papers, Yale University.

21. Rose Pastor Stokes, "Autobiography," p. 115, Victor Jerome Papers, Yale University. Rose's comparison of Stokes to Siddhartha does not appear in the copy of her "Autobiography" in her own papers. See Rose Pastor Stokes, "Autobiography," p. 115, RPS Papers, Yale University.

22. Hans Torwesten, *Vedanta: Heart of Hinduism*, adapted by Loly Rosset from a translation by John Phillips (New York: Grove Weidenfeld, 1991), 12, 14. See also Donald S. Lopez Jr., ed. *Religions of India in Practice* (Princeton, N.J.: Princeton University Press, 1995), 47. There is considerable information contained in the Vedanta folders in Box 89 of the JGPS Papers, Columbia University.

23. Baba P. Bharati to J. G. Phelps Stokes, 15 March 1906, James Graham Phelps Stokes Papers, Yale University (herafter JGPS Papers, Yale University).

24. J. G. Phelps Stokes to the Rev. Louis W. Pitt, 7 May 1948, Ledger 29, JGPS Papers, Columbia University. See also certificate "Baptized, Confirmed, First Communion," Box 96, JGPS Papers, Columbia University.

25. Rose Pastor Stokes, "Autobiography," pp. 122–23, Victor Jerome Papers, Yale University. J. G. Phelps Stokes to Anson Phelps Stokes [Jr.], 29 May 1905, Rose Pastor Stokes Papers, Socialist Collections in the Tamiment Library, 1872–1956, New York University.

26. *New York Sun*, 6 April 1905, clipping, Box 75, JGPS Papers, Columbia University.

27. *New York Press*, 7 April 1905, clipping, Box 75, JGPS Papers, Columbia University. There did not seem to be any opposition in either family. The *New York Press* quoted Mrs. Pastor as saying: "I am a Jew but I approve of this marriage. I am proud of Mr. Stokes." Anson Stokes and his wife were traveling in Europe when, according to their grandson, they read the news in the Paris edition of the *New York Herald*. The elder Stokes is recalled as having said, "If Graham wants to marry Rose, I'll see they have the best wedding possible." Anson P. Stokes [III] to J. M. Whitcomb, 28 April 1955, John M. Whitcomb Correspondence. Whitcomb material was in his possession when the author used it but now the collection is at Yale University.

28. Rose Pastor Stokes, "Autobiography," p. 118, Victor Jerome Papers, Yale University.

29. For Hearst's takeover of the Municipal Ownership movement in New York City, see W. A. Swanberg, *Citizen Hearst: A Biography of William Randolph Hearst* (New York: Charles Scribner's Sons, 1961), 247–77. For Stokes's involvement, see list of "sundry movements" compiled by J. G. Phelps Stokes, Box 83, and C. J. Mar to J. G. Phelps Stokes, 3 November 1903, Box 19, JGPS Papers, Columbia University.

30. Untitled draft of J. G. Phelps Stokes statement about "accepting Mr. Hearst's invitation to co-operate with him in the approaching political campaign" [1905]; JGPS papers, Yale University. This document is intriguing because it is typewritten with many handwritten changes that may not be in Stokes's hand. The changes mute a document that has a Marxist class-struggle tone. For example, quoted words "the people as a whole" originally appeared as "the masses." In an earlier sentence, "Insistence upon 'the rights of property' so blinds us, that we commonly fail to distinguish vested rights from vested wrongs," became the less inflammatory "The just rights of property must be jealously preserved but insistence upon those rights must not blind us to the difference between 'vested rights' and vested wrongs." There is Stokes's handwritten note at the end of the document: "Send to me at 184 Eldridge St for OK."

31. John Spargo to J. G. Phelps Stokes [ca. 11 October 1905], and J. G. Phelps Stokes to John Spargo, 30 October 1905, Box 19, JGPS Papers, Columbia University.

32. J. G. Phelps Stokes, "autobiographical notes," pp. 16–17, Box 25, JGPS Papers, Columbia University.

33. Circular, n.d., containing a reprinted letter from Thomas Wentworth Higginson to *Harper's* magazine, 14 July 1905, Box 25, JGPS Papers, Columbia University.

34. Margin note, ca. 1955, by J. G. Phelps Stokes on a printed letter to members issued by Jack London, 20 September 1905, Box 25, JGPS Papers, Columbia University.

35. The X [membership list], 26 October 1905, JGPS Papers, Yale University; W. J. Ghent to X Club [1906?], JGPS Papers, Columbia University.

36. For the full story of the 1905 and 1906 conferences and the Gorky Affair, see the first chapter of the author's "The Millionaire Socialists: J. G. Phelps Stokes and His Circle of Friends" (Ph. D. dissertation, University of South Carolina, 1974).

37. *New York Herald*, 5 March 1906, 4.

38. Rose Pastor Stokes, "Autobiography," p. 138, Victor Jerome Papers, Yale University; J. G. Phelps Stokes Appointment Book 1906, Box 2, JGPS Papers, Columbia University; J. Stitt Wilson to Rose Pastor Stokes, 28 August 1906, Box 3, Rose Pastor Stokes Papers, Tamiment Library, New York University; *New York Evening Call*, 1 June 1906, clipping, Box 75, JGPS Papers, Columbia University.

39. Rose Pastor Stokes, "Autobiography," p. 138, Victor Jerome Papers, Yale University. There is no correspondence to support Rose's account, but the existing material with the Hearst organization for the summer of 1906 is sparse and may be incomplete. See Box 19, JGPS Papers, Columbia University.

40. *Milwaukee Record Herald*, 13 July 1906, 4; *New York Worker*, 14 July 1906, 1.

41. John Spargo to J. G. Phelps Stokes, 14 July 1906, JGPS Papers, Yale University.

42. Uncle Will [W. E. D. Stokes] to Graham [JGPS], 14 July 1906, JGPS Papers, Yale University.

43. U. Solomon to J. G. Phelps Stokes, 7 August 1906, JGPS Papers, Yale University.

44. U. Solomon to J. G. Phelps Stokes, 13, 19 September 1906; and "The Chase-Stokes Tour" itinerary, 30 September to 10 October [1906], JGPS papers, Yale University. See also *New York Worker*, 13 October 1906, 1.

45. Robert B. Ringler to J. G. Phelps Stokes, 16 December 1906, and Stokes to Ringler, 18 December 1906, JGPS Papers, Yale University.

46. E. H. Thomas, Victor Berger, and H. W. Bistorius to J. G. Phelps Stokes, 25 September 1906. See also *Chicago Daily Socialist* to Stokes, 12 July 1907; *The World* to Stokes, 20 August 1907; and *Worker* to Stokes, 3 August 1907, JGPS Papers, Yale University. Stokes contributed or purchased stock in most of the publishing ventures along the lines suggested by the solicitations.

47. An article titled "Our Millionaire Socialists" by Gustavus Myers appeared in some copies of *Cosmopolitan*, 51 (October 1906): 596–603. It contained profiles of Stokes, Patterson, Lloyd, Hunter, Walling, and Nelson O. Nelson, a wealthy St. Louis-area co-operative plumbing manufacturer. The article was withdrawn during publication of the journal and another article was substituted. The exact reason is unclear, but that issue of the journal was the center of a campaign against muckraking. For a detailed account of the events surrounding the suppression of "Our Millionaire Socialists," see the author's doctoral dissertation or his "The 1906 Campaign to Sway Muckraking Periodicals," *Journalism Quarterly* 56 (Autumn 1979): 513–20, 589.

48. Lillian Baynes Griffin, "Mrs. J. G. Phelps Stokes at Home," *Harper's Bazaar* 40 (September 1906): 795; *New York Worker*, 2 February 1907, 1; Mrs. J. G. Phelps Stokes (the former Lettice Lee Sands), interview with author, 15 November 1971, New York City. One measure of Stokes's sincerity about not using unearned income was his refusal to accept the position of trustee of the I. N. Phelps estate, which yielded about $2,000 a year. Anson Phelps Stokes, *Stokes Records* (New York: Privately printed, 1915), 4:119, 129. Stokes did,

however, receive help from his mother and others in the family when he made large purchases such as houses.

49. Edgar S. Wiers to J. G. Phelps Stokes, 27 July, 10 October 1906, JGPS Papers, Yale University. Among the speeches Stokes gave to church audiences was one titled "Am I My Brother's Keeper?" The Rev. Leighton Williams to J. G. Phelps Stokes, March 1907, JGPS Papers, Yale University.

50. J. G. Phelps Stokes to the Rev. E. E. Carr, 14 May 1907, JGPS Papers, Yale University.

51. "J. G. Phelps Stokes Explains Why He Is a Socialist," 16 January [1907?], *The Record*, Box 75, JGPS Papers, Columbia University.

52. J. G. Phelps Stokes to Robert C. Ogden, 13 May 1907, Box 17, JGPS Papers, Columbia University.

53. Charlotte Teller, "The National Socialist Convention," *Arena* 40 (July 1908): 34; *Socialist Party: Proceedings of the National Convention, 1908* (Chicago: Socialist Party, 1908), 99.

54. Newspaper clipping, 30 October 1908, Harry W. Laidler Papers, Tamiment Library, New York University; *Ayer's Directory: 1909* (Albany, N.Y.: J. B. Lyon, 1909), 888.

55. J. G. Phelps Stokes to Morris Hillquit, 2, 13, 15 December 1909, reprinted in *International Socialist Review* 10 (January 1910): 656–58, 660–62. The letters also appeared in the *New York Call*, 19 December 1909.

56. William English Walling to Eugene V. Debs, 12 February 1910, and Walling to H. M. Hyndman, 19 February 1910, Box 1, William English Walling Papers, State Historical Society of Wisconsin.

57. Kent, *It's Me O Lord*, 194–95; Rockwell Kent to John M. Whitcomb, 2 February 1963, Whitcomb Material, Rose Pastor Stokes Papers, Yale University; Elizabeth Gurley Flynn, *I Speak My Own Piece: Autobiography of the "The Rebel Girl"* (New York: Masses & Mainstream, 1955), 105.

58. Rose Pastor Stokes, "Autobiography," p. 194–95, Victor Jerome Papers, Yale University.

59. J. G. Phelps Stokes to William J. Schieffelin, 16 February 1916, and Schieffelin to Stokes, 1 March 1916, Schieffelin & Co. Archives, New York City. Marketed in 1919, the product proved very successful and is still produced.

60. William English Walling, *Socialism as It Is* (New York: Macmillan, 1912), vi; Robert Hunter, *Socialists at Work* (New York: Macmillan, 1908), ix; William English Walling et al., *The Socialism of To-Day: A Source-Book of the Present Position and Recent Development of the Socialist and Labor Parties in All Countries, Consisting Mainly of Original Documents* (New York: Henry Holt, 1916).

61. "What Haywood Says on Political Action," *International Socialist Review* 13 (February 1913): 623.

62. Rose Pastor Stokes Diary, February 1913, Whitcomb Material, Rose Pastor Stokes Papers, Yale University.

63. J. G. Phelps Stokes to W. E. D. Stokes, 14 January 1916, Box 25, JGPS Papers, Columbia University.

64. J. G. Phelps Stokes, "Tentative Draft of proposal for formation of a Social Democratic League," 24 April 1917, Box 26, JGPS Papers, Columbia University.

65. J. G. Phelps Stokes and Rose Pastor Stokes to Local, Stamford Socialist Party, 9 July 1917, Box 27, JGPS Papers, Columbia University.

66. J. G. Phelps Stokes, "Universal Service in Peace and War," *Intercollegiate Socialist* 6 (December–January 1917–1918): 11–15, original copy in Box 28, JGPS Papers, Columbia University. The article was also printed in the *New York Times Magazine* section under the

title "Nonresidence and Anarchy Closely Allied: An Arraignment of the Selfishness and Immorality of the Pacifists' Attitude When Their Country Calls for Help," 25 November 1917.

67. J. G. Phelps Stokes to William English Walling, 12 December 1917, Box 29, JGPS Papers, Columbia University.

68. See Robert D. Reynolds Jr., "Pro-War Socialists: Intolerant or Blood-thirsty?" *Labor History* 17 (Summer 1976): 413–16.

69. "Unofficial War Activities of Captain J. G. Phelps Stokes, CA—ORC," compiled at the request of Captain C. Hockwell Cole, Secretary to the Adjunct General of New York, December 1922, JGPS Papers, Columbia University.

70. J. G. Phelps Stokes to Norman Thomas, 29 July 1918, Box 30–31, JGPS Papers, Columbia University.

71. Mrs. J. G. Phelps Stokes, interview with author, 24 November 1972, New York City.

72. Life Extension Institute Medical Report [J. G. Phelps Stokes], 7 August 1931, Box 93, JGPS Papers, Columbia University.

73. Colonel William D. Lynch to Mrs. J. G. Phelps Stokes, 27 July 1960, Grace Church Archives, General, Box X, II A–30–8. See also *Class of '92 Sheff: Supplementary Record*, 58–59 and *Class of '92 Sheff: Third Supplementary Record*, 53–54. The Stokes Papers at Columbia University contain almost twenty boxes of material relating to Stokes's military career and the military-related organizations in which he held membership.

74. Letterhead of the Himalayan organization, 22 November 1938. Swami Omkar to J. G. Phelps Stokes, 1 March 1943, 12 December 1949, 18 November 1954, Box 88, JGPS Papers, Columbia University.

75. J. G. Phelps Stokes to his mother, 17 July 1929; see also membership cards and other material related to the organization, Box 89, JGPS Papers, Columbia University.

76. J. G. Phelps Stokes to John O'Neill, 9 November 1929, Box 88, JGPS Papers, Columbia University.

77. Lettice S. Phelps Stokes to Friends of "the Gatherings," 18 January 1944, and Virginia Horner to J. G. Phelps Stokes, 19 December 1958, Box 93, JGPS Stokes Papers, Columbia University.

78. J. G. Phelps Stokes, *The One Lord of East and West* (Sivananda Nagar Post. [Himalayas] India: The Yoga Vedanta Forest University, April 1956), 1. Other Stokes pamphlets published by Yoga-Vedanta Forest in the 1950s were *The Ever-Returning Christ* and *The Awakening*.

79. For information about Stokes's gift and his ties to Grace Church, see the J. G. Phelps Stokes files in the Grace Church Archives; and Edyth McKitrick and Kate McMullan, *Grace Church School, 1894–1994: The Story of the First Hundred Years* (New York: Friends of Grace Church, 1994), 50–53.

80. J. G. Phelps Stokes to the Rev. Louis W. Pitt, 7 May 1948, Ledger 29, JGPS Papers, Columbia University.

81. Letter fragment, n.d., Box 1, William English Walling Papers, State Historical Society of Wisconsin. Although this letter is incomplete and undated, internal evidence makes inescapable that the author was Rose Strunsky and the date late 1912 or early 1913.

82. J. G. Phelps Stokes to Swami Omkar, 9 December 1955, Box 88, JGPS Papers, Columbia University.

Essay on Sources

Materials for the study of the many relationships between American Christianity and socialism are widely scattered and frustratingly uneven. Mainstream religious leaders commented and wrote much about socialism, yet their private papers and the proceedings of the denominations contain, with few exceptions, little more than traces of interest. Socialist periodicals contain abundant coverage of religion as both a spiritual element in human history and social institution, viewing it sometimes as potential or actual enemy and sometimes as potential or actual ally. Many socialists, moreover, came from Christian traditions that they either continued to embrace in some fashion or found it impossible to escape. Yet the researcher in socialist records encounters many lacunae. Intriguing trails abruptly end, fascinating individuals disappear without explanation, and the historian's skills as detective are put to the severest test.

All this notwithstanding, the subject deserves—and research materials will support—more thorough treatment than it has received since Robert T. Handy surveyed it in "Christianity and Socialism in America, 1900–1920," *Church History* 21 (March 1952): 39–54. The situation with respect to sources is not utterly bleak, as the contributors to this volume demonstrate. Even for individuals who left behind no private manuscripts whatsoever, it is possible to track their activities as socialists through periodicals and probe their worldviews through published accounts of their messages, and thus limn biographical sketches of scholarly significance. Approaches to the Christian-socialist engagement other than the biographical are likewise promising.

MANUSCRIPT COLLECTIONS

The major general collections of socialist material are the Socialist Party of America Papers in the Perkins Library at Duke University and the Socialist

Collections in the Tamiment Library, 1872–1956, at New York University. Both collections are available on microfilm. The Tamiment collections, part of broader holdings that include labor and communist materials, originated with the Rand School of Social Science (founded in 1906 with the financial support of George D. Herron's second mother-in-law); they include records of that school as well as of the Intercollegiate Socialist Society, the Socialist Party in New York city and state, and individuals such as Herron, Algernon Lee, Lena Morrow Lewis, and Rose Pastor Stokes. Christian participation in the socialist movement is evident in the ISS, Rand School, and New York Local records, and the New York materials throw light on religion as an issue in that setting.

Though richest for later decades, the SPA collection at Duke offers a valuable biographical guide through which one can locate the correspondence of some religious radicals before the mid-1920s. The issue of religion, and especially Catholic anti-socialism, has a high profile in the national office papers for 1911–1914, when former minister Carl D. Thompson was information director for the SPA. Some state and local files in the Duke collection are useful for probing religious influences in particular locales.

Both the Tamiment and Duke repositories also hold publications by socialist Christians and socialist periodicals that took note of their work. Both are well organized and exceptionally well serviced.

Other manuscript collections are relevant to particular aspects of the subject. The Eugene V. Debs Collection in the Cunningham Memorial Library at Indiana State University at Terre Haute reveals much about Debs's attitude toward religion, as expressed in his writings and letters, and about his contacts with people of religious bent, including ministers. Augmented by Debs material from many other libraries, that collection is available in a microfilm collection edited by J. Robert Constantine, who also edited *Letters of Eugene V. Debs*, 3 vols. (Urbana, Ill.: University of Illinois Press, 1990), which contains representative selections. Indiana State University also holds a very extensive collection of pamphlets not included in the microfilm project.

Two collections at the State Historical Society of Wisconsin in Madison, those of Richard T. Ely and Henry Demarest Lloyd, contain important correspondence to and from religious radicals with socialist political tendencies, which is especially valuable for the 1890s and early 1900s, before the Socialist Party of America became a viable outlet for their energies. William Dwight Porter Bliss is an especially important case in point. Both collections are on microfilm.

The John Spargo Papers in the Bailey/Howe Library at the University of Vermont include numbers of letters between him and Franklin S. Spalding, J. G. Phelps Stokes, Mary Sanford, Alexander Irvine, George D. Herron, Walter Rauschenbusch, and other figures mentioned in this study, but they are mostly routine exchanges. A far richer collection on Christianity and socialism is to be found in the papers of Roland D. Sawyer, a clergyman and Socialist candidate for governor in Massachusetts, and later a longtime Democratic assemblyman, which are held at the University of New Hampshire Library. Thus far little explored, Sawyer's life awaits a conscientious biographer. The Samuel Colgate—American

Baptist Historical Society Library in Rochester, New York, holds the papers of Walter Rauschenbusch, one of the Social Gospel's most incisive thinkers. This collection contains important correspondence with European and American socialist Christians like Rufus W. Weeks, as well as with non-religious party members, all underscoring the depth of Rauschenbusch's interest in and sympathy for socialism. No other Social Gospel collection, including the sizeable Washington Gladden Papers at the Ohio Historical Society in Columbus, approaches the Rauschenbusch collection for value in the study of socialism.

Few local socialist records have survived, many having been destroyed by governmental and private vigilante actions during World War I or in the Red Scare of 1919–1920. The Socialist Party-Social Democratic Federation (SP-SDF) Collection of the Milwaukee Public Library includes some minutes through which it is possible to trace the activities of the ministers Harvey Dee Brown, Winfield Gaylord, Frederick G. Strickland, and Carl D. Thompson in the party. Records of Local Dayton (Ohio), including a small collection of the papers of Frederick G. Strickland, in the Dunbar Library at Wright State University in Dayton, illustrate the immense value of looking at socialist history locally. In the case of Dayton, a middle-American city in which socialists had strong appeal, the power of an ethical posture by the party is very evident.

Some of the most influential individuals in religion-based socialism left no private papers. W.D.P. Bliss remains thus without a comprehensive biography, though numerous authors have written chapter- or article-length studies of him. George D. Herron also awaits a full-life study that would span the 1890s and his cooperation with the Wilson administration during and after World War I in Europe, to which the Herron collection at the Hoover Institution at Stanford University is primarily devoted.

Edward Ellis Carr, who more than anyone else organized the Christian Socialist Fellowship and kept it going, left no known collection, and this author's efforts to locate his descendants have proven futile. Scores of second-tier activists who in other enterprises would have been important enough to preserve personal collections, did not do so. Peripatetic careers and a concentration on action rather than record-keeping are at least partial explanations in many cases.

Of the seven subjects of this volume, Irwin St. John Tucker and J. G. Phelps Stokes were the most indefatigable record-keepers. Early in the century, Tucker's father initiated a system of weekly letter-writing, in which each family member wrote a general letter, with additional comments to particular members, which he then circulated among them all. Not all, but a very extensive selection of these letters has survived, and they document Tucker's experiences, insights, motives, responses to criticism, and setbacks beginning at about the age of sixteen. A diary begun in boyhood, despite several gaps, is also detailed, far-reaching, and candid. The Tucker Papers at the University of Illinois at Chicago is surely one of the best collections for a twentieth-century American religious figure. It also includes copies of his many writings, photos and scrapbooks, and many newspaper and magazine clippings about newsworthy events in his life. A smaller but important set of materials on Tucker and St. Stephen's Church is in the Archives of the Episcopal

Diocese of Chicago; a Tucker collection at the Seabury-Western Theological Seminary in Evanston, Illinois, includes some valuable but not well-processed materials on non-socialist aspects of his life.

The major bodies of Stokes's papers are at Columbia and Yale universities. The collection at Columbia, begun by Stokes before his death in 1959 and later supplemented by his widow, documents the many social, political, civic, and philanthropic organizations with which he was associated but unfortunately contains few documents directly related to the Socialist Party. Yale University holds the papers of Rose Pastor Stokes, his first wife, which include some materials pertinent to his socialist years. The J. G. Phelps Stokes Files and Rose Pastor Stokes Files, obtained by Yale in 1990, are of considerable significance. These papers include much correspondence from the years 1903–1910 involving the Stokeses' decision to join the Socialist Party and their early years of party activity. Other materials may be found in the Stokes Family Papers at Yale, the Rose Pastor Stokes Collection at the Tamiment Institute Library at New York University, the Grace Church (New York City) Archives, and scattered other socialist collections. The location of an unpublished autobiography by J. G. Phelps Stokes, once in the possession of his widow but not deposited at Columbia, is unknown.

Surprisingly, there are no known collections of personal papers for J. Stitt Wilson, Franklin S. Spalding, George Washington Woodbey, or Bouck White. There is probably little extant information about Woodbey that Philip S. Foner failed to discover. Douglas Firth Anderson's work on Wilson rests on periodicals, published writings, and secondary works, except for a few boxes of Berkeley election materials in the Bancroft Library of the University of California at Berkeley; the same is true for John R. Sillito's research on Spalding, except for Spalding scrapbooks at the Colorado Historical Society in Denver and the Denver Public Library, and for Mary E. Kenton's on White, except for a few items in the Widener Library at Harvard. In White's case, an important cache of clippings, interview notes, photographs, and other material collected in 1948–1950 by Irvin G. Wyllie, who intended to write a comprehensive biography before other professional responsibilities intervened, was given to Kenton by Wyllie's widow, Harriet Wyllie, in 1977 and remains in her possession. Kate Richards O'Hare would likely have left a plentiful array of personal papers had they not been destroyed twice by others, including Frank P. O'Hare, at the time of their divorce. Sally M. Miller has located O'Hare letters and other materials at the Missouri and Kansas state historical societies in St. Louis and Topeka, respectively, and at the University of Missouri at Columbia library. O'Hare's many published writings and generous press coverage of her life, supplemented by what correspondence remains, enabled Miller to produce *From Prairie to Prison: The Life of Social Activist Kate Richards O'Hare* (Columbia, Mo.: University of Missouri Press, 1993).

PERIODICALS

In the absence of correspondence and diaries, newspapers and magazines often must supply the skeleton of the story of Christian-socialist encounter. Fortunately, socialists saw themselves as having an essential educational mission to perform in order to bring about revolution through the ballot box, and they appreciated the contribution the press might make to spreading their message and binding their movement together. For the Christian socialism of the 1890s, Bliss's *Dawn* (1889–1896) is indispensable. It chronicles the fragile history of the Society of Christian Socialists, Bliss's formation of a socialist Church of the Carpenter in Boston, his work on behalf of the Anglican Christian Social Union, and his attempt to build a broad-based reform movement in alliance with the People's Party and disenchanted labor forces. Bliss's interest in creating an American Fabian movement, devoted to education in socialism, is reflected in the first two years of the *American Fabian* (1895–1900), which he helped found and which carried the same material as the *Dawn* during the period in which they overlapped.

Religious ideals were prominent, though not linked with Bliss's Christian socialism, in another radical paper of the 1890s, the *Coming Nation* (1893–1903), begun by Julius A. Wayland before he undertook his greatest publishing venture, the *Appeal to Reason*. Long associated with the Ruskin Commonwealth colony in Tennessee, and with a broader socialist interest in cooperative colonies, the *Coming Nation* drew deeply from Jeffersonian, populistic, and evangelical Christian sources.

If the *Dawn* is crucial to any study of Bliss's Christian socialism, so the *Social Crusader* (1898–1901) and *Socialist Spirit* (1901–1903) provide the essential narrative structure for the movement toward socialism of J. Stitt Wilson, Carl D. Thompson, and other Chicago-based radical ministers at the turn of the century. These periodicals enable one to reconstruct this group's relationship with George D. Herron, their campaigns across the United States and in Britain, and their important work in promoting the movement for socialist unity that culminated in organization of the Socialist Party of America in 1901. Unlike the *Dawn*, which judged the churches by a radical standard of justice but remained loyal to them as institutions, these periodicals often breathed fire at a Christianity that had betrayed its founder's spirit and ideals. Closely related in personnel and outlook to Herron and his circle was the *Comrade* (1901–1905), edited by John Spargo and linking the arts, socialism, and emancipation from religious tradition. Its "How I Became a Socialist" accounts, published in 1902–1903, illustrate the mixture of religious with other factors found frequently in conversions to socialism.

The *International Socialist Review* (1900–1918), published by Charles H. Kerr, was a journal of serious Marxist theoretical discourse in its early years, and after 1908 a staunch proponent of revolutionary class struggle. Kerr also published many classic works of the socialist movement (sometimes for the first time in English) and a popular "Pocket Library of Socialism" that included such titles by socialist Christians as George H. Strobell's *A Christian View of Socialism,* Robert W. Webster's *The Kingdom of God and Socialism*, and others by Charles H. Vail, William Thurston Brown, and George D. Herron. In its first year, the *Review* had a regular column on "Socialism and Religion" directed by George D. Herron. Though Herron's personal difficulties brought that column to an end, articles and book reviews involving religion appeared across the years that followed. The

Review gave voice to authors who attacked religion as anachronistic in an age of science and as hostile to the interests of the workers, and to others, like J. Stitt Wilson, Owen R. Lovejoy, Thomas C. Hall, and Lucien V. Rule, who saw in socialism the spirit of Christ. It also reflected socialist attitudes toward Roman Catholicism and responses to Catholic attacks on socialism.

Much folksier in style, the *Appeal to Reason* (1895–1922) reflected the popular political and moral culture of the Southwest and Midwest but also won a national and urban readership through an imaginative system of distribution (and even newsstand sales). It was a truly mass circulation publication, with elements of humor, sarcasm, parody, and common sense that eased readers' digestion of its serious contents, contents that tapped into the protean moral ideal of a cooperative commonwealth. Along with the *National Rip-Saw* (1904–1917), it was a key forum for the writings of Kate Richards O'Hare and Eugene V. Debs. Widely admired by socialist Christians, the *Appeal* extolled a working-class Jesus while castigating the religion of the privileged classes, and expressed particular antagonism toward Roman Catholicism.

The *Masses* (1911–1917), put out by cosmopolitan cultural rebels in Greenwich Village, far from the socialist encampments of the Southwest, likewise took note of the social impact of religion and distinguished sharply between Jesus and the churches. Editor Max Eastman was the son of Congregational ministers, and others on the staff had religious backgrounds that were never completely shaken. Carl Sandburg first published his poem attacking evangelist Billy Sunday, the "bunkshooter," in its pages, while cartoonist Art Young lampooned expensive church conventions and sketched a Jesus who "stirr[ed] up the people," and Sara Cleghorn memorialized Jesus as a party comrade. Representative selections appear in William L. O'Neill, ed., *Echoes of Revolt: THE MASSES, 1911–1917* (Chicago: Ivan R. Dee, 1989 repr. ed.).

Among other national socialist publications, the *Intercollegiate Socialist* (1913–1919), directed toward the largely native-born, middle-class campus audience sought by the Intercollegiate Socialist Society, repays examination for its general tenor of intellectual idealism, as well as for contributions by socialist Christians such as Walter Rauschenbusch and Vida D. Scudder.

Urban socialist newspapers are a rich mine of information about the activities of religious socialists, debates over religion within party forums, and reactions to Catholic attacks. The *New York Call* (1909–1923) and the *Chicago Socialist* (1902–1912), each of which was a daily for some period, are but the two most prominent examples. For both Bouck White and Irwin St. John Tucker, the *Call*'s coverage was frequent enough to establish details about their work in New York City unavailable in other sources. For J. Stitt Wilson and northern California religious radicals, the *San Francisco Call* (1895–1913) performs a similar function. Outside metropolitan centers, socialist papers like the *Miami Valley Socialist* (1912–1925) in mid-sized Dayton are often the sole source for coverage of religious issues and such public enterprises as Frederick G. Strickland's "Workers' Ethical Platform."

No periodical is more significant for the study of Christianity and socialism, of course, than the *Christian Socialist* (1903–1922). Its use by historians of socialism has been cursory, and few if any historians of American religion seem to have perused it in its entirety. When socialist Christians split over American intervention in World War I, E. E. Carr, who took a pro-war stance, renamed the badly damaged paper *Real Democracy*. He attempted unsuccessfully to revive it in 1932. The *Christian Socialist* regularly covered developments in the socialist movement; its greater importance, however, is as the pre-eminent source for the Christian Socialist Fellowship's history, the identity of often isolated Christians who became socialists, the participation of Christians in party affairs, and the panoply of theological and practical rationales used by Christians on behalf of socialism. Its numerous autobiographical accounts of conversion to socialism offer a substantial comple-ment to the "How I Became a Socialist" articles published earlier in the *Comrade*. Considerably less important in scope and substance, the *Social Preparation for the Kingdom of God* (1914–1924) was vital to Episcopalians in their Church Socialist League.

The *Outlook, Independent, Forum, Arena, Literary Digest,* and *North American Review* are among the many general periodicals of the time that carried occasional articles and editorials, too numerous to cite here, on socialism and religion.

SOCIALIST AND WORKING-CLASS HISTORIES

General studies of American socialism typically relegate religion to a rather minor role in the movement's history, when they do not ignore it. An important exception, Howard H. Quint's pathbreaking *The Forging of American Socialism: Origins of the Modern Movement* (Indianapolis, Ind.: Bobbs-Merrill, 1953), gives religious radicals like Bliss and Herron their due, but extends only through the creation of the Socialist Party of America in 1901. David A. Shannon's *The Socialist Party of America: A History* (New York: Macmillan, 1955) and James Weinstein's *The Decline of Socialism in America, 1912–1925* (New York: Monthly Review Press, 1967) fairly describe the Christian socialists in opening chapters that survey the SPA's makeup but mention them only rarely thereafter. In *The American Socialist Movement, 1897–1912* (New York: Columbia University Press, 1952), Ira Kipnis briefly acknowledges the Christian contingent but mistakenly implies that it was uniformly on the party's Right, toward which he is unsympathetic.

Several broad interpretations of American radical history allow little place to religion: Paul Buhle, *Marxism in the United States: Remapping the History of the American Left* (London: Verso, 1987); Milton Cantor, *The Divided Left: American Radicalism, 1900–1975* (New York: Hill and Wang, 1978); John Patrick Diggins, *The Rise and Fall of the American Left* (New York: W. W. Norton, 1992 ed.); and David Herreshoff, *American Disciples of Marx: From the Age of Jackson to the Progressive Era* (Detroit, Mich.: Wayne State University Press, 1967). One such work in which it receives an entire chapter, Bernard K. Johnpoll with Lillian Johnpoll, *The Impossible Dream: The Rise and Demise of the American Left*

(Westport, Conn.: Greenwood Press, 1981) is erratic in coverage and unreliable in judgment.

The excellent *Encyclopedia of the American Left* (Urbana, Ill.: University of Illinois Press, 1992), edited by Mari Jo Buhle, Paul Buhle, and Dan Georgakas, contains only a brief entry on Christian socialism by Paul Buhle and John Cort; limitations of space, however, not lack of interest, explain the absence of other articles relevant to the subject.

In her sweeping effort to demolish radical historiography, *The Radical Persuasion: Aspects of the Intellectual History and the Historiography of Three American Radical Organizations* (Baton Rouge, La.: Louisiana State University Press, 1981), Aileen S. Kraditor argues that leftist leaders failed to understand the priorities of an archetypal John Q. Worker she posits. While recognizing that religion often held a prominent place in workers' culture and aspirations, and thus might yield support for her argument, she nevertheless makes no assessment of its impact on their acceptance or rejection of socialism.

Monographic studies of socialism provide considerable insight into religious dimensions of the socialist experience. Mari Jo Buhle's *Women and American Socialism, 1870–1920* (Urbana, Ill.: University of Illinois Press, 1981), underscores the Protestant reformist backgrounds of native-born women who became socialists and provides numerous biographical leads. The religious and moral framework in which Southwestern socialists understood their politics receives careful analysis in Garin Burbank, *When Farmers Voted Red: The Gospel of Socialism in the Oklahoma Countryside, 1910–1924* (Westport, Conn.: Greenwood Press, 1976), and James R. Green, *Grass-Roots Socialism: Radical Movements in the Southwest, 1895–1943* (Baton Rouge, La.: Louisiana State University Press, 1978). Elliott Shore's *Talkin' Socialism: J. A. Wayland and the Role of the Press in American Radicalism, 1890–1912* (Lawrence, Kans.: University Press of Kansas, 1988) sheds much light on the the man and the publications, especially the *Appeal to Reason*, that helped bind folks in that region and elsewhere to the socialist movement. Though its contributors do not give religion the emphasis it deserves, *Socialism in the Heartland: The Midwestern Experience* (Notre Dame, Ind.: Notre Dame University Press, 1986), edited by Donald T. Critchlow, is a valuable starting point for further exploration of socialism in places like Dayton, Flint, Marion (Indiana), Minneapolis, and Milwaukee.

The importance that Herbert Gutman attributed to religion as a force that bolstered working-class resistance to capitalist encroachments on traditional values in the late nineteenth century, in particular in his *Work, Culture, and Society in Industrializing America* (New York: Alfred E. Knopf, 1976), has stimulated the interest of labor historians. This interest has been particularly prominent in the works of Ken Fones-Wolf, including *Trade Union Gospel: Christianity and Labor in Industrial Philadelphia, 1865–1915* (Philadelphia: Temple University Press, 1989), which indicate that workers, in their contests with employers over the social meaning of religion, often grounded their critique of capitalism in a religious and moral foundation. Donald E. Winters' *The Soul of the Wobblies: The I. W. W., Religion, and American Culture in the Progressive Era, 1905–1917* (Westport,

Conn.: Greenwood Press, 1985), utilizing the conceptual tools of contemporary religion studies, finds religious symbols and values diffused throughout the movement culture—the music, legends, martyrs, poetry, enemies, and the like—of the most radical labor union of the period. Attempts to measure working-class religiosity, however defined, have been rare. In "Revival and Upheaval: Religion, Irreligion, and Chicago's Working Class in 1886," *Journal of Social History* 25 (Winter 1991): 233–53, Bruce C. Nelson reports high rates of indifference, and in some ethnic communities of hostility, toward religion. Kevin Christiano's *Religious Diversity and Social Change: American Cities, 1890–1906* (Cambridge, England: Cambridge University Press, 1987), which makes careful use of U. S. religious censuses, is not primarily concerned with working-class religious adherence but indicates the strong persistence of religious loyalties in urban areas. Further studies of this important subject are needed for the twentieth century.

Max Horn's *The Intercollegiate Socialist Society, 1905–1921: Origins of the Modern Student Movement* (Boulder, Colo.: Westview Press, 1979) substantiates the appeal a major socialist educational venture had to privileged Christians and the contributions they made to its work. A superb analysis of the role of religion in the lives of those associated with the *Masses* and of its treatment within that journal is to be found in Leslie Fishbein, *Rebels in Bohemia: The Radicals of the Masses, 1911–1917* (Chapel Hill, N.C.: University of North Carolina Press, 1982).

AUTOBIOGRAPHIES AND BIOGRAPHIES

Socialist autobiographies and biographies are another fruitful source for the study of Christianity and socialism. Some indicate that Christian influences made a significant contribution to their subjects' becoming socialists. Allen Ruff's *"We Called Each Other Comrade": Charles H. Kerr & Company, Radical Publishers* (Urbana, Ill.: University of Illinois Press, 1997) explores the pilgrimage of America's pre-eminent publisher of socialist literature, from childhood in a family of antislavery Congregationalists, through Chicago-based radical Unitarianism, with which he began his publishing career, to socialism. For Algie M. Simons, first editor of Kerr's *International Socialist Review*, who grew up a Baptist, studied under Social Gospel economist Richard T. Ely at the University of Wisconsin, and worked in settlements in Chicago before joining the socialist movement, Kent and Gretchen Kreuter's *An American Dissenter: The Life of Algie Martin Simons, 1870–1950* (Lexington, Ky.: University of Kentucky Press, 1969) is very useful. The Kreuters' essay on Simons' wife, May Wood Simons, who aspired to be a Christian missionary, and Mari Jo Buhle's essay on Lena Morrow Lewis, devout daughter of a Presbyterian minister, both in Sally M. Miller's *Flawed Liberation: Socialism and Feminism* (Westport, Conn.: Greenwood Press, 1981), tell similar stories. Anna Louise Strong, daughter of a socially liberal Congregational minister, tells her story of involvement in radical labor circles in Seattle and favorable accounts of the Soviet Union in *I Change Worlds* (New York: Holt, Rinehart and Winston, 1935; Seattle: Seal Press, 1979). Ella Reeve Bloor's religious background receives scattered but revealing emphasis in her *We Are Many: An Autobiography*

(New York: International Publishers, 1940), as does Sara N. Cleghorn's in *Threescore: The Autobiography of Sarah N. Cleghorn* (New York: Harrison Smith & Robert Haas, 1936). Iowa socialist and national party secretary John M. Work revealed a lifelong belief in a supreme being and personal immortality in his chatty *Letters to a Lady* (New York: Exposition Press, 1951).

Religion as a force in the early life of muckraking journalist and socialist Upton Sinclair, and as a continuing preoccupation for him, can be found in William Andrew Bloodworth Jr., "The Early Years of Upton Sinclair: A Study of the Development of a Progressive Christian Socialist" (Ph.D. dissertation, University of Texas, 1972); in Sinclair's autobiographical *American Outpost: A Book of Reminiscences* (New York: Farrar & Rinehart, 1932) and "The Reminiscences of Upton Sinclair" (Oral History Research Office, Butler Library, Columbia University, 1963); in his condemnatory *The Profits of Religion: An Essay in Economic Interpretation* (Pasadena, Calif.: Published by the author, 1918); and in his fantastic novel of Jesus' arrival in class conflict-ridden Los Angeles after World War I, *They Call Me Carpenter: A Tale of the Second Coming* (Pasadena, Calif.: Upton Sinclair, 1922). Sinclair credited George D. Herron with providing financial support for him as a struggling writer and bringing him into the socialist movement.

Ray Ginger's *The Bending Cross: A Biography of Eugene Victor Debs* (New Brunswick, N.J.: Rutgers University Press, 1949) and the more recent *Eugene V. Debs: Citizen and Socialist* (Urbana, Ill.: University of Illinois Press, 1982), by Nick Salvatore, throw light on the most popular American socialist's perspective on religion and mythic role as a religious figure within the socialist movement. Harold W. Currie systematizes Debs's thinking in "The Religious Views of Eugene V. Debs," *Mid-America* 54 (July 1972): 147–56. For the best-known and most popular woman in the movement, Sally M. Miller has provided indispensable coverage in *From Prairie to Prison: The Life of Social Activist Kate Richards O'Hare* (Columbia, Mo.: University of Missouri Press, 1993) and, edited with Philip S. Foner, *Kate Richards O'Hare: Selected Writings and Speeches* (Baton Rouge, La.: Louisiana State University Press, 1982). O'Hare's religious experience also receives attention in Neil K. Basen, "Kate Richards O'Hare: The 'First Lady' of American Socialism, 1901–1917," *Labor History* 21 (Spring 1980): 165–99.

The case of a minister who, like J. Stitt Wilson, won a mayor's office on the Socialist Party ticket, receives attention in Kenneth E. Hendrickson Jr., "George R. Lunn and the Socialist Era in Schenectady, New York, 1909–1916," *New York History* 47 (January 1955): 22–40, and Hendrickson, "Tribune of the People: George R. Lunn and the Rise and Fall of Christian Socialism in Schnectady," in Bruce Stave, ed., *Socialism and the Cities* (Port Washington, N.Y.: Kennikat Press, 1975). Lunn's denomination was the (Dutch) Reformed Church in America. Jerry W. Calvert examines the administration of Lewis J. Duncan, a former Unitarian minister who became a Socialist mayor, in *The Gibraltar: Socialism and Labor in Butte, Montana, 1895–1920* (Helena, Mont.: Montana Historical Society Press, 1988), without much emphasis on religion, except for the Catholic opposition.

The Irish-born preacher, sailor, and man of many other occupations, Alexander Irvine, who was active in church work, settlements, and the Socialist Party in and around New York City in the Progressive Era, wrote two book-length accounts of his life, *From the Bottom Up: The Life Story of Alexander Irvine* (New York: Doubleday, Page, 1910) and *A Fighting Parson: The Autobiography of Alexander Irvine* (Boston: Little, Brown, 1930). Kathryn Oberdeck subjects him to careful cultural analysis in "Labor's Vicar and the Variety Show: Popular Religion, Popular Theatre, and Cultural Class Conflict in Turn-of-the-Century America" (Ph.D. dissertation, Yale University, 1991).

Previous biographical work on subjects of this volume includes the following. For Spalding: John H. Melish's admiring *Franklin Spencer Spalding: Man and Bishop* (New York: Macmillan, 1917), and two articles by John M. Sillito, " 'Prove All Things, Hold Fast That Which is Good'—Franklin Spencer Spalding, a Christian Socialist Dissenter From Capitalist Values," *Weber Studies* 1 (Spring 1984): 39–49, and, with Martha S. Bradley, "Franklin Spencer Spalding: An Episcopal Observer of Mormonism," *Historical Magazine of the Protestant Episcopal Church* 54 (December 1985): 339–50. For J. G. Phelps Stokes, Robert D. Reynolds Jr., "The Millionaire Socialists: J. G. Phelps Stokes and His Circle of Friends" (Ph.D. dissertation, University of South Carolina, 1974), and Patrick Renshaw, "Rose of the World: The Pastor-Stokes Marriage and the American Left, 1905–1925," *New York History* 62 (October 1981): 415–38. For Irwin St. John Tucker: Jacob H. Dorn, "Episcopal Priest and Socialist Activist: The Case of Irwin St. John Tucker," *Anglican and Episcopal History* 61 (June 1992): 167–96. For Bouck White: Mary E. Kenton, "Soul on the Open Road—Bouck White: The Life of an American Social Agitator" (M.A. thesis, Wright State University, 1978). For J. Stitt Wilson: Douglas Firth Anderson, "The Reverend J. Stitt Wilson and Christian Socialism in California," in Carl Guarneri and David Alvarez, eds., *Religion and Society in the American West: Historical Essays* (Lanham, Md.: University Press of America, 1987); and Michael Hanika, "J. Stitt Wilson: California Socialist" (M.A. thesis, California State University at Hayward, 1972). For George Washington Woodbey: Philip S. Foner, "Reverend George Washington Woodbey: Early Twentieth Century California Black Socialist," in Randall K. Burkett and Richard Newman, eds., *Black Apostles: Afro-American Clergy Confront the Twentieth Century* (Boston: G. K. Hall, 1978), and Foner, ed., *Black Socialist Preacher: The Writings of the Rev. George Washington Woodbey* (San Francisco: Synthesis Publications, 1983).

Both W.D.P. Bliss and George D. Herron have been perennial favorites of religious historians, though neither has received a full biography. Much of the writing is duplicative. The standard older studies of American social Christianity by James Dombrowski (*The Early Days of Christian Socialism in America* [New York: Columbia University Press, 1936]), Charles Howard Hopkins (*The Rise of the Social Gospel in American Protestantism, 1865–1915* [New Haven, Conn.: Yale University Press, 1940]), and Henry F. May (*Protestant Churches and Industrial America* [New York: Harper & Row, 1949]) all emphasize these two men's efforts to stir Protestantism to face the challenges of a new urban-industrial society. Like Howard Quint's *Forging of American Socialism*, however, Dombrowski and May venture little beyond the nineteenth century, which badly truncates our understanding of Bliss's and Herron's socialist work, and Hopkins also neglects Bliss after 1900. Other works that either minimize their socialism or do not track their activities in the early twentieth century are: John C. Cort, *Christian Socialism: An Informal History* (Maryknoll, N.Y.: Orbis Books, 1988); Peter J. Frederick, *Knights of the Golden Rule: The Intellectual as Christian Social Reformer in the 1890s* (Lexington, Ky.: University Press of Kentucky, 1976); and Robert H. Craig, "Seek Ye First the Political Kingdom: Christians and Socialism in the United States, 1890–1940" (Ph.D. dissertation, Columbia University, 1975), and *Religion and Radical Politics: An Alternative Christian Tradition in the United States* (Philadelphia: Temple University Press, 1992). An article that encompasses Bliss's entire life, without sufficiently probing his socialism, is Christopher L. Webber, "William Dwight Porter Bliss (1856–1926): Priest and Socialist," *Historical Magazine of the Protestant Episcopal Church* 28 (March 1959): 9–39. Most satisfactory is the work of Richard B. Dressner: "William Dwight Porter Bliss's Christian Socialism," *Church History* 47 (March 1978): 66–82, which stresses his work for the Christian Socialist Fellowship, and "Christian Socialism: A Response to Industrial America in the Progressive Era" (Ph.D. dissertation, Cornell University, 1972), in which Bliss is one of three subjects.

Three early doctoral dissertations on Herron remain valuable. Robert T. Handy's "George D. Herron and the Social Gospel in American Protestantism, 1890–1901" (Ph.D. dissertation, University of Chicago, 1949), a condensed version of which appeared as "George D. Herron and the Kingdom Movement," *Church History* 19 (June 1950): 97–115, is exhaustive for the years it covers, but unfortunately leaves Herron's twentieth-century work in limbo. A wide-ranging exploration of Herron's influence in the Socialist Party and the Protestant churches marks Phyllis A.Nelson's "George D. Herron and the Socialist Clergy, 1890–1914" (Ph.D. dissertation, State University of Iowa, 1953), and Herbert R. Dieterich probes the entire life in "Patterns of Dissent: The Reform Ideas and Activities of George D. Herron" (Ph.D. dissertation, University of New Mexico, 1957). Finally, there is an excellent assessment of Herron in Robert D. Crunden, *Ministers of Reform: The Progressives' Achievement in American Civilization, 1889–1920* (New York: Basic Books, 1982).

WORKS ON RELIGION AND SOCIAL ACTION; RELIGIOUS PERSPECTIVES ON SOCIALISM

Works on social Christianity have commonly acknowledged that its rise and the rise of socialism were interconnected, though they have not always been precise about what socialism meant. Following the lead of late nineteenth-century Christians whose use of "socialism" was amorphous, for example, James Dombrowski's *Early Days of Christian Socialism* includes reformist figures and ventures that were not politically socialist. Henry May structured his *Protestant Churches and Industrial America* along lines of conservative, moderate, and radical forms of social Christianity that religious historians continue to find useful. He was thus able to distinguish clearly between the emerging Social Gospel (the moderate form) and socialist Christianity (the radical form) without making them mutually exclusive. Charles Howard Hopkins recognized the differences as well. Both May and Hopkins believed that rising working-class discontent and the threat of social disorder contributed to the formulation of Social Gospel reformism as an alternative. Theological influences were undoubtedly fundamental: newer approaches to the Bible that emphasized its socio-historical context and socio-ethical significance, an immanentist view of God's relationship to humanity, and the core rubric of the coming Kingdom of God as the cornerstone of Christian teaching. Socialism, however, was a challenge to the churches—to their teachings as well as their social influence. Hopkins called it "the midwife and nurse" to the Social Gospel, while May referred to the Christian socialists as "stimuli or irritants" to their moderate fellow believers. Neither author, however, pointed to the reverse impact, which is evident in several chapters in this volume: Moderate social Christianity could open experiential and intellectual doors to more radical orientations. The Kingdom of God on earth might well be not a reformed and tamed capitalism, but an egalitarian cooperative commonwealth. Jesus' message of the "Fatherhood of God" and the "Brotherhood of Man" might well require ownership by all of the nation's capital plant. Despite the importance of this dialectical relationship between Social Gospel and socialist Christianity, the most closely researched recent study of the Social Gospel in denominational and ecumenical organizations, Donald K. Gorrell's *The Age of Social Responsibility: The Social Gospel in the Progressive Era, 1900–1920* (Macon, Ga.: Mercer University Press, 1988), reveals almost no consideration of socialism in those quarters, which may suggest the predominance of the Social Gospel agenda or simple institutional inertia.

Protestant leaders wrote much about socialism across four decades or more. The late nineteenth-century commentary commonly suffers from vaporous definitions of socialism. Negative reactions to both socialism and Christian socialism came from Roswell D. Hitchcock, a Union Theological Seminary professor, in *Socialism* (New York: Anson D. F. Randolph, 1879); from Brooklyn Congregational pastor A. J. F. Behrends, in *Socialism and Christianity* (New York: Baker & Taylor, 1886); and from Nicholas Paine Gilman, a Boston Unitarian devoted to profit-sharing, in *Socialism and the American Spirit* (Freeport, N.Y.: Books for Libraries Press reprint, [1893], 1971). The broad-scale dismissal of socialism as theoretically and practically unsound continued into the twentieth century, with Harvard Unitarian and Social Gospel thinker Francis Greenwood Peabody contributing *Jesus Christ and the Social Question: An Examination of the Teaching of Jesus in Its Relation to Some of the Problems of Modern Social Life* (New York: Macmillan, 1900) and other works. In contrast, Washington Gladden, a Congregational pastor in Ohio, usually balanced criticisms with affirmations in various assessments he published in the 1880s and 1890s and in *Christianity and Socialism* (New York: Eaton & Mains, 1905). Even more ungrudging affirmations came from Walter Rauschenbusch in *Christianity and the Social Crisis* (New York: Macmillan, 1907) and *Christianizing the Social Order* (New York: Macmillan, 1912), both devastating assessments of American capitalism, and from Henry C. Vedder of the

Baptist Crozer Theological Seminary in *Socialism and the Ethics of Jesus* (New York: Macmillan, 1912). A recent intellectual study of the Social Gospel-socialist Christian relationship, focusing on a wide array of the writings of three of these authors, is Jacob H. Dorn's "The Social Gospel and Socialism: A Comparison of the Thought of Francis Greenwood Peabody, Washington Gladden, and Walter Rauschenbusch," *Church History* 62 (March 1993): 82–100.

Conservative evangelicals left a much thinner body of commentary. Charles R. Erdman of Princeton Seminary, a leader in the emerging Fundamentalist movement, contributed a chapter on "The Church and Socialism" to *The Fundamentals: A Testimony to the Truth*, edited by R. A. Torrey and A. C. Dixon in twelve volumes between 1910 and 1915, which was distributed without charge in hundreds of thousands of copies. Though free of hysteria about socialist atheism and free love, Erdman refused to grant that socialism and Christianity had much in common. Edward R. Hartman, an author committed to premillennial prophetic views common to the rising Fundamentalist movement, refused as well, but in less reasoned terms than Erdman, in *Socialism Versus Christianity* (New York: Cochrane Publishing, 1909).

Roman Catholic writing was unremittingly hostile to socialism, even when most temperate. Representative works are: John Lancaster Spalding, *Socialism and Labor and Other Arguments* (Chicago: A. C. McClurg, 1902); David Goldstein, *Socialism: The Nation of Fatherless Children* (Boston: Union News League, 1903); William Stang, *Socialism and Christianity* (New York: Benziger Brothers, 1905); John Ming, *The Characteristics and the Religion of Modern Socialism* (2nd ed., New York: Benziger Brothers, 1908); Bernard Vaughan, *Socialism from the Christian Standpoint: Ten Conferences* (New York: Macmillan, 1912); and John A. Ryan, *Alleged Socialism of the Church Fathers* (St. Louis: B. Herder, 1913), a demonstration that the Church Fathers' criticisms of unjust and oppressive wealth were not the same as socialism. Ryan's extended debate with New York socialist leader Morris Hillquit in *Everybody's Magazine*, published as *Socialism: Promise or Menace?* (New York: Macmillan, 1914), is an intelligent, courteous juxtaposition of arguments between two informed, skilled debaters. For another "debate," between the Jesuit president of Boston College and a Massachusetts Socialist politician, see *The "Menace of Socialism," Being a Report of an Address by The Rev. Thos. Gasson, S.J., and a Reply Thereto by Hon. James F. Carey, Delivered in Faneuil Hall, Boston, Mass., February 27, 1911* (Milwaukee: Social Democratic Publishing, 1912).

The Catholic-socialist relationship is the subject of Robert E. Doherty, "The American Socialist Party and the Roman Catholic Church, 1901–1917" (Ed.D. dissertation, Columbia University Teachers College, 1959). Doherty is also the author of an important study of one of the few Catholic priests to join the socialist movement, "Thomas J. Hagerty, the Church, and Socialism," *Labor History* 3 (Winter 1962): 39–56. The Catholic campaign against socialism receives an extended critique in Marc Karson, *American Labor Unions and Politics, 1900–1918* (Carbondale, Ill.: Southern Illinois University Press, 1958). Karson's work appears in condensed form, with a response from Catholic historian Henry J.

Brown, in John H. M. Laslett and Seymour M. Lipset, eds., *Failure of a Dream? Essays in the History of American Socilaism* (Garden City, N.Y.: Anchor Press/Doubleday, 1974). Important conclusions about the effectiveness of this campaign in one state may be found in Henry D. Bedford, *Socialism and the Workers in Massachusetts, 1886–1912* (Amherst, Mass.: University of Massachusetts Press, 1966). In the growing literature on Catholic social action, Aaron I. Abell's *American Catholicism and Social Action: A Search for Social Justice* (Notre Dame, Ind.: University of Notre Dame Press, 1960), remains a useful survey.

Several works cited above with reference to W.D.P. Bliss and George D. Herron have broader significance and are important general sources. John Cort's *Christian Socialism*, a work by a Catholic socialist with long experience in Dorothy Day's Catholic Worker and the socialist movements, encompasses the early Christian Fathers and the twentieth century, Europe as well as the United States. What it accomplishes in breadth, it sometimes loses in thoroughness, but it is well worth reading. Robert Craig's *Religion and Radical Politics* seeks relevance for present social-justice action in the past, and thus judges past radicals by standards of racial and gender equality they might have difficulty understanding, but it is also a compassionate, well-researched book that brings Christian radicals in from the shadows. A superb recent work by Paul T. Phillips, *A Kingdom on Earth: Anglo-American Social Christianity, 1880–1940* (University Park, Pa.: Pennsylvania State University Press, 1996), is stronger on the English than on the American side and gives greater attention to Anglicanism than to other denominations, but it demonstrates the value of comparative, trans-Atlantic studies and synthesizes a great deal of information about correlations between theological developments and political action.

Index

Contributors

DOUGLAS FIRTH ANDERSON teaches history at Northwestern College in Iowa, where he is also chairman of the Department of History. He publishes regularly in the fields of the history of the U.S. West and U.S. religious history. He is working on a book tentatively titled *"A Different Civilization": Anglo-American Protestants in Metropolitan San Francisco during the Progressive Era.*

JACOB H. DORN is professor of history at Wright State University in Dayton, Ohio, where he teaches courses on American religious history, modern American radical movements, and the United States in the twentieth century. His publications focus on Protestant social thought and action in the nineteenth and twentieth centuries and include *Washington Gladden: Prophet of the Social Gospel* (1967).

PHILIP S. FONER was an extraordinarily prolific author in the fields of labor and African-American history, pioneering in areas previously neglected by scholars and producing important monographs, such as *American Socialism and Black Americans: From the Age of Jackson to World War II* (1977), and editions of the writings of Jack London, Helen Keller, George Washington Woodbey, and others.

MARY E. KENTON is associate director of the Wright State University Honors Program, with which she has been affiliated for many years, and she occasionally teaches in that program and for the Department of English at Wright State. Her graduate training in history emphasized social and intellectual topics and included a thesis on Bouck White.

SALLY M. MILLER is professor of history at the University of the Pacific. She is the author or editor of ten books and many articles in social history, including *From Prairie to Prison: The Life of Social Activist Kate Richards O'Hare* (1993) and

Kate Richards O'Hare: Selected Writings and Speeches (1982). Among her honors are Fulbright appointments in New Zealand (1986) and Finland (1996).

ROBERT D. REYNOLDS JR. is archivist at the George Meany Memorial Archives and managing editor of its illustrated quarterly historical journal, *Labor's Heritage*. His writing has appeared in such publications as *Journalism Quarterly, Labor History,* the *American Archivist,* and *SAOTHAR.* He is a contributor to the second edition of the *Encyclopedia of the American Left* (1998).

JOHN R. SILLITO is archivist and professor of libraries at Weber State University, Ogden, Utah. He is the author of articles on Utah and socialist history, and with John S. McCormick is editor of *A World We Thought We Knew: Readings in Utah History* (1995). Sillito and McCormick are working on a study of the Socialist Party in Utah.

ISBN 0-313-30262-6

EAN

9 780313 302626

HARDCOVER BAR CODE